Client Psychology

Client Psychology

CHARLES R. CHAFFIN, EdD
EDITOR

WILEY

Library of Congress Cataloging-in-Publication Data:

ISBN 978-1-119-43626-3 (Hardcover)
ISBN 978-1-119-44090-1 (ePDF)
ISBN 978-1-119-44091-8 (ePub)
ISBN 978-1-119-44089-5 (oBook)

Printed in the United States of America

10 9 8 7 6 5 4 3 2 1

Contents

CHAPTER 11

Automated Decision Aids: Understanding Disuse and Designing for Trust, with Implications for Financial Planning

167

Jason S. McCarley, PhD, Oregon State University

CHAPTER 12

Self-Determination Theory and Self-Efficacy in Financial Planning

181

Charles R. Chaffin, EdD, CFP Board Center for Financial Planning

CHAPTER 13

Marriage and Family Therapy, Financial Therapy, and Client Psychology

189

Kristy Archuleta, PhD, and Sonya Britt-Lutter, PhD
Kansas State University

CHAPTER 14

Client Diversity: Understanding and Leveraging Difference to Enhance Financial Planning Practice

203

Quinetta Roberson, PhD, Villanova University

Acknowledgments

A work of this magnitude could not happen without the commitment and dedication of an esteemed group of contributors. Each of these 23 researchers and scholar-practitioners brought a different perspective to the same subject, the human client. They are all leaders in their respective fields and I was fortunate to have the privilege to collaborate with each of them over the course of 2017 to write this book. There is something truly fascinating about diverse lenses examining the same topic—challenging assumptions and providing innovative ideas, all with a common purpose in mind. I am grateful to each of them for their trust and commitment to this new idea.

Thank you to Sheck Cho and all of my friends at John Wiley & Sons for their continued partnership throughout this yearlong endeavor. Wiley continues to be a great partner to the CFP Board Center for Financial Planning and I hope this book is representative of that impactful partnership.

I would like to thank the board of directors at CFP Board for their unwavering commitment to this project. Thank you as well to members of the Executive Leadership Team at CFP Board for their support of this work.

Thank you to Kevin Keller, CEO of CFP Board, and Marilyn Mohrman-Gillis, Executive Director of the CFP Board Center for Financial Planning for their commitment to the Academic Home for the Center for Financial Planning. This work started in 2011 with a vision—a platform where members of academe from multiple disciplines as well as practitioners from across financial planning could present, publish, consume, and discuss research that impacts our academic discipline—our profession—in new and profound ways. It is truly satisfying to see that vision come to fruition.

Thank you to all of those individuals and organizations who support the CFP Board Center for Financial Planning, particularly TD Ameritrade Institutional for their support as Lead Founding Sponsor and Northwestern Mutual as Founding Sponsor. We are grateful to all of the firms, CFP® professionals, and friends from across business models and professions who have joined us on this journey to build the Academic Home for the profession of personal financial planning.

In the end, I take responsibility for this work—a work that I hope will help serve as a catalyst for expanding the financial planning body of knowledge to include the biases, behaviors, and perceptions of the individuals who entrust this profession with their life's work: the client. The objective of this book is not to be the last word in client psychology, but the first word. I hope that the text found within these pages will fuel both new lines of inquiry and innovative approaches to financial planning practice, making our profession more impactful, relevant, and most important, client-centered.

Charles R. Chaffin, EdD
Editor

Preface

Financial planning is, at face value, a quantitative endeavor. There is a host of numbers that exist within a financial plan, representing a client's savings, debt, investments, retirement, insurance, and other numeric values associated with his or her financial well-being. In the proposed changes to the CFP® Board Standards of Professional Conduct, the CFP Board defines financial planning as ". . . a collaborative process that helps maximize a Client's potential for meeting life goals through Financial Advice that integrates relevant elements of the Client's personal and financial circumstances" (Proposed CFP Board Standards of Professional Conduct, 2017). Inherent within that definition are both the steps of the financial planning process as well as the content areas, essentially the necessary competencies of a CFP® professional, to provide competent and ethical financial planning.

The role of the financial planner is challenging and with it comes a high level of responsibility. Beyond the numbers, clients entrust not only their goals and dreams to their CFP® professional, but also the accumulation of their life's work. Years, and in some cases decades, of long hours in the office and careful investing culminate into a specific set of numbers on a spreadsheet. Clients bring into the financial-planning process their vision for the future as well as their vision for those closest to them. Conversely, clients also bring concerns regarding the current and future well-being of their loved ones. The financial planner is sometimes the first to hear the good news and is also the first phone call or text message when bad news arises, both of which require frank conversation, careful planning, action, and sometimes, thoughtful inaction. Therefore, financial planning is, at its core, a human endeavor.

So what about these clients? How do we help them discover (and then communicate) their hopes and dreams? What about the goals for their spouses, partners, or families? How do the interactions with those around them affect their decisions and financial well-being? How do relationships and communication with their advisors impact the financial-planning process? What do we know about individual behaviors such as spending, debt, planning, and saving relative to a variety of client profiles and contexts? How does stress impact the dialogue between the client and planner . . . what can the planner do to mitigate this stress? How do the cognitive load and attention resources of the client during the development and presentation of a financial plan impact the client's relationship with the planner? How does technology impact a client's willingness to communicate more freely with their financial planner? What about the sociological issues that are inherently part of the relationship between client and planner? Beyond these questions, there are hundreds more that financial planners encounter each and every day, many of which have a direct impact on planner efficacy and client success.

Behavioral finance helps answer some of these questions. It brings elements of cognitive and behavioral psychology to both economics and finance to examine why investors make irrational financial decisions. These irrational decisions in many cases stem from heuristics, or mental shortcuts, that involve only one aspect of a complex program or phenomenon, leading to errors in judgment, or biases. In behavioral finance, the focus is on the individual and not the market. Essentially, and at the risk of oversimplifying, the tidiness of modern portfolio theory becomes rather messy with the arrival of the human and all of his thoughts and actions. Behavioral finance helps explain some of that messiness with an underlying premise that the individuals making the decisions are complex and not always well-informed. All of these ideas are relevant to financial planning. Practitioners need to know about concepts such as choice architecture, anchoring, and availability bias, all of which have an impact in the daily life of serving clients and are helpful in explaining some of these irrational decisions.

But are these decisions actually irrational? From the outside looking in, it may appear so, but it is also possible that these decisions can be explained by a host of other factors. Many psychologists, including preeminent scholars such as Skinner and Freud, saw many of the actions of the individual based predominantly on environmental factors and those within the psyche of the individual. Skinner saw the environment as solely determining the actions of the individual. Essentially, the individual does not make any decisions on her or his own—the environment does it for them. Freud saw the unconscious—the automated and visceral elements of the self and thought processes—as a key determinant of behavior and decision-making. Although Freud and Skinner saw many elements of psychology quite differently (and there are many aspects of their work that have been both confirmed and refuted in recent years), their work identifies multiple factors that impact human behavior and decision-making. Therefore, what is an irrational decision to one may be the best decision, given the circumstance, to another. So perhaps irrational is in the eye of the beholder.

The body of literature from behavioral finance is critical to our current and future work in serving clients (as well as important parts of this book), but perhaps we should think more broadly. We need to further investigate stress, cognition, interpersonal relationships, communication, identity, and other basic elements, all within the framework of financial planning. We need to invite researchers from fields such as clinical and cognitive psychology, sociology, education, and others to better understand the rationale behind client perceptions, behaviors, and decision-making and then specifically outline the implications of this work (the "So what?") in an effort to help practitioners and CFP® professionals do their work better.

In medicine, evidence-based practice is where medical professionals use relevant data to make healthcare decisions for individual patients. Clinical practice, patient values, and the best available research and data are all integrated to formulate a healthcare plan. Perhaps most importantly, individual characteristics and preferences—so essentially what works best for each patient physically, psychologically, emotionally, and spiritually—are primary drivers in determining treatment. It is not, therefore, merely a matter of one-size-fits-all nor a sole focus on the action of the physician, but rather, a personalized approach to medicine based upon the patient's health status, research, and desired outcomes: a patient-centered approach.

Similarly, in education, the classroom approach for decades was teacher-centric, where the actions and knowledge of the teacher were considered the primary drivers in determining the success of an educational offering or program of study. If the instructor performed his or her actions well, then the assumption was that the students must be successful. But then, a few decades ago, educational psychologists identified key attributes associated with cognition and learner development to help better understand the student learner. These advances placed the focus of teaching pedagogy (essentially, the practice of teaching) on what works for the learner, not the teacher. We now almost universally define success in education as not what the teacher knows or does, but rather, by whether the student learned a concept or not: a student-centered approach.

Perhaps we are at a similar juncture in financial planning, where the profession has begun to realize that the knowledge and actions of the planner are critical, but useless if the client is unsuccessful. No financial planner says, "My client failed to reach her lifetime goals, but not to worry, I myself was competent throughout the financial planning process." We as a profession can follow medicine and education and develop deeper insights into our practice and focus more closely on the individual. Ultimately, taking this evidence-based approach to financial planning, specifically the characteristics of the client, would yield new findings that could help prepare future generations with the competencies and skills that directly relate to the human element of this profession. The basic fundamentals of investments, taxation, insurance, estate planning, communication, and so on would still and likely always be vital, but these content areas and competencies can be developed and refined solely with the client in mind: a client-centered approach.

Against that backdrop, I present *Client Psychology*. This book brings together the expected research areas such as financial planning, behavioral finance, communication, and financial therapy. Just as importantly, client psychology invites new fields (or those new to financial planning) such as sociology, cognitive psychology, education, social work, and others. This interdisciplinary approach, bringing diverse fields, methodologies, and researchers together to focus on the financial planning client, can lead to new knowledge that has a significant impact on our profession. As we all know, all of this new knowledge has limited relevance if we cannot answer the "So what?" question. We hope to do so here.

There is an added dimension to this work given the influence of technology in financial planning. As the use and access of artificial intelligence and technology expand, there are a multitude of opportunities and threats to the profession as it strives to be relevant to the population it serves (and perhaps is hoping to serve). The profession has the opportunity to be creative in delivering competent and ethical financial planning through a combination of in-person and electronic delivery, all based upon client needs and preferences. In order to fully serve each client and maximize market potential, the profession needs to have a full awareness of the tendencies and perceptions of the user. In addition, at the tap of a smartphone or tablet, clients now have access to increasing amounts of data, whether their own accounts or financial advice from others, potentially altering the complexion of (and potentially the need for) the client-planner relationship. Taking an evidence-based approach to financial planning, we can use much of the body of literature found within client psychology and then utilize or build technology that fits the needs of our current and future clients. As we all know, learning as much as possible about clients will make our profession more relevant to clients.

Client Psychology is not the final and definitive word in financial planning. Rather, it is a commencement to an approach that brings together many fields of study that can have some impact on the financial planning client, always with their best interests in mind. Our attempt is to provide a new theoretical underpinning through a body of literature from across the academy. Each chapter represents a formal introduction of these new concept areas to a broad audience of practitioners and scholars. As you read each chapter, my hope is that you will be drawn to the argument as to why each of these diverse topics is important to our field. Some chapters draw explicit connections to financial planning and others ask the reader to infer where specific concepts fit into daily practice. I hope that scholars from within and beyond financial planning will be challenged to think about new lines of inquiry within this framework that help us as a profession become more client-centered. To summarize this book and at the risk of giving away the plot, it is a new theoretical framework with contributions from a variety of academic disciplines to enable financial planning to become more client-centered.

So let us begin. I hope that you find *Client Psychology* both challenging and illuminating, but perhaps more importantly, I hope that you finish the book with more questions than when you started. We all still have so much to learn.

Charles R. Chaffin, EdD
Editor

REFERENCES

Code of Ethics and Standards of Conduct. (2017). Retrieved from https://www.cfp.net/docs/default-source/for-cfp-pros—professional-standards-enforcement/2017-proposed-standards/final-standards-for-public-comment.pdf?sfvrsn=2.

About the Contributors

Charles R. Chaffin, EdD, is Director of Academic Initiatives, CFP Board Center for Financial Planning, leading academic initiatives such as the Academic Research Colloquium; executive editor of the academic journal *Financial Planning Review*; editor of the CFP Board book series; and the program lead for the Columbia University–CFP Board Teaching Program. For seven years prior to that appointment, Chaffin provided guidance and oversight to the over 300 CFP Board Registered Programs across the United States. He holds a graduate degree from the University of Michigan and a doctorate from the University of Illinois.

Kristy Archuleta, PhD, is an associate professor and program director of the personal financial planning program at Kansas State University and a licensed marriage and family therapist. She has been quoted in media outlets such as the *New York Times, Glamour, Parade,* and *NPR Marketplace.* She is the editor of the *Journal of Financial Therapy* and has coedited two books related to assessment and financial therapy.

Sarah Asebedo, PhD, CFP®, is an assistant professor at Texas Tech University. With extensive financial planning experience, her goal is to connect research and financial planning practice. She is spearheading research focused on personality, positive psychology, and financial behavior, and how mediation and principled negotiation techniques can be employed to resolve money arguments. Asebedo's work has been recognized with the 2016 Montgomery-Warschauer Award (FPA/JFP), 2014 and 2017 Best Applied Research Award (FPA/JFP), 2017 Top 40 Under 40 Award (Investment News), 2017 AARP Public Policy Institute Financial Services and the Older Consumer Award (ACCI), and 2017 Robert O. Hermann Outstanding Dissertation Award (ACCI). Asebedo currently serves as President of the Financial Therapy Association. She earned her PhD from Kansas State University.

Sonya Britt-Lutter, PhD, CFP®, is an associate professor of personal financial planning at Kansas State University. She holds degrees from Kansas State University and Texas Tech University. Her research has been featured in news outlets such as the *New York Times,* the *Wall Street Journal,*

Kiplinger's, and *Yahoo! Finance*. Dr. Britt-Lutter recently wrote a love and money curriculum and a forthcoming book for couples.

Swarn Chatterjee, PhD, is an associate professor of financial planning at the University of Georgia. He has published more than 40 peer-reviewed papers and teaches classes in wealth management and behavioral economics. His research interests include studying performance evaluation across different stages of the financial planning process and identification of factors that improve financial decision-making among millennials and the elderly.

Jonathan Fox, PhD, is the Ruth Whipp Sherwin Professor of Human Development and Family Studies at Iowa State University, where he teaches courses in financial counseling and planning. His research in financial socialization appears in journals such as the *Journal of Financial Therapy* and the *Journal of Consumer Affairs*. He received his PhD in Consumer Economics from the University of Maryland.

Joseph Goetz, PhD, is an associate professor of financial planning at the University of Georgia. He is an award-winning professor, practitioner, and researcher in the area of financial planning and wealth management. His primary professional objectives are to assist individuals and families in reaching their financial life goals, and to support the development of future financial planners who will participate in the positive transformation of the financial planning profession.

John Grable, PhD, CFP®, holds an Athletic Association Endowed Professorship at the University of Georgia. Dr. Grable served as the founding editor for the *Journal of Personal Finance* and the founding coeditor of the *Journal of Financial Therapy*. His research interests include financial risk-tolerance assessment, evidence-based financial planning, and behavioral financial planning. He is Director of the Financial Planning Performance Laboratory at the University of Georgia and a coeditor of *Financial Planning Review*.

Stuart J. Heckman, PhD, CFP®, is an assistant professor of personal financial planning at Kansas State University. He earned his BS in Personal Financial Planning from Kansas State University and his MS and PhD in Family Resource Management from The Ohio State University. His research focuses on professional financial planning and on risky financial decisions among young adults.

Edward Horwitz, PhD, CFP®, ChFC, CLU, FBS®, is the Mutual of Omaha Endowed Executive Director in Risk Management at Creighton University's

Heider College of Business and an associate professor of practice in behavioral finance. He also serves as Director for Creighton's Financial Planning and Financial Psychology programs. Prior to academia, his career in the insurance industry spanned over 25 years.

Zhuo Jin is scheduled to complete her master's degree in 2018, in Organizational Management from George Washington University and earned her bachelor's degree in Psychology in 2014 from the University of Nebraska, Lincoln. Zhuo's primary research interests are in consumer and donating behaviors, technology, social media–inspired creativity and lifestyle branding, and social media celebrity. She plans to pursue a doctoral degree in either Marketing or Human Computer Interaction in the fall of 2018.

Bradley T. Klontz, PsyD, CFP®, is an associate professor of practice in financial psychology at Creighton University Heider College of Business and a managing principal at Your Mental Wealth Advisors™. Dr. Klontz is coeditor/author of five books on the psychology of money, including *Financial Therapy* (Springer, 2015), *Mind Over Money* (Broadway Business, 2009), and *Facilitating Financial Health* (NUCO, 2016).

Jodi Letkiewicz, PhD, is an assistant professor at York University in Toronto, Ontario. She teaches, researches, and publishes in the areas of consumer finance, financial planning, and financial well-being. She received an MS and PhD in Family Resource Management at The Ohio State University.

Michael J. Liersch, PhD, is a behavioral scientist and financial planning executive. He holds a PhD in Cognitive Psychology from University of California, San Diego and an AB from Harvard in Economics. He has spent time in both academia and business. As an academic, Dr. Liersch was a postdoctoral fellow at University of California, San Diego Rady School of Business and a visiting professor at New York University Stern School of Business. In business, he held positions as head of behavioral finance in the Americas at Barclays Wealth, head of behavioral finance and goals-based consulting at Merrill Lynch, and most recently, head of financial planning at JPMorgan Chase.

HanNa Lim, PhD, is an assistant professor of personal financial planning at Kansas State University. Her research focuses on households' financial decision-making and college students' financial wellness. She earned her BA and MA in Consumer Science from Seoul National University, and her PhD in Family Resource Management from The Ohio State University.

Meghaan R. Lurtz is a financial psychology specialist at Kaleido Creative Studio, an assistant adjunct professor of finance at the University of Maryland University College, and a PhD student at Kansas State University. She graduated from the University of Kansas with a bachelor's degree in Philosophy, Psychology, and Spanish. Her master's degree was in Industrial Organizational Psychology.

Jason McCarley, PhD, is a professor in the School of Psychological Sciences at Oregon State University. He holds a BA in Psychology from Purdue University and a PhD in Experimental Psychology from the University of Louisville, and has held positions at the Naval Postgraduate School, the University of Illinois, and Flinders University of South Australia. He conducts research in engineering psychology, with interest in models of attention, decision-making, and human–automation interaction. His work has appeared in outlets including *Human Factors* and *Journal of Experimental Psychology: Applied*, and he is coauthor of the book *Applied Attention Theory* (Wickens & McCarley, 2008).

Nils Olsen, PhD, is an assistant professor of organizational sciences at George Washington University and conducts research within the following domains: (a) individual decision-making (e.g., medical, financial, legal); (b) strategic decision-making (e.g., Olympic Games); and (c) procedural justice (e.g., physician-patient, lawyer-client); and has publications appearing in the *Journal of Personality and Social Psychology*, *Academic Emergency Medicine*, and *Handbook of the London 2012 Olympic and Paralympic Games*. Before joining the faculty at GWU, Professor Olsen worked as a researcher at the Developmental Psychology Laboratory of the National Institute of Mental Health and worked collaboratively with the American Bar Foundation. Professor Olsen holds a BS in Psychology from the University of Wisconsin, an MA from the University of Iowa, and PhD from the University of North Carolina at Chapel Hill.

Vanessa Gail Perry, MBA, PhD, is professor of marketing, strategic management and public policy at the George Washington University School of Business. Her research is focused on consumers in financial and housing markets, public policy, and marketplace discrimination, and has been widely published in scholarly and industry-oriented outlets. Professor Perry has served as senior advisor to the secretary of the U.S. Department of Housing and Urban Development, as an expert appointee at the U.S. Consumer Financial Protection Bureau, and as a consultant to numerous public and private sector clients. Before joining the faculty at GWU, Professor Perry was a senior economist at Freddie Mac. Professor Perry holds a BA in Philosophy from American University, an MBA from Washington University in St. Louis, and a PhD from the University of North Carolina at Chapel Hill.

Quinetta Roberson, PhD, is the Fred J. Springer Endowed Chair in Business Leadership in the School of Business at Villanova University. Prior to her current position, she was an associate professor of human resource studies at Cornell University. Professor Roberson has over 15 years of experience teaching courses and workshops globally on leadership, talent management, and diversity. She has published over 20 scholarly journal articles and book chapters and edited *Handbook of Diversity in the Workplace,* published by Oxford Press in 2013. Her research interests center on developing organizational capability and enhancing effectiveness through the strategic management of people, particularly diverse work teams. Dr. Roberson's research and work with organizations is informed by her background in finance, having worked as a financial analyst and small business development consultant prior to obtaining her PhD in Organizational Behavior from the University of Maryland. She also holds a BS in Finance and Accounting from the University of Delaware and an MBA in Finance and Strategic Planning from the University of Pittsburgh.

Deanna L. Sharpe, PhD, CFP®, CRPC®, CRPS®, is an associate professor in the Personal Financial Planning department at the University of Missouri. Her teaching and research focus on factors affecting later-life economic well-being. She has provided leadership for the American Council on Consumer Interests, the Association of Financial Counseling and Planning Education, and the Certified Financial Planner Board of Standards Education Task Force.

Abigail Sussman, PhD, is an associate professor of marketing at the University of Chicago Booth School of Business. Sussman's prior experience includes work at Goldman Sachs in its equity research division. She earned a bachelor's degree from Brown University in Cognitive Science and Economics, and a joint PhD from the psychology department and the Woodrow Wilson School of Public and International Affairs at Princeton University.

Faith Zabek is a PhD candidate in School Psychology at Georgia State University. She is currently completing her doctoral internship at the APA-accredited Hawaii Psychology Internship Consortium, where she has contributed to research investigating the impact of experiential financial therapy on savings behaviors.

C. Yiwei Zhang, PhD, is a postdoctoral fellow at the University of Chicago Booth School of Business. Prior to joining the University of Chicago, Zhang worked as an economist in the Office of Research at the Consumer Financial Protection Bureau. She earned bachelor's degrees in Economics and in Mathematics from the Massachusetts Institute of Technology and earned her PhD from the University of Pennsylvania, Wharton School's program in Applied Economics.

CHAPTER 1

Client Psychology

Charles R. Chaffin, EdD
CFP Board Center for Financial Planning

Jonathan J. Fox, PhD
Iowa State University

Ben (59) and Colleen (49) Orr are not entirely uncommon clients in the practice of financial planning. While they are entrenched in a successful family business and rewarding careers, they are typical clients with a host of financial challenges, somewhat undefined long- and short-term goals, and a family with complex interpersonal dynamics.

This is the second marriage for both. Ben has three children with his first wife, Nina (58). Nina retained 33% ownership of the private cleaning supplies corporation that she and Ben started 25 years ago and she remains actively involved in company management. Ben and Colleen almost never discuss Nina's continued involvement in the business and family. Of Ben and Nina's three children, Mary Jo (34) and Ernest (32) are principals in the family business and both are married and have children of their own. Their 29-year-old son, Jacob, resides in a local community serving adults with developmental disabilities.

Colleen's first spouse was killed in an automobile accident soon after their second anniversary. With modest life insurance benefits, she completed graduate school and now loves her work as a professor of math education at the state university. She currently has no plans or intentions for retirement. She and Ben married 15 years ago, and have two children, John (14) and Joan (10).

Ben and Colleen are committed to planning for Jacob's needs for the rest of his life. Ben would like to retire in 7 years and wants to transfer ownership of the company to his adult children Mary Jo and Ernest, but he doesn't know what Nina wants to do with her interest in the company. Ben has no clear plans for what he may do in retirement. He just knows the work of the company is all-consuming and he needs a change. Ben and

Colleen are committed to setting aside some funds in a separate account to help support John and Joan when they attend college and believe they have adequate resources to do so.

Another looming concern for Ben and Colleen is Ben's 81-year-old father, Jack. Ben lost his mother to cancer 10 years ago. Since that time, Jack has lived alone in a town about an hour's drive from Ben and Colleen. Ben visits when he can, but makes a point to call and talk with his father at least once a week. Jack is in relatively good health and enjoys several volunteer activities and golfing with friends. Lately, though, Ben has noticed that his father has become more forgetful and he is not sure if what he is seeing is a normal part of aging or the early signs of dementia or Alzheimer's. Ben worries that his father might forget to pay his bills or become vulnerable to fraud. He knows Jack meets with a financial advisor a few times a year. Ben wonders if he should give his father's financial advisor a call, to share his concerns and see what she has noticed during client appointments with his dad. Under most objective measures, Ben and Colleen are financially healthy. Not including the value of the cleaning supplies company, their net worth is approximately $2,600,000. This is comprised of approximately $3,000,000 in assets and $400,000 in debt, in the form of a home mortgage and a personal loan taken to grow the business. A recent independent valuation of the business came in just under $9,000,000. The bulk of their financial assets are in conservative, income-driven investments within qualified retirement plans. Ben has never been a fan of financial risk and equity investing. He still talks about the few equity funds he held, and quickly sold, in 2008. He is more comfortable with direct control over his company assets and has never been open to others controlling his money. Most of the retirement assets are Ben's with Colleen designated as the beneficiary. Colleen considers herself more of a risk taker when it comes to investing and her retirement assets (approximately $110,000) are mostly invested in small cap index funds within her university's 403(b) plan.

Colleen believes Ben spends too much on travel, company and family celebrations, and charity. She is the primary manager of the family budget and tries to keep their spending on track but has been frustrated lately that their annual rate of saving is almost zero, excluding retirement contributions through the company and the university. They own a four-bedroom home in a neighborhood of homes valued between $250,000 and $300,000. Their mortgage balance is approximately $175,000.

Ben and Colleen believe they have adequate protection against the risk of financial loss, but it has been at least 5 years since they have given insurance coverage significant thought. Both are so busy that the thought of evaluating life, home, automobile, health, disability, umbrella liability, and long-term care options seems overwhelming, yet it is something they know they need to do. Colleen has life insurance through the university with benefits of 2.5 times her $88,000 annual salary. She is not sure who her beneficiaries are for the policy. Ben has a $3,000,000 term life policy connected to the family business, with Nina as the primary beneficiary and their three adult children as secondary beneficiaries. They are covered under a group health plan connected to Colleen's university and have homeowner and automobile policies but don't remember the last time they reviewed coverage and costs. Ben and Colleen each drive older, reliable vehicles with no automobile loans. They have a $1,000,000 umbrella liability policy but no disability or long-term care insurance.

Ben and Colleen have simple wills and healthcare power of attorney documents that were drafted 13 years ago, just after the birth of John. In their 15 years of marriage, Ben and Colleen have never committed to working with a financial planner. Ben is hesitant to turn everything over to one person or company. He likes bouncing ideas off his many financial advisors (accountant, attorney, retirement investment advisor, and insurance agent), but prefers to make his own decisions in the end. Colleen is growing increasingly frustrated with the lack of coordination between the finances of the business and their household. She has been suggesting that they use the services of a Certified Financial Planner™ (CFP) for years. They have visited with a few planners for initial consultations, but never made the commitment. Ben and Colleen's situation is complex: There are not only difficult decisions to make, but the number of decisions is overwhelming.

As you move through the methods of inquiry in this book, keep a case family like the Orrs in mind. Keep asking yourself, "What really guides Ben and Colleen's decisions? How have these decisions been shaped by both mathematical calculations as well as gut-level intuition? When is it mostly about money, and when is it family relations that matter most? How do clients' understanding of risk impact the decisions they make? How do the dynamics of marriage and communication patterns impact the formulation of life plans and goals? How do personalities, upbringing, and personal identities influence spending and saving patterns and retirement investment choices? How often and in what ways do clients like Ben and Colleen communicate with one another about their goals and vision for the future, and to what extent should that communication matter to you as their counselor and advisor?

Ben and Colleen are in mid-life, but Ben is a decade older than Colleen. How might the aging process affect their decision-making capacities now and in years to come? Will the age difference matter more or less in later life? At what point might each be at risk of cognitive decline and loss of financial capacity? Since Ben is older, what should Colleen understand about age-related changes in cognition? What makes them, and clients like them, more or less willing to trust your advice?

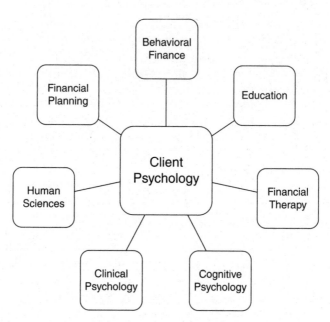

FIGURE 1.1   The Academic Disciplines of Client Psychology

These are the types of questions this book is attempting to address. By working more systemically and holistically beyond the tenets of optimal resource allocation theory and behavioral finance, we find new approaches to the deeply human questions defining the financial lives of Ben and Colleen. All of these questions require an in-depth analysis of multiple academic disciplines to help better serve Ben, Colleen, and their family that goes beyond the traditional content areas associated with financial planning, such as estate planning, taxation, and investments. This leads us to client psychology.

For the purpose of this book, client psychology is defined as the biases, behaviors, and perceptions that impact client decision-making and financial well-being. By anyone's standards, that is a broad umbrella. However, holistically serving a financial planning client requires a broad approach, taking multiple academic disciplines, research methodologies, and traditions from various programs of study and professions. Biases are our inclinations for or against a certain object or person. Client biases may relate to interpersonal matters and could be based upon one's past experiences. Behaviors are our responses to a given situation and stimulus, which, in a client context, are more likely to be observable. Perceptions are recognitions of the lived experiences of the individual, the lenses by which they look at the environment around them. Essentially, it is not just what the client does, it is also her perceptions: perceptions of her spouse and family; her motivations; and of herself that impact almost all aspects of her as a client. The first three words of this working definition purposely represent a broad approach to understanding the attitudes and behaviors of the client. Implicit within this broad umbrella are a variety of research methodologies needed to answer many of the questions about our clients, including any combination of quantitative, qualitative, theoretical, experimental, or historical approaches.

Behavioral finance is an important component of our working definition of client psychology and certainly this book. It is a product of cognitive and behavioral psychology within the context of economics and finance to examine why humans, in this case the individual client, make what would appear to be irrational financial decisions when compared to a pure economic or optimization model. Heuristics, or mental shortcuts, are a big cause of these irrational decisions and lead to inherent biases on the part of the individual, particularly when the problem is complex and motivation to think slowly and deliberately is low.

Chapters of this book focus on the foundational elements of behavioral finance, heuristics and biases, prospect theory, mental accounting, choice architecture, and personality and financial behavior. The approach within client psychology is not only to present a theoretical framework for each of these content areas, but also outline the implications of this theory specifically for the field of financial planning and the financial-planning client.

Education is also critical in the field of financial planning, exploring topics such as self-determination theory and self-efficacy, both of which have roots in cognitive psychology but have evolved further in the more practitioner-based profession of education. Self-determination theory focuses on the motivation of the individual with a specific focus on innate psychological needs (Ryan & Deci, 2000). Bandura (1994) defines self-efficacy as "people's beliefs about their capabilities to produce designated levels of performance that exercise influence over events that affect their lives" (p. 1). Self-efficacy is a focus on the individual's perception of their own ability to perform a certain task within a specific task setting. A financial planner should have a keen understanding of self-determination theory, as knowing the intrinsic motivation of the client can be a powerful tool in helping keep client behaviors on track and consistent with the client's long-term financial goals. Self-efficacy and client financial literacy are intertwined. If individuals feel that they have knowledge and aptitude with regard to their own financial decision-making and overall well-being, they are more likely to both seek out a financial planner and stay the course as life challenges intervene.

Financial therapy is a key component to client psychology; as with other aspects of client psychology, it focuses on client behaviors, but from the perspective of the influences of personal relationships. Grounded in the practice and theory of couples and family counseling, financial therapy draws from the relational life of the client. While financial professionals have long acknowledged that advising is a relationship business, the focus has been mainly on the relationship between planner and client. The body of knowledge within the financial therapy discipline continues to grow and has been an integral part of financial planning practice. The inter-relational elements of client decision-making and financial well-being have a powerful impact on the client, with equally powerful implications for advisors working with clients dealing with complex family relationships.

Cognitive psychology focuses on mental processes such as attention, memory, and creativity, and has provided the theoretical underpinning for educational psychology and behavioral finance. The amount of cognitive load that a client, or planner for that matter, uses during the presentation of a financial plan or articulation of goals may have a significant impact on the success of a given client–planner interaction. Similarly, cognitive psychology has a deep impact on the motivations of the individual, which is useful in defining why clients make decisions that enable their long-term financial well-being, or even why they seek a financial planner in the first place. Obviously, behavioral finance topics such as heuristics and biases, anchoring, and mental accounting are greatly influenced by work in cognitive psychology.

Clinical psychology is defined by the American Psychological Association as the "psychological specialty that provides continuing and comprehensive mental and behavioral health care for individuals and families; consultation to agencies and communities; training, education and supervision; and research-based practice" (American Psychological Association, 2017). Within this book, we explore financial psychology, which blends aspects of broader elements of psychology with behavioral finance.

The human sciences add an ecological perspective to the field of financial planning. At the individual level, human sciences includes the biological, psychological, and cultural aspects of life. It is by definition an interdisciplinary approach, incorporating sociology, biochemistry, neurosciences, psychology, and other disciplines to better understand the context of human development and family health. A human sciences perspective brings together an understanding of the individual (what is going on in the clients' minds), their near environments (relationships with family and friends), the financial marketplace, and the wider cultural and political environments.

The traditional building blocks of financial planning are also key components of this book. The core aspects of financial planning, including investments, taxation, retirement planning, insurance, and communication, are integral parts of client decision-making and overall financial health. Client psychology and financial planning are joined at the hip from both theory and application perspectives. For our purposes, the context for client psychology *is* financial planning. What differentiates client psychology is that the focus is purely on the client and all of her, his, or their biases, behaviors, and perceptions, whereas the focus of much of the body of knowledge and practical applications of financial planning are planner-centered.

As outlined in the introduction to this book, our journey to becoming a client-centered profession is along the same path of other professions, whether the evidence-based practice of medicine or the evolution of education from teaching to learning. Our objective is to evaluate our actions, efforts, competency, and ultimately our success as a profession on the outcomes of the client.

Through technology, clients have access to all of their account information on their phones or tablets. Access to this information, as well as advice via multiple means, is readily available whether at two in the afternoon or during a sleepless night. To compensate for the ever-increasing availability and effectiveness of financial technology, the planner has to exploit the uniquely human elements of the financial planning process. Dealing with uniquely human factors like emotions and empathy becomes particularly important in ensuring that the CFP® professional continues to be relevant to the population. Technology, already providing basic quantitative client account information and low-level advice, will require the CFP® professional to perform higher-order cognitive thinking, working expertly in what is often referred to as the "soft-skills" of financial planning. Ironically, these soft-skills are difficult to develop and one's effectiveness in the practice of client psychology is not easy to measure.

In reference to our working definition of client psychology, the information contained in this book is designed for the purpose of helping clients meet their goals of financial success. It is designed to enable planners to focus more on the well-being of their clients. This is an important distinction, as it is not designed to trick clients or discover vulnerabilities of a client in order to take advantage. The contents of this book are designed with the fiduciary in mind, learning as much as possible about the client in context in order to better serve an ever-diversifying clientele.

Practitioners reading this book have the opportunity to infer from a variety of different disciplines how uniquely human factors impact client financial success. We hope that practitioners will consider how areas such as marriage, family therapy, and cognition can potentially impact new advisor-training programs, mentorship, and even the methods by which we prepare the next generation of CFP® professionals. Saying that financial planning is an art is no longer good enough. The stakes are too high. We are talking about the life's work of our clients. We as a profession must challenge assumptions, question best practices, and learn more about the dynamics that exist within the minds of our clients and the widely varied contexts influencing family financial decision-making.

Just as with practitioners, researchers in financial planning need to accept the challenge of working with unobservable outcomes. Little in consumer psychology comes down to a specific number or set threshold value. There are few accepted rules of thumb to quantitatively assess personal financial well-being. With financial health and well-being as the outcomes of interest, measurement becomes the researcher's first concern. To start filling this gap, the Consumer Financial Protection Bureau (CFPB) recently developed a financial well-being scale linking an individual's financial situation, skills, and knowledge to their sense of financial security and freedom of choice.

The Consumer Financial Protection Bureau Financial Well-Being Scale (2017) contains items similar to previous studies of financial stress or strain. Scale items such as "I have money left over at the end of the month" and "My finances control my life" have long been used in the study of finances in a family or social context. However, for the first time, a scale based on multiple waves of testing, including the use of item response theory, has been shown to be a reliable measure of unobservable financial health and well-being. The work of the CFPB on the scale sets an example and standard for researchers interested in questions related to client psychology. What a client may be thinking will never be directly observable, nor will it be easily quantifiable, and researchers in the field of financial planning will have to become comfortable with studies involving unobservable variables with complex measurement models.

Related to the measurement issue is selection of the unit of analysis in research. With a client-centered approach, the unit of analysis should be obvious. The outcomes and research questions center on the client's personal financial health. For example, assessing a client's level of self-efficacy in a study of the use of financial planners brings the focus to personal motivation as opposed to a study where the complexity of a client's portfolio is considered the driving factor in using a planner. Certainly both questions are of interest to financial planners, and perhaps the best study is one presenting competing hypotheses between personal and portfolio considerations. The point here is that with a client-centered approach, research questions focus on the person, and the personal, as the units of analysis.

Long-practicing financial planners know that it's never just about the money. While retirement account balances, savings rates, and rates of return are easily observed, such values are only meaningful in context. Moreover, the questions stemming from a typical case like the one introduced in the start of this chapter cannot be answered in dollars and rates of return. How a family communicates about money is a descriptive study that likely involves little quantitative analysis. How financial decisions are made depends on similarly unobservable factors such as personality, communication strategy, cognitive ability, and self-efficacy. Moreover, the outcomes that matter most to clients are equally unobservable. A safe and secure life for a child with special needs or the successful transition from a long business career into retirement are examples of outcomes with deep meaning for client and planner alike. Research that identifies the best interventions to build family financial well-being is in great demand. Moreover, studies linking a personal sense of increased security and freedom of choice (financial well-being) to the higher-order needs of life (the real things clients care about besides money) can make the most meaningful contributions to the field of financial planning.

REFERENCES

American Psychological Association. (2017). *Clinical psychology.* Retrieved from http://www.apa.org/ed/graduate/specialize/clinical.aspx.
Bandura, A. (1994). Self-efficacy. In V. S. Ramachaudran (Ed.), *Encyclopedia of human behavior* (Vol. 4, pp. 71–81). New York: Academic Press. (Reprinted in H. Friedman [Ed.], *Encyclopedia of mental health.* San Diego: Academic Press, 1998).
Consumer Financial Protection Bureau. (2017). *Financial well-being scale.* Retrieved from http://files.consumerfinance.gov/f/201512_cfpb_financial-well-being-user-guide-scale.pdf.
Ryan, R. M., & Deci, E. L. (2000). Self-determination theory and the facilitation of intrinsic motivation, social development, and well-being. *American Psychologist, 55*(1), 68–78.

CHAPTER 2

Behavioral Finance

Swarn Chatterjee, PhD, and Joseph Goetz, PhD
University of Georgia

Knowledge of behavioral finance can be useful to financial planners and counselors trying to understand their clients' financial goals, objectives, and behavior patterns (Chatterjee & Goetz, 2015). For example, going back to the discussion of Ben and Colleen, a financial planner who works with this couple should understand that Ben and Colleen's perception of their finances and financial well-being are just as important for them as the objective measures of these characteristics. In psychology, this is known as anchoring (Tversky & Kahneman, 1974). Findings from a study by Ariely, Loewenstein, and Pelec (2003) would suggest that most individuals do not know how much money they need to maintain a standard of living that would maximize their utility either in the current period or in the future. Therefore, in many cases, well-intentioned people such as Ben and Colleen may use sub-optimal reference points from which they are anchored, particularly when this anchoring was based on observing their friends, relatives, and acquaintances to determine their optimal financial needs. Irrespective of how the broader market is performing, Ben and Colleen's financial expectations and financial satisfaction may be anchored to the expectations and satisfaction of their friends, acquaintances, and their life experiences.

Additionally, the works of Richard Thaler (winner of the 2017 Nobel Prize in Economics) and other behavioral economists find that investors suffer from what is known as myopic loss aversion (Benartzi & Thaler, 1995). Myopic loss aversion is defined as a tendency of investors to compare the performances of their investment portfolios from the perspective of avoiding a possible loss rather than from the perspective of potential gains. This behavior is based on the amount of risk they perceive having taken within their investments. Other studies indicate that investors who frequently checked the performances of their portfolios were also more likely to sell off their securities after experiencing a market drop. This runs counter to the rational investment notion of buying securities when prices fall and selling the securities when prices rise. Loss aversion can also explain the decision of Ben and Colleen to sell their investment portfolio soon after the markets fell in 2008. As a result of this tendency, many individual investors tend to exit the market after it has fallen and deny their portfolios an opportunity to recover when the market subsequently rebounds.

Some knowledge of behavioral finance can help in improving counselors' understanding of their clients' financial behaviors when providing them financial advice. Ben and Colleen's perception of financial preparedness, like that of most people, will be shaped by their unique cognitive biases, financial attitudes, and their previous experiences with money and wealth. This chapter defines and discusses key concepts in behavioral finance as they relate to the financial planning process. The discussions in this chapter revolve around the integration of some of these key behavioral finance–based concepts within the advisors' counseling and communication techniques, and how these techniques can be useful in improving the quality of advice planners provide to their clients.

WHAT IS BEHAVIORAL FINANCE?

Behavioral finance can be defined as an interdisciplinary area that utilizes components of economics, finance, and psychology to examine the implications and outcomes of financial decisions made by individual investors and traders in the market. These individuals are often constrained by their emotional biases and cognitive abilities to rationally process sophisticated financial information (Mullainathan & Thaler, 2000). The findings from the area of behavioral finance indicate that many of the financial decisions made by people are better understood when the assumption of rational decision-making by all parties involved in the decision is dropped.

In a perfect world, all individuals are expected to be rational in their financial decision-making. And neoclassical economics assume that these optimal decisions are made after individuals have carefully weighed the costs and benefits of the expected outcomes (Becker, 2013). The rational choice theory also assumes that people have stable and consistent intertemporal preferences and their decisions are based on an underlying desire to maximize their utility. However, numerous studies conducted by Amos Tversky and Daniel Kahneman challenged this assumption of rational human behavior. These authors found that people do not always make rational decisions. In fact, peoples' decisions depend on the context of the situation and framing of the choices when decisions are presented to them. The authors found that people tend to be more risk averse when they have to make a financial decision in the domain of gains, and are more risk taking when they are faced with a potential loss-making scenario. The authors also found that people disliked taking a loss more than they liked an equivalent amount of gain; this finding provided the foundation for what became known as prospect theory (Kahneman & Tversky, 1979). The authors also found that people were more likely to make impulsive decisions, which are often more risky and possibly financially more harmful, when they are facing a loss-related scenario. As a result of this fear of loss, many investors hold on to their loss-making stocks a lot longer than they hold on to their profitable stocks; this is known as the disposition effect (Shefrin, 2001). This fear of loss and the unknown also manifests in peoples' decisions to resist change and drives peoples' preference for *the status quo*. The status quo bias is also known as mental inertia (Kahneman, Knesch, & Thaler, 1991; Samuelson & Zeckhauser, 1988). Extant literature finds that status quo bias can prevent people from changing their financial behaviors. Ariely and Wortenbroch (2002) found in one study that individuals continue to show a preference for the status quo bias when they have to make important decisions, the outcome of which is not known ahead of time. Ariely and Wortenbroch argue that this aversion to the unknown is also the reason why people procrastinate when they have to act on important financial decisions.

The process of financial planning involves numerous meetings and communications between the financial planners and their clients. Scholars of behavioral finance describe this type of communication, which forms a big part of the client-planner relationship, at two levels (Evans, 2008; Kahneman & Klein, 2009). Benartzi (2013) differentiates the two levels as *reflective* and *intuitive* decision-making. The intuitive decision-making process is quick, impulsive, and less thoughtful than the reflective decision-making process. The reflective decision-making process is slower, but more thoughtful and rational.

In the opening case, where Ben Sanford is averse to seeking the services of a financial planner, the Sanfords have seen a number of planners but have not yet committed. During these initial meetings with the respective planners, it is likely that the Sanfords (especially Ben because of his aversion to using financial planners), may have used an intuitive decision-making process to evaluate the financial planners and have not found anyone with whom they were able to commit to a long-term engagement. An intuitive decision-making process is less thoughtful and quick, and is often influenced by the perceived biases and past experiences to which an individual may be anchored. According to Kahneman and Klein (2009) the two types of decision-making are reconciled initially where the reflective decision-making process agrees with the intuitive decision process until proven wrong. One practical challenge to this two-system decision-making process is that the outcome of the decision is not known until later in the future. Since the outcome is not known it causes uncertainty, and in the absence of evidence to disprove, the reflective mind usually agrees with the decisions that the intuitive mind makes initially. If the outcome is found to be undesirable in the future, many individuals are left to regret the mistakes they made in their financial decisions at some later point in time.

APPLICATIONS OF BEHAVIORAL FINANCE IN UNDERSTANDING AND CHANGING CLIENTS' BEHAVIOR

As discussed earlier, emotional and cognitive biases can constrain peoples' abilities to make rational financial decisions. The intuitive decision-making system, which is our quick but emotional and impulsive decision-making system, relies on certain mental shortcuts to make quick decisions. These are known as heuristics (Kahneman, 2003). Heuristics rely on peoples' biases developed from their life experiences, preferences, and perceptions. For example, it is not uncommon for planners to find their clients apply at least some form of heuristics or biases based on their attitudes toward finances when making important financial decisions. In extreme cases, decisions made by some clients are deeply emotional and could conflict with the financial planner's recommendations. Later in the book, there will be further discussion on the theory behind heuristics and biases.

When clients make emotional but irrational decisions based on their preconceived notions and perceptions, it can be more challenging for financial planners to change their clients' behavior. According to Klontz, Kahler, and Klontz (2008), financial planners need to have detailed discussions with their clients and gradually bring about changes to help reduce their clients' stress during the transition process. Financial therapists believe that various counseling techniques can reduce clients' biases and resistance to the changes recommended by the financial planners (Goetz & Gale, 2014). Similarly, Thaler and Sunstein (2008) suggest that counselors can help their clients make better financial decisions by providing them with good recommendations and timely follow-up and feedback to help keep their clients on track toward achieving their financial goals.

Risk Tolerance, Risk Capacity, and Client Risk Perceptions

Financial risk tolerance can be defined as an individual's willingness to take financial risks. People who are less worried when taking greater levels of risk within their portfolios are considered to have a high risk tolerance, whereas people who are less willing to take financial risks within their portfolios are considered risk averse. According to Ricciardi (2008), people's perceptions of risk may not be the same as their risk tolerance.

Risk capacity is a person's ability to take financial risk based on their financial resources (Cordell, 2002). Risk tolerance can be measured using psychometrically developed risk tolerance scales (e.g., Barsky, Juster, Kimball, & Shapiro, 1997; Grable & Lytton, 2003; Roszkowski & Davey, 2010). Financial advisors also have to measure their clients' risk tolerance before they can provide portfolio recommendations to their clients. In practice, financial planners can obtain more risk-related information from clients using a standardized scale.

Financial planners can also discuss the risk and return characteristics of various asset classes before making financial recommendations in order to get a true sense of a client's risk perception and risk capacity that may not be captured with a regular risk tolerance scale. Financial planners can further counsel their clients to correct their clients' misperceptions of risk tolerance and help align their clients' portfolios closer to their clients' actual risk tolerance.

Overconfidence Bias

On many occasions, clients' expectations of their expected standard of living upon retirement do not align with the amount of money they have saved for this purpose. The amount of wealth individuals can accumulate over time is constrained by their levels of risk tolerance and their investment time horizons. Furthermore, many individuals do not have sufficient financial literacy to correctly assess their true financial situations. Individual investors frequently overestimate the amount of wealth they can accumulate across time. Consequently, many individual investors fail to follow normative investment principles, and overestimate the securities selection and market timing abilities within their portfolios (Barber & Odean, 2002). Other studies have found that people overestimate their abilities to predict future returns (Bondt & Thaler, 1994; Heath & Tversky, 1991). The advent of social media and the internet have transformed the investment management industry over the past two decades. However, Barber and Odean (2000) find that increased access to and the availability of this very large amount of financial data have resulted in the unintended consequence of investor overconfidence and have resulted in substantial loss of wealth for investors who attempt to time the market (Barber & Odean, 2000).

Just as in the case of financial markets, people also underestimate the potential for loss from very low probability but financially burdensome adverse events that can otherwise be mitigated through insurance coverage (Eisner & Strotz, 1961). Conversely, Finkelstein and McGarry (2006) found that people who overestimated their probabilities of needing nursing care were more likely to purchase long-term care insurance. These errors can be linked to the average person's inability to understand the true magnitude or probability of the potential risk of loss to which they could be exposed (De Bondt, 1998).

Financial Literacy and Financial Capability

The concept of financial literacy includes financial planning–related knowledge and skills, people's perceptions of knowledge about their finances, financial behavior, and financial education (Finke & Huston, 2014). Financial capability is closely related to financial literacy. *Financial capability* is defined as "an individual's capacity based on knowledge, skills, and access, to manage financial resources effectively" (GAO, 2012). According to Nicolini, Cude, and Chatterjee (2013), making financial education available when consumers are making important, task-specific financial decisions may be the most efficient method of improving the quality of financial decisions that people make. Based on these studies, financial planners who educate their clients about the potential risks and returns of different investment choices are more likely to lead clients in making better financial decisions than planners who do not provide this type of task-specific financial education to their clients.

SUMMARY

Although behavioral finance has been around for a few decades, its applications in client psychology, and especially in the context of financial planning, has been limited. The applications of behavioral finance to financial planning can be useful in improving client–planner interactions in many ways. Knowledge of some of the key concepts of behavioral finance, such as loss aversion, mental accounting, and applications of heuristics, as discussed in this chapter, can be useful for financial planners in identifying clients' strengths and weaknesses when it comes to financial decision-making. The academic findings from behavioral finance suggest that reducing a client's level of stress during their meetings with financial planners can help improve the outcomes of the meeting for both the client and the planner. The association between stress reduction and quality of engagement with a client holds promise for potential future possibilities when stress reduction techniques can be integrated within the client communication process to further improve the outcome of financial planning recommendations for clients.

REFERENCES

Barber, B. M., & Odean, T. (2000). Trading is hazardous to your wealth: The common stock investment performance of individual investors. *The Journal of Finance, 55*(2), 773–806.

Barber, B. M., & Odean, T. (2002). Online investors: Do the slow die first? *Review of Financial Studies, 15*(2), 455–488.

Barsky, R. B., Juster, F. T., Kimball, M. S., & Shapiro, M. D. (1997). Preference parameters and behavioral heterogeneity: An experimental approach in the health and retirement study. *Quarterly Journal of Economics, 112*(2), 537–579.

Becker, G. S. (2013). *The economic approach to human behavior.* Chicago: University of Chicago Press.

Benartzi, S. (2013). *Behavioral finance: Two minds at work.* Retrieved from https://www.allianzglobalinvestors.de/MDBWS/doc/13–03–048+BR+Two+Minds+at+work_EN-01.pdf?c02045b621c5f293e0ab72de72a63fa12ab7055c.

Benartzi, S., & Thaler, R. H. (1995). Myopic loss aversion and the equity premium puzzle. *The Quarterly Journal of Economics, 110*(1), 73–92.

Chatterjee, S., & Goetz, J. W. (2015). Applications of behavioral finance in financial planning. In C. Chaffin (Ed.), *Financial Planning Competency Handbook II* (pp. 751–762). Hoboken, NJ: John Wiley & Sons.

Cordell, D. M. (2002). Risk tolerance in two dimensions. *Journal of Financial Planning, 15*(5), 30.

De Bondt, W. F. (1998). A portrait of the individual investor. *European Economic Review, 42*(3), 831–844.

Eisner, R., & Strotz, R. H. (1961). Flight insurance and the theory of choice. *The Journal of Political Economy,* 355–368.

Evans, J. S. B. (2008). Dual-processing accounts of reasoning, judgment, and social cognition. *Annual Review of Psychology, 59,* 255–278.

Finke, M. S., & Huston, S. J. (2014). Financial literacy and education. *Investor Behavior: The Psychology of Financial Planning and Investing,* 63–82.

Finkelstein, A., & McGarry, K. (2006). Multiple dimensions of private information: Evidence from the long-term care insurance market. *American Economic Review, 96*(4), 938–958.

Goetz, J., & Gale, J. (2014). Financial therapy: De-biasing and client behaviors. In H. K. Baker & V. Ricciardi (Eds.), *Investment behavior: The psychology of financial planning and Investing* (pp. 227–244). Hoboken, NJ: John Wiley & Sons.

Government Accountability Office. (2012). *Financial literacy: Strengthening partnerships in challenging times.* Retrieved from https://www.gao.gov/assets/590/588448.txt.

Grable, J. E., & Lytton, R. H. (2003). The development of a risk assessment instrument: A follow-up study. *Financial Services Review, 12*(3).

Heath, C., & Tversky, A. (1991). Preference and belief: Ambiguity and competence in choice under uncertainty. *Journal of Risk and Uncertainty, 4*(1), 5–28.

Kahneman, D. (2003). A perspective on judgment and choice: Mapping bounded rationality. *American Psychologist, 58*(9), 697.

Kahneman, D., & Klein, G. (2009). Conditions for intuitive expertise: A failure to disagree. *American Psychologist, 64*(6), 515.

Kahneman, D., Knetsch, J. L., & Thaler, R. H. (1991). Anomalies: The endowment effect, loss aversion, and status quo bias. *The Journal of Economic Perspectives, 5*(1), 193–206.

Kahneman, D., & Tversky, A. (1979). Prospect theory: An analysis of decision under risk. *Econometrica, 47*(2), 263–292.

Klontz, B., Kahler, R., & Klontz, P. (2008). *Facilitating financial health: Tools for financial planners, coaches, and therapists.* Erlanger, KY: National Underwriter Company.

Mullainathan, S., & Thaler, R. H. (2000). *Behavioral economics* (No. w7948). Cambridge, MA: National Bureau of Economic Research.

Nicolini, G., Cude, B. J., & Chatterjee, S. (2013). Financial literacy: A comparative study across four countries. *International Journal of Consumer Studies, 37*(6), 689–705.

Roszkowski, M. J., & Davey, G. (2010). Risk perception and risk tolerance changes attributable to the 2008 economic crisis: A subtle but critical difference. *Journal of Financial Service Professionals, 64*(4).

Samuelson, W., & Zeckhauser, R. (1988). Status quo bias in decision making. *Journal of Risk and Uncertainty, 1*(1), 7–59.

Shefrin, H. (2001). Do investors expect higher returns from safer stocks than from riskier stocks? *The Journal of Psychology and Financial Markets, 2*(4), 176–181.

Thaler, R., & Sunstein, C. (2008). *Nudge: The gentle power of choice architecture.* New Haven, CT: Yale.

Tversky, A., & Kahneman, D. (1974). Judgment under uncertainty: Heuristics and biases. *Science, 185*(4157), 1124–1131.

CHAPTER 3

Understanding Client Behavior

Rational or Irrational?

Swarn Chatterjee, PhD, and Joseph Goetz, PhD
University of Georgia

The field of neoclassical economics has traditionally assumed that people are utility maximizers. According to neoclassical economics, people are rational and make decisions without being biased by their emotions, and people can accurately weigh the costs and benefits of the choices they make. The conceptual frameworks applied in the conventional economic models to study decisions made by people ignored the behavioral anomalies found by social scientists who studied human behavior from a psychological or social perspective. However, the emergence of behavioral economics has challenged this idea of rational human behavior. The rigorous research that emerged from this field identified various instances when people's behavior deviated from the normative model. Furthermore, these studies confirmed that human behavior is a significant factor and requires inclusion in economic models that study economic decisions made by people (Mullainathan & Thaler, 2000). This chapter examines the rational and irrational decisions made by people based on the concept of bounded rationality. This chapter discusses how bounded rationality can be used to study financial decision-making of households. Other cognitive errors associated with related biases such as sunk cost fallacy and flat rate bias are also presented.

BOUNDED RATIONALITY

Herbert Simon (1972) helped reconcile the debate between rational and biased decision-making by using the term *bounded rationality*. Bounded rationality can be defined as rational decisions that people make within the constraints of their biases and abilities to access and process information. For example, investors usually do not know the future returns of securities when investing in them. But their investment decisions are based on an expected return they compute from the available data and information available to them at the time of investment.

Usage of the term *bounded rationality* is relatively new—it is only a few decades old—but the concept of bounded rationality goes back a few centuries. According to a study by Camerer, Loewenstein, and Rabin (2011) many philosophers, going as far back as the 18th century, tried to investigate the linkage between human behavior and the laws of economics. However, the neoclassical economists who followed these early 18th-century philosophers showed a preference for studying economic outcomes of decisions made with the assumption that the decisions made were rational, all else being equal. It wasn't until the second half of the 20th century that works of Herbert Simon, Amos Tversky, Daniel Kahneman, and others tried to bridge this gap in the literature between rational and irrational decision-making. Burgeoning research related to bounded rationality studied rational decision-making within the constraints of the psychological biases that individuals often succumbed to when making decisions under conditions of uncertainty and in changing environments. These studies found that decisions made by people were in many cases suboptimal. These decisions were constrained by limitations in the human abilities to process information and compute the payoffs from outcomes accurately on a consistent basis (Kahneman, 2003; Simon, 1982).

Studies by Gigerenzer and Goldstein tried to explain bounded rationality in another way. The authors found that people try to make rational decisions within the limitations of their cognitive abilities and biases. The authors described humans as being ecologically rational because they made optimized decisions within the constraints of their information-processing abilities (Gigerenzer & Goldstein, 1996). The notions of people's constraints to rationality were empirically tested by Tversky and Kahneman. These studies found that people often used mental shortcuts or heuristics to overcome the limitations of their information accessing and processing abilities (Tversky & Kahneman, 1974). This process is known today as anchoring, where people use a random reference point to compare and guide their perceptions of value and success from a decision (Ariely, Loewenstein, & Prelec, 2003). After nearly three decades of the line of work started by Tversky and Kahneman, this idea of bounded rationality has become mainstream and is considered by scholars, policymakers, and practitioners when developing tools and policies to influence normative decision-making in the population. These studies have contributed particularly to the area of individuals' and households' financial decision-making. Heuristics and biases are discussed in greater details in the later chapters of this book.

Mullainathan and Thaler (2000) extend the concept of bounded rationality by including bounded willpower, a concept that captures the choices made by people that may not be in their long-term interest. The authors also introduce the concept of bounded self-interest to indicate that people are not driven solely by the profit motive, and many people willingly make sacrifices at the cost of their welfare to help out others. The authors find that many times people know what is in their best interest yet fail to act desirably because of a lack of self-regulation. When forced to make a complex decision under uncertainty, people also tend to procrastinate and delay their decision to act on the issue. Banks, Blundell, and Tanner (1998) found in their study that many individuals violated the assumptions of the life-cycle hypothesis (Ando & Modigliani, 1963). Life-cycle hypothesis postulates that people initially borrow to maintain their standard of living when younger and when their income is low, and then start saving for the future as their income rises, and finally draw down from their savings upon retirement. But the Banks, Blundell, and Tanner study found that people's consumption patterns tracked their current income very closely. As a result, people did not have adequate savings and required a drastic cut to their standard of living upon retirement. Mullainathan and Thaler (2000) attribute this behavior to the concepts of bounded rationality and bounded willpower, as saving for retirement is cognitively challenging and a self-regulation problem.

An example of bounded rationality is also evident in the opening case of Ben and Colleen Sanford. The couple understands the importance of risk management, yet they have not reviewed their insurance needs in nearly half a decade and believe they have adequate coverage to protect against the risk of loss. In this case, the Sanfords are probably making their decisions constrained perhaps by their lack of knowledge in the area of financial planning. They have also prioritized other things while procrastinating on the decision to review their insurance coverage over the previous 5 years.

Thaler and Sunstein (2008) recommend providing people with access to good information, experience in the market, and prompt feedback as solutions to reduce the negative effects of bounded rationality when people make decisions. Good financial planners often practice these virtues as part of the comprehensive financial planning process by educating their clients about the risks and returns of securities and asset classes, sharing their own experience in the markets, and by periodically reviewing the financial situations of their clients. Providing feedback is important in investment planning because the clients would not know the outcome of their investment decision until much later in life when it may be too late for individuals to correct course. In the general population, policies related to the financial well-being of people have relied on providing generic financial education at different levels that are aimed at encouraging behavior change. However, financial planners add greater value by providing more customized and timely feedback specifically catered to meeting the financial goals and objectives of their clients.

SUNK COST FALLACY

Sunk cost fallacy is a term used to describe people's tendency to continue holding on to an investment, asset, or project because they have previously committed resources (financial, time, or emotional) to this asset or effort (Arkes & Blumer, 1985; Goetz & Gale, 2014). Belsky and Gilovich (2010) find that sunk cost fallacy happens when individual decisions are bounded by the resources that they have already committed to an investment or a project. People also tend to anchor their decision on future investments to the number of resources they have previously committed to the specific investment or project. According to Thaler (1999) this fallacy is associated with both status quo bias (a bias where individuals are reluctant to change from an ongoing commitment) and loss aversion (avoidance of uncertainty because of the potential for loss). Sunk cost fallacy is irrational because in many cases if costs outweigh the potential benefits, it is probably not a project or an investment worth pursuing. Thaler (1999) explains that people are vulnerable to the sunk cost fallacy because they tend to hold the potential benefits, the expected costs, and the unexpected expenses incurred in separate mental accounts. Another explanation for sunk cost fallacy is that people hold on to their loss-making projects or investments longer hoping to recover from the losses (Kahneman & Tversky, 1982). Doody (2013) explains that individuals demonstrate sunk cost fallacy because they care about their resources, including the ones committed to the failing project or endeavor. Strough, Mehta, McFall, and Schuller (2008) find that older adults are less likely to have sunk cost fallacy when compared with younger, college-age adults. The authors attribute this age difference in sunk cost fallacy to the fact that older adults are less loss averse than younger adults, since sunk cost fallacy is, in part, a manifestation of loss aversion. According to Garland and Newport (1991) there are two types of sunk costs—the first being the total dollar amount or absolute sunk costs and second being the relative sunk cost or the dollars already spent as a percentage of the overall budget of the project. The authors find that the probability of individuals falling into the trap of sunk cost was significantly higher when the relative sunk costs were higher.

FLAT RATE BIAS

Flat rate bias is a type of consumer fallacy where people prefer to choose a fixed payment or income option over a variable payment or income option. Mitomo, Otsuka, & Nakaba (2009) link people's preference for flat rates to their loss aversion. People generally prefer certainty over uncertainty and since the flat rate structure is more certain than a variable rate structure, people prefer the fixed rate option. Loss-averse individuals are willing to pay a premium for the relative certainty of a flat rate income or payment (Herwig & Mierendorff, 2011). According to Thaler (1999), mental accounts could be another reason why people show a preference for flat rate charges. Cognitive mistakes happen when costs are decoupled from consumption in people's minds. Many telecommunications companies, health clubs, and other service providers tend to take advantage of this bias by offering customers a much higher flat fee for an amount of service that a consumer is unlikely to be able to fully consume. Due to the flat rate bias, many clients of financial planners are likely to prefer a pre-established retainer fee or even a fixed assets-under-management fee as compared to an hourly fee when the number of hours required on a periodic basis is unknown. In addition, employees may prefer salary increases rather than large bonuses when those bonuses are based on firm growth and market movement, given the inherent uncertainty with these factors.

SUMMARY

This chapter discussed the concepts of bounded rationality, sunk cost fallacy, and flat rate bias. Overall, these are cognitive errors that we make as humans that have implications for financial planners (Chatterjee & Goetz, 2015). As discussed earlier, financial planners can add value through the process of financial planning by providing clients with timely feedback when their actions deviate from attaining their financial goals and objectives. Financial planners can also help reduce the information gap by educating clients about their finances, correcting inaccurate perceptions, reframing information, and providing clients with prudent financial advice (Goetz & Gale, 2014). Loss aversion is an underlying factor that also drives people's sunk cost fallacy and flat rate bias. Knowledge of these concepts can help financial planners to recognize these cognitive errors early and provide recommendations to promptly correct these behaviors in their clients.

REFERENCES

Ando, A., & Modigliani, F. (1963). The "life cycle" hypothesis of saving: Aggregate implications and tests. *The American Economic Review, 53*(1), 55–84.

Ariely, D., Loewenstein, G., & Prelec, D. (2003). "Coherent arbitrariness": Stable demand curves without stable preferences. *Quarterly Journal of Economics, 118*, 73–105.

Arkes, H. R., & Blumer, C. (1985). The psychology of sunk costs. *Organizational Behavior and Human Decision Processes, 35*, 124–140.

Banks, J., Blundell, R., & Tanner, S. (1998). Is there a retirement-savings puzzle? *American Economic Review, 88*(4), 769–88.

Belsky, G., & Gilovich T. (2010). *Why smart people make big money mistakes—and how to correct them: Lessons from the life-changing science of behavioral economics* (Rev. ed.). New York: Simon & Schuster.

Camerer, C., Loewenstein, G., & Rabin, M. (Eds.). (2011). *Advances in behavioral economics*. Princeton, NJ: Princeton University Press.

Chatterjee, S., & Goetz, J. W. (2015). Applications of behavioral finance in financial planning. In C. Chaffin (Ed.), *Financial planning competency handbook II* (pp. 751–762). Hoboken, NJ: John Wiley & Sons.

Doody, R. (2013, November 1). *The sunk cost "fallacy" is not a fallacy*. (Manuscript). Retrieved from http://www.mit.edu/~rdoody/TheSunkCostFallacy.pdf.

Garland, H., & Newport, S. (1991). Effects of absolute and relative sunk costs on the decision to persist with a course of action. *Organizational Behavior and Human Decision Processes, 48*(1), 55–69.

Gigerenzer, G., & Goldstein, D. G. (1996). Reasoning the fast and frugal way: Models of bounded rationality. *Psychological Review, 103*, 650–669.

Goetz, J., & Gale, J. (2014). Financial therapy: De-biasing and client behaviors. In H. K. Baker & V. Ricciardi (Eds.), *Investment behavior: The psychology of financial planning and investing* (pp. 227–244). Hoboken, NJ: John Wiley & Sons.

Kahneman, D. (2003). Maps of bounded rationality: Psychology for behavioral economics. *The American Economic Review, 93*, 1449–1475.

Kahneman, D., & Tversky, A. (1982). The psychology of preference. *Scientific American, 246*, 160–173.

Mitomo, H., Otsuka, T., & Nakaba, K. (2009). A behavioral economic interpretation of the preference for flat rates: The case of post-paid mobile phone services. In B. Preissl, J. Haucap, & P. Curwen (Eds.), *Telecommunication markets: Drivers and impediments* (pp. 59–73). Heidelberg, Germany: Physica-Verlag HD.

Simon, H. A. (1972). Theories of bounded rationality. *Decision and Organization, 1*(1), 161–176.

Simon, H. A. (1982). *Models of bounded rationality*. Cambridge, MA: MIT Press.

Strough, J., Mehta, C. M., McFall, J. P., & Schuller, K. L. (2008). Are older adults less subject to the sunk-cost fallacy than younger adults? *Psychological Science, 19*(7), 650–652.

Tversky, A., & Kahneman, D. (1974). Judgment under uncertainty: Heuristics and biases. *Science (New Series), 185*, 1124–1131.

CHAPTER 4

Heuristics and Biases

Jodi Letkiewicz, PhD

York University

It is common knowledge that human beings do not always make good financial decisions. Many fail to save, do not buy adequate insurance, delay investing, and accumulate serious debt. It is not that people do not understand the benefits of savings or the risks associated with not having adequate insurance, so why aren't they doing these things? Research in the areas of judgment and decision-making sheds some light on how people make decisions, why they sometimes make suboptimal decisions, and how to improve the decision-making process. The work is this area has been so impactful that two researchers, Daniel Kahneman (in 2002) and Richard Thaler (in 2017), were awarded the Nobel Prize in Economic Sciences for their contributions.[1]

The study of judgment and decision-making is primarily comprised of three strands of research. Normative studies identify the courses of action to elicit the best outcomes in line with the decision-makers' values and intentions. Descriptive studies observe actual behaviors and compare those behaviors to normative standards. Prescriptive interventions study ways to help individuals make better decisions, attempting to close the gap between the actual decisions we make and the choices that are in our best interest. The research arises primarily from psychology but is also grounded in economics, philosophy, and management science (Fischhoff, 2010).

Applying this field of study to financial planning provides us with a framework to examine the way people make decisions concerning their money and financial situation. Financial planners can play a key role in helping individuals make good financial decisions. In order to do so, we must first understand the mechanisms behind how people make decisions.

---

[1] Amos Tversky collaborated extensively with Daniel Kahneman but died in 1996, making him ineligible for the prize.

SYSTEM 1 AND SYSTEM 2

Stanovich and West (2000) introduced the specific concepts of System 1 and System 2, two process-based theories of reasoning. The researchers propose that the brain operates using two different systems. System 1 is described as "automatic, largely unconscious, and relatively undemanding of computational capacity" (Stanovich & West, 2000, p. 658). System 1 is fast, instinctive, emotional, and both contextualized and personalized. System 1 is highly efficient, but prone to systematic errors. System 2 is slow, deliberate, logical, and demanding of cognitive capacity. System 2 is taxing; it takes tremendous energy to engage System 2 so we often rely on System 1. The more frantic our lives are, the more we tend to rely on System 1. We are busy people with lots on our minds, which is why System 1 can be handy to have around. As Kahneman (2011) explains, System 1 can be tremendously helpful and it allows us to make rather complex decisions in a very short time.

Let us consider an example. Imagine you are on a walk through the woods. You turn a corner and see a snake at your feet. For most people, a surge of adrenalin kicks in and maybe a moment of panic. Before you even fully processed that it is a snake, your brain sent a warning message to your body. From an evolutionary perspective, this is a very handy warning system. We could stop and consider the markings on the snake, or the shape of the snake's head to determine if it is poisonous. Doing so would take time, time you might not have. What you felt in that first moment was System 1 doing its job. System 1 alerted you to the danger of a snake. Using System 2, you might have concluded that it was not poisonous, but as a protective measure, System 1 responded first.

We can use the System 1–System 2 framework to gain a better under-standing of how we make decisions. System 1 is on automatically while System 2 is in stand-by mode, preserving energy for more challenging tasks. When System 1 runs into trouble or is deemed insufficient, System 2 kicks in. Once System 2 is engaged, it can override the instincts (and potential errors) of System 1. Usually this arrangement works well and the two sys-tems are in sync, but System 1 is prone to systematic errors that can often go undetected by System 2.

System 1 is useful for things like choosing which food staples to buy or the best route to take to work. These are decisions that we do not actively have to contemplate. If System 2 was used for these everyday decisions, we would reach decision fatigue and be unlikely to accomplish what we intended. Can you imagine how exhausting and time-consuming grocery shopping would be if you stopped to inspect every brand of jam or cereal?

In our daily lives, we face many complex financial decisions. For example, whether or not to attend college, buy a house, how much to save for retirement, or what kind of investments to make. These complex problems require System 2. Several shortcuts have been developed over the years to help make financial decisions more efficient. For example, the advice to save 10% of your income toward retirement or that an emergency fund should be about 3 to 6 months of your income. These shortcuts were developed because financial decisions are difficult, with many factors to consider. These shortcuts, often referred to as *heuristics* (explained next); they are back-of-the-envelope calculations that are usually reasonable approximations and sometimes lead to the right answer. Heuristics are usually biased, meaning they can lead to incorrect estimates and, sometimes, serious errors.

HEURISTICS

The term *heuristic* comes from a Greek word meaning "to find out or to discover." It is an adjective defined as "enabling a person to discover or learn something for themselves" and "proceeding to a solution by trial and error or by rules that are only loosely defined." In the process of learning and discovering, we use our experiences and observations to develop shortcuts that can be relied on to make decisions more efficiently. In psychology, the term *heuristic* is used to denote a shortcut or efficient strategy that does not correspond to the normative model of solving a problem, but is usually quite sufficient (Tversky & Kahneman, 1975). Tversky and Kahneman (1975) demonstrated that people rely on a number of common heuristic principles when making decisions and that, while they can be extremely useful, they can also lead to serious errors in judgment.

Kahneman (2011) asserts that heuristics are associated with System 1 thinking. Individuals use heuristics to simplify complex problems that might otherwise require more time and consideration. The shortcuts (or rules of thumb) are referred to as heuristics and the underlying systematic errors associated with them are *cognitive biases*. Shefrin (2002, p. 312) summarizes the relationship between heuristics and biases concisely using the availability principle and the tendency to incorrectly assess risks as the example:

> *Availability is the principle; judging the frequency of occurrence by the number of instances that come readily to mind is the heuristic rule of thumb; being predisposed to ease of recall resulting from distortions in media coverage is the bias; and judging homicide to be a more frequent cause of death than stroke is the error.*

Think for a moment about the decision-making process most people use when making an investment. Do they consider every piece of information available? Do they pore over financial statements, earning reports, and mission statements? For most people, the answer is no. Investments are generally evaluated using a select set of criteria. Perhaps we hear of a company that is doing something innovative in an area we know a lot about. We then look at the financial statements for a few key statistics, maybe price-to-earnings ratio or earnings per share and decide whether to invest. This is what Herbert Simon (1956) originally called "satisficing." It is the idea that we use just enough information to make a reasonable decision.

Heuristics have been studied extensively, originating in psychology but with applications in other fields including medicine, criminal justice, and marketing. Heuristics are helpful at reducing the complexity of assessing certain situations and probabilities and predicting values, but can sometimes lead to severe and systematic errors. Researchers are interested in how heuristics arise and the various implications the use of heuristics has on decision-making. Tversky and Kahneman (1975) first introduced three heuristics: representativeness, availability, and anchoring and adjustment.

Representativeness

One of the most important principles affecting financial decisions is known as representativeness.

—Shefrin (2002, p. 14)

The representativeness heuristic is the tendency to overgeneralize from a few characteristics or observations. It is an example of attribute substitution in judgment. Probability is difficult to understand and interpret; therefore, we substitute *similarity* for *probability*. This is an entirely reasonable behavior. This substitution frequently results in reasonable probability estimates, but sometimes it does not. Many judgment mistakes are due to the inappropriate substitution of one aspect (e.g., similarity) for another (e.g., probability).

If asked, "What is the probability that event *A* originates from process *B*?" probabilities will be evaluated by the degree to which *A* is representative of *B*. As such, when *A* is highly representative of *B*, the probability that *A* originates from B is judged to be very high (Tversky & Kahneman, 1975). This can be a useful and efficient way to make judgments, but probability should be based on other factors, such as base rates and sample sizes, so limiting our judgment to just similarity can lead to serious errors.

Representativeness is present in a multitude of financial decisions, such as predicting the market, picking stocks, choosing mutual funds, selecting money managers, and buying insurance. Ignoring base rates and regression to the mean are two errors that can arise from the representativeness heuristic and can lead to serious financial mistakes. First, we will consider base rate neglect. Base rate neglect is ignoring underlying percentages or sample sizes.

In his book, *Thinking Fast and Slow,* Daniel Kahneman (2011, pp. 6–7) proposes the following scenario:

> *Steve is very shy and withdrawn, invariably helpful, but with little interest in people or the social world. A meek and tidy soul, he has a need for order and structure and a passion for detail. Is Steve more likely to be a librarian or a farmer?*

Most people, when posed this scenario, decide that Steve is a librarian based on the stereotypes we have about librarians. Kahneman points out that farmers outnumber librarians 20 to 1, so Steve is statistically more likely to be a farmer. If you chose librarian you were using the representativeness heuristic.

Our tendency for substituting similarity for probability is only part of the problem. Humans fundamentally struggle with understanding statistical information. As Gigernezer and Edwards (2003) point out, the inability to understand statistics is not a mental deficiency; in fact, some of the brightest people find it difficult. The misinterpretation is largely due to poor presentation of the information. Statistical information presented in a way that is difficult to decipher can lead to serious errors, particularly when assessing risk. These challenges can lead us to opt for the shortcuts we have developed—to look for similarity or recency of events rather than doing calculations. In the Kahneman example, whether we ignored the base rates or simply did not know them, we still ignored statistical information available to us. Another complicating factor is that base rates are pallid so we tend to overlook them. Individuating information, on the other hand, is vivid and stimulating. We are drawn to the story and interesting details, which leads us to focus on that rather than the boring statistical information.

Ignoring base rates is a common problem in financial decisions. When deciding on insurance deductibles, many people choose a low deductible and end up paying more in premiums over time. They do this because they want to avoid large out-of-pocket expenses. They do not take into consideration the small probability of making a claim in any given year. The money they save each year on lower premiums can easily offset the higher deductible in the rare event they need to make a claim.

Let us consider another similar example. Tversky and Kahneman (1983, p. 11) conducted a number of experiments using the following (edited) scenario:

Linda is 31 years old, single, outspoken, and very bright. She majored in philosophy. As a student, she was deeply concerned with issues of discrimination and social justice, and also participated in antinuclear demonstrations. Please check off the most likely alternative.

1. Linda is a bank teller.
2. Linda is a bank teller and is active in the feminist movement.

Linda is obviously more likely to be a bank teller than she is to be a bank teller *and* active in the feminist movement, but more students chose option 2—that she is both a bank teller and a feminist. Choosing option 2 violates the most basic laws of probability theory. People chose that answer because the description was constructed so that Linda would be more *representative* of a feminist than a bank teller. Tversky and Kahneman (1983) explain that the addition of feminist activities to her job as a bank teller improves the match of Linda's activities to her profession, leading students to choose the conjunction rather than the single activity.

Regression to the mean is an important concept that the representativeness heuristic can complicate. Regression to the mean is a technical way of saying that things will balance out in the end. It means that even though we might have days of record high temperatures, or historically high returns in the stock market, eventually both temperatures and the stock market will correct and regress back to the mean. One bias arising from this is the gambler's fallacy: the tendency to believe that if something occurs several times during a certain period of time it will happen less frequently in the future and vice versa. A common example of this is a heads/tails simulation. If I just flipped nine coins and they were all heads, you might predict that the next toss will be tails, even though each toss is still a 50–50 chance. Here we expect the next flip to regress us back to the mean. However, regression to the mean has nothing to do with the past; it is simply the tautological observation that we expect the average outcome with each iteration. As Shefrin (2002) explains it, people misunderstand the law of averages, otherwise known as the law of large numbers. People tend to attribute the same principles of large samples to small samples. The problem is that people grossly underestimate the sample size necessary for convergence to the mean.

Availability

The availability heuristic is another substitution heuristic, similar to representativeness. This heuristic describes the way in which people assess the frequency of a class or the probability of an event by the *ease* with which they can remember similar events or occurrences (Tversky & Kahneman, 1975). Like most heuristics, this is a very sensible strategy. Information that is presented more frequently is more easily retrieved from our memory. It is also sensible to assume that the more easily we retrieve something from our memory, the more likely it is to be true. The availability heuristic is a useful cue for assessing frequency or probability; however, other factors can influence retrieval and these factors can obscure probability estimates and lead to a number of problematic biases. Some biases that come about as a result of the availability heuristic include the false consensus effect (Ross, Greene, & House, 1977) and the validity effect (Boehm, 1994).

A common effect of the availability heuristic is referred to as the false consensus effect (Ross, Greene, & House, 1977). This leads us to believe other people think like we do because our opinion dominates our considerations. This can cause confusion and sometimes discomfort, and is something to be aware of when talking with clients.

The validity effect (Boehm, 1994) is the tendency for something to become more valid simply because it is repeated often. Kahneman (2011) says that repeating information is powerful because familiarity is not easily distinguished from truth. This phenomenon can be used for both good and evil. Certainly authoritarian regimes and marketers understand this fact. Planners, with their clients' best interests in mind, can use the validity effect to influence their decisions. This should be kept in mind when deciding on client touch points. What misconception is important to dispel? It might be wise to highlight long-term trends in both bull and bear markets so clients get the message consistently and it does not come across as reactive. Other communication tools can be used so the messages get through to different audiences. Storytelling and the use of video-based resources can be effective tools to convey memorable information. Note that people also tend to trust people who look like them (Farmer, McKay, & Tsakiris, 2014). If it is important to communicate something, consider your audiences and tailor your communications appropriately so that the message is trustworthy and memorable.

The availability heuristic can also lead us to incorrectly assess the frequency of events. Let us consider the 2008–2009 financial crisis. Events like the housing and financial crisis are rare events, but they may be at the forefront of our mind when we consider buying a new house or investing in the stock market. Clients may exhibit more risk aversion after these events, leading them to withdraw from the market or choose less risky investments. This can be a very costly mistake.

Anchoring and Adjustment

To demonstrate anchoring and adjustment, we will start with a question: What is the population of the city of Toronto?

Perhaps you live in Toronto and readily know the answer. Most people are unlikely to know this off the top of their head. In order to answer the question, you start considering things you do know. Maybe you know that the population of your city is 200,000 and Toronto is much larger than that, so you say 1 million. Maybe you know that the population of New York City is 8 million and think Toronto is probably smaller than that, so you say 5 million. In both cases, you started with what you know and adjusted from that number. The adjustment gets you closer to the right answer but is likely insufficient. This is what is known as the anchoring and adjustment heuristic. Some psychologists like to joke that it is the anchoring and insufficient adjustment heuristic! (Note: The population of Toronto is approximately 2.8 million.)

The anchoring heuristic is used when making estimates about an unknown value. As demonstrated, people generally start with an initial value, something they know, and then adjust to yield a final answer. Different starting points yield different estimates and the subsequent adjustments are generally insufficient. This typically leads to a bias toward the initial value (Tversky & Kahneman, 1975).

Anchoring and adjustment is very common in financial decisions and is evident in many domains. For example, an investor anchoring to the original price they paid for a stock or a home buyer latching onto an arbitrary posted sales price are both examples of anchoring and adjustment. Similarly, credit card minimum payments can lure a consumer into paying less than they should because the minimum payment is so low (Agarwal, Chomsisengphet, Mahoney, & Stroebel, 2014; McHugh & Ranyard, 2016).

The anchoring and adjustment principle can help explain the tendency to base future expectations on past performance. A study by Kaustia, Alho, and Puttonen (2008) found that both students and investment professionals anchored future expectations to prior performance. When they administered the study to professionals with more investment experience, the effect was reduced but did not disappear completely. Most investment professionals are aware of the vast amount of research showing that past performance does not predict future performance (Malkiel, 1995) but they have trouble overcoming this innate bias and are susceptible to the same errors as novice investors.

Several biases arise from anchoring and adjustment. We will discuss status quo bias, loss aversion, and sunk costs. The status quo bias is the path of least resistance. It is simply exhibiting a preference for the current state of affairs. The current status or baseline is a reference point and the "disadvantages of moving from it loom larger than the advantages" (Kahneman, Knetsch, & Thaler 1991, pp. 197–198). In one of the first studies on the topic, Samuelson and Zeckhauser (1988) conducted a series of experiments to test the status quo bias. In one experiment, two scenarios were presented to participants. The first was a neutral scenario: "You are a serious reader of the financial pages but until recently you have had few funds to invest. That is when you inherited a large sum of money from your great-uncle. You are considering different portfolios." The participants were given four choices: a moderate-risk company, a high-risk company, treasury bills, or municipal bonds. Descriptions were provided for each type of investment. In the status quo scenario, participants were told that a significant portion is invested in the moderate risk Company A and the wording on the first choice was changed to "Retain the investment in Moderate Company A." As expected, the researchers found that participants were far more likely to choose the moderate company when it was presented as the existing investment.

The status quo bias has been demonstrated in multiple domains including organ donation (Johnson & Goldstein, 2003), car insurance (Johnson, Hershey, Meszaros, & Kunreuther, 1993), and utility service (Hartman, Doane, & Woo, 1991). It has been identified as a significant issue in retirement planning with several important findings. In a study of retirement accounts at a prominent university, Samuelson and Zeckhauser (1988) found that more than half of retirement plan participants never changed from their initial asset allocation. Madrian and Shea (2001) found that only about half of employees enrolled in a company's 401(k) plan when they had to take action to enroll and that participation increased dramatically when enrollment was automatic. Thaler and Benartzi (2004) proposed a retirement plan called Save More Tomorrow (SMarT) designed to exploit the tendency to stick to the status quo. First, employees are automatically enrolled into a retirement plan. Then they are defaulted into an option to increase the amount they save each year. In order to change this designation, they must take action to do so. Doing nothing keeps them in the retirement savings plan and increases their savings each year. In their study, the SMarT program led to substantial increases in the savings rates of employees.

Daniel Kahneman once said, "The concept of loss aversion is certainly the most significant contribution of psychology to behavioral economics." In prospect theory, Kahneman and Tversky (1979) demonstrated that individuals do not evaluate their wealth in absolute terms, but rather to a reference point (i.e., the status quo). Loss aversion contributes to the status quo bias (Kahneman, Knetsch, & Thaler 1991). The status quo becomes the reference point from which gains and losses are evaluated. Any deviation from that may be considered a loss.

Loss aversion motivates a lot of financial decision-making and can be the dominant rationale for risky decisions. Myopic loss aversion is the worry of suffering imminent losses and can contribute to the reluctance to invest or save for retirement. Some individuals may choose to hold their savings in a low interest bank account rather than investing in financial markets. This is a loss aversion bias grounded in their life history or personal psychology. A prior experience of selling assets during a market decline or investing just before a market decline can create a sense of fear of repeating the error.

Loss aversion is also to blame for something called the disposition effect (Shefrin & Statman, 1985). This is the tendency to hold onto a losing stock because you do not want to realize the loss. Odean (1998) found that it can be surprisingly difficult to sell a stock that has fallen in value. On the other side, investors also have the tendency to panic when the market falls and may wish to sell off some of their securities. In these situations, it is important to return to fundamentals and make strategic decisions based on reason rather than emotion. Loss aversion might also be the reason people with the capacity to take risk choose a low-risk profile.

Sunk cost is simply "throwing good money after bad." It is the "tendency to continue an endeavor once an investment in money, effort, or time has been made" (Arkes & Blumer, 1985, p. 124). We put considerable weight on previously spent resources that are irrelevant to current or future decisions. Economists classify this behavior as irrational because it can lead to a misallocation of resources. No matter how we decide to proceed, the money we already spent is gone.

BIAS REDUCTION

When I moved to Canada a few years ago, I faced some of the unique challenges that many Americans living abroad face. The Internal Revenue Service places restrictions on the types of investments Americans can make outside of Canada or, rather, places onerous reporting requirements on certain investments. Therefore, the simplest way to invest is to buy individual stocks. This was new to me since in the past I almost exclusively held exchange-traded funds, and mutual funds. I started buying shares in a few Canadian companies. I know all of the psychological pitfalls of investing—I teach it, read about it, and just wrote a chapter on it. That did not stop me from making some serious mistakes. I panicked when a stock price fell and I sold the stock, only to see it rebound and I bought it again at a higher price.

I held on to certain stocks because the price fell and I was fixated on the price I paid for it rather than considering if the new price accurately reflected the financials and outlook of the company. I am aware of the normative rules of investing and that this is the *exact opposite* of what I am supposed to do, but I still fell into the trap. If I know I am predisposed to these kinds of mistakes and struggled to stop it, that should give us some understanding for how people who are not aware of these heuristics and biases might behave.

I am not alone in this. A study by Haigh and List (2005) found that traders exhibited behaviors consistent with myopic loss aversion to a greater extent than a comparable group of undergraduate students. Mullainathan, Noeth, and Schoar (2012) found that financial advisors encouraged returns-chasing behavior and pushed for funds with higher fees, even if their client started with a diversified, low-fee portfolio.

That brings us to the topic of *bias reduction* and how to stop ourselves—and our clients—from making financial mistakes. Soll, Milkman, and Payne (2013) wrote a comprehensive chapter in the *Handbook of Judgment and Decision Making* that is used as the basis for the following discussion but modified with financial planning in mind. For more information on debiasing, I recommend reading their chapter in full. Soll, Milkman, and Payne (2013) use Stanovich and West's (2000) System 1–System 2 framework to identify strategies that can be effective at improving decision-making. Before determining which strategies might work, it's important to determine the readiness of the decision-maker. The researchers outline three determinants of decision readiness: fatigue and distraction effects, visceral influences, and individual differences.

When someone is fatigued, distracted, or pressed by time engaging System 2 to override System 1 becomes increasingly difficult. Research in the area shows that when people are distracted they are more likely succumb to temptation (Shiv & Fedorikhin, 1999) and when people are depleted they are less able to exercise self-control (Baumeister, Vohs, & Tice, 2007; Milkman, 2012). The lesson here to is pay attention to the distress and distraction of your clients in order to encourage optimal environments for good decision-making.

Visceral reactions are System 1's way to ensure survival. It is the instinct to recoil in fear when seeing a snake or being started in the middle of the night when you hear a sound. System 1 reacts before System 2 has a chance to kick in. This can be a very valuable reaction, but can lead us to make unsound decisions. This is why we buy high caloric food when we are hungry (Read & Van Leeuwen, 1998). Paying attention to emotional reactions of clients can help a planner decide what kinds of decisions they may be able to make. Suggesting a cooling-off period before doing something extreme, like divesting when the market is low, can be effective at limiting the effect.

Individual differences are the variability between different people in terms of their intelligence, knowledge, and thinking styles. While some biases correlated with intelligence, many do not (Stanovich & West, 2000). Engaging System 2 is more related to thinking styles than to intelligence or cognitive ability. Even when people are aware of their erroneous responses, they may not have the knowledge to know what steps to take to make a better choice. This can be highly relevant in the field of financial planning, where clients are aware of their emotional reactions but unsure the best financial decisions to make.

Soll, Milkman, and Payne (2013) suggest there are two ways to go about bias reduction. The first, referred to as "modify the decision-maker," involves education and tools in an attempt to shift a decision-maker's thinking from System 1 to System 2. The second, referred to as "modify the environment," involves changing the environment to encourage optimal decision-making.

Modify the Decision-Maker

Modifying the decision-maker requires shifting from System 1 and engaging System 2. This requires focused attention and effort on the part of the decision-maker. It requires us to actively engage and work harder when making decisions, which may be not be an easy process. Researchers have identified several strategies to modify the decision-maker to encourage optimal decision-making.

One key debiasing technique is through education. It should be noted that types of education and presentation of information can have very different impacts. McKenzie and Liersch (2011) found that novel way to debias the notion that investments grow linearly as opposed to exponentially, a bias that causes people to delay saving for retirement or other future goals. They found that knowing the normative rule is not a guarantee that someone will use it. They found that the best intervention was a graphical representation highlighting the benefits of saving early and the associated downsides of delaying.

Another debiasing technique to modify the decision-maker is to encourage taking an alternative view or an outsider's perspective. This can help to overcome the problem of narrow thinking. Taking an outsider's perspective involves removing oneself from a specific situation (Kahneman & Lovallo, 1993) and can help reduce overconfidence (Gigerenzer, Hoffrage, & Kleinbölting, 1991). It can also be effective to ask an outsider when evaluating a decision. Another intervention is to consider the opposite of whatever decision they plan to make. Planning an investment property and expect it to increase 10% a year for the next several years? What if it doesn't? Is it still an investment you would make? These different methods can help to reduce overconfidence and the hindsight bias (Larrick, 2004).

The use of tools or models can be helpful in reducing bias. Checklists that provide a list of specific actions, steps, or criteria can help reduce errors due to memory failure or limited attention (Hales & Pronovost, 2006). Checklists have been incorporated into medical environments and aviation with positive effects (Hart & Owen, 2005; Myburgh, Chapman, Szekely, & Osborne, 2005). While checklists are generally recommended in high-pressure settings where best practices might be overlooked (Hales & Pronovost, 2006), they can also be useful for financial planners. There are often many variables involved, both known and unknown, when making complex financial decisions. Identifying the specific areas that are more onerous and emotionally fraught, for example, estate planning, can help improve decisions around complex and sometimes sensitive decisions.

Change the Decision-Making Environment

Rather than trying to shift thinking from System 1 to System 2, this strategy attempts to modify the environment so that System 1 thinking will yield good outcomes. Thaler and Sunstein (2008) popularized these methods, and discuss them at length, in their book *Nudge* (2008). They call these strategies nudges because they attempt to nudge decision-makers into the optimal direction.

Perhaps one of the most important contributions to the judgment and decision-making literature is the power of defaults. When default options are set, people are far more likely to stick with the default option. As pointed out earlier in the chapter, defaults have predicted everything from retirement savings to organ donation. The default option plays off our tendency to procrastinate and our preference for the status quo. When faced with difficult choices, sometimes it is easier not to choose at all. As Dan Ariely (2008) points out in his TED Talk, the problem (regarding organ donation) isn't that people don't care or think it is not important; it's that we *do* care and *do* think it's important! The choice is difficult and we truly do not know what to do, so we do nothing and the default becomes our choice. Defaults have been effective at enrolling employees into retirement plans (Madrian & Shea, 2001) and increasing savings over time (Thaler & Bernartzi, 2004).

Defaults can be an important tool for financial planners. From a normative standpoint, we know what our clients *should* be doing to meet their financial goals. Think of the things your clients struggle with the most: Is it taking action on buying adequate insurance? Starting an investment or individual retirement account? Is there a way you can grease the skids or nudge them into taking those actions? Consider presenting options to them in a way that puts them on a path where they actively need to disengage rather than engage.

Another nudge involves constructing and presenting information. Information ought to be presented in an intuitive and easily interpreted format. Similar to the suggestion earlier on presenting vivid graphs, sometimes information (and numbers, more specifically) need to be presented in a user-friendly format. For example, translating information into monthly retirement income might be more easily understood than a large lump-sum amount. "Saving $400 more per month now will increase your monthly income in retirement by $550" is more easily interpreted than "Saving an additional $5,000 per year will result in an additional $175,000 at retirement." Pictorial displays can be an effective tool (Galesic, Garcia-Retamero, & Gigerenzer, 2009).

Comprehending relative frequency and proportions is particularly difficult for humans. Recall the Linda problem presented earlier. The scenario faced much criticism for wording and framing, leading to several adjustments and experiments over time. Hertwig and Gigerenzer (1999) found that changing to a frequency format was successful at reducing the mistakes. When the wording of the Linda problem was changed to—"There are 100 persons who fit the [Linda] description above. How many of them are: (a) Bank tellers, (b) Bank tellers and active in the feminist movement."—the effect was significantly reduced; decreasing from 85% in Tversky and Kahneman's original study to 22% in a study by Fiedler (1988). Hasher and Zacks (1984) explain why frequencies are easier for human beings to process. The researchers found that frequency encoding is automatic; it does not improve over time or change with age or training. Probability was a 17th-century invention and can be difficult for humans to adapt and comprehend. The lesson here is that we need to be mindful about how information, more specifically probability, percentages, and frequencies, are presented to clients to limit the mistakes they are prone to make.

Providing new information can be useful in certain situations. Studies have found, for example, that showing caloric information at restaurants reduced the average calories per order at chain restaurants (Bollinger, Leslie & Sorenson, 2010). Iyengar and Lepper (2000) caution that providing too much information can lead to analysis paralysis and act as a deterrent. A study by Cain, Loewenstein, and Moore (2005) offers some cautionary advice for financial planners around disclosure. The researchers found that financial advisors tended to act more in their own self-interest upon disclosing possible conflicts of interest, feeling entitled after having fairly warned their clients. As for the clients, Sah, Loewenstein, and Cain (2013) found that clients may have increased pressure to comply with advice upon disclosure either in an effort to satisfy the personal interests of their advisor or because they do not want to insult their financial advisor. So, carefully consider the information you share with clients, particularly with respect to conflicts of interest.

Finally, nudges that induce future-focused thinking can help overcome the tendency to place more weight on immediate rewards and lower weight on our long-term goals (referred to as present bias). Making choices in advance (Rogers & Bazerman, 2008), using precommitment devices (Thaler and Bernatzi, 2004), and imagining oneself aging (Hershfield et al., 2011) are all effective strategies. Choosing in advance allows people to engage System 2 to make a decision without the emotional effects from System 1 interfering.

How did I stop the cycle of irrationality that I laid out earlier in the chapter I paused and reflected on the decisions I was making and recognized the biases that were entrapping me and leading me to make poor decisions. I focused on available information and normative rules and decided to take a different approach. I made sure the stocks I invested in diversified me sufficiently, rebalanced my portfolio, and left it alone. I check in every three months to see if I need to make any adjustments, but I otherwise ignore it. Essentially, making myself aware of my biases helped me stop making mistakes. I engaged System 2 and then set rules in place to limit the instincts driven by System 1.

REFERENCES

Agarwal, S., Chomsisengphet, S., Mahoney, N., & Stroebel, J. (2014). Regulating consumer financial products: Evidence from credit cards. *The Quarterly Journal of Economics, 130*(1), 111–164.

Ariely, D. (2008). *Are we in control of our own decisions?* Retrieved from https://www.ted.com/talks/dan_ariely_asks_are_we_in_control_of_our_own_decisions/transcript?language=en.

Arkes, H. R., & Blumer, C. (1985). The psychology of sunk cost. *Organizational Behavior and Human Decision Processes, 35*(1), 124–140.

Baumeister, R. F., Vohs, K. D., & Tice, D. M. (2007). The strength model of self-control. *Current Directions in Psychological Science, 16*(6), 351–355.

Boehm, L. E. (1994). The validity effect: A search for mediating variables. *Personality and Social Psychology Bulletin, 20*(3), 285–293.

Bollinger, B., Leslie, P., & Sorensen, A. (2010). Calorie posting in chain restaurants. *American Economic Journal: Economic Policy, 3*(1), 91–128.

Farmer, H., McKay, R., & Tsakiris, M. (2014). Trust in me: Trustworthy others are seen as more physically similar to the self. *Psychological Science, 25*(1), 290–292.

Fiedler, K. (1988). The dependence of the conjunction fallacy on subtle linguistic factors. *Psychological Research, 50*(2), 123–129.

Fischhoff, B. (2010). Judgment and decision making. *WIREs Cognitive Science, 1*, 724–735. doi:10.1002/wcs.65.

Galesic, M., Garcia-Retamero, R., & Gigerenzer, G. (2009). Using icon arrays to communicate medical risks: Overcoming low numeracy. *Health Psychology, 28*(2), 210–216.

Gigerenzer, G., & Edwards, A. (2003). Simple tools for understanding risks: From innumeracy to insight. *British Medical Journal, 327*(7417), 741.

Gigerenzer, G., Hoffrage, U., & Kleinbölting, H. (1991). Probabilistic mental models: A Brunswikian theory of confidence. *Psychological Review, 98*(4), 506.

Haigh, M. S., & List, J. A. (2005). Do professional traders exhibit myopic loss aversion? An experimental analysis. *The Journal of Finance, 60*(1), 523–534.

Hales, B. M., & Pronovost, P. J. (2006). The checklist—A tool for error management and performance improvement. *Journal of Critical Care, 21*(3), 231–235.

Hart, E. M., & Owen, H. (2005). Errors and omissions in anesthesia: A pilot study using a pilot's checklist. *Anesthesia & Analgesia, 101*(1), 246–250.

Hartman, R. S., Doane, M. J., & Woo, C. K. (1991). Consumer rationality and the status quo. *The Quarterly Journal of Economics, 106*(1), 141–162.

Hasher, L., & Zacks, R. T. (1984). Automatic processing of fundamental information: The case of frequency of occurrence. *American Psychologist, 39*(12), 1372.

Hershfield, H. E., Goldstein, D. G., Sharpe, W. F., Fox, J., Yeykelis, L., Carstensen, L. L., & Bailenson, J. N. (2011). Increasing saving behavior through age-progressed renderings of the future self. *Journal of Marketing Research, 48*(SPL), S23-S37.

Hertwig, R., & Gigerenzer, G. (1999). The "conjunction fallacy" revisited: How intelligent inferences look like reasoning errors. *Journal of Behavioral Decision Making, 12,* 275–305.

Iyengar, S. S., & Lepper, M. R. (2000). When choice is demotivating: Can one desire too much of a good thing? *Journal of Personality and Social Psychology, 79*(6), 995–1006.

Johnson, E. J., & Goldstein, D. (2003). Do defaults save lives? *Science, 302*(5649), 1338–1339.

Johnson, E. J., Hershey, J., Meszaros, J., & Kunreuther, H. (1993). Framing, probability distortions, and insurance decisions. *Journal of Risk and Uncertainty, 7*(1), 35–51.

Kahneman, D. (2011). *Thinking, fast and slow.* London, England: Macmillan.

Kahneman, D., Knetsch, J. L., & Thaler, R. H. (1991). Anomalies: The endowment effect, loss aversion, and status quo bias. *The Journal of Economic Perspectives, 5*(1), 193–206.

Kahneman, D., & Lovallo, D. (1993). Timid choices and bold forecasts: A cognitive perspective on risk and risk taking. *Management Science, 39,* 17–31.

Kaustia, M., Alho, E., & Puttonen, V. (2008). How much does expertise reduce behavioral biases? The case of anchoring effects in stock return estimates. *Financial Management, 37*(3), 391–412.

Larrick, R. P. (2004). Debiasing. In D. J. Koehler & N. Harvey (Eds.), *Blackwell handbook of judgment and decision making.* Oxford, England: Blackwell.

Madrian, B. C., & Shea, D. F. (2001). The power of suggestion: Inertia in 401(k) participation and savings behavior. *The Quarterly Journal of Economics, 116*(4), 1149–1187.

Malkiel, B. G. (1995). Returns from investing in equity mutual funds 1971 to 1991. *Journal of Finance, 50*(2), 549–572.

McHugh, S., & Ranyard, R. (2016). Consumers' credit card repayment decisions: The role of higher anchors and future repayment concern. *Journal of Economic Psychology, 52*, 102–114.

McKenzie, C. R., & Liersch, M. J. (2011). Misunderstanding savings growth: Implications for retirement savings behavior. *Journal of Marketing Research, 48*(SPL), S1–S13.

Milkman, K. L., Chugh, D., & Bazerman, M. H. (2009). How can decision making be improved? *Perspectives on Psychological Science, 4*(4), 379–383.

Milkman, K. L. (2012). Unsure what the future will bring? You may overindulge: Uncertainty increases the appeal of wants over shoulds. *Organizational Behavior and Human Decision Processes, 119*(2), 163–176.

Mullainathan, S., Noeth, M., & Schoar, A. (2012). *The market for financial advice: An audit study (No. w17929)*. Cambridge, MA: National Bureau of Economic Research.

Myburgh, J. A., Chapman, M. J., Szekely, S. M., & Osborne, G. A. (2005). Crisis management during anaesthesia: Sepsis. *Quality and Safety in Health Care, 14*(3), e22–e22.

Odean, T. (1998). Are investors reluctant to realize their losses? *The Journal of Finance, 53*(5), 1775–1798.

Read, D., & Van Leeuwen, B. (1998). Predicting hunger: The effects of appetite and delay on choice. *Organizational Behavior and Human Decision Processes, 76*(2), 189–205.

Rogers, T., & Bazerman, M. H. (2008). Future lock-in: Future implementation increases selection of "should" choices. *Organizational Behavior and Human Decision Processes, 106*(1), 1–20.

Ross, L., Greene, D., & House, P. (1977). The false consensus effect: An egocentric bias in social perception and attribution processes. *Journal of Experimental Social Psychology, 13*, 279–301.

Sah, S., Loewenstein, G., & Cain, D. M. (2013). The burden of disclosure: Increased compliance with distrusted advice. *Journal of Personality and Social Psychology, 104*(2), 289.

Samuelson, W., & Zeckhauser, R. (1988). Status quo bias in decision making. *Journal of Risk and Uncertainty, 1*, 7–59.

Shefrin, H. (2002). *Beyond greed and fear: Understanding behavioral finance and the psychology of investing*. New York: Oxford University Press.

Shefrin, H., & Statman, M. (1985). The disposition to sell winners too early and ride losers too long: Theory and evidence. *The Journal of Finance, 40*(3), 777–790.

Shiv, B., & Fedorikhin, A. (1999). Heart and mind in conflict: The interplay of affect and cognition in consumer decision making. *Journal of Consumer Research, 26*(3), 278–292.

Simon, H. A. (1956). Rational choice and the structure of the environment. *Psychological Review, 63*(2), 129.

Soll, J. B., Milkman, K. L. and Payne, J. W. (2013) A User's Guide to Debiasing, in G. Keren and G. Wu (eds), *The Wiley Blackwell Handbook of Judgment and Decision Making*, Chichester, UK: John Wiley & Sons. doi: 10.1002/9781118468333.ch33.

Stanovich, K. E., & West, R. F. (2000). Individual differences in reasoning: Implications for the rationality debate? *Behavioral and Brain Sciences*, 23(5), 645–665.

Thaler, R. H., & Benartzi, S. (2004). Save more tomorrow™: Using behavioral economics to increase employee saving. *Journal of Political Economy*, 112(S1), S164–S187.

Thaler, R. H., & Sunstein, C. R. (2008). *Nudge: Improving decisions about health, wealth, and happiness*. New York: Penguin Books.

Tversky, A., & Kahneman, D. (1975). Judgment under uncertainty: Heuristics and biases. In *Utility, probability, and human decision making* (pp. 141–162). Springer: Netherlands.

Tversky, A., & Kahneman, D. (1983). Extensional versus intuitive reasoning: The conjunction fallacy in probability judgment. *Psychological Review*, 90(4), 293–315. doi:10.1037/0033-295X.90.4.293.

CHAPTER 5

Decision-Making under Risk

HanNa Lim, PhD

Kansas State University

Decision-making under risk is extremely complex because the number of risky events around us is large and the information processing procedure is complicated (Chavas, 2004). There have been continuous efforts to explain how people make decisions under risk. Among those efforts, expected utility theory has been considered as the major paradigm and it has been developed with various modifications as to how utility and probability are treated in the models (Schoemaker, 1982).

EXPECTED UTILITY THEORY

The key to expected utility theory is that a rational decision-maker makes choices so as to maximize the sum of expected utilities. The utilities of outcomes are weighted by their probabilities. This utility maximization problem is expressed as Max $\sum p_i u(x_i)$. The outcome from the event i is denoted as x_i, the utility function is denoted as u, and the probability associated with the event i is denoted as p_i. Individual risk preference is reflected in the utility function u. If a decision-maker prefers a gamble (e.g. 50% chance to receive $10 and 50% chance to receive nothing) to its expected monetary value for sure (e.g., certain $5), the individual is regarded as risk-seeking (Schoemaker, 1982). On the contrary, if a decision-maker prefers the sure thing to the gamble of equal expected value, the individual is risk-averse. A concave utility function in expected utility theory implies risk-averse preferences (Schoemaker, 1982).

Expected utility theory is based on four assumptions, which are cancellation, transitivity, dominance, and invariance (Tversky & Kahneman, 1986). Tversky and Kahneman (1986) documented these four assumptions as follows. First, under the cancellation assumption, individuals ignore the states that yield the same outcomes regardless of one's choice and only consider the states that yield different outcomes. Second, if option A is preferred to option B and option B is preferred to option C, then option A is preferred to option C, according to the transitivity assumption (Kahneman &Tversky, 1984). Third, if one option is better than other options in one state and at least as good as other options in all other states, that option is the dominant option. Fourth, the assumption of invariance implies that the preference between options should be independent of the way the options are represented.

VIOLATIONS OF EXPECTED UTILITY THEORY

Despite its normative role in a decision-making model, research found failures of expected utility theory in describing how individuals actually make decisions under risk. In particular, violations of invariance and dominance have been discussed as evidence of the failure of expected utility theory (Barberis & Thaler, 2003). The examples presented next are from Tversky and Kahneman's (1981) article, and show how invariance and dominance principles are violated in experiments.

> *Problem 1 [N = 152]: Imagine that the U.S. is preparing for the outbreak of an unusual Asian disease, which is expected to kill 600 people. Two alternative programs to combat the disease have been proposed. Assume that the exact scientific estimates of the consequences of the programs are as follows:*
>
> *If Program A is adopted, 200 people will be saved. [72 percent]*
>
> *If Program B is adopted, there is a one-third probability that 600 people will be saved and a two-thirds probability that no people will be saved. [28 percent]*
>
> *Which of the two programs would you favor? (Tversky & Kahneman, 1981, p. 453)*

> *Problem 2 [N = 155]: If program C is adopted, 400 people will die. [22 percent]*
>
> *If program D is adopted, there is a one-third probability that nobody will die and a two-thirds probability that 600 people will die. [78 percent]*
>
> *Which of the two programs would you favor? (Tversky & Kahneman, 1981, p. 453)*

Problem 1 and Problem 2 are basically identical except that Problem 1 uses a survival frame and Problem 2 uses a mortality frame (Tversky & Kahneman, 1981). According to the invariance assumption in expected utility theory, individuals are expected to show consistent risk preference across the problems. Those who choose Program A from Problem 1 are expected to choose Program C from Problem 2, showing their consistent risk-aversion. On the other hand, those who choose Program B from Problem 1 are expected to choose Program D from Problem 2, showing their consistent risk-seeking. However, it turns out that the survival frame versus mortality frame evokes the inconsistency in preferences: 72% of respondents to Problem 1 chose Program A, but 78% of respondents to Problem 2 chose Program D (Tversky & Kahneman, 1981). This means that the majority is found to be risk in one frame (the survival frame) and seek risk averse in the other frame (the mortality frame), which is an obvious violation of invariance. The next example is the evidence showing violation of the dominance principle.

Problem 3 [N = 150]: Imagine that you face the following pair of concurrent decisions. First examine both decisions, then indicate the options you prefer.
Decision 1. Choose between:
A. a sure gain of $240 [84 percent]
B. 25% chance to gain $1,000, and 75% chance to gain nothing [16 percent]
Decision 2. Choose between:
Choose between:
C. a sure loss of $750 [13 percent]
D. 75% chance to lose $1,000, and 25% chance to lose nothing [87 percent] (Tversky & Kahneman, 1981, p. 454)

The majority (73%) of the respondents chose option A from Decision 1 and option D from Decision 2, and only 3% of the respondents chose option B from Decision 1 and option C from Decision 2 (Tversky & Kahneman, 1981). Apparently, options A and D are preferred to options B and C. The combination of options A and D can be expressed as: a 25% chance to win $240 and a 75% chance to lose $760. The combination of options B and C can be expressed as: a 25% chance to win $250 and a 75% chance to lose $750. When options are combined, the preferred combination is actually surpassed by the unpopular combination (Tversky & Kahneman, 1986). This example shows the violation of dominance. However, when the aggregated form, which is the transparent version of combination of options, was presented as follows, 100% of respondents chose options B and C (Tversky & Kahneman, 1981).

Problem 4 [N = 86]. Choose between:
A & D. 25% chance to win $240 and 75% chance to lose $760 [0 percent]
B & C. 25% chance to win $250 and 75% chance to lose $750 [100 percent] (Tversky & Kahneman, 1981, p. 454)

PROSPECT THEORY

Overview

While expected utility theory contributed to prescribing how rational individuals should make decisions under risk, it was confronted with many empirical challenges. In empirical works, individuals were found to behave differently than the axioms of expected utility theory. There have been attempts to explain these violations and one of them, which is considered the most successful, is prospect theory (Barberis & Thaler, 2003). Prospect theory provides an explanation of how individuals, who are not perfectly rational as assumed in economics, make decisions under risk. It has been mostly applied to finance and insurance, where attitudes to risk play a crucial role (Barberis, 2013).

Ever since prospect theory was introduced in 1979 as a descriptive model of decision-making under risk, it has been modified and extended to encompass not only choice between risky prospects with a small number of outcomes, but also uncertain prospects with any number of outcomes (Tversky & Fox, 1995; Tversky & Kahneman, 1992). Under the risk, the probabilities associated with possible outcomes are assumed to be known, but the probabilities are not assumed to be known under uncertainty (Tversky & Fox, 1995). This extension toward cumulative representation under uncertainty brings more reality into the original model since, in the real world, it is common that decision-makers do not know the probability of each option.

Like the equations of expected utility theory are formed with utilities (u) and probabilities (p), the equations of prospect theory are formed with values (v) and weighted probabilities, which are called decision weights (π). It is notable that in prospect theory, probability is in the weighting function.

Expected utility theory: $\sum p_i u(x_i)$

Prospect theory: $\sum \pi(p_i) v(x_i)$

In his review of over 30 years of prospect theory in economics, Barberis (2013) summarized four elements of prospect theory: reference dependence, diminishing sensitivity, loss aversion, and probability weighting. The first three are related to the value function and the last one is related to the weighting function. In the following sections, the properties of the value function and the probability weighting function are discussed.

Value Function

Kahneman and Tversky (1979) proposed three properties of the value function. The value function is (1) defined on deviations from the reference point, (2) concave for gains and convex for losses, and (3) steeper for losses than for gains. These properties are explained below and reflected in the asymmetric S-shaped value function (see figure 1 in Barberis [2013], p. 176).

First, in prospect theory, people derive utility from gains and losses, measured relative to a reference point, rather than from absolute levels of wealth (Barberis, 2013). This so-called *reference dependence* is widely experienced in our perceptual system—people respond differently to the same level of brightness, loudness, or temperature, depending on the reference point (Barberis, 2013; Kahneman & Tversky, 1979). Kahneman (2011) described a small experience in his book. Prepare three bowls of water: one with ice water; one with water at room temperature; and one with warm water. Put your left hand in the ice water and your right hand in the warm water for about a minute. Then put both hands in the room temperature water. Even though both of your hands are in the same temperature water, you will feel heat in your left hand and cold in the right hand because the reference points are different to each of your hands (Kahneman, 2011).

In the value function, the horizontal axis represents gain or loss x, and the vertical axis represents the value $v(x)$ people derive from that gain or loss (Barberis, 2013). The point that the horizontal and vertical dotted lines cross at is the reference point. The positive change from the reference point is perceived as a gain and the negative change from the reference point is perceived as a loss. The widely used reference points are the status quo, break-even point, expectation level, and purchasing price.

Second, the marginal sensitivity to changes from the reference point diminishes and the value function is concave for gains and convex for losses. People feel the change between a $100 gain and a $200 gain as greater than the change between a $1,100 gain and a $1,200 gain even though the actual amount of changes are equal and the same is true of the domains of losses (Kahneman & Tversky, 1979). This is applied to the risky context as well. Following are the rewritten version of risky choices problems used in Kahneman and Tversky (1979) and the outcomes are noted to refer to Israeli currency in the original version.

Problem 5 [N = 68]. Choose between:
   A: 25% chance to win 6,000 [18%]
   B: 25% chance to win 4,000 and 25% chance to win 2,000 [82%]

> *(Source: From Kahneman & Tversky [1979, p. 278] and rewritten following the style used for the problem above)*

Problem 6 [N = 64]. Choose between:
C: 25% chance to lose 6,000 [70%]
D: 25% chance to lose 4,000 and 25% chance to lose 2,000 [30%]

(Source: From Kahneman & Tversky [1979, p. 278] and
rewritten following the style used for the problem above)

Expected utility theory predicts individuals to be indifferent to the options in both problems. However, in their hypothetical choice experiments to university students and faculty members, Kahneman and Tversky (1979) found that 82% of respondents chose option B from Problem 5 and 70% of respondents chose option D from Problem 6. This means, in Problem 5, $\pi(.25)\upsilon(6,000) < \pi(.25)[\upsilon(4,000) + \upsilon(2,000)]$, which is $\upsilon(6,000) < \upsilon(-4,000) + \upsilon(2,000)$, and in Problem 6, $\pi(.25)\upsilon(-6,000) > \pi(.25)[\upsilon(-4,000) + \upsilon(-2,000)]$, which is $\upsilon(-6,000) > \upsilon(-4,000) + \upsilon(-2,000)$ (Kahneman & Tversky, 1979). Kahneman and Tversky (1979) noted that these preferences are consistent with the property that the value function is concave for gains and convex for losses.

The concavity for gains and the convexity of losses are reflected in the S-shaped value function. The concavity over gains implies that people tend to be risk averse in the domains of gains and the convexity over losses implies that people tend to be risk seeking in the domains of losses. This pattern is labeled as the reflection effect, since the preference between losses is the mirror image of the preference between gains (Kahneman & Tversky, 1979).

Last, people are much more sensitive to losses than to gains of the same magnitude. This is called loss aversion. Kahneman and Tversky (1979) explained that most people find symmetric bets of a 50% chance of getting money and a 50% chance of losing same amount of money unattractive and that this aversion to symmetric fair bets generally increases with the size of the stake. The value function is steeper in the domain of losses compared to the domain of gains.

About the magnitude of loss aversion, it is typically known that pain from losses is about twice as steep as pleasure from gains. The loss aversion coefficient has been estimated in experiments and is usually in the range of 1.5 to 2.5 (Kahneman, 2011). Tversky and Kahneman (1991) estimated the median loss aversion coefficient as 2.25, which indicates that when the possible loss increased by 1 unit, the compensating gain must be increased by about 2.25 units. The level of loss aversion varies across individuals. Professional risk takers in the financial markets are more tolerant of losses. When participants in an experiment were instructed to think like a trader, they became less loss averse and their emotional reaction to losses was sharply reduced (Kahneman, 2011).

Probability Weighting Function

Prospect theory is distinguished from expected utility theory not only in its treatment of preference patterns described in the previous section but also in its treatment of probabilities. In prospect theory, the value of each outcome is multiplied by its decision weight. While subjective expected utility theory attempted to encompass subjective attributes of probability, decision weights in prospect theory are not probabilities (Schoemaker, 1982). Decision weights measure the impact of events on the desirability of prospects, not the perceived likelihood of these events (Kahneman & Tversky, 1979). Kahneman (2011) presented a simple example to show how decision weights work differently from probabilities.

> *Problem 7. In the four examples below, your chances of receiving $1 million improve by 5%. Is the news equally good in each case?*
> *A. From 0% to 5%*
> *B. From 5% to 10%*
> *C. From 60% to 65%*
> *D. From 95% to 100% (Kahneman, 2011, p. 311)*

Despite the equal increase in probability, individuals feel that option A and option D are more impressive than option B and option C. The overweighted impact of option A demonstrates the possibility effect and another overweighted impact of option D demonstrates the certainty effect (Kahneman, 2011). When an event turns from impossibility to possibility and possibility to certainty, the impact is greater compared to the comparable amount of possibility change in the middle (Kahneman & Tversky, 1984). Kahneman and Tversky (1984) collectively named this end-tail sensitivity as a category-boundary effect. The possibility effect and the certainty effect are reflected in the probability weighting function as being steep at the ends and flatter in the middle (see figure 2 in Barberis [2013], p. 177.)

The main property of the weighting function is that low probabilities are generally overweighted, while moderate and high probabilities are underweighted. Below are the examples showing how low probabilities are overweighted in the hypothetical choice problems.

> *Problem 8 [N = 72]. Choose between:*
> *A: 0.1% chance to gain 5,000 [72%]*
> *B: a certain gain of 5 [28%]*
>
> > *(Source: From Kahneman & Tversky [1979, p. 281] and rewritten following the style used for the problem above)*

Problem 9 [N = 72]. Choose between:
C: 0.1% chance to lose 5,000 [17%]
D: a certain loss of 5 [83%]

> *(Source: From Kahneman & Tversky [1979, p. 281] and*
> *rewritten following the style used for the problem above)*

The participants prefer option A in Problem 8, which can be viewed as a purchase of a lottery ticket, and option D in Problem 9, which can be viewed as a payment of an insurance premium (Kahneman & Tversky, 1979). Overweighting unlikely extreme events explains the preference for lottery tickets and insurance, which were considered as anomalies in expected utility theory.

Combining the properties of the value function with the properties of the probability weighting function, prospect theory presents a fourfold pattern of risk attitudes (see Table 5.1). Depending on whether the event is perceived as a gain or loss from the reference point and whether the probability of the event is low or not, the risk attitudes differ. Individuals seek risk for gains and are risk averse for losses when the probabilities are low. On the other hand, when the probabilities are moderate or high, individuals are risk-averse for gains and seek risk for losses. The bottom row of Table 5.1 reflects the general properties of the value function but the top row shows the opposite risk attitudes, reflecting the category-boundary effect. The top left (when the probability is low for losses) explains why lotteries are popular and the top right (when the probability is low for losses) explains why people buy insurance (Kahneman, 2011). Kahneman (2011) considered this fourfold pattern of risk attitudes as one of the core achievements of prospect theory. Table 5.2 summarizes the differences between expected utility theory and prospect theory.

TABLE 5.1   The Fourfold Pattern of Risk Attitudes

Probability	Gain	Loss
Low	Risk seeking	Risk aversion
Moderate-High	Risk aversion	Risk seeking

Source: Slightly modified from Tversky and Fox (1995, p. 270).

TABLE 5.2   Expected Utility Theory versus Prospect Theory

	Expected Utility Theory	Prospect Theory
Objects of choice	Probability distributions over the states of wealth	Prospects framed in terms of gains and losses
Valuation rule	Expected utility	Two-part cumulative functional
Characteristics of the functions	Concave function of wealth	Asymmetric S-shaped value function and inverse S-shaped weighting function

Source: Author created based on discussions in Tversky and Kahneman (1992).

EFFECTS IN PROSPECT THEORY

Due to the unique properties of the value function and the weighting function, prospect theory explains some interesting phenomena that the standard economic model fails to answer. Camerer (1998) described the ten patterns in the field which can be explained by prospect theory: equity premium, disposition effect, downward-sloping labor supply, asymmetric price elasticities, insensitivity to bad income news, status quo bias, favorite-longshot bias, end-of-the-day effect, buying insurance against telephone wire damages, and demand for lotto. In this section, summaries and discussions of the endowment effect, status quo bias, and disposition effect are presented.

Endowment Effect

Individuals tend to value goods that are included in their endowment more highly than others and Thaler (1980) referred to this pattern as the endowment effect. This effect is noted as a manifestation of loss aversion (Kahneman, Knetsch, & Thaler, 1990). According to Barberis (2013), the term *endowment effect* actually refers to two distinct findings, which are exchange asymmetries and the willingness to accept (WTA) and willingness to pay (WTP) gap. He noted each of Kentsch's (1989) mug–candy bar exchange experiment and Kahneman, Knetsch, and Thaler's (1990) experiment as the standard references for exchange symmetries and WTA/WTP gap.

In his experiment, Knetsch (1989) gave a coffee mug to each participant in the first group and gave a candy bar to each participant in the
second group. After completing a short questionnaire, the participants
in the first group were asked whether they wanted to keep their mugs
or exchange them for candy bars. The second group, on the other hand,
was asked whether to keep their candy bars or trade for mugs. The third
group was a control group. They were simply asked to choose between
a mug and a candy bar, without initial entitlement or a reference point.
The preference of the control group was fairly evenly spread between a
mug and a candy bar: 56% preferred a mug and 44% preferred a candy
bar. However, 89% of those who initially received a mug (the first group)
declined to give it up for a candy bar and 90% of those who were initially
given a candy bar (the second group) refused to exchange for a coffee
mug. This dramatic asymmetry in valuations is the evidence for reference points and loss aversion. Participants view an exchange as losing
the item that they were initially given and gaining the other item. Since
the pain from losses is greater than the pleasure from gains, most of the
participants feel the exchange is unattractive and stick with their initial
endowment (Barberis, 2013).

In one of the experiments by Kahneman, Knetsch, and Thaler (1990),
half of the participants were given mugs and designated as sellers. The sellers were asked for each of the possible prices listed to indicate whether they
would receive the money and sell their mugs or not. The other half of the
participants were designated as buyers. For each of the listed prices they
were asked to indicate whether they would pay the money and buy the
mugs or not. The listed prices ranged from $0 to $9.50, with increments of
$0.50. The participants were instructed that one of the listed prices would
be selected at random and exchanges would take place at that price. The
random selection of the price implied that the participants' decision had
no effect on the price so they indicated their true preferences, rather than
bargained over the prices (Kahneman, Knetsch, & Thaler, 1990). While the
median WTP was $2.25, the median WTA was $5.75, which was over twice
of the median WTP. Since giving up a mug is a loss to sellers and getting
one is a gain to buyers, participants demanded much more money than they
were willing to pay in order to get one (Barberis, 2013).

There has been a controversy on the conditions in which the endowment effect disappears. Kahneman, Knetsch, and Thaler (1990) pointed out
that individuals would not overvalue their owned goods when the goods
are purchased for resale rather than for utilization. Also, consumers with
significant market experience were found not to exhibit the endowment
effect in a field experiment List (2004) conducted in the sports card market.

Regarding the role of experience, DellaVigna (2009) interpreted the role of experience in the endowment effects in two ways. One is that experience leads individuals to become aware of their loss aversion and counteract it. The other is that experience does not affect loss aversion, but it impacts the reference-point formation.

Status Quo Bias

Individuals have a strong tendency to do nothing or maintain their current or previous decision. This tendency is called status quo bias (Samuelson & Zeckhauser, 1988). Kahneman, Knetsch, and Thaler (1991) argued that individuals exhibit status quo bias because the disadvantages of leaving the status quo loom larger than advantages.

Samuelson and Zeckhauser (1988) conducted both experiments and field studies to test for status quo effect. In their investment decision-making experiments, Samuelson and Zeckhauser (1988) designed two versions of the decision questions. One was the neutral version that the participants faced a new decision and were asked choose one from several alternatives. The other was the status quo version, in which one of the alternatives is the position of the status quo. The main findings from the experiments were that individuals disproportionately adhere to the status quo choices (Samuelson & Zeckhauser, 1988). In the field studies regarding decisions on individual health-plan choice and retirement fund allocation of Harvard University employees and faculty members, strong status quo bias was observed as well (Samuelson & Zeckhauser, 1988). New enrollees to the health plan are naturally exposed to the neutral setting while continuing plan enrollees are not free of status quo bias. When new health plan options were added, continuing enrollees chose the status quo option more frequently and chose the new plans less frequently compared to new enrollees across all age groups. In the allocation choices between bonds and stocks, a participant can change the distribution between the funds at no cost. However, the changes in allocations year by year were found to be insignificant despite large variations in the rates of return.

From Samuelson and Zeckhauser's (1988) work, the number of alternatives and the amount of changes from the status quo were found to affect the preference. In the investment decision-making experiment, the degree of status quo bias increased with the number of alternatives in the choice set. In the field study of health-plan choice, enrollees who did transfer from the originally most popular plan tended to favor a new variant of that plan over other new alternatives. Tversky and Kahneman (1991) noted that small changes from the status quo were favored over larger changes.

Disposition Effect

Shefrin and Statman (1985) named the tendency of individuals to sell the winning stocks too soon and hold the losing stocks too long the disposition effect. Barberis and Thaler (2003) explained this reluctance to realize losses using the concavity over gains and convexity over losses property of the value function in prospect theory. The purchase price is assumed to be the reference point in this example. First, suppose that an investor purchased a stock at \$50 and it is currently trading at \$55. The utility from selling the stock now is $\upsilon(5)$. Or the investor can wait another period, when the stock price is expected to drop to \$50 or rise to \$60 with equal probability. The expected value of waiting and selling next period is then $0.5\ \upsilon(0) + 0.5\ \upsilon(10)$. Since the value function υ is concave in the region of gains, that is, $\upsilon(5)$ is greater than $0.5\ \upsilon(0) + 0.5\ \upsilon(10)$, the investor is more inclined to sell it now. On the other hand, suppose that a stock is currently selling at \$45. This means, the utility from selling it now is $\upsilon(-5)$. In the next period, the stock is expected to decline further to \$40 or regain its original price of \$50 with equal probability. If the investor waits and sells it in the next period, the utility will be $0.5\ \upsilon(-10) + 0.5\ \upsilon(0)$. Since the value function υ is convex in the region of losses, $0.5\ \upsilon(-10) + 0.5\ \upsilon(0)$ is greater than $\upsilon(-5)$. The investor tends to hold on to the stock, expecting the stock will eventually break even and he can avoid a painful loss (Barberis & Thaler, 2003).

Odean (1998) analyzed the individual trading records from a discount brokerage house. For tax purposes, investors are expected to postpone taxable gains and realize tax losses by holding winning investments and selling losing investments. With an assumption of purchase prices as investors' reference points, individual investors were found to tend to sell their winners and hold their losers over the entire year. There was an exception in December. Investors tended to sell losers more in December than during the rest of the year because they engaged in tax-motivated trading. Ivkovii, Poterba, and Weisbenner (2005) analyzed the trading behaviors of investors who had stocks in both taxable accounts and tax-deferred accounts. At short horizons, they found that the disposition effect is present in both taxable and tax-deferred accounts tradings, and that the effect is more pronounced in tax-deferred accounts. However, with longer holding periods, the tax-motivated loss realization became prevalent (Ivkovii, Poterba, & Weisbenner, 2005).

Frazzini (2006) argued that professional traders are not free from the disposition effect, even though greater investor sophistication was found to be less susceptible to the disposition effect. Using the data on mutual fund holdings, he found an asymmetric pattern that mutual fund managers were reluctant to realize losses facing bad news but actively realized gains facing good news. This pattern is consistent with the disposition effect and it leads the gradual market response to new information (Frazzini, 2006).

IMPLICATIONS FOR RESEARCH AND PRACTICE

Research

Utilize Prospect Theory to Solve the Puzzles

There exist various puzzles that literature is not consistent with the predictions from traditional economic theories. Traditional economic theories assume rational human beings but irrationalities abound in the real world. Researchers can contribute to solving the unresolved puzzles by applying behavioral perspectives.

One example is the limited annuity demand. While annuities have been considered an ideal vehicle to insure people against longevity risk in economics (Yarri, 1965), the demand for annuities is limited. This mismatch is called the *annuity puzzle*. Recent works take prospect theory's loss aversion concept into consideration to understand the limited demand for annuities (Benartzi, Previtero, & Thaler, 2011; Brown, 2009; Gottlieb, 2012; Hu & Scott, 2007).

According to Brown (2009), people view annuity products as a risky gamble, rather than as a risk-reducing strategy. In the absence of the annuity, for example, the individual has $100,000 for certain, but with the annuity there is some possibility that the individual will receive only a part of $100,000 or receive more than $100,000. This setting makes individuals ask themselves, "Will I live long enough for this to pay off?" (Benartzi, Previtero, & Thaler, 2011). Since the losses (in case the individual dies earlier than expected) from the annuity loom larger than the gains (in case the individual lives longer than expected), the attractiveness of annuities is reduced. Also, Benartzi, Previtero, and Thaler (2011) found that the participants in a traditional defined benefit plan, where an annuity is framed as consumption (in the form of monthly or annual income), are more likely to choose an annuity than the participants in cash balance plans, where annuity is framed as investment (in the form of account balances).

As noted earlier, prospect theory-induced preferences are pronounced with unexperienced decision-makers and decisions with complexity. Since annuity decisions involve complicated estimations and most people start thinking about them nearing retirement age without having chances to accumulate experience (Benartzi, Previtero, & Thaler, 2011), limited annuity demand can be explained well with the concepts in prospect theory.

Explore with Individual-Level Survey Data

In his review and assessment of prospect theory in economics, Barberis (2013) noted that while prospect theory describes risk attitudes well in experimental settings, there is doubt whether it accurately predicts individual behaviors outside the laboratory. Besides typical classroom experiments, there have been studies that show how prospect theory successfully explains individual behavior observed in field data (summarized in Camerer (2000)). While the reference dependent preferences can be inferred from observed behaviors, the direct link between the properties from prospect theory and individual behaviors is still missing.

Recently certain survey data, such as American Life Panel and Health and Retirement Study (HRS), provided researchers, who have been suffering from a lack of individual-level empirical evidence, the opportunities to utilize this information on key concepts of prospect theory. There are ample opportunities with the use of the HRS data, because responses in the prospect theory module in the 2012 HRS could be combined with other rich information on respondents' health and wealth from the core survey.

The HRS interviews a nationally representative sample of older people every other year and in each wave, and experimental modules are randomly assigned to a subset of respondents (Gottlieb & Mitchell, 2015). One of the modules conducted in the 2012 HRS is the prospect theory module that Gottlieb and Mitchell developed. Based on Tversky and Kahneman's (1992) experiment, a series of hypothetical risky investment questions are asked, and researchers can measure individuals' loss aversion level using the responses to these questions below.

Suppose that a relative offers you an investment opportunity for which there is a 50–50 chance you would (NV011) receive $115 or have to pay $100.
(NV012) receive $107 or have to pay $100.
(NV013) receive $130 or have to pay $100.
(NV014) receive $103 or have to pay $100.
(NV015) receive $110 or have to pay $100.
(NV016) receive $120 or have to pay $100.
(NV017) receive $300 or have to pay $100.
Would you agree to this investment? (2012 HRS questionnaire)

The questions are asked as follows (documented in Hwang [2017]): Not all seven questions are asked to respondents. First, all respondents are asked to choose whether to accept or reject the offer of the 50% chance

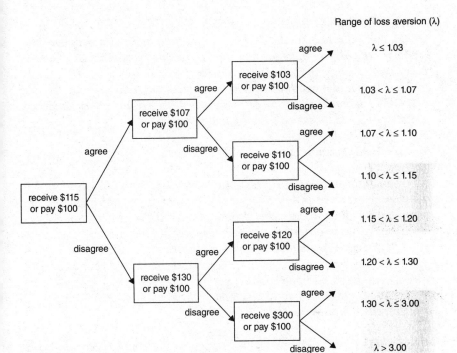

Range of loss aversion (λ)

FIGURE 5.1   Measurement of Loss Aversion from the 2012 HRS
Source: Author created based on the prospect theory module in the 2012 HRS and
discussions in Hwang (2017).

of receiving $115 and 50% chance of paying $100. Depending on their
responses, the subsequent questions are decided. If the respondent accepts
this offer, then lesser-gain option is offered. On the other hand, if the respondents reject the offer, then greater-gain option is offered. Figure 5.1
shows the flow of the questions asked in the 2012 HRS and the estimated
range of loss aversion based on the responses to the questions. Using this
data, Hwang (2017) found that loss-averse individuals are less likely to own
term-life insurance and more likely to own whole-life insurance, which is
consistent empirical evidence with prospect theory's prediction.

Also, the prospect theory module of the 2012 HRS provides information
on whether the respondents are subject to narrow framing or not. Based on
Tversky and Kahneman's (1981) experiment, these two hypothetical questions are asked to the respondents.

Imagine that the United States is preparing for the outbreak of an epidemic expected to kill 600 people. Two alternative programs to combat the disease have been proposed. Scientists estimate that the outcome of each program is as follows:

If Program A is adopted, 300 people will be saved.

If Program B is adopted, there is a 50–50 chance that either 600 people will be saved or none will be saved.

Which program would you favor: Program A or Program B? (2012 HRS questionnaire)

Imagine that the United States is preparing for the outbreak of an epidemic expected to kill 600 people. Two alternative programs to combat the disease have been proposed. Scientists estimate that the outcome of each program is as follows:

If Program A is adopted, 300 people die.

If Program B is adopted, there is a 50–50 chance that either none will die or 600 people will die.

Which program would you favor: Program A or Program B? (2012 HRS questionnaire)

As discussed for Problems 1 and 2 earlier in this chapter, the two problems are basically identical except in the way they are framed. The first problem is framed as survival and the second one is framed as mortality. Based on the responses from these two problems, Gottlieb and Mitchelle (2015) constructed a narrow framing measure (the concept of narrow framing is discussed later in the chapter). If the respondents choose Program A from Problem 1 and choose Program B from Problem 2, the respondents are regarded as having narrow framing. It is found that 25% of respondents were categorized as having narrow framing from Gottlieb and Mitchelle's (2015) analysis. With the information of narrow framing, they found behavioral explanation about why people underinsure their later-life care needs (Gottlieb & Mitchell, 2015). Tremendous potential exists for researchers to explore how the properties of prospect theory are related to an individual's health, employment, and financial behaviors.

Practice

Identify Clients' Loss Aversion Level

The first implication for the financial practitioner is that it is important to identify how much your clients are loss averse. Like risk tolerance acts as a key concept in expected utility theory, loss aversion is a key feature in prospect theory. In research, the loss aversion coefficient has been estimated as about 2.25 (Tversky & Kahneman, 1992). However, there exists a wide range of loss aversion. Using data from the experimental module of the 2012 HRS, Hwang (2017) conducted an analysis on the differences in the degree of loss aversion by respondents' demographics. While the author failed to find statistical significance, females, those aged 70 or older, those who are less educated, and those with fewer children tend to be more loss averse compared to their counterparts. Loss aversion is known to be related to important investor attitudes and behaviors such as holding losing stocks and selling winning stocks (Odean, 1998), reluctance to make a change in investment (Samuelson & Zeckhauser, 1988), and preferences on increasing consumption profile (Loewenstein & Thaler, 1989). Therefore, accurate knowledge about clients' loss aversion levels will enhance financial practitioners' ability to predict clients' preferences and behaviors overtime.

To assess how loss averse clients are, the hypothetical choice problems in the experimental module of the HRS can be used as a base measure. As various risk tolerance measures have been proposed by financial planners and investment advisors (Hanna, Guillemette, & Finke, 2013), future efforts are expected for accurate assessments of loss aversion.

Make Choices Transparent

One of the important roles of the financial practitioner is to make the choices transparent for clients. Similar discussion was noted by Hanna, Guillemette, and Finke (2013) that financial advisors can help their clients to overcome cognitive illusions. Decision-making depends on how the choices are represented. In transparent situations, individuals tend to make rational decisions, while in nontransparent situations, there exist violations of the axioms of rational choice (Tversky & Kahneman, 1986). Tversky and Kahneman (1986) emphasized the importance of transparency using the well-known Müller-Lyer illusion. In the Müller-Lyer illusion example (see figure 3-4 in Tversky & Kahneman [1986], pp. S266–S267), the top line looks longer than the bottom line, but drawing a rectangular frame makes it apparent that the bottom line is actually longer than the top one. The role of financial practitioners is to draw a rectangular frame to the Müller-Lyer illusion so that clients can clearly recognize which line is longer.

Financial professionals might be able to add transparency to investors' choices in the cross-sectional aspects and in the temporal aspects. In the cross-sectional way, financial practitioners might be able to help clients by suggesting a broad framing. In the temporal way, financial practitioners can help clients by presenting a long-term view, which is the temporal version of broad framing. Selected recommendations from Kahneman and Riepe (1998) to financial advisors are presented below.

Broad Framing

Broad framing is the opposite of narrow framing. Narrow framing occurs when an individual evaluates a risk separately rather than in combination with other concurrent or preexisting risks (Barberies, 2013). Narrow framing recently received attention from researchers. Barberis, Huang, and Thaler (2006) argued that narrow framing may be a more important feature than previously thought, and DellaVigna (2009) proposed this as the fifth feature of prospect theory, along with the four features discussed earlier. Kahneman (2011) noted that "the combination of loss aversion and narrow framing is a costly curse" and that the broad framing is beneficial since it alleviates the pain from losses and increases the willingness to take risks.

Kahneman and Riepe (1998) noted that rational decision-making is possible by adopting broad frames and by focusing on states rather than on changes. Following are recommendations by Kahneman and Riepe (1998) for financial advisors regarding narrow framing.

- *Encourage clients to adopt as broad a frame as possible when making investment decisions.*
- *When developing a client's investment policy, follow a top-down process, which accounts for all the investor's objectives simultaneously. Avoid the common bottom-up approach in which a separate policy is set up for each investor objective.*
- *Alert the client to the costs of narrow frames.*
- *Don't go overboard. While broad frames are preferable, using mental accounts is probably the better option for those investors who use mental accounting as an instrument of self-control or who would suffer undue stress over losing money from a safe account.*
- *Broad framing helps, because it often allows one to point out gains that offset the losses that are the current focus of regret. Redesign account statements to give greater prominence to the performance of the overall portfolio. Downplay what happened to each piece of the portfolio over the most recent reporting period. (Kahneman & Riepe, 1998, p. 61)*

Long-Term Views

In terms of time frame, financial practitioners can make choices transparent by presenting long-term views. The costs of having short-term views have been documented in previous research. Benartzi and Thaler (1995) referred to the combination of loss aversion and a short evaluation period as the myopic loss aversion and explained that due to myopic loss aversion, individuals demand a large equity premium. Considering the variability of returns in risky assets, stock returns are negative much more frequently than bond returns, and this makes loss-inverse investors demand a large equity premium or be reluctant to participate in the stock market (Barberis, 2013; Camerer, 2001). Benartzi and Thaler (1995) simulated the evaluation period at which the decision between stock and bond becomes transparent and it was one year. Ivkovič, Poterba, and Weisbenner (2005) also provided support for the importance of long-term views, showing that the disposition effect was more pronounced with a short horizon. Next are recommendations by Kahneman and Riepe (1998) for financial advisors regarding time frame.

- *Teach the investor the importance of taking a long-term view.*
- *Many clients like to talk long-term and act short-term. Pay more attention to what investors have done in the past than what they say they'll do in the future.*
- *Recognize early which clients will find it most difficult to stay the course and to live with a long-term commitment.*
- *Don't let account statements reinforce short-term thinking. Design statements that give less prominence to the most recent quarter, and more to what has happened over the lifetime of the account.*
- *The advisor and the investor should agree ahead of time on a set of procedures to follow in the event that the investor is tempted to make a portfolio alteration based on a hunch or knee-jerk reaction to recent events.*
- *If the investor does cave in and drastically alters a portfolio based on short-term considerations, and the trades do not turn out well, the advisor should tactfully point out the consequences of these actions the next time the urge arises. (Kahneman & Riepe, 1998, p. 62)*

Kahneman and Riepe (1998) presented a checklist for financial advisors at the end of their article in the journal of portfolio management. The checklist asks how frequently financial advisors do each of 10 tasks. This checklist will provide financial planners an opportunity to self-evaluate how effectively they incorporate the implications from prospect theory in the field.

Checklist: How Frequently Do You Do Each of These Tasks?

1. *Encourage clients to adopt a broad view of their wealth, prospects, and objectives.*
2. *Encourage clients to make long-term commitments to investment policies.*
3. *Encourage clients not to monitor results too frequently.*
4. *Discuss the possibility of future regret with your clients.*
5. *Ask yourself if a course of action is out of character for your client.*
6. *Verify that the client has a realistic view of the odds, particularly when a normally cautious investor is attracted to a risky venture.*
7. *Encourage the client to adopt different attitudes toward risk for small and for large decisions.*
8. *Attempt to structure the client's portfolio to the shape that the client likes best (such as insuring a decent return with a small chance of large gain).*
9. *Make clients aware of the uncertainty involved in investment decisions.*
10. *Identify the aversion of your clients to the different aspects of risk, and incorporate their risk aversions when structuring an investment program. (Kahneman & Riepe, 1998, p. 64).*

REFERENCES

Barberis, N. (2013). Thirty years of prospect theory in economics: A review and assessment. *Journal of Economic Perspectives, 27*(1), 173–195.

Barberis, N., Huang, M., & Thaler, R. H. (2006). Individual preferences, monetary gambles, and stock market participation: A case for narrow framing. *American Economic Review, 96*(4), 1069–1090.

Barberis, N., & Thaler, R. H. (2003). A survey of behavioral finance. In G. M. Constantinides, M. Harris, & R. Stulz (Eds.), *Handbook of the economics of finance* (Vol. *1B*, pp. 1053–1123). Amsterdam, The Netherlands: Elsevier B.V.

Benartzi, S., Previtero, A., & Thaler, R. H. (2011). Annuitization puzzles. *Journal of Economic Perspectives, 25*(4), 143–164.

Benartzi, S. & Thaler, R. H. (1995). Myopic loss aversion and the equity premium puzzle. *Quarterly Journal of Economics, 110*(1), 73–92.

Brown, J. R. (2009). Understanding the role of annuities in retirement planning. In A. Lusardi (Ed.), *Overcoming the saving slump: How to increase the effectiveness of financial education and saving programs* (pp. 178–208). Chicago: University of Chicago Press.

Camerer, C. F. (1998). Prospect theory in the wild: Evidence from the field. In D. Kahneman & A. Tversky (Eds.), *Choices, values, and frames* (pp. 288–300). Cambridge, England: Cambridge University Press.

Chavas, J.-P. (2004). *Risk analysis in theory and practice*. San Diego: Academic Press.

DellaVigna, S. (2009). Psychology and economics: Evidence from the field. *Journal of Economic Literature, 47*(2), 315–372.

Frazzini, A. (2006). The disposition effect and underreaction to news. *Journal of Finance, 61*(4), 2017–2046.

Gottlieb, D. (2012). Prospect theory, life insurance, and annuities. *The Wharton School Research Paper* No. 44.

Gottlieb, D., & Mitchell, O. S. (2015). *Narrow framing and long-term care insurance* (No. w21048). Cambridge, MA: National Bureau of Economic Research.

Hanna, S. D., Guillemette, M. A., & Finke, M. S. (2013). Assessing risk tolerance. In H. K. Baker & G. Filbeck (Eds.), *Portfolio theory and management* (pp. 99–120). New York: Oxford University Press.

Hu, W. Y., & Scott, J. S. (2007). Behavioral obstacles in the annuity market. *Financial Analysts Journal, 63*(6), 71–82.

Hwang, I. D. (2017, February 27). *Behavioral aspects of household portfolio choice: Effects of loss aversion on life insurance uptake and savings.* Bank of Korea Working Paper No. 2017–8.

Ivkovii, Z., Poterba, J., & Weisbenner, S. (2005). Tax-motivated trading by individual investors. *American Economic Review, 95*(5), 1605–1630.

Kahneman, D. (2011). *Thinking, fast and slow.* New York: Macmillan.

Kahneman, D., Knetsch, J. L., & Thaler, R. H. (1990). Experimental tests of the endowment effect and the Coase theorem. *Journal of Political Economy, 98*(6), 1325–1348.

Kahneman, D., Knetsch, J. L., & Thaler, R. H. (1991). Anomalies: The endowment effect, loss aversion, and status quo bias. *Journal of Economic Perspectives, 5*(1), 193–206.

Kahneman, D., & Riepe, M. W. (1998). Aspects of investor psychology. *Journal of Portfolio Management, 24*(4), 52–65.

Kahneman, D., & Tversky, A. (1979). Prospect theory: An analysis of decision under risk. *Econometrica, 47*(2), 263–291.

Kahneman, D., & Tversky, A. (1984). Choices, values, and frames. *American Psychologist, 39*(4), 341–350.

Knetsch, J. L. (1989). The endowment effect and evidence of nonreversible indifference curves. *American Economic Review, 79*(5), 1277–1284.

List, J. A. (2004). Neoclassical theory versus prospect theory: Evidence from the marketplace. *Econometrica, 72*(2), 615–625.

Loewenstein, G., & Thaler, R. H. (1989). Anomalies: Intertemporal choice. *Journal of Economic Perspectives, 3*(4), 181–193.

Odean, T. (1998). Are investors reluctant to realize their losses? *Journal of Finance*, 53(5), 1775–1798.

Samuelson, W., & Zeckhauser, R. (1988). Status quo bias in decision making. *Journal of Risk and Uncertainty*, 1(1), 7–59.

Schoemaker, P. J. (1982). The expected utility model: Its variants, purposes, evidence and limitations. *Journal of Economic Literature*, 20(2), 529–563.

Shefrin, H., & Statman, M. (1985). The disposition to sell winners too early and ride losers too long: Theory and evidence. *Journal of Finance*, 40(3), 777–790.

Thaler, R. H. (1980). Toward a positive theory of consumer choice. *Journal of Economic Behavior and Organization*, 1(1), 39–60.

Tversky, A., & Fox, C. R. (1995). Weighing risk and uncertainty. *Psychological Review*, 102(2), 269–283.

Tversky, A., & Kahneman, D. (1981). The framing of decisions and the psychology of choice. *Science*, 211, 453–458.

Tversky, A., & Kahneman, D. (1986). Rational choice and the framing of decisions. *Journal of Business*, S251–S278.

Tversky, A., & Kahneman, D. (1991). Loss aversion in riskless choice: A reference-dependent model. *Quarterly Journal of Economics*, 106(4), 1039–1061.

Tversky, A., & Kahneman, D. (1992). Advances in prospect theory: Cumulative representation of uncertainty. *Journal of Risk and Uncertainty*, 5(4), 297–323.

Yaari, M. E. (1965). Uncertain lifetime, life insurance, and the theory of the consumer. *Review of Economic Studies*, 32(2), 137–150.

CHAPTER 6

The Role of Mental Accounting in Household Spending and Investing Decisions

C. Yiwei Zhang, PhD, and Abigail B. Sussman, PhD

The University of Chicago Booth School of Business

Traditional accounting refers to the way that businesses or corporations track and evaluate financial activities. In contrast, mental accounting refers to the way that people perform these same activities in their own lives. Defined by Thaler (1999) as "the set of cognitive operations used by individuals and households to organize, evaluate, and keep track of financial activities," mental accounting describes the way that people group expenses into categories, assign funds to these categories, determine budgets, and perform elements of cost–benefit analyses.

In this chapter, we focus on mental accounting within the context of consumer financial decision-making. Specifically, we examine how mental accounting influences budgeting, spending, and investment decisions.[1] As part of our review, this chapter highlights some of the notable work in this growing field. However, we do not cover aspects of these decisions beyond mental accounting (e.g., we do not discuss how goal-setting affects budgeting efficacy) nor do we examine elements of mental accounting that do not have relevance for these decisions.

---

[1] See Soman and Ahn (2011) for a review of mental accounting research with particular attention to the relationship between mental accounting and framing effects. See also Frydman and Camerer (2016) for a review of the psychology and neuroscience behind financial decision-making.

The chapter proceeds as follows. First, we provide an overview of the categorization process that underlies mental accounting. We extend this discussion of categorization to describe methods for categorizing funds, such as grouping funds based on their sources and uses or grouping funds based on the timing in which income is received or lost. Next, we move to discuss applications of these concepts. We initially focus on the budgeting process, explicating potential benefits as well as potential costs of utilizing this approach. In addition to discussing specific spending decisions, we consider how mental accounting for assets and debt influences wealth perceptions as well as decisions to take on or avoid debt. We then turn to implications of the mental accounting process for investing, discussing the relevance of opening and closing accounts and choices about which assets to purchase. Finally, we conclude by laying out an agenda for future research in the area.

MENTAL ACCOUNTING AS CATEGORIZATION

The categorization of funds into different groups is one of the defining elements of mental accounting. People might, for example, group any expenses they incur on a trip to Florida into a vacation-spending category or categorize any money received as a wedding gift as savings for their future home. Prior research has argued that this categorization of funds is driven by similar cognitive processes to those that underlie the categorization of objects and events more generally. Consequently, mental accounting can be understood through the cognitive principles of categorization (Heath & Soll, 1996; Henderson & Peterson, 1992). This approach highlights important reasons why individuals might engage in mental accounting, especially within the domain of consumer finance. Namely, categorizing funds helps facilitate the processing of information in ways necessary for evaluating spending opportunities. In the absence of such categorization, people would need to assess their full financial portfolio when faced with nearly any consumption decision, such as the affordability of a given purchase (e.g., "Is this something I can buy?") or the appropriate allocation of resources toward various goods (e.g., "How much can I spend?"). This evaluation would require integrating across present and future wealth as well as incorporating all debts and anticipated expenses.

By organizing information into groups based on commonalities, categorization can facilitate the quick recall and judgment of relevant information, thus reducing the cognitive effort required to evaluate the decision at hand (Henderson & Peterson, 1992). For example, when deciding how much to spend on an upcoming trip, a person could consider how much money she has available to spend over the course of her lifetime and from there, how much would be available for the trip based on all anticipated current and future expenses and opportunity costs. Alternatively, incorporating principles of mental accounting, she can focus her decision on a given accounting period (e.g., a year) and consider how much she believes is reasonable to spend on travel given her income and expenses, how much she has already spent on vacation or travel, and how much more she expects to spend on these costs in the given period. The latter calculation is manageable for most people whereas the former is not.

While categorizing funds can help ease the burdens associated with financial decision-making, it also has implications for how people choose to spend and save their money and can lead to systematic errors. According to traditional economic theory, categorizing funds into various mental accounts should have no effect on subsequent behavior since the boundaries of mental accounts are only notionally set. Yet a wealth of evidence indicates that how funds are grouped and labeled influences individual preferences for spending. In other words, mental accounting violates the economic principle of fungibility—the notion that money is interchangeable (Abeler & Marklein, 2017; Shefrin & Thaler, 1988; Thaler, 1990, 1999). Even in instances where the only categorization of funds is the method of payment used (cash or credit), differences in the marginal propensity to spend and consume across separate categories persist (Soman, 2003). Below, we highlight several notable studies from the growing body of research documenting the many ways in which people categorize funds and how this categorization can in turn alter spending. We organize our discussion of these studies by focusing on two primary methods for categorizing funds: (1) categorizing the sources and uses of funds and (2) categorizing choices and outcomes involving funds.

METHODS FOR CATEGORIZING FUNDS

Sources and Uses of Funds

In assigning funds to different mental accounts, people may consider the inflow of resources (income, capital gains, etc.), the stock of resources available (retirement savings, housing wealth, etc.), and the outflow of expenditures (food, clothing, etc.) from the household (Thaler, 1999). One common practice in mental accounting is to categorize funds based on the origin or source of those funds. Early studies considered common ways in which an individual's wealth might change (e.g., receiving a raise or anticipating a future inheritance check) and proposed three broad categories that might intuitively comprise that person's wealth over her lifetime: current income, current assets (e.g., savings or housing equity), and future income (Shefrin & Thaler, 1988; Thaler, 1990, 1994, 1999). Though each of these three categories belong to the more global category of wealth, people exhibit differential marginal propensities to consume across the three groups, with the marginal propensity to consume typically highest out of current income and lowest out of future income (Courant, Gramlich, & Laitner, 1986; Shefrin & Thaler, 1988). In other words, people are differentially tempted to spend (consume) a dollar of wealth depending on whether that dollar is from their current income, current assets, or future income. Receiving a raise today will lead to a greater increase in spending than will an increase in a future inheritance check of the same amount, even though standard economic theory suggest that people should treat wealth the same regardless of its source (i.e., the marginal propensity to consume out of different categories of wealth should be the same).

Funds may be categorized by their source within these three partitions of wealth as well. For instance, the allocation of current assets across specific accounts (e.g., "money in my wallet" versus "money in my bank account") can alter spending decisions, even after controlling for overall wealth (Morewedge, Holtzman, & Epley, 2007). Similarly, numerous studies suggest that people categorize changes in current income as either regular income or a more irregular windfall (Arkes et al., 1994; Milkman & Beshears, 2009; O'Curry, 1999; O'Curry & Strahilevitz, 2001; Shefrin & Thaler, 1988; Thaler, 1999). Whether a change in income is coded as a windfall gain or simply regular income depends on a number of factors, including but not limited to the size of the gain relative to regular income receipts (Thaler, 1990), the typicality or regularity of the income, or the degree to which a person anticipates the change in income (O'Curry & Strahilevitz, 2001). For example, a work bonus is likely to be considered distinct from an individual's regular salary (Ishikawa & Ueda, 1984), as are unpredictable tips and commissions (O'Curry, 1999).

One of the most frequently cited examples of windfall income is the tax refund. Each year, more than three-quarters of taxpayers overwithhold taxes from their paychecks and, as a result, receive a lump-sum tax refund (Internal Revenue Service, 2017). While the reasons for overwithholding vary, people often treat their annual tax refund as a windfall distinct from their regular earnings and exhibit a greater marginal propensity to consume out of their tax refund than out of other funds (Souleles, 1999; Thaler, 1994). Marketers recognize that people treat a tax refund as a windfall gain, with some stores capitalizing on tax refund season by advertising opportunities to spend the newly found money. Research further shows that people are even more likely to spend this windfall when it is described as a bonus than as a rebate (Epley, Mak, & Idson, 2006). An income receipt that is not labeled differently but is received infrequently may also be categorized as its own mental account, separate from that of regular and frequent income. For example, biweekly paid workers receive two paychecks in most months. However, there are about two months a year when they receive three paychecks as a predictable consequence of the distribution of days in the calendar. These workers have been shown to spend more in the months following these "extra" third paychecks, treating them as a windfall (Zhang, 2016). Although the type of windfall income varies by context, these studies indicate that people are consistently more likely to spend windfall income than regular income.

Beyond affecting the marginal propensity to consume, categorizing funds by their source can also influence the types of goods that people are likely to purchase with the money. Windfall gains are more likely to be spent on luxury goods (e.g., eating an expensive meal) than on more essential goods (e.g., purchasing groceries) when given the choice (O'Curry, 1999). Moreover, this preference for spending on luxury rather than essential goods can be amplified in contexts where there is heightened anticipation of acquiring the good (O'Curry & Strahilevitz, 2001). However, funds that evoke emotional feelings, particularly negative ones, are more generally spent on essential goods rather than luxury goods (Levav & McGraw, 2009). For example, a widow is more likely to spend life insurance funds from the death of her spouse on school supplies for her children than on upgrading her television set. In this case of emotional accounting, spending money on virtuous expenditures allows people to reduce negative feelings associated with windfall gains. Recent research on mental money laundering suggests that people exploit flexibility in mental accounting to justify selfish use of funds. Specifically, people will seek out opportunities to dissociate earnings from undesirable sources when it allows them to rationalize less virtuous spending (Imas, Loewenstein, & Morewedge, 2017).

A second common practice in mental accounting is categorizing funds based on the intended use of the money, for example, based on the type of good it will be used to purchase.[2] Households, for instance, may set budgets for various expenses (e.g., a food budget or a gas budget) and treat funds between the accounts tagged for each purpose as distinct and imperfectly substitutable (Hastings & Shapiro, 2013; Heath & Soll, 1996; Thaler, 1985). In some cases, this categorization arises naturally, based on the congruence between a labeled source of income and possible uses of that money

---

[2] See Markman and Brendl (2000) for analysis of the organization of mental accounts around active goals.

(i.e., how typical a good is of goods generally purchased with those funds). That is, people spend money on purchases that align with the source of the funds used. One study finds that spending on children's clothing is significantly more sensitive to funds designated for spending on children (in this case, child benefit payments from the Dutch government that help defray the costs of raising a child) than to other sources of income (Kooreman, 2000). When child benefit payments increase, spending on children's clothing increases more than when other sources of income increase by the same amount. Similarly, Supplemental Nutrition Assistance Program (SNAP) beneficiaries who receive restricted-use funds for purchasing food exhibit a much higher marginal propensity to consume SNAP-eligible food out of their SNAP benefits than out of cash (Hastings & Shapiro, 2017). Related findings from a lab study suggest that this behavior may stem from a greater discomfort in spending unrestricted funds rather than restricted-use funds on goods belonging to a restricted-use category (André, Reinholtz, & Lynch, 2017). Reinholtz, Bartels, and Parker (2015) observe similar behavior in a retail context; people who receive a retailer-specific gift card express a greater preference for products highly congruent with the purpose of the mental account (i.e., typical of that retailer; e.g., jeans from a Levi's store) than those that are less congruent (e.g., sweaters from a Levi's store) in comparison to people who received an unrestricted-use gift card. Even in the absence of an externally imposed designation, people are more likely to spend on goods whose category aligns with the source of the income (O'Curry, 1999).

Sets of Choices and Outcomes

Another method by which people categorize funds is by grouping a set of choices or event outcomes together. These groupings can take many forms. Choice bracketing refers to the way people group together or bracket a set of individual choices (Read, Loewenstein, & Rabin, 1999). Brackets can be defined broadly over large sets of choices or narrowly over very small sets of choices. For instance, an individual deciding whether or not to purchase a particular item may consider only the purchases she has made thus far in this trip to this store (narrow bracketing) or she may consider every purchase she has made that week in all stores (broad bracketing). Importantly, narrow bracketing facilitates the defining of separate mental accounts.

One of the most common ways in which choice bracketing behavior manifests is temporal bracketing: people bracket funds based on the timing of when those funds will subsequently be used. In particular, they can choose whether to temporally combine or separate different expenditures into the same or distinct mental accounts (Linville & Fisher, 1991;

Thaler & Johnson, 1990). Consistent with temporal bracketing behavior, the temporal distance between outcomes can influence cognitive integration. Outcomes that are temporally separate are more likely to be segregated across different mental accounts; in contrast, outcomes that are temporally proximate are more likely to be integrated into the same mental account. The most immediate form of temporal bracketing is perhaps the setting of household budgets where people must determine the period (e.g., daily, monthly, annually, etc.) over which their mental accounts are evaluated and consequently should be spent (Read et al., 1999; Thaler, 1999). These budgeting periods can have a direct influence on financial decisions and judgments. As Ülkümen, Thomas, and Morwitz (2008) show, the period over which consumers evaluate their household budgets can affect their estimates of how much they expect to spend and therefore how much of their resources they need to budget in the future. The authors find that people significantly underestimate their actual spending when budgeting for the following month; in contrast, budgets planned over the upcoming year are much closer to actual recorded expenses. While the frequency with which a mental account is evaluated is generally endogenously chosen, temporal bracketing can sometimes be exogenously imposed by others with meaningful effects. For instance, temporal decoupling of expenditures (e.g., the payment of a tax and the later use of tax revenue) can potentially affect attitudes toward the eventual use of those funds (Sussman & Olivola, 2011).

In some cases, key elements of prospect theory (Kahneman & Tversky, 1979) have implications for mental accounting and can affect the way people form or evaluate groups of outcomes. People may evaluate events in relation to a reference point, with changes coded as either a gain or loss relative to that point. For example, a homeowner deciding whether or not to sell her home might consider whether the nominal current market value of her house exceeds its original purchase price (i.e., whether selling her house would result in a capital gain), and be less likely to sell if it does not (Genesove & Mayer, 2001).In other words, the homeowner would be creating a mental account for her home and grouping money paid in the initial purchase (the reference point) with money received in the final sale. An implication of prospect theory is that spending decisions can be driven not just by the market price of a potential purchase but also by how good of a deal that purchase would be. Under this model of behavior, people evaluate a purchase by its transaction utility: the perceived value from the relative difference between the amount to be paid (the market price) for a given product and the reference price for that product (Thaler, 1985). For instance, a person may be willing to pay $5 for a bottle of water at a movie theater but only $2 for the same bottle of water at the grocery store, even though the bottle of water being consumed in each scenario is the same.

While paying $5 for a bottle of water at the movie theater may be expected, paying that same price at the store would seem like a bad deal when compared to the typical reference price of a bottle of water at the store.

In addition to evaluating events relative to a reference point, people experience diminishing sensitivity to any gains or losses and exhibit loss aversion (losses loom larger than gains) under this framework. For example, the difference in added value to the homeowner between selling her home for $50,000 and $100,000 seems bigger than the difference between selling her home for $800,000 and $850,000 (diminishing sensitivity to gains), and selling her home at a $50,000 loss hurts more than selling her home at a $50,000 gain yields happiness (loss aversion).

Importantly, prospect theory has implications for how people prefer to group gains and losses (Thaler, 1980, 1985, 1999). Because people experience diminishing sensitivity to gains and losses, they will prefer to segregate gains and integrate losses. For example, if someone wins two small lottery prizes, she may prefer to receive each win separately (segregating gains) whereas if someone incurs two small parking tickets, she may choose to incur both tickets on the same day (integrating losses). The process of naturally segregating and integrating events with these preferences in mind is known as hedonic editing. However, these specific patterns are constrained by whether the two incidents are perceived as belonging to the same category. Recent research shows that when two events are perceived to be in different categories (e.g., performance on a test in school vs. the outcome of a social interaction), people cannot book them to the same account and evaluate the two events separately (Evers, Imas, & Loewenstein, 2017). Given any positive time discounting, this leads to people preferring gains from different categories close together in time and to spread apart losses from different categories.

When considering mixed outcomes (i.e., both gains and losses), people should prefer to integrate small losses with larger gains and segregate smaller gains from larger losses (Jarnebrant, Toubia, & Johnson, 2009). However, this rule does not explain reactions in all cases and treatment of mixed outcomes can be complex. For example, Wu and Markle (2008) find that people treat gambles with both positive and negative potential outcomes differently than gambles that involve only gains or losses, placing different weights on probability differences. Additionally, people tend to care about the composition of a given, realized outcome. People place more weight on losses after receiving a net gain but more weight on gains after receiving a net loss, rather than focusing only on the net outcome (Sussman, 2017).

Important research remains to be done to build a full account of how mental accounting categories are formed. However, these studies offer a helpful framework for understanding some of the cognitive underpinnings of elements that influence the grouping of items into mental accounts. In what follows, we cover some of the existing research on the implications of mental accounting for consumer behavior, focusing on two important personal financial management practices: budgeting and investing.

BUDGETING

Financial decisions involve trade-offs between different bundles of goods and between consumption today versus in a future period. The processes by which individuals make these trade-offs have meaningful implications for the overall well-being of households. In this section, we focus on household budgeting both as the foundation for making many of these decisions and as an important process for which mental accounting provides especially useful insights. We provide a brief overview of the literature on mental budgeting before discussing both the potential benefits and pitfalls that arise from segregating funds.

Implications for Financial Planning Practice

A budget is a financial plan by which individuals, companies, or institutions allocate present and future funds to various uses such as expenses, savings, investments, and debt repayment. More generally, budgeting is the process used to segregate and track the allocation and use of funds against different accounts with implicit or explicit spending limits or budgets (Galperti, 2016). In the case of individuals or households, mental accounting guides this process. Budgets can play an important role in the management of a household's financial life, both for short term (e.g., prioritizing spending across different categories) and for long-term financial planning (e.g., determining how much money to set aside for the future). Outside of the household, consumer budgets can shape demand for various products and services.

Informal financial advice often encourages households to budget, and a number of financial products are designed to facilitate the budgeting process. Furthermore, Heath and Soll (1996) propose a cognitive framework in which new purchases will only impact a budget if they are first noticed (i.e., booked) and then assigned to a meaningful account (i.e., posted). Booking relies on attention and memory while posting relies on evaluations of similarity and categorization. However, relatively little is known about how households actually budget. How do people form and maintain budgets, what might influence the budgeting process, and what are the effects of budgeting on household financial well-being? Surveys on household budgeting behavior that do exist primarily aim to capture engagement: whether or not individuals have a budget. For example, roughly 46% of survey respondents for the University of Michigan's 2001 Surveys of Consumers report using a spending plan or budget (Hilgert, Hogarth, & Beverly, 2003). More recently, the 2015 National Financial Capability Study, a nationally representative survey administered by the Financial Industry Regulatory Authority, estimated that just over half of individuals (56%) report having a household budget (Lin et al., 2016).[3,4]

Beyond the propensity to budget, a small number of surveys also ask respondents what financial planning horizon is of greatest importance and whether individuals are able to fit their budget or make ends meet. Rather than parsing different short-term horizons for budgeting (e.g., daily vs. weekly vs. monthly), these surveys often focus on less granular differences, for example whether people keep budgets over the period of a few months versus a few years. For longer-term financial planning, a survey of TIAA participants by Ameriks, Caplin, and Leary (2013) finds that roughly 39% of respondents agree or strongly agree that they have spent a significant amount of time developing a financial plan and 27% of respondents have gathered and reviewed their household's financial information in detail to formulate a specific plan for their household's long-term future.

While survey evidence suggests that roughly half of individuals have a budget or financial plan of some form, emerging studies underscore the numerous ways in which households might budget, especially when financially constrained. For instance, one strategy that people can undertake to cope with a financial shortfall is to stretch their financial resources (*efficiency planning*) to make the most of what they have. A person might place an order with a friend to split delivery costs or run several errands at once rather than take multiple trips. An alternative strategy is to identify and sacrifice less important goals (*priority planning*), recognizing the trade-offs inherent when allocating resources to different goals (Fernbach, Kan, & Lynch, 2015). Priority planning can extend beyond goals to sources of funds and expenses more generally as well. A related study provides suggestive evidence that financially constrained households, much like companies, may

---

[3] Similarly, the 2014 Canadian Financial Capability Survey administered by Statistics Canada estimates that almost half of Canadians (46%) have a budget (FCAC, 2015).

[4] A number of industry surveys also capture engagement. Using a random sample of adults across the United States, a 2013 Gallup poll found that roughly one-third of households use a detailed written or computerized household budget each month to track their income and expenditures. Similarly, the 2013 Household Financial Planning Survey and Index by the Consumer Federation of America (CFA, 2013) reports that around 57% of surveyed households have a budget, even if informally, and 32% of surveyed households have a budget that is written down.

cope with financial shocks to their budget by establishing a "pecking order" of sources of funds to turn toward when constrained (Lusardi, Schneider, & Tufano, 2011). For example, households may try to borrow from friends and family before turning toward using their credit cards when strapped for cash. Similarly, households may establish a pecking order of expenses, choosing which bills to prioritize over others.

Although there is little systematic survey evidence on household budgeting, much of what we do know about household budgeting is tied to our understanding of mental accounting behavior and how individuals segregate funds. Principles of mental accounting can operate through informal or implicit budgets and thus likely influence how people choose to spend money even in cases where they do not keep a formal or explicit budget. For example, in one seminal study of framing effects by Tversky and Kahneman (1981), a group of participants was told to imagine that they were about to purchase a calculator that cost either $15 or $125. The calculator was on sale for either $10 or $120 in a store 20 minutes away. Participants were asked whether they would travel to the other store to buy the calculator at the discounted price. Participants were much more likely to travel to save money on the $15 than $120 item (68% vs. 29%). Mental accounting led to this pattern, even in the absence of explicit budgeting. Participants in all cases were asked their willingness to travel 20 minutes to save $5. However, rather than considering the dollar cost in absolute terms, which would have led to similar responses across conditions, they considered the dollar cost as a percent of the total cost of the item.

Assets versus Debts

Beyond choosing which items to purchase or forego, mental accounting has implications for how people view their household balance sheets and financial wealth more generally by influencing how people bracket these funds. Much like that of a business, a household balance sheet provides an overview of a household's finances, and more specifically its assets and liabilities. Perceptions of this balance sheet can influence how much people feel they can afford to spend and how they choose to finance purchases. Thus, while understanding the balance sheet is not a traditional component of budgeting, it provides groundwork for how much money is available overall, with clear relevance for budgeting decisions.

Under standard economic theory, people borrow to move consumption forward from the future to the present, and their willingness to borrow depends entirely on the relative value of consumption today versus consumption in the future and the cost of moving consumption from the future to the present (interest rate). However, a number of studies provide empirical evidence of debt aversion and suggest that such behavior can stem from a psychological aversion to debt, rather than from financial trade-offs. To explain debt-averse behavior, Prelec and Loewenstein (1998) proposed a double-entry mental accounting model where people engage in two important behaviors. First, people associate or couple the consumption and payment of a good (to varying degrees), making two mental entries: (1) the overall utility derived from consumption after subtracting the disutility of associated payments, and (2) the overall disutility of payments after subtracting the utility of associated consumption. For example, driving a car will bring to mind all the payments required to pay for the car while paying for a car will bring to mind all the future enjoyment that will be experienced while driving the car. Second, people engage in prospective accounting, where consumption that has already been paid for can be enjoyed as if it were free, and the pain of payment prior to consumption is mitigated by thoughts of the future pleasure of that consumption. Under this model, paying in advance (prepayment) decouples the immediate pain of paying from the pleasure of consumption so that the car owner can enjoy driving the car as if it were free and any pain of prepayment is buffered by thoughts of the future enjoyment of driving.[5] In other words, the double-entry mental accounting model predicts a preference for paying for consumption in advance, namely, a debt aversion.

Hirst, Joyce, and Schadewald (1994) likewise address debt aversion in their study on the role of temporal contiguity in mentally accounting. Drawing on prior research on individual preferences for integrating gains and losses (Linville & Fischer, 1991; Thaler, 1980, 1985) and research indicating that outcomes that occur contemporaneously are more likely to be integrated in the same mental account (Thaler & Johnson, 1990), they provide evidence suggesting that people will prefer to borrow for goods where the repayment of the associated debt corresponds with the timeline of consumption benefits for that good. Because debt can vary significantly in the timing of future payments, such a preference can lead to a reluctance to borrow or debt aversion. For instance, students may be resistant to taking out a loan for school in light of the fact that loan repayment typically extends far past the period during which students are in school.

---

[5] There is a large body of research exploring the pain of paying experienced when spending money and its role in influencing individual decision-making. In addition to Prelec and Loewenstein (1998), see, for example, Zellermayer (1996); Knutson, Rick, Wimmer, Prelec, and Loewenstein (2007); Rick et al. (2007); Thomas et al. (2011); Shah, Eisenkraft, Bettman, and Chartrand (2016); Kan, Lynch, and Fernbach (2015); and Mažar, Plassmann, Robitaille, and Lindner (2017).

In some cases, rather than exhibiting behavior that is consistent with debt aversion, people hold debt while simultaneously holding liquid assets (e.g., Gross & Souleles, 2002). One area of recent research has focused on how the relationship between assets and debts can influence perceptions of wealth. All else equal, individual perceptions of personal wealth should be driven by overall net worth (the difference between one's assets and debts) and should not depend on the level of assets and debts. Sussman and Shafir (2012) find, however, that people differentially perceive the relative wealth of financial profiles with equal total net worth but different asset and debt levels. In particular, financial profiles with higher asset and debt levels are viewed as wealthier when the overall net worth of those individuals is negative (e.g., $50,000 in assets and $100,000 in debt is preferred to $20,000 in assets and $70,000 in debt) while financial profiles with low asset and debt levels are viewed as wealthier when the overall net worth is positive (e.g., $70,000 in assets and $20,000 in debt is preferred to $100,000 in assets and $50,000 in debt). The authors further find that these differences in perceived wealth can in turn affect financial decisions, such as the willingness to take on additional debt. By providing evidence of individuals differentially focusing on their assets (or debts) when their net worth is negative (or positive), these findings suggest that individuals may consider the two sides of their balance sheet as psychologically distinct when judging their overall wealth. This finding provides one factor that may contribute to debt-averse behavior among many while also accounting for debt-seeking behavior in some cases.

Potential Benefits

While the benefits of mental accounting and segregating funds more generally are numerous, we focus our discussion on the primary benefits that have received the most attention in the literature thus far. First, segregating funds can help simplify the often overwhelming process of financial planning by limiting the complexity of choices households face (Thaler, 1999). Budgeting can make spending rules clear while also increasing the pain of paying, helping people stay on track in some cases (Kan, Lynch, & Fernbach, 2015; Rick, Cryder, & Loewenstein, 2007). As mentioned at the outset of this section, most consumer financial decisions involve making trade-offs between competing uses for funds. Segregating funds can facilitate making these trade-offs by narrowing the set of choices under consideration that may compete for use of allocated funds (Read et al., 1999; Simon, 1947).

Second, segregating funds can help households maintain financial discipline (Shefrin & Thaler, 1988). There is a large body of research in both psychology and economics documenting individuals' struggles with managing their self-control problems (Soman et al., 2005; Thaler & Shefrin, 1981).

Within the consumer finance domain, self-control problems typically arise in one of two circumstances: when choosing what type of good to consume (e.g., a luxury good versus a necessity good) and when choosing when to consume (e.g., spend today versus save for the future). In either case, self-control problems can lead individuals to overconsume or overspend relative to what would otherwise be optimal, which, for individuals trying to financially plan, can lead to failure to meet both short- and long-term goals.

In the face of such self-control problems, segregating funds allows people to resist the temptation of immediate consumption opportunities by precommitting their spending or otherwise limiting their ability to overspend (i.e., setting a budget; Heath & Soll, 1996). For instance, a person may set an entertainment budget and allocate a certain amount of money to be spent on entertainment expenses, such as attending a play or a sporting event. The segregation of funds can thus facilitate the creation of heuristic decision rules that govern how and when to spend (Shefrin & Thaler, 1988; Thaler & Shefrin, 1981). Such budgeting rules could include going out to dinner only once a month or purchasing lattes only when meeting with friends. Similar rules might designate certain funds, for example, funds earmarked as savings toward a house down payment as off-limits for current spending. Budgeting rules may even govern the accumulation of debt. For example, people may choose to prohibit borrowing except for financing the consumption of specific goods (e.g., purchasing a car) or the consumption of specific classes of goods (e.g., emergency spending) (Thaler & Shefrin, 1981; Wertenbroch, Soman, & Nunes, 2001). They may also choose to follow a budgeting rule that allows spending only from current income, which would prohibit borrowing to smooth consumption as it declines over the pay period (Huffman & Barenstein, 2005) or the life cycle (Friedman, 1957). Segregating funds and creating explicit mental budgets can make consumption goals more concrete as well. Reinforcing or increasing the salience of the goals tied to mental budgets can help facilitate self-control, particularly when the mental budget is associated with a goal of limiting overconsumption (Krishnamurthy & Prokopec, 2010; Soman & Cheema, 2011).

In some instances, funds are segregated into physically separate accounts. Early papers on mental accounting often point to the observed habit of households placing cash into separate envelopes, each labeled with a specific spending category or use (Thaler, 1985; 1999; Zelizer, 1994). Formally segregating funds in this way can help in the management of self-control problems by increasing the psychological cost required to transfer funds. For example, Soman and Cheema (2011) find that partitioning funds earmarked as savings into two distinct accounts (sealed envelopes) increased the overall level of savings by participants, thus helping households maintain financial discipline and better reach their savings goals. Beyond the decreased fungibility of funds arising from psychological barriers, formal segregation can also introduce real frictions (e.g., bank-processing delays or transfer fees) that discourage transferring funds outside of a given account (Shefrin & Thaler, 1988). For this reason, formally segregating funds may be especially useful when trying to encourage long-term saving behavior where people face current temptation to spend out of those savings (Thaler, 1999).

Potential Errors

While the previous section details several ways in which segregating funds can benefit households, doing so also has the potential to lead to errors in decision-making. These errors can occur either because mental accounts are too flexible or because they are too rigid.

Though individuals may segregate funds as a way of establishing internal rules on spending, mental accounts are in fact often malleable (Cheema & Soman, 2008). In particular, mental accounts may fail to strictly segregate funds when the classification of expenses is unclear or ambiguous. For instance, an expense could be classified as belonging to more than one mental account (e.g., dinner while traveling for work may be classified as a food expense or a work expense). In the absence of a crisp categorization of expenses and funds, individuals who are motivated to do so are able to circumvent the self-control imposed by budgeting rules and convince themselves to overspend. Even in the absence of a motivation to evade one's budgeting rules, expenses that are hard to classify may lead to errors in decision-making. An expense that seems exceptional (unusual or infrequent) may be more difficult to classify than an expense that is more ordinary. Consequently, people are more likely to place these exceptional items into smaller or ad hoc budget categories that lack sufficient context to be meaningful. For example, people are likely to consider spending money on a present for a friend's birthday, on a weekend with relatives visiting from out of town, or on tickets for a favorite band as unique expenses that will occur only once rather than as part of a broader category of expenses (e.g., spending on infrequent festivities). When people believe an expense is unusual and will either not recur or will recur infrequently, they may fail to record or record incompletely the expense when posting the expense to their mental budget (Sussman & Alter, 2012; Sussman, Sharma, & Alter, 2015).[6] Failure to appropriately account for an expense can lead to increased spending.

---

[6] See also Sussman, Paley, and Alter, (2017) for an examination of mental accounting for exceptional items in the context of food consumption.

People tend to spend more on exceptional expenses because they are infrequent, even when they are large. However, in a reverse case, people will ignore even frequent expenses when they are small because people tend to ignore costs they consider trivial (Gourville, 1998). People will be more likely to make an identical large purchase when the payment is described in small installments (e.g., as "pennies-a-day"). In both cases, people ignore an expense because they fail to recognize how the individual spending incident fits into a broader spending category.[7]

A failure to appropriately account for an expense can extend to other contexts as well. In a recent study, Cheng and Cryder (2017) provide evidence that people engage in double mental discounting, a phenomenon where people mentally deduct a single gain multiple times when that single gain is associated with multiple purchases. For instance, individuals who receive a gift card for future spending in return for current spending mentally discount the gift card funds from both the current purchase and the future purchase, even though in reality, the gift card funds can only be applied toward one of those two purchases.

A related pitfall of segregating funds stems from the potential mismatch in the timing of when budgets are set and when consumption opportunities arise. Budgets that are set in advance of consumption serve as useful precommitments against the temptation of overspending. For the budget to effectively facilitate self-control, the budgeting rules must by nature be fairly inflexible. However, this nonfungibility of funds can yield suboptimal behavior, particularly when it is difficult to anticipate consumption needs in advance. Not only can this inflexibility in budget adjustment lead people to overconsume or underconsume goods, but it can also affect the types of goods that are consumed. Purchases that are highly typical of the associated mental account can lead people to consume less on goods within that category. More generally, an inflexible budget prevents individuals from reallocating funds to other categories in response (Heath & Soll, 1996). For instance, Hastings and Shapiro (2013) find that when global conditions cause the price of gas to fall by roughly 50%, consumers responded by substituting regular gasoline with premium-grade gasoline, rather than by purchasing other types of goods. And, not only did consumers shift to purchasing premium-grade gasoline, but that shift far exceeded what would normally be expected from consumers had they instead received an increase

---

[7] Installment pricing can also alter the mental representation of a contract's benefits, leading people to think of these as more separate and discrete. This change in representation can increase expected benefits when there are diminishing returns to scale for the benefits (over time or other aggregation). This process can increase purchase intentions even for nontrivial costs (Atlas & Bartels, 2017).

in their income equivalent to the savings from gas prices falling. In other words, inflexibility in consumers' adjustment of their gas budgets led them to overspend on gas relative to what would be optimal had they not segregated funds for a gas budget in this way.

While categorizing and segregating funds can facilitate making trade-offs by narrowing the set of choices to consider (and the associated cognitive burden), doing so can lead to myopic decision-making. For example, while it is important for people to set aside money for future savings, earmarking funds for specific savings purposes can lead people to maintain these savings even when doing so means incurring high interest rate debt (Sussman & O'Brien, 2016). In another example, Camerer, Babcock, Loewenstein, and Thaler (1997) study how the behavior of New York City taxi drivers changes in response to changes in the demand for taxi services (e.g., temporary demand shocks from weather changes, conventions, etc.). When the demand for taxi services increases, drivers can spend less time searching for their next customer; as a result, when demand increases, driver earnings per hour also increase. The authors find that taxi drivers segregate their earnings at the daily level. In other words, they decide how long to drive by aiming for a daily income target. This means they simply quit working once they reach that target on high demand days, even though they would earn more by working longer hours when the hourly wage is high (i.e., when demand is high).[8] By focusing on a very narrow time horizon rather than a broader time horizon of one week or month, the drivers effectively leave money on the table that they otherwise could have made. This behavior is not specific to taxi drivers by any means; Rizzo and Zeckhauser (2003) observe similar narrow bracketing behavior with doctors. In general, broad bracketing or less segregation of funds allows people to consider a more complete set of information, though it comes with a trade-off of higher cognitive costs for decision-making (Read et al., 1999).

Treatment of windfall gains as distinct from other funds can also lead to overly narrow decision-making. In an examination of restitution payments after World War II among Israelis as an example of windfall gains, Landsberger (1966) finds that groups receiving the largest windfalls spent less than 25% of the amount received. However, those receiving the smallest windfalls spent more than twice the amount of the windfall, suggesting that a narrow focus on these funds led people to spend more than they otherwise

---

[8] Subsequent research on the income targeting has yielded mixed results (see Farber, 2015 for an overview of the literature). While several papers have found evidence in support of income-targeting (Chang & Gross, 2014; Crawford & Meng, 2011; Fehr & Götte, 2007), others have failed to find supporting evidence (Chen & Sheldon, 2015; Farber, 2005; 2008; 2015; Oettinginer, 1999; Stafford, 2015).

would (see also Milkman & Beshears, 2009). Additionally, recent research shows that people are more likely to take out a sizable loan for an automobile in months adjacent to receiving a bonus, even when this bonus amount is less than $500. This pattern is consistent with differential treatment of the bonus as a windfall gain. However, people who take out auto loans during this period are also more likely to become delinquent on these loans one year after origination, suggesting that focusing on this bonus amount may lead people to spend beyond their means (Chan, Jiang, & Zhang, 2017).

IMPLICATIONS FOR INVESTING

In addition to influencing how people spend current funds and choices around how much debt to hold, mental accounting can influence the types of investment decisions that people make, as well as the timing of those decisions. Investing is typically thought of as a long-term financial behavior and requires making a trade-off between consumption today and consumption in the future. Over a long time horizon, earmarking funds across different time periods can help prevent overconsumption in the present due to self-control problems. On the other hand, segregating funds and more generally treating funds as nonfungible across mental accounts can also lead to suboptimal behavior. In this section, we explore the implications, both positive and negative, of mental accounting and the cognitive processes that underlie investment behavior.

Opening and Closing Accounts

Temporal labels allow for the crisp categorizations of funds. For example, there is no ambiguity in what time horizon a day represents. However, the choice of when an account is considered open versus closed can be quite flexible (Thaler, 1999). As noted in the discussion on budgeting, flexibility in the categorization process and in the evaluation of funds can result in malleable mental accounting (Cheema & Soman, 2006). This malleability in the temporal bracketing of a mental account has implications for how individuals choose to invest. In particular, the practice of investing often features paper gains and paper losses—unrealized changes in the value of an investment. Once an investment is sold, any changes in the value of the investment are then realized, with funds being transferred between accounts (e.g., cashing out a stock after a sale). Shefrin and Statman (1987) first proposed a model of an investor who opens a mental account when she makes an investment and then closes that mental account when she subsequently sells the investment. As long as she has not sold the investment, the mental account remains open regardless of what paper gains or losses she experiences. The authors suggest that the nominal purchase price is the natural reference point for the value of the investment against which the investor will evaluate the relative gain or loss. Investors tend to be reluctant to realize a loss (and eager to realize a gain) and any changes in value are realized when the asset is sold and the mental account therefore closed. Consequently, investors sell winners too early and ride losers too long, a tendency that is now referred to as the *disposition effect* (Barberis & Xiong, 2009; Shefrin & Statman, 1987). Later research has documented this behavior both in the laboratory (Weber & Camerer, 1998) and in the field for individual traders (Odean, 1998) as well as for professional traders, market makers, and mutual fund managers (Coval & Shumway, 2005; Frazzini, 2006; Locke & Mann, 2000; Shapira & Venezia, 2001; Wermers, 2003). Taken together, this research suggests an important role for financial advisors to help individual investors who may suffer from this behavioral bias.

To avoid experiencing the disutility that comes with realizing a loss, investors may sometimes roll a mental account from one investment to another by selling the original asset and buying a new asset, all within a short window of time (Frydman, Hartzmark, & Solomon, 2017). By allowing some flexibility in the framing of mental accounts, rolling the mental account allows investors to avoid realizing the loss that would have been associated with closing the mental account after the sale of the initial asset. By making the sale of the initial asset and subsequent purchase of the new asset quickly, the mental account remains open with same reference point linked to the purchase price of the initial asset. Looking at the behavior of individual investors, Frydman et al. (2017) find that investors do indeed display behavior consistent with rolling mental accounts: Investors are more likely to sell a new asset if its value exceeds that of the initial asset investment, regardless of whether the value of the new asset exceeds or is at a loss relative to its own initial purchase price. Consistent with the notion that the timing of the sale of the initial asset and the purchase of the new asset must occur within a sufficiently short window of time to be bracketed into the same mental account, the authors further find that the longer the gap in time between the initial sale and subsequent purchase, the greater the likelihood of observing the disposition effect. These findings lend further support to the influence of mental accounting on investor behavior.

The psychological distinction between a paper loss and a realized loss, and thus between an open mental account and a closed mental account has implications for risk-taking behavior as well. In a series of laboratory experiments, Imas (2016) documents a differential effect of paper versus realized losses on risk-taking behavior. In particular, the author finds that people take on more risk after a paper loss and less risk after a realized loss and that the increased risk after a paper loss represents a deviation from individuals' original planned risk-taking strategies. That is, after a paper loss, individuals are reluctant to realize a loss in their investments and instead take on more risk than they otherwise preferred prior to experiencing the paper loss. Such behavior can result in serious consequences for the individual investor and highlight a need for careful monitoring of these types of investor behaviors.

The effect of prior outcomes on risk-taking behavior extends outside of paper versus realized changes to gains and losses more generally. Specifically, individuals engage in more risk-seeking behavior following a prior gain and exhibit more risk-aversion when following a prior loss (Thaler & Johnson, 1990). A commonly cited example of this behavior is the gamblers' tendency to reference "playing with house money" when their current winnings exceed the initial investment they made to play. By reframing the winnings (house money) as separate from their initial investment to play (own money), they can mentally recode any losses incurred as reductions in the gain from winning as if the disutility associated with losing house money is less than the disutility associated with losing one's own money. In support of this proposed mental accounting, studies have documented greater risk-seeking behavior in a setting where house money accounting is possible relative to a setting where it is not (Battalio, Kagel, & Jiranyakul, 1988; Thaler & Johnson, 1990). Similarly, a prior loss can lead individuals to engage in more risk-seeking behavior when faced with an opportunity to return to the original reference level (the initial investment) and break even (Thaler & Johnson, 1990). In general, whether an individual decides to follow an initial (sunk) investment by increasing her investment (escalating commitment) or decreasing her investment (de-escalating commitment) can depend both on whether the individual has set a mental budget and how difficult it is to mentally track any additional investments against that budget (Heath, 1995; Thaler, 1980). The more difficult it is to track and account for additional investments against a mental budget, either because the additional investments differ from the initial sunk investment in the type of resource or in their timing and format, the more likely the individual is to respond by escalating commitment.

Investor behavior can be influenced not only by when they consider a mental account to be open or closed but also by the frequency with which they evaluate the mental account (and thus reset their reference point for an investment). When an investor is differentially sensitive to losses (loss averse), the more frequently she evaluates an investment or counts her money, the less attractive a risky asset will appear. In other words, investors may exhibit *myopic loss aversion*, a tendency to take an overly short-term view on an investment (Benartzi & Thaler, 1995). This myopic loss aversion can help explain one of the most striking facts about the behavior of the

U.S. stock market: the financial phenomenon referred to as the equity premium puzzle. Historically, the observed returns on stocks are much higher than that of government bonds (i.e., there is a significant equity premium), so much so that it suggests a surprisingly high level of risk aversion among investors. Though the persistence of the equity premium remains an ongoing puzzle for researchers, myopic loss aversion can help explain why investors may appear especially risk averse when it comes to holding stocks.

What Assets to Purchase

Mental accounting, and in particular the bracketing or grouping of items, also has implications for the set of investments people choose to consider and the variety of that set of investments. For instance, individuals may assign different investments to different mental accounts rather than consider their portfolio as a whole. Individuals may consider company stock from their employer as belonging to a unique, separate mental account from other funds they hold (Benartzi & Thaler, 2001). They may choose the asset allocation for their own retirement savings contributions separately from the allocation for the employer's matched retirement savings contributions (Choi, Laibson, & Madrian, 2009). And they may fail to reallocate "old money" already invested (current accumulated assets) despite reallocating "new money" (future funds not yet contributed) (Ameriks & Zeldes, 2000; Benartzi & Thaler, 2007).

Whether a set of choices is presented together (e.g., a set of investment options in a portfolio) or separately (e.g., several individual investment opportunities) can also affect which options are eventually chosen. Specifically, people exhibit diversification bias—a preference for greater variety when making choices in combination (i.e., when choices are bracketed together) than when making choices separately (Read & Loewenstein, 1995; Simonson, 1990). For example, consider an individual who goes to purchase three yogurts. A person with diversification bias would be more likely to purchase a variety of yogurt flavors on a single trip to the supermarket when buying three yogurts all at once than if she were to buy a single yogurt on three separate trips to the store. Additional research has shown that this diversification bias extends to the realm of investing. Benartzi and Thaler (1998) find evidence that some people exhibit an extreme version of diversification bias, or what they call the "$1/n$ heuristic": when presented with n funds, individuals have a tendency to roughly allocate an even split of their resources ($1/n$ of their money) to each of the available funds. This tendency suggests that their allocation of resources across asset types will be strongly influenced by the set and the number of funds offered. More generally, the choices and allocations people make over money or consumption depends on the subjective grouping of the options under consideration (Fox, Ratner, & Lieb, 2005). An individual may allocate her funds differently across the same set of investment options when shown those options grouped by asset class versus grouped by economic sector.

CONCLUDING REMARKS AND FUTURE RESEARCH

Consumer financial behavior has long been used to gauge the overall well-being of individuals and their households. Why and how people choose to spend, borrow, save, and invest and the plans they make for engaging in these behaviors has direct implications not only for their personal well-being but also for the various companies and financial institutions they interact with in making these decisions. To complicate matters further, people often seek advice from financial advisors, planners, and other experts as well as from nonexperts such as friends and family, thus expanding the potential set of influences driving consumer financial behavior.

In this chapter, we discuss a number of ways in which financial decision-making is informed by mental accounting. Our understanding of mental accounts depends crucially on understanding what leads individuals to form the mental accounts that they do, the conditions under which the associated mental accounting rules remain effective, and the subsequent influence of mental accounting on outcomes. Despite its prevalence and importance, there remains a sizeable gap in our understanding of mental accounting and its effects on financial well-being. Below, we sketch some of the current gaps in knowledge and suggest a few promising avenues of research for the future.

Formation and Evolution of Mental Accounts

Research on the flexibility of mental accounts has largely focused on self-driven malleability in mental accounts in settings where people can exploit flexibility in classifying ambiguous expenses or in accommodating unclassified expenses to sidestep the self-control imposed by mental accounting budgeting rules (Cheema & Soman, 2008). However, much of the existing research takes certain mental accounts as given (e.g., a food account, an entertainment account, or a gas account), and additional research is needed to better understand how people select accounts and how accounts may evolve over time and as a result of environmental factors. For example, there has been minimal attention devoted to how external forces can strengthen or weaken the categorization of funds. In situations where mental accounting facilitates self-control, any external weakening of mental accounts presents a potentially serious concern. These concerns especially hold when the weakening of mental accounts is accompanied by financial costs.

Consider, for example, defined contribution retirement savings plans such as a 401(k). Under these plans, pretax contributions are deducted directly from an employee's paycheck and placed in a 401(k) account with the option to be invested. In addition to those funds being earmarked as retirement savings, withdrawals from a 401(k) account prior to age 59½ are generally subject to an early withdrawal financial penalty to discourage the cashing out of funds from the account. Recent evidence suggests, however, that this separate account may not be sufficient in light of premature leakage of funds from these retirement savings plans (Beshears, Choi, Hurwitz, Laibson, & Madrian, 2015). While some of the channels through which leakage occurs, such as early withdrawal or the taking out of 401(k) loans, may be due to liquidity needs, other channels can arise as a result of seemingly innocuous outside factors. Most notably, workers have the option to cash out funds from their retirement accounts when leaving a job. A study by Aon Hewitt of over 1.8 million employees found that nearly 42% of employees who left their job in the prior year chose to cash out their retirement accounts rather than remain in their current plan or rollover those funds to an Individual Retirement Account (IRA) or a 401(k) plan with their new employer (Aon Hewitt, 2011). Though some of those who choose to cash out when leaving their job may need immediate access to cash, the prevalence of this behavior suggests that separating from a job works in part to undo both the formal and informal segregation of those funds. Outside of the 401(k) account, those leaked funds can be easily spent and may now be categorized as cash-on-hand rather than as retirements savings for the future. Recent research has explored interventions to enhance the effectiveness of earmarking on savings and finds that using a visual reminder of the savings goal (in this case, a picture of the household's children) and physically segregating funds into sealed envelopes significantly increased the rate of savings for participants (Soman & Cheema, 2011). Taken together, these studies highlight a need for additional research on what factors, both internally and externally motivated, can influence the effectiveness of mental accounts.

Mental Accounting Interactions

While there is some research describing how the categorization of funds varies by different individual characteristics (e.g., Abeler & Marklein, 2017; Paul, Parker, & Dommer, 2017; Shah, Shafir, & Mullainathan, 2015), the evidence on such relationships is relatively sparse, and little is known about how past experiences inform mental accounting behavior. Even less attention has been devoted to how households, rather than individuals, form mental accounts, especially in the face of potentially different preferences and categorization processes between members of the same household. The financial well-being of a household often depends on the decision-making input of multiple members within the household. Yet, most research to date on mental accounting has overlooked how intrahousehold decisions may inform the construction of household mental accounts and has instead either focused on individual decision-making or has treated households as if they can be thought of as a single, unified unit. While this latter assumption can greatly ease the complexity in studying mental accounting behavior, it ignores potentially important intrahousehold dynamics that may influence household outcomes. For instance, a household budget for a married couple depends on the inflow of resources from both spouses, which may vary in amount, timing, and reliability, as well as the outflow of expenditures from the household, which may be purchased jointly or separately by both spouses. Potential intrahousehold conflicts can arise not only from differences in the inflow and outflow of funds across spouses but also by differences in personal tradeoffs and priorities as well as household-specific financial management structures (Ashraf, 2009). Within the domain of consumer finance, researchers have only recently begun to extend mental accounting to the financial decision-making of couples. In a recent study, Garbinsky and Gladstone (2017) explore whether couples spend differently out of different types of financial accounts. They find that couples are more likely to purchase essential goods and less likely to purchase luxury goods when spending from a joint account (rather than a separate account) and provide evidence suggesting that these spending patterns are driven by a differential need to justify purchases when spending out of pooled funds (the joint account). These findings underscore a critical need for additional research that can shed light on how households form and manage mental accounts.

Mental Accounting and Technology

Another underexplored area of research is the role of recent technological advances in the financial services sector, or FinTech, and how such technology can help facilitate or hinder mental accounting. Emerging technology presents both threats and opportunities to consumers as they grapple with their household finances in an ever-evolving financial environment. For instance, recent advances in payments and expense tracking by financial institutions allow consumers to see not only how much they spend each month but also how much of their spending goes to eating out versus retail shopping. In the realm of budgeting, personal financial management applications and personal budgeting software act as financial aggregators and allow consumers to connect different financial accounts to help track spending and saving over time within self-set budget categories. Indeed, some banking institutions now allow customers to open multiple savings accounts and label each with a different savings goal, effectively providing their customers with the ability to make mental accounting behavior more explicit. In the investing realm, automated investing platforms encourage people to designate certain funds (e.g., the round-up difference between a purchase and the next integer dollar amount) for investing. These platforms often aim to engage people who may otherwise not invest on their own. As technological advances change the financial landscape that consumers face, there is an increasing need for research on how consumer financial behavior will adapt and how our understanding of the role of mental accounting behavior evolves as well.

Mental Accounting and Well-Being

Finally, and perhaps most important, there is a pressing need for additional research on how mental accounting and its associated behaviors directly link to overall financial well-being. While our review highlights the role mental accounting can play in influencing financial decision-making in various settings and the potential benefits and pitfalls that can occur as a result, establishing a direct link between mental accounting and economic outcomes, particularly in the long term, remains an ongoing challenge.

REFERENCES

Abeler, J., & Marklein, F. (2017). Fungibility, labels, and consumption. *Journal of the European Economic Association, 15*(1), 99–127.

Ameriks, J., Caplin, A., & Leary, J. (2013). Wealth accumulation and the propensity to plan. *The Quarterly Journal of Economics, 118,* 1007–1047.

Ameriks J., & Zeldes, S. (2000). *How do household portfolio shares vary with age?* Working paper, Columbia University and TIAA-CREF.

André, Q., Reinholtz, N., & Lynch, J. G. (2017). *As good as money? How less fungible resources affect budgeting decisions.* Working paper, INSEAD and Leeds School of Business, University of Colorado.

Aon Hewitt. (2011). *Leakage of participants' DC assets: How loans, withdrawals, and cashouts are eroding retirement income.* London, England. Retrieved from http://www.aon.com/attachments/thought-leadership/survey_asset_leakage.pdf.

Arkes, H. R., Joyner, C. A., Pezzo, M. V., Nash, J. G., Siegel-Jacobs, K., & Stone, E. (1994). The psychology of windfall gains. *Organizational Behavior and Human Decision Processes, 59*(3), 331–347.

Ashraf, N. (2009). Spousal control and intra–household decision making: An experimental study in the Philippines. *American Economic Review, 99*(4), 1245–1277.

Atlas, S. & Bartels, D. (2017). *Periodic pricing and perceived contract benefits.* Working paper, University of Rhode Island and University of Chicago, Booth School of Business

Barberis, N., & Xiong, W. (2009). What drives the disposition effect? An analysis of a long-standing preference-based explanation. *The Journal of Finance, 64*(2), 751–784.

Battalio, R. C., Kagel, J. H., & Komain, J. (1990). Testing between alternative models of choice under uncertainty: Some initial results. *Journal of Risk and Uncertainty, 3*(1), 25–50.

Benartzi, S., & Thaler, R. H. (1995). Myopic loss-aversion and the equity premium puzzle. *The Quarterly Journal of Economics, 110*(1), 75–92.

Benartzi, S., & Thaler, R. H. (1998). *Illusory diversification and retirement savings.* Unpublished manuscript, University of Chicago and UCLA.

Benartzi, S., & Thaler, R. H. (2001). Naive diversification strategies in defined contribution saving plans. *The American Economic Review, 91*(1), 79–98.

Benartzi, S., & Thaler, R. H. (2007). Heuristics and biases in retirement savings behavior. *The Journal of Economic Perspectives, 21*(3), 81–104.

Beshears, J., Choi, J. J., Hurwitz, J., Laibson, D., & Madrian, B. C. (2015). *Liquidity in retirement savings systems: An international comparison.* Working paper, JFK School of Government, Harvard University.

Camerer, C., Babcock, L., Loewenstein, G., & Thaler, R. H. (1997). Labor supply of New York City cabdrivers: One day at a time. *The Quarterly Journal of Economics, 112*(2), 407–441.

Chan, T., Jiang, Z., & Zhang, D.T. (2017). *Bonus induced durable goods consumption and its unintended consequence.* Working paper, Olin Business School, Washington University in St. Louis.

Chang, T., & Gross, T. (2014). How many pears would a pear packer pack if a pear packer could pack pears at quasi-exogenously varying piece rates? *Journal of Economic Behavior & Organization, 99*, 1–17.

Cheema, A., & Soman, D. (2006). Malleable mental accounting: The effect of flexibility on the justification of attractive spending and consumption decisions. *Journal of Consumer Psychology, 16*(1), 33–44.

Cheema, A., & Soman, D. (2008). The effect of partitions on controlling consumption. *Journal of Marketing Research, XLV*, 665–675.

Chen, M. K., & Sheldon, M. (2015). *Dynamic pricing in a labor market: Surge pricing and flexible work on the Uber platform.* Working paper, Anderson School of Management, University of California Los Angeles and University of Chicago.

Cheng, A., & Cryder, C. (2017). *Double mental discounting: When a single price promotion feels twice as nice.* Working paper, The Pennsylvania State University and Olin Business School, Washington University in St. Louis.

Choi, J. J., Laibson, D., & Madrian, B. C. (2009). Mental accounting in portfolio choice: Evidence from a flypaper effect. *American Economic Review, 99*(5), 2085–95.

Consumer Federation of America. (2013). Financial planning profiles of American households: The 2013 Household Financial Planning Survey and Index. http://www.consumerfed.org/pdfs/HPI-Report-2013.pdf.

References

91

Courant, P., Gramlich, E., & Laitner, J. (1986). A dynamic micro estimate of the life-cycle model. In H. G. Aaron & G. Burtless (Eds.), *Retirement and economic behavior* (pp. 832–857). Washington, DC: Brookings Institution.

Coval, J. D., & Shumway, T. (2005). Do behavioral biases affect prices? *The Journal of Finance, 60*, 1–34.

Crawford, V. P., & Meng, J. (2011). New York City cab drivers' labor supply revisited: Reference-dependent preferences with rational expectations targets for hours and income. *The American Economic Review, 101*(5), 1912–1932.

Epley, N., Mak, D., & Idson, L. C. (2006). Bonus or rebate?: The impact of income framing on spending and saving. *Journal of Behavioral Decision Making, 19*(3), 213-227.

Evers, E. R. K., Imas, A., & Loewenstein, G. (2017). *Mental accounting and preferences over the timing of outcomes.* Working paper, University of California, Berkeley, Haas School of Business and Carnegie Mellon University.

Farber, H. S. (2005). Is tomorrow another day? The labor supply of New York City cabdrivers. *Journal of Political Economy, 113*(1), 46–82.

Farber, H. S. (2008). Reference-dependent preferences and labor supply: The case of New York city taxi drivers. *American Economic Review, 98*(3), 1069–1082.

Farber, H. S. (2015). Why you can't find a taxi in the rain and other labor supply lessons from cab drivers. *The Quarterly Journal of Economics, 130*(4), 1975–2026.

Fehr, E., & Götte, L. (2007). Do workers work more if wages are high? Evidence from a randomized field experiment. *The American Economic Review, 97*(1), 298–317.

Fernbach, P. M., Kan, C., & Lynch Jr, J. G. (2015). Squeezed: Coping with constraint through efficiency and prioritization. *Journal of Consumer Research, 41*(5), 1204–1227.

Field, E. (2009). Educational debt burden and career choice: Evidence from a financial aid experiment at NYU law school. *American Economic Journal: Applied Economics, 1*(1), 1–21.

Financial Consumer Agency of Canada. (2015). *Managing money and planning for the future: Key findings from the 2014 Canadian Financial Capability Survey.* https://www.canada.ca/content/dam/canada/financial-consumer-agency/ migration/eng/resources/researchsurveys/documents/managing-money-key-findings.pdf.

Fox, C. R., Ratner, R. K., & Lieb, D. S. (2005). How subjective grouping of options influences choice and allocation: Diversification bias and the phenomenon of partition dependence. *Journal of Experimental Psychology: General, 134*(4), 538–551.

Frazzini, A. (2006). The disposition effect and underreaction to news. *The Journal of Finance, 61*(4), 2017–2046.

Friedman, M. (1957). *A theory of the consumption function.* Princeton, NJ: Princeton University Press.

Frydman, C., & Camerer, C. F. (2016). The psychology and neuroscience of financial decision making. *Trends in Cognitive Sciences, 20*(9), 661–675.

Frydman, C., Hartzmark, S., & Solomon, D. (2017, June 12). Rolling mental accounts. *Review of Financial Studies.* hhx042.

Galperti, S. (2016). *A theory of personal budgeting.* Working paper, University of California, San Diego.

Garbinsky, E. N., & Gladstone, J. J. (2017). *The consumption consequences of couples pooling financial resources.* Working paper, University of Notre Dame and University College London.

Genesove, D., & Mayer, C. (2001). Loss aversion and seller behavior: Evidence from the housing market. *The Quarterly Journal of Economics, 116*(4), 1233-1260.

Gourville, J. T., (1998). Pennies-a-day: The effect of temporal reframing on transaction evaluation. *Journal of Consumer Research, 24,* 395–408.

Gross, D. B., & Souleles, N. S. (2002). Do liquidity constraints and interest rates matter for consumer behavior? Evidence from credit card data. *Quarterly Journal of Economics, 117*(1), 149-185.

Hastings, J. S., & Shapiro, J. M. (2013). Fungibility and consumer choice: Evidence from commodity price shocks. *The Quarterly Journal of Economics, 128*(4), 1449–1498.

Hastings, J. S., & Shapiro, J. M. (2017). *How are SNAP benefits spent? Evidence from a retail panel.* Working paper, Brown University.

Heath, C. (1995). Escalation and de-escalation of commitment in response to sunk costs: The role of budgeting in mental accounting. *Organizational Behavior and Human Decision Processes, 62,* 38–54.

Heath, C., & Soll, J. B. (1996). Mental budgeting and consumer decisions. *Journal of Consumer Research, 23*(1), 40–52.

Henderson, P. W. & Peterson, R. A. (1992). Mental accounting and categorization. *Organizational Behavior and Human Decision Processes, 51,* 92–117.

Hilgert, M. A., Hogarth, J. M., & Beverly, S. G. (2003). Household financial management: The connection between knowledge and behavior. *Federal Reserve Bulletin, 89,* 309.

Hirst, D. E., Joyce, E. J., & Schadewald, M. S. (1994). Mental accounting and outcome contiguity in consumer-borrowing decisions. *Organizational Behavior and Human Decision Processes, 58,* 136–152.

Huffman, D. & Barenstein, M. (2005). *A monthly struggle for self-control? Hyperbolic discounting, mental accounting, and the fall in consumption between paydays.* Working paper, University of Pittsburgh and Federal Trade Commission.

Imas, A. (2016). The realization effect: Risk-taking after realized versus paper losses. *The American Economic Review, 106*(8), 2086–2109.

Imas, A., Loewenstein, G., & Morewedge, C. K. (2017). *Mental money laundering: A motivated violation of fungibility.* Working paper, Carnegie Mellon University and Boston University, Questrom School of Business.

Ishikawa, T. & Ueda, K. (1984). The bonus payment system and Japanese personal savings. In M. Aoki (Eds.), *The economic analysis of the Japanese firm* (pp. 133-192). North Holland, Amsterdam: Elsevier Science.

Internal Revenue Service. (2017). 2017 Statistics of Income. https://www.irs.gov/newsroom/filing-season-statistics-for-the-week-ending-december-30-2016.

Jarnebrant, P., Toubia, O., & Johnson, E. (2009). The silver lining effect: Formal analysis and experiments. *Management Science, 55*(11), 1832-1841.

Kan, C., Lynch, J., & Fernbach, P. (2015). How budgeting helps consumers achieve financial goals. In K. Diehl & C. Yoon (Eds.), *North American advances in consumer research* (Vol. *43*). Duluth, MN: Association for Consumer Research.

Kahneman, D., & Tversky, A. (1979). Prospect theory: An analysis of decision under risk. *Econometrica: Journal of the Econometric Society*, 263–291.

Knutson, B., Rick, S., Wimmer, G. E., Prelec, D., & Loewenstein, G. (2007). Neural predictors of purchases. *Neuron, 53*(1), 147–156.

Kooreman, P. (2000). The labeling effect of a child benefit system. *The American Economic Review, 90*(3), 571–583.

Krishnamurthy, P., & Prokopec, S. (2010). Resisting that triple-chocolate cake: Mental budgets and self-control. *The Journal of Consumer Research, 37*(1), 68–79.

Landsberger, M. (1966). Windfall income and consumption: Comment. *American Economic Review, 56*, 534–539.

Levav, J., & McGraw, A. P. (2009). Emotional accounting: How feelings about money influence consumer choice. *Journal of Marketing Research, 46*(1), 66–80.

Lin, J. T., Bumcrot, C., Ulicny, T., Lusardi, A., Mottola, G., Kieffer, C., & Walsh, G. (2016). *Financial capability in the United States 2016. FINRA Investor Education Foundation*. Retrieved from http://www.usfinancialcapability.org/downloads/NFCS_2015_Report_Natl_Findings.pdf.

Linville, P. W., & Fischer, G. W. (1991). Preferences for separating or combining events. *Journal of Personality and Social Psychology, 60*(1), 5.

Locke, P., & Mann, S. C. (2000). *Do professional traders exhibit loss realization aversion?* Working paper, Texas Christian University, M. J. Neeley School of Business.

Lusardi, A., Schneider, D., & Tufano, P. (2011). Financially fragile households: Evidence and implications. *Brookings Papers on Economic Activity*, 83–134.

Markman, A. B., & Brendl, C. M. (2000). The influence of goals on value and choice. *Psychology of Learning and Motivation, 39*, 97-128.

Mažar, N., Plassmann, H., Robitaille, N., & Lindner, A. (2017). *Pain of paying?— A metaphor gone literal: Evidence from neural and behavioral science*. Working paper, Rotman School of Management, University of Toronto, INSEAD, Queen's University, and the Institute for Clinical Brain Research.

Milkman, K. L., & Beshears, J. (2009). Mental accounting and small windfalls: Evidence from an online grocer. *Journal of Economic Behavior & Organization, 71*(2), 384–394.

Morewedge, C. K., Holtzman, L., & Epley, N. (2007). Unfixed resources: Perceived costs, consumption, and the accessible account effect. *Journal of Consumer Research, 34*(4), 459-467.

O'Curry, S. (1999). Consumer budgeting and mental accounting. In P. E. Earl & S. Kemp (Eds.), *The Elgar companion to consumer research and economic psychology* (pp. 280–284). Cheltenham, UK: Edward Elgar.

O'Curry, S., & Strahilevitz, M. (2001). Probability and mode of acquisition effects on choices between hedonic and utilitarian options. *Marketing Letters, 12*(1), 37–49.

Odean, T. (1998). Are investors reluctant to realize their losses? *The Journal of Finance, 53*(5), 1775–1798.

Oettinger, G. S. (1999). An empirical analysis of the daily labor supply of stadium vendors. *Journal of Political Economy, 107*(2), 360–392.

Paul, I., Parker, J. R., & Dommer, S. L. (2017). *Don't forget the accountant: Role-integration increases the fungibility of mentally accounted resources.* Working paper, Georgia Tech, Scheller College of Business and Georgia State University, J. Mack Robinson College of Business.

Prelec, D., & Loewenstein, G. (1998). The red and the black: Mental accounting of savings and debt. *Marketing Science, 17*(1), 4–28.

Read, D., & Loewenstein, G. (1995). Diversification bias: Explaining the discrepancy in variety seeking between combined and separated choices. *Journal of Experimental Psychology: Applied 1*(1), 34–49.

Read, D., Loewenstein, G., & Rabin, M. (1999). Choice bracketing. *Journal of Risk and Uncertainty, 19*(1–3), 171–197.

Reinholtz, N., Bartels, D. M., & Parker, J. R. (2015). On the mental accounting of restricted-use funds: How gift cards change what people purchase. *Journal of Consumer Research, 42*(4), 596–614.

Rick, S. I., Cryder, C. E., & Loewenstein, G. (2007). Tightwads and spendthrifts. *Journal of Consumer Research, 34*(6), 767–782.

Rizzo, J. A., & Zeckhauser, R. J. (2003). Reference incomes, loss aversion, and physician behavior. *The Review of Economics and Statistics, 85*(4), 909–922.

Shah, A. K., Shafir, E., & Mullainathan, S. (2015). Scarcity frames value. *Psychological Science, 26*(4), 402–412.

Shah, A. M., Eisenkraft, N., Bettman, J. R., & Chartrand, T. L. (2016). "Paper or plastic?": How we pay influences post-transaction connection. *Journal of Consumer Research, 42*(5), 688–708.

Shapira, Z., & Venezia, I. (2001). Patterns of behavior of professionally managed and independent investors. *Journal of Banking & Finance, 25*(8), 1573–1587.

Shefrin, H. M., & Statman, M. (1987). The disposition to sell winners too early and ride losers too long. *Journal of Finance, 40*, 777–790.

Shefrin, H. M. & Thaler, R. H. (1988). The behavioral life-cycle hypothesis. *Economic Inquiry, 26*, 609–643.

Simon, H. A. (1947). *Administrative behavior: A study of decision-making processes in administrative organization.* New York: Macmillan.

Simonson, I. (1990). The effect of purchase quantity and timing on variety-seeking behavior. *Journal of Marketing Research, 32*, 150–162.

Soman, D. (2003). The effect of payment transparency on consumption: Quasi-experiments from the field. *Marketing Letters, 14*(3), 173–183.

Soman, D., & Ahn, H. K. (2011). Mental accounting and individual welfare. In K. Gideon (Ed.), *Perspectives on framing.* New York: Psychology Press.

Soman, D., Ainslie, G., Frederick, S., Li, X., Lynch, J., Moreau, P., et al. (2005). The psychology of intertemporal discounting: Why are distant events valued differently from proximal ones? *Marketing Letters, 16*(3), 347–360.

Soman, D., & Cheema, A. (2011). Earmarking and partitioning: Increasing saving by low-income households. *Journal of Marketing Research, XLVIII*, S14–S22.

Souleles, N. S. (1999). The response of household consumption to income tax refunds. *The American Economic Review, 89*(4), 947–958.

Stafford, T. (2015). What do fishermen tell us that taxi drivers don't? An empirical investigation of labor supply. *Journal of Labor Economics, 33*(3), 1–24.

Sussman, A. B. (2017). Valence in context: Asymmetric reactions to realized gains and losses. *Journal of Experimental Psychology: General, 146*(3), 376–394.

Sussman, A. B., & Alter, A. L. (2012). The exception is the rule: Underestimating and overspending on exceptional expenses. *Journal of Consumer Research, 39,* 800–814.

Sussman, A. B., Paley, A., & Alter, A. L. (2017). *Mentally accounting for food: Booking, posting, and reconciling exceptional consumption.* Working paper, Booth School of Business, University of Chicago, New York University, Stern School of Business, and Ohio State University, Fisher College of Business.

Sussman, A. B., & O'Brien, R. L. (2016). Knowing when to spend: Unintended financial consequences of earmarking to encourage savings. *Journal of Marketing Research, 53,* 790–803.

Sussman, A. B., & Olivola, C. Y. (2011). Axe the tax: Taxes are disliked more than equivalent costs. *Journal of Marketing Research, XLVIII,* S91–S101.

Sussman, A. B., & Shafir, E. (2012). On assets and debt in the psychology of perceived wealth. *Psychological Science, 23*(1), 101–108.

Sussman, A. B., Sharma, E., & Alter, A. L. (2015). Framing charitable donations as exceptional expenses increases giving. *Journal of Experimental Psychology: Applied, 21*(2), 130.

Thaler, R. (1980). Toward a positive theory of consumer choice. *Journal of Economic Behavior & Organization, 1*(1), 39–60.

Thaler, R. (1985). Mental accounting and consumer choice. *Marketing Science, 4*(3), 199–214.

Thaler, R. H. (1990). Anomalies: Saving, fungibility, and mental accounts. *The Journal of Economic Perspectives, 4*(1), 193–205.

Thaler, R. H. (1994). Psychology and savings policies. *The American Economic Review, 84*(2), 186–192.

Thaler, R. H. (1999). Mental accounting matters. *Journal of Behavioral Decision Making, 12*(3), 183.

Thaler, R. H., & Johnson, E. J. (1990). Gambling with the house money and trying to break even: The effects of prior outcomes on risky choice. *Management Science, 36*(6), 643–660.

Thaler, R. H., & Shefrin, H. M. (1981). An economic theory of self-control. *Journal of Political Economy, 89*(2), 392–406.

Thomas, M., Desai, K. K., & Seenivasan, S. (2011). How credit card payments increase unhealthy food purchases: Visceral regulation of vices. *Journal of Consumer Research, 38*(1), 126–139.

Tversky, A., & Kahneman, D. (1981). The framing of decisions and the psychology of choice. *Science, 211,* 453–458.

Ülkümen, G., Thomas, M., & Morwitz, V. G. (2008). Will I spend more in 12 months or a year? The effect of ease of estimation and confidence on budget estimates. *Journal of Consumer Research, 35*(2), 245–256.

Weber, M., & Camerer, C. F. (1998). The disposition effect in securities trading: An experimental analysis. *Journal of Economic Behavior & Organization, 33*(2), 167–184.

Wermers, R. (2003). *Is money really "smart?": New evidence on the relation between mutual fund flows, manager behavior, and performance persistence.* Working paper, University of Maryland.

Wertenbroch, K., Soman, D., & Nunes, J. (2001). *Debt aversion as self-control: Consumer self-management of liquidity constraints.* Working paper, INSEAD, Hong Kong University of Science and Technology, and Marshall School of Business, University of Southern California.

Wu, G., & Markle, A. (2008). An empirical test of gain–loss separability in prospect theory. *Management Science, 54,* 1322–1335.

Zelizer, V. A. (1994). The creation of domestic currencies. *The American Economic Review, 84*(2), 138–142.

Zellermayer, O. (1996). *The pain of paying.* Unpublished dissertation, Carnegie Mellon University.

Zhang, C. Y. (2016). *Consumption responses to pay frequency: Evidence from "extra" paychecks.* Working paper, Booth School of Business, University of Chicago.

CHAPTER 7

Intentional Choice Architecture

Michael J. Liersch, PhD

People who design environments for decision-makers are choice architects. As a financial planning professional, there is no question that you are a choice architect: You gather clients' personal information on a variety of topics and translate that data into information that facilitates critical financial decisions. From the way in which you elicit responses to questions, to the way in which you present choices, you can influence your clients in profound and predictable ways. So rather than asking *if* you are a choice architect, the question is: Are you an *intentional* choice architect? An intentional choice architect aims to identify the outcomes that they—and the decision-makers that they serve—desire. They also attempt to understand whether the way in which the design of the decision environment they have architected helps facilitate those outcomes. There is an opportunity to continuously evaluate and align architecture with desired outcomes in a way that enhances value to decision-makers.

There is also an opportunity for financial planning professionals to collaborate with researchers—and vice versa. Researchers can bring the theoretical knowledge they have tested in laboratory environments and validate them in real-world decision environments with the help of practitioners. You will see examples of this approach throughout this chapter (e.g., in my own work with my former PhD advisor, Professor Craig McKenzie). Purposeful collaboration between academic and practitioner communities can also inspire academics in different fields to come together, too. For example, how do the social (e.g., interpersonal family dynamics), psychological (e.g., cognitive overload), economic (e.g., choices we know people should make) and policy (e.g., tax law) environments interact to (de)motivate people to engage in planning? The beginnings of these types of collaborations are highlighting the value of presenting simple, default goals-based frameworks to clients. Using intuitive frameworks—rather than the planning itself—as an entry point can create structure around complex problems that helps people understand the value of the choices they are making, and overcome inertia (Wesley, Liersch, & Cooper, 2017). Further exploration of these types of approaches can enhance the choice architecture—and outcomes—that clients experience.

As you read this chapter, I encourage you to think about the role you play in architecting financial planning choices for human beings. How can you better the environment in which you help people make the financial decisions that are most important to them?

ARE YOU AN INTENTIONAL CHOICE ARCHITECT?

Imagine that after a long run in hot weather, you come across a person who offers you a glass of water. You are thirsty. Oddly, the glass is only at the halfway (50%) mark. Would it affect your decision to sip the water if the person described the glass to you as half empty (rather than half full)? What inferences might you make? For example, could the person be telling you that someone else had already drank from the (previously full) glass? Or that you should drink at your own risk? Juxtapose this with a person who tells you that the glass of water is half full. Would it be relatively more appealing? If a person describes a glass as half full, is it more likely that it has not been touched or tampered with by another human being?

Notice that the way the information is framed may actually change your decision (Tversky & Kahneman, 1981). One reason framing may influence you is that you might assume that the choice to describe the glass as half full or half empty—on some level (above or below conscious awareness)—is providing information to you about the glass of water (Sher & McKenzie, 2006). This is a very basic example of choice architecture: The way in which the information provider chooses to describe (or frame) information can influence the choices of the decision-maker. In this case, you can think of the information provider as the choice architect, and the decision-maker as being influenced by that architecture. As such, *choice architecture* can be broadly defined as the ways in which different choice designs predictably influence decision-makers.

Framing options is just one way a choice architect can design decision environments. Other common design elements range from setting a default option (i.e., the choice that is made for the decision-maker if they do nothing) to the number of options presented to the decision-maker (i.e., one or many). Like framing, the default option and number of options have a predictable effect on behavior: As you might expect, in many cases, people tend not to opt out of the default option (for better and worse; see Johnson & Goldstein, 2003) and when there are too many choices, people tend to struggle to make a decision in a variety of ways (see Iyengar & Lepper, 2000).

Given that choice architecture can predictably influence decisions, how intentional are choice architects? Should we assume that the way decision environments are designed is providing us with information about what we should or should not do? Unfortunately, evidence suggests that choice architects may not be as intentional as we might assume (Thaler & Sunstein, 2008).

To bring this closer to home—as a financial professional and a choice architect—I would encourage you to answer four basic questions to evaluate your level of intentionality in your practice:

1. What are the one or two most important outcomes that your decision environment is designed to facilitate? (E.g., are you trying to get the individual to drink the glass of water or not?)
2. Once someone enters your decision environment, can you describe the experience in detail from the very start of the interaction to the very end of the interaction? (E.g., how are you framing, or describing, the glass of water?)
3. Does the experience you described best facilitate the outcomes you and the decision-maker desire? (E.g., did the thirsty individual drink the glass of water?)
4. How can you make small adjustments over time to get closer to the desired outcomes and improve the decision environment? (E.g., can you reframe how the glass of water is described to get closer to your and the decision-maker's desired outcome?)

If, for example, the most important outcome that you are trying to facilitate is goal attainment of your clients (question 1), you might think about how you interact with your clients to make that happen (question 2): You may have an assessment process where you gather information about risk preferences, goals, cash flows, family circumstances, and the balance sheet. Once that data is gathered, you may input it into some type of financial planning software and produce exhibits that reflect whether your clients' goals are feasible. After the exhibits are created, you may schedule a client meeting to walk through them and discuss the dynamics of those exhibits— and whether any trade-offs need to be made (e.g., adjust the asset mix; save more; spend less; reallocate resources across the balance sheet; work longer; give less). As the relationship progresses, you may also have a process whereby the plan is reevaluated and revisited.

In thinking about the decision environment for your clients, consider whether it helps your clients reach their goals (question 3). Be critical. How long are the questionnaires that you ask clients to complete in the assessment process? Are the questions framed in a way that reveal clients' true answers? Is technology employed to help gather real-time balance sheet and cash flow data? Do the exhibits you use contain the most relevant information needed for your clients to make the trade-offs that will get them to where they need to go? What is your process to help clients pre-commit to the trade-offs they need to make? How do you follow-up in a way that holds clients accountable? Do you have a system to always include relevant family members (e.g., spouses and partners)?

By authentically examining the environment you have architected, you can quickly begin to identify key ways to improve your approach (question 4). For example, maybe you notice that you do not truly use all of the data in the questionnaires that you send to clients, thereby revealing an opportunity to simplify the process for you and your clients. Decreasing this additional effort could reduce both your and your clients' inertia around planning. Or you might recognize that you do not send clients a follow-up email asking them to confirm the trade-offs that they have agreed to make. As you might imagine, asking people to formally precommit to savings choices can help them stick with their plan (see Thaler, 2015, for extensive discussions around precommitment and inertia).

If you are able to identify a number of opportunities to be an intentional choice architect, you are joining a rapidly growing movement led by scientists, business leaders, and policymakers. Indeed, choice architecture is a burgeoning concept, which was first brought to the mainstream in 2008 by Richard Thaler and Cass Sunstein in their book *Nudge*. (Richard Thaler, a professor at the University of Chicago Booth School of Business, is known as the father of behavioral finance/economics and is the 2017 Nobel Prize laureate in Economics. At its core, behavioral finance/economics is the study of how real humans actually make financial decisions. Cass Sunstein is a Harvard Law School professor, and was the administrator of the White House Office of Information and Regulatory Affairs in the Obama administration from 2009 to 2012.)

The idea of a nudge is to design a choice architecture that facilitates decisions with desirable outcomes, but that also maintains people's freedom to choose. One example that we will cover in much more detail later in this chapter is employee retirement savings. The traditional format for employees deciding to enroll in a company's 401(k)-type retirement plan is to opt in. In other words, if employees do nothing, they are not enrolled. Alternatively, employers can change things up and make the default enrollment in the plan. In this situation, if employees do nothing, they save for retirement. Since employees can still opt out of the plan, choice is preserved. In this way, the nudge potentially improves employee retirement savings (since employees tend to stay with default options) while maintaining employees' options.

Thaler and Sunstein's ideas were heavily influenced by the behavioral scientists Daniel Kahneman and Amos Tversky (Thaler, 2016), who put forth evidence that due to a variety of constraints—e.g., time; cognitive limitations; information—human beings often use rules of thumb, or heuristics, to guide their decision-making (Tversky & Kahneman, 1974). Their insights were so revolutionary that Daniel Kahneman won the Nobel Prize in 2002 for his and Amos Tversky's (who passed in 1996) contribution in the field of Economics. Specifically, they found that the heuristics people use lead to very predictable ways in which people evaluate and ultimately make decisions. In some cases these heuristics lead people to good decisions, and in other cases decisions that are not so good (see also Kahneman, 2011; for a third-party narrative of Daniel Kahneman and Amos Tversky's enormous scientific contribution, see Lewis, 2016).

For example, one heuristic that human beings tend to apply to many situations is the notion of loss aversion: People would prefer to avoid losing something (e.g., losing $1,000) rather than having an equal opportunity to get that same thing (e.g., gaining $1,000; Tversky & Kahneman, 1979). You may have heard the adage "losses hurt more than gains feel good" and may have also directly experienced this feeling with your clients!

Loss aversion could be one reason why people tend to stick with the status quo: Giving up the status quo may be perceived as a loss (Johnson, Hershey, Mezaros, & Kunreuther, 1993). Now imagine that an employee encounters a default choice—which many consider the status quo option—to *not* enroll in their retirement plan. If the employee stays with the default choice and it is in line with their preferences, that may constitute good decision-making. However, if the employee stays with the default choice, and it does not fit their preferences, that may constitute a poor decision. Knowledge of these human rules of thumb—and their implications—can be a great asset as a choice architect, as we will see later in this chapter.

With a high-level appreciation for how the mind works, the choice architect should keep (at least) two principles at the forefront when designing a decision environment. (For elaboration on some of the following themes, note that Thaler & Sunstein's *Nudge* [2008] provide six principles of good choice architecture.)

PRINCIPLE 1: HUMANS HAVE LIMITATIONS

It should come as no surprise that when making decisions, human beings cannot carefully evaluate every option and trade-off presented to them—and therefore employ mental shortcuts (i.e., heuristics) to make many decisions. With this in mind, the choice architect should carefully examine the signal-to-noise ratio of a decision environment. The decision environment should help the decision-maker focus on the signal, or the most relevant aspects of the decisions that are being facilitated—while letting the noise, or less relevant information, fall to the wayside. Otherwise put, the choice architect wants the signal-to-noise ratio to be high: More signal, less noise.

Being aware that the number of decisions people are confronted with is important, too. Many human beings make thousands of decisions per day (if this is difficult to believe, we make hundreds of decisions daily about food alone; Wansink & Sobal, 2007). Unfortunately, as the number of decisions increases, most human beings experience what is called decision fatigue. Researchers have shown that decision fatigue not only negatively affects the quality of choices people make (e.g., by diminishing self-control; Vohs et al., 2008), but also affects other aspects of the human experience such as the decision-makers' mood (see Baumeister, 2002). (Former) President Barack Obama, recognizing this issue in his own life, architected his choices by only wearing gray or blue suits in order to reduce the number of decisions he makes (Lewis, 2012). As a financial planning choice architect, deliberately examining everything from the relevance of the information you present, to the quantity of decisions that you ask clients to make, can make a difference.

The fact that the human mind is even able to navigate extreme complexity in our world today, and with a surprising level of accuracy, is quite amazing. To that end, empathy and recognition of the bounded nature of decision-making should drive the core creation of any decision environment (Gigerenzer & Reinhard, 2002). You might be encouraged to find that if you design an environment that acknowledges human limitations, the people within your decision environment may take notice and appreciate it. If you are a courageous choice architect, you could even ask decision-makers for their feedback on how you could further improve it.

And the feedback could be more productive than you may think. Human beings seem to be aware that they have limitations—with clever approaches to address them—even at young ages. In studies with 4-year-olds, researchers wanted to see if children could delay the consumption of treats (e.g., a marshmallow) for the opportunity to get more treats later (Mischel, Shoda, & Rodriguez, 1989). While some children ate the treats immediately, others were able to deliberately delay gratification by employing strategies such as covering their eyes (see Benartzi & Levin, 2012, for an entertaining discussion of these experiments). But it does not just stop at childhood and sweets. Many adults formally self-impose strategies to delay gratification with an even more important consumable item: money. For example, you may have seen people bucket—allocate—their money across four categories: investing, giving, saving, and spending. (The creation of mental accounts is a very common human strategy that can lead to productive and unproductive financial choices; see Thaler, 2016.) This self-control strategy is so popular, you can even buy children's piggy banks formally segmented using this exact four-bucket approach. The buckets, in essence, help people defer consumption (i.e., budget) for their (and others') future selves—and we intuitively know it works. The recent rise of goals-based wealth management (GBWM) can be said to be a more sophisticated form of this type of self-control strategy by explicitly dedicating saving and investment strategies to distinct goals (e.g., annual spending; retirement; education; bequest; see Brunel, 2015, for an extensive discussion of GBWM).

It is almost as if people are aware that they have competing selves—one that is more impulsive and present-biased, while the other is more deliberative and plans (see Thaler, 2016, for an excellent discussion of the notion of competing selves—what he calls the planner and the doer). Indeed, one of the primary reasons financial planning exists is to help people manage limitations around self-control of the more impulsive self. But limits to deferring consumption are not only caused by traditional self-control issues. For example, researchers surmised that one of the primary reasons young people do not save more is the difficulty in imagining the (negative) effects on one's future self (Hershfield et al., 2011). (And it is not surprising that young people find it hard to imagine the future: They have never been there.) Instead of presenting complex financial plans and information about what their future would be like if they saved more, the researchers decided to take a less overwhelming route. They showed young people digitally aged avatars of themselves. In essence, the researchers were helping young people connect to their future selves in a quick, relevant, and intuitive way (perhaps it was even fun!). Indeed, this simple tool did not require a great deal of effort on the decision-makers' part, but still resulted in young people allocating a significantly larger amount of money toward their retirement. The upshot: Helping people who have limited time, cognitive capacity, and information should focus on pleasant and simple—not painful and complicated—choice architecture.

PRINCIPLE 2: HUMANS USE REFERENCE POINTS TO MAKE DECISIONS

When making decisions, humans often evaluate potential outcomes based on a reference point—for example, whether the future decision may result in a gain or a loss from where they are at now. Different people come to the table with different reference points based on a number of factors including their past experiences, current situation, goals, etc. For example, an individual with hundreds of millions of dollars may think very differently about a $1 million investment relative to someone with a net worth of $2 million.

Of course—and critically for the choice architect—the way in which the decision environment is designed may establish reference points as well. We illustrated this at the start of the chapter with the glass of water at the half-way mark: How the glass of water is described—half full or half empty—can influence the decision-maker. In essence, the description is setting the reference point (i.e., the glass is relatively full or empty). Default options can also be said to establish a reference point for decision-makers: The default is the status quo option—and any movement away from that reference point could be perceived as a loss.

I would be remiss if I did not mention the most classic example of how people's decision-making can be influenced via reference points: risky choice framing effects. While Amos Tversky and Daniel Kahneman (1981) developed the seminal "risky choice framing" examples (e.g., in the domain of human lives), for our purposes, we will use a scenario created by researcher X. T. Wang (1996). Consider the following:

> *Imagine that you bought $6,000 worth of stock from a company that has just filed a claim for bankruptcy. The company now provides you with two alternatives to recover some of your money. If you choose alternative A, you will save $2,000 of your money.*
>
> *If you choose alternative B, you will take part in a random drawing procedure with exactly a one-third probability of saving all of your money, and a two-thirds probability of saving none of your money.*
>
> *Which of the two alternatives would you favor?*

In Wang's study, 91% of experimental participants went with the sure thing (alternative A). Here is where it gets interesting. Now, imagine the same scenario, but with reframed options X and Y:

> *If you choose alternative X, you will lose $4,000 of your money.*
>
> *If you choose alternative Y, you will take part in a random drawing procedure with exactly two-thirds probability of losing all of your money, and one-third probability of not losing any of your money.*
>
> *Which of the alternatives would you favor?*

For alternatives X and Y, only 66% of the experimental participants chose the sure thing (alternative X). Note that the outcomes of alternatives A and X are monetarily equivalent (in both cases, you receive $2,000 for sure), as are alternatives B and Y (in both cases, there is a one-third chance that you receive $6,000 and a two-thirds chance that you receive $0). So the choices are identical—it is only the frame that is different. A and B describe the risky choice in terms of gains (i.e., what could be saved) whereas X and Y describe it in terms of losses. The fact that less people chose the sure thing when the options are described in terms of losses (rather than gains) illustrates the tendency for people to be relatively risk seeking for losses compared to gains. Another way to put this is that people are relatively risk averse for gains compared to losses (see Tversky & Kahneman, 1981). If you are skeptical that framing risky choices in terms of gains and losses matters, this tendency is found in a number of real-world situations, including investing. For example, investors are more likely to sell winning stocks and hold on to losing ones (the disposition effect, Shefrin & Statman, 1985). Interestingly enough, tax policies (a form of choice architecture) actually cause the disposition effect to go away in December, presumably due to the tax benefits of selling losers and holding winners (Odean, 1998).

Understanding people's reference points—and how reference points affect decision-making—can help the choice architect intentionally design a decision environment that facilitates decisions in line with desired outcomes. To directly apply this concept to the choice architecture of financial planning, consider the endowment effect, whereby people can assign a greater value to things simply because they own them (Kahneman, Knetsch, & Thaler, 1991). As a financial planning professional, when constructing a clients' balance sheet, knowing that the reference point of mere ownership may cause clients to overvalue their homes, cars, boats and even investments could be important: By having a client articulate the value of these items, it could result in an overestimation of the financial resources they have available to reach their goals. Architecting a process where data-driven, third-party estimates (e.g., Zillow estimates for homes) are used to build out the balance sheet could be a more accurate reflection of the assets' true value.

As we leave the topic of reference points, it is important to note that it can be advantageous to remain nonjudgmental when it comes to the reference points people use. Remaining nonjudgmental can increase the chance that the decision-maker will authentically reveal their reference points to you—which can allow you to facilitate decision-making aligned with desired outcomes.

To illustrate this point, I often ask groups the following question: "Would you rather have $20 for sure from me right now, or flip a coin for an equal chance of $0 (heads) or $100 (tails)?" People choosing the sure thing are typically in the minority. They tend to say that $20 is meaningful to them and they do not want to give up the bird in hand. If these people were my clients, this would be very good information for me to know! However, the risk takers in the group are typically quick to judge, and articulate how obvious it is that the coin flip is the better choice. I remind the group that without knowledge of their specific objectives, the dollar amounts that are important to them, their levels of loss aversion and the like, it would be impossible to know which decision was wrong or right (Liersch & Etheridge, 2015). I go on to illustrate the point by posing a new choice to the group: "Would you rather have $2 million for sure from me right now, or flip a coin for an equal chance of $0 (heads) and $10 million (tails)?" Under these circumstances, the majority of the group chooses the sure thing. While the idea of losing $20 was not very meaningful to the former risk takers, the idea of losing $2 million is. Here is the fun part: To the surprise of many, there are inevitably one or two people who still stay with the coin flip—even at these high stakes. If these people were my clients, this would *also* be very good information for me to know! I always highlight to the group that based on the context of their lives and preferences, sticking with the risky choice may be perfectly right for these individuals. What is wrong is the assumption that the same reference points share the same meaning for everyone.

THE CHOICE ARCHITECT'S OPPORTUNITY

There is an extraordinary opportunity to (re)define the value that you deliver by considering yourself a choice architect. In particular, once you have articulated your desired outcomes and defined the existing experience, you can much more easily identify any mismatches between your intentions and the outcomes that your existing architecture facilitates. In this way, you can immediately begin to redesign a choice architecture that better aligns with what you (and your clients) would like to accomplish.

This not only creates value for you and your clients—it also has the potential to differentiate your practice. Why? The outcomes that clients desire are not necessarily ubiquitous. Otherwise put, different types of clients have different needs, concerns, and goals. Reestablishing why you do what you do and why your clients work with you can bring to life the unique aspects of your decision environment that you should highlight to existing and prospective clients.

To drive this point home, imagine that your and your clients' primary focus is to reach your clients' goals via a formal financial plan. If so, making markets and investment performance the anchor of your client interactions—and putting the onus on your clients to proactively request to revisit their plan—may not be the ideal architecture. Instead, you and your clients may want to precommit to a scheduled quarterly or annual interaction where the review of your clients' plan is a default part of the agenda. In your review meetings, it may also be important to discuss the plan first before getting to the details of the accounts or portfolio, so that the investment performance is in context of what your clients are trying to accomplish. And designing a formal follow-up surrounding next steps (e.g., spending less; saving/investing more; setting-up tax advantage wealth structures) via human or technological interaction may be essential to the success of the plan.

However, if you and your clients' focus is investment outperformance, you might architect a completely different approach. First, you might want to set up a formal process to precommit to the performance benchmark that will help measure the level of out- or underperformance—along with trading and investing guidelines that you and your clients will follow (i.e., an investment policy). Rather than quarterly or annual review meetings focused on a financial plan, you may set up regular, but very brief, check-ins with your clients every few weeks focused on potential market opportunities. These touch bases could help ensure that you do not miss anything that you or your clients may be interested in. Additionally, you may consider proactively, rather than reactively, sending market updates to your clients and providing on-demand access to their investment performance (in addition to attribution of what caused out- or underperformance).

Of course, in both contexts, there is much more that could be done from a design perspective. The point is that intentional choice architecture centered on desired outcomes not only has the potential to increase the likelihood of those outcomes, but it can actually change the very nature of the client experience and your value: Clients who do not want to have a planning relationship could be unhappy with a financial planning architecture, but happy with an investment outperformance architecture—and vice versa for clients who do want to have a planning relationship. Of course, you could focus on multiple desired outcomes. For instance, you could focus on both client goals and investment outperformance. Recall, though, the limits of human decision-making: having multiple focal points could have a number of negative effects from taxing the decision-maker with additional time to overwhelm or confusion (e.g., what are you and your client managing to: a goals-based or a market-based benchmark?). Much like architecture in areas outside of finance—think about office and residential buildings, which help separate work and living spaces for a variety of reasons—there can be value in a smaller set of focal points rather than trying to design an experience that is too broad.

THE CASE FOR INTENTIONAL CHOICE ARCHITECTURE: RETIREMENT SAVINGS

Being an intentional choice architect is far from easy. However, when done well, it can be enormously effective. Indeed, marketers have been intentional choice architects for quite some time now and have played their role well.

You may have noticed, for example, how candy and magazines are almost always prominently displayed at every checkout aisle at the grocery store, with the candy at kids' level and the magazines at adult height. Or how digital boxes are sometimes prechecked online when you are asked to verify a choice to receive future marketing information from a company. And perhaps you are very familiar with the surprising simplicity and accuracy with which online stores make recommendations about purchases you could make while you are shopping.

However, the extent of choice architects' influence on critical human decisions—from increasing rates of organ donation to improving retirement savings decisions—has only been recently examined. The results over the past decade have been so profound in this short time that governments around the world (including the United States and the UK) set up behavioral centers to examine choice architecture and how it influences the decisions people make.

One of the most well-known, real-world examples of the effects of intentional choice architecture is in the domain of employee retirement plans—a context extremely relevant to financial planners and their constituents. Since many of you help clients realize their retirement goals—my hope is that you can relate to, and draw inspiration from, this example in your own practices. What do your clients truly want to accomplish in collaboration with you? How can you make simple, yet effective, changes to your decision environment to help them?

As you may know, U.S. corporations have been steadily moving from defined benefit (e.g., pension-like plans) to defined contribution (e.g., 401[k]-like plans) over the past handful of decades. And the choices that employees make to set aside money for their future does not just have implications for the individual, but for Americans at a much broader socioeconomic level. This means that the ways in which employees are offered information and choices—about whether to participate in a plan, how much to contribute, and whether to increase those contributions over time—matter to all of us.

What is most interesting is that—as we mentioned earlier—for many years, plan design focused on an opt-in format for plan participation: If an employee wanted to participate in their company's defined contribution plan, they needed to actively choose to participate. There were a variety of reasons for this, ranging from the perception that people would opt in if they wanted to participate in the plan (e.g., if an employee truly had a preference to invest for retirement, why would they do nothing?) to the regulatory environment for employers, or plan sponsors, as fiduciaries (e.g., would companies be legally protected if they automatically enrolled employees in a 401[k]?).

As choice architects, let us take the most basic assumption here and challenge it: When employees are confronted with an opt-in decision, do they make choices that reflect their true preferences? To examine the answer to this question, it is useful to describe the major opt-in choices that an employee is confronted with in a defined contribution plan—specifically a 401(k)—when they first become eligible to participate. Of course, there is the initial choice to participate (or not). But it does not stop there: With a choice to participate also comes a decision related to the initial deferral rate (how much should I contribute now?) and the investment options (which investments are right for me at this point in my life?). Do not forget that these choices will also evolve over time as the individual gets closer to retirement, their financial circumstances change, and so on.

Needless to say, an employee who would like to participate in the plan has a lot to consider. The effort itself (e.g., the paperwork)—especially for a busy individual who is not a financial expert—may be overwhelming and cause an employee to abandon ship. No doubt that we have all had this type of experience at some point in our lives: Do your best to think back to a particular choice that you wanted to pursue, but for whatever reason the (immediate or future) effort involved somehow prevented you from moving forward (e.g., trust and estate planning). Remember our first principle of choice architecture: Humans have limitations. Interestingly, though, research has shown that when confronted with a default, effort alone does not explain people's inertia (Johnson & Goldstein, 2003). You may recall that there may be other factors at play such as feeling that the default represents the status-quo option—and that giving up the status-quo option may be perceived as a loss (Johnson, Hershey, Mezaros, & Kunreuther, 1993). Since people are generally loss-averse (Tversky & Kahneman, 1991), this might also contribute to the reason people stay with the default. Taking this idea further, employees may even feel that the default option might be some type of "implied recommendation" from the plan sponsor: If the plan was something the employer thought all employees should consider participating in, they would have automatically enrolled all employees; since they did not design enrollment in this way, employees may assume that the employer is telling employees that participation is not the recommended option. Remember our second principle of choice architecture: Humans use reference points to make decisions. Indeed, Craig McKenzie (my PhD advisor), Stacy Finkelstein, and I (2006) found that in some cases, people thought that the plan default (automatically enrolled versus not enrolled) implied the recommended course of action from a company to its employees.

Given that saving more for retirement is probably a good thing that many employees want to do, how might you rethink plan design as a choice architect to facilitate the desired outcome?

PLAN PARTICIPATION, DEFERRAL RATES, AND DEFAULT INVESTMENT OPTIONS

If the retirement savings of American workers is critical to both individual and macro success—on a qualitative (e.g., happiness) and quantitative (e.g., economic) level—it would seem reasonable to assume that increasing participation in plans would be a core consideration of the choice architect. When trying to increase plan participation, the choice architect might focus on enrollment—since participation is the first decision the employee is confronted with. How might you best remove inertia and provide information to the employee that participating in the plan is a good option? Changing the default is a good start. Instead of an opt-in plan, you could make it opt out by automatically enrolling employees: If an employee did not want to participate in their company's defined contribution plan, they would need to actively choose not to participate. In this way, a choice architect is intentionally using the effects of a choice default in a way that could predictably drive behavior to the desired outcome. Indeed, when choice architects employ plan participation as the default, participation rates often dramatically increase (Benartzi & Thaler, 2013). In case you are a skeptic, a seminal study by researchers Brigitte Madrian and Dennis Shea (2001) found that automatic enrollment nearly doubled plan enrollment of new employees. Today, opt-out rather than opt-in 401(k) plans are considered to be one of the most effective ways to reliably increase employee participation (Beshears, Choi, Laibson, & Madrian, 2009).

However, automatic enrollment presents a number of issues. First, to automatically enroll an employee, a default deferral rate needs to be set. Theoretically, the default deferral rate could range from 0% to 100% of an employee's eligible compensation. (Ultimately, employee contributions are capped at the annual elective contribution limits.) Since we know that people tend to stick with defaults, we would want to avoid setting the default too low or too high. Setting the default too low might actually harm overall levels of saving: Employees who would have already participated within an opt-in format may adhere to the default deferral rate and save at lower levels than they otherwise would have. Or employees could be generally undersaving for retirement. Conversely, setting the default too high may actually lower participation because employees may opt out due to concern that they would be oversaving or saving at a level that just felt was too high. And it gets even more complex. Whereas it feels safe to say that many—if not most—employees should participate in their 401(k) plan at some level, the extent to which they should participate is a very open question. For example, as a plan sponsor, you may actively want to avoid a situation where employees defer essential cash flow into a 401(k) that they actually need now (i.e., money they may need to pay their bills). Deferring money required to pay bills into the plan could create a situation where the employee may have to pay penalties or borrow money. An approach some have taken to address this issue is to set the default deferral rate at a relatively low level (e.g., 3%) or to make the default deferral rate equal to the maximum employee match (so that employees do not leave retirement money on the table).

And what about the future deferral rate? If employees tend to stick with the default deferral rate, how could you facilitate increased employee saving over time? Richard Thaler (who we discussed earlier in this chapter) and Shlomo Benartzi (a professor at University of California, Los Angeles Anderson School of Management)—two of the foremost choice architects in our lifetime—came up with an extremely clever solution: Save More Tomorrow (SMT). Under SMT, employees precommit to escalating their deferral rate in the future so that the initial deferral rate is not set for life. Instead, saving rates increase over time in conjunction, for example, with raises. This can enable default rates set at a lower level (e.g., 3%) to increase to a level that can further help employees successfully replace their income in retirement (e.g., 10%). Thaler and Benartzi reasoned that framing employees' decision to give up future income now would be much better received relative to giving up present income now. You can think of it in this way: Committing to spend less later is likely to be much easier than committing to spend less now. In addition, if the increase in saving coincides with an increase in wages, then this can help diminish the effects of loss aversion (since the increase in savings is offset by the increase in compensation). Finally, the idea of formal precommitment to increase deferral rates takes advantage of inertia—similar to the effort avoidance involved in opting out of the default that causes people to stay with it. In other words, inertia can make it much less likely that employees will back out of future increases in savings once they have precommitted. Indeed, the first company to implement the SMT feature more than tripled employee savings rates in about three years (Thaler & Benartzi, 2004). A more generic version of SMT is in the form of automatic escalation, where the default deferral rate (e.g., 3%) automatically increases annually by a set rate (e.g., 1%) to a predetermined cap (e.g., 10%). Benartzi and Thaler (2013) estimate that automatic escalation features have boosted annual savings rates of employees by over $7 billion.

Increasing retirement savings over time is not just limited to automatic increases in deferral rates. Much like the precommitment decision, how the information to save is framed seems to matter quite a bit, too. In collaboration with Jodi DiCenzo of Behavioral Research Associates, Craig McKenzie and I (2011) found that providing employees at a Fortune 100 company with information about the amount of savings they could have in the future increased their desire to save. In fact, this type of information display is so effective, you may have noticed that projections of future account values are often used on 401(k) statements. The reason it is so effective is fairly intuitive: Estimating money growth is not easy. In fact, human beings tend to estimate money growth in a linear way that causes them to vastly underestimate the amount of money they will have in the future if they invested now. So, framing their decision in terms of the amount of money their 401(k) could have in the future is extremely critical to influencing their decision to save more today. For example, in another study, Craig McKenzie and I (2011) asked people how much they would have if they saved $400 per month for 40 years at a 5% annually compounded interest rate. The prototype answer was around $200,000. But the real answer is over $600,000! As a choice architect, understanding that financial concepts that may feel basic to a financial professional are not actually basic to normal humans is a critical insight. This is one of the main challenges to the choice architect, however, who has the curse of knowledge: once a choice architect knows something, they may assume that decision-makers have a similar level of understanding. However, that assumption can be flawed. Think back to when you were not a financial professional: Did you understand the complexities of money growth over time? Or even know what a Monte Carlo simulation represented?

With respect to plan participation, not only do deferral rates need to be addressed, but so does investment selection: What investment will plan participants' retirement savings be automatically deferred to? As with plan participation and deferral rates, defaults can play an important role, but with increasing complexity because there are so many potential investment options. Which option should be the default? Thankfully, regulators via the Pension Protection Act of 2006 (by amending the Employee Retirement Income Security Act, or ERISA) have laid out investment options that are Qualified Default Investment Alternatives (QDIAs; e.g., life-cycle/target-date funds, balanced funds, or professionally managed accounts). The main goal of the QDIA is to focus on diversification to minimize the risk of investment loss. For example, in a target-date fund, a diversified portfolio shifts its investment mix along a glide-path that reallocates to a heavier weighting in cash-like/fixed-income investments—and away from equities—as the investor gets closer to their retirement date. In this way, even if the investor does nothing, the goal is to move investments toward a more conservative risk profile as the time horizon of the investor diminishes.

Default investments can bring into question whether choice architecture is playing too heavy of a hand in investor decision-making: Should plans be making investment decisions for people? To thoughtfully consider this question, it is important to know that when employees are in a position to select their own investments, they have been shown to experience extreme difficulties. For example, as the number of investment options increases within a plan, it has been shown that plan participation decreases (Iyengar, Huberman, & Jiang, 2004). This result may be intuitive to many, but it flies in the face of the traditional economic perspective that more choice is preferred to less. In this case, more actually equates to less. In fact, researchers have illustrated that while people prefer more choice, more choice can lead to less decisiveness—likely due to overwhelm or what is coined as choice overload (Iyengar & Lepper, 2000). And when participants do select investments, they can (mis)apply rules of thumb like dividing their retirement savings equally among all of the different available investments (Benartzi & Thaler, 2001). In the absence of expertise or knowledge of what is best based on their circumstances, what else would the employee be expected to do?

Given these facts, the number of choices that a plan participant should be presented with raises a difficult consideration for the choice architect. They know that people desire choice, but that too many choices can be detrimental to good decision-making. In this way, the choice architect's design choices quickly veer into the domain of ethics: Is the participation rate or the feeling of the decision-maker more relevant? This is why intention is so critical for the choice architect to formally define. If the desired outcome is to increase participation rates of American employees, it would seem that facilitating decision-making via narrowing choice would be the ideal decision environment. However, if the desired outcome is to enhance the positive feelings of employees about the number of choices they have in their retirement plan, more options may be better.

It cannot be repeated enough: Intent is arguably the most critical factor behind choice architecture. Especially from an ethical standpoint, there is real power in a choice architect's ability to formally articulate the rationale behind the design choices of the decision environment. This will help the decision-maker determine whether the choice architect is facilitating decisions that are in line with their intent as well. It can also help avoid controversy around whether the choice architect is good or bad because the intent is fully transparent. Indeed, choice architects with the perception of bad intent have been shown to be less effective. For example, in one of our experiments, Craig McKenzie and I showed that when decision-makers were primed to distrust the choice architect, they tended to reject default options (Liersch & McKenzie, 2009). Otherwise put, skeptical or distrustful decision-makers can make the choice architect's efforts ineffective or perhaps even facilitate unintended outcomes.

FROM AWARENESS TO ACTION

As a choice architect, you can choose to be intentional or unintentional. If you choose to be intentional, the two principles we described earlier—the fact that humans have limitations and that they are reference-dependent—can help you assess your choice architecture in the following way:

Is it as simple as possible to reach the desired outcomes? Consider the needs, concerns, and goals of your clients. Many clients interested in financial planning are trying to address basic questions such as: Do I have enough? Your decision environment can facilitate the answer to those questions, and help them make the right trade-offs. For example, if they do not have enough, perhaps they can spend less or work longer; if they have just enough, you can help them create and stick to a budget or "bucketed" investment strategy; or if they have more than enough, you may encourage them to engage in more complex trust and estate planning. But do you immediately cut through the noise to address the basic questions about whether they can reach their goals? Or do you start with topics such as the details of their balance sheet, the tax implications of their investment strategy, the other investment choices they can consider, or their investment performance? In addition to the questions you are trying to help your clients answer, take a look at the complexity of your overall process: Examine the questions you ask, the planning exhibits that you use, and what your clients see when they log in online to view their progress to their goals. Try to narrow down the questions to what is essential, trim the number of exhibits you present, and see that when your clients log in, they are greeted with relevant information that will help them make decisions when you may not be available.

Are you using tools and technology to their greatest effect? Ultimately, tools and technologies that facilitate financial planning can be considered decision aids. These decision aids are being incorporated in a vast number of contexts at an alarming rate, and can have an enormous influence on the decisions that people make (Johnson et al., 2012). When you think about your financial planning software or the online capabilities available to you and your clients—are they being utilized in a way that facilitates the outcomes you and your clients desire? Ideally, tools and technologies can be leveraged in a way that enhances advice. For example, architecting an environment where you can share a screen with your clients as you walk through their financial plan—making real-time changes to the data elements to illustrate trade-offs—can be extraordinarily powerful. Or using voice technology to immediately capture your notes (like doctors do) after every client meeting can be both efficient and help you to avoid difficulty in recalling key action items from the meeting.

What is your default process? As you outline the approach you take with your clients, you may find that you do things a little differently for everyone. While bespoke interactions can be a valuable service element, they can also be difficult to scale in a way that enables repeatability (which can reduce the likelihood of missing things) and facilitates the evaluation of quality (application of standard processes can help identify what is working and what is not). For example, you could apply a default that *every* client receives a standard agenda prior to a meeting—unless the client opts out by indicating that they do not want or need one. Of course, the agenda can always be tailored to the unique needs of the client, but this default can serve as a core foundation for what is covered. Such a foundation may have enormous downstream implications to your client experience: It may help you and your clients better prepare for meetings, arrange the most productive topic order, address the most important decisions first, and create structure for your follow-up with the client after the meeting.

Are you empathetic and nonjudgmental? Clients come to you with a variety of different experiences and circumstances. This not only influences the reference points that they use to evaluate choices, but also the other heuristics they apply to decisions. These heuristics are imperfect and can lead to biases, or predictable errors, ranging from overconfidence in investment decision-making (which can lead to overtrading; Barber & Odean, 2001) to impulsive investment choices (which financial professionals can help prevent; Maymin & Fisher, 2011). As a financial planning professional, being empathetic to your clients' humanity can help you nonjudgmentally assess what choice architecture could be most valuable to them. For example, perhaps you have clients who think they know more than they actually do about the planning process. Instead of telling them they know less, you could architect a decision environment that intentionally incorporates other decision-makers (e.g., family members) that can open the door to more realistic, deliberative, collaborative, and successful investment decisions (Liersch & Suri, 2017).

Do you ask for feedback? Clearly, choice architecture is not just about the choice architect. It is also a collaboration with the decision-makers operating in the decision environment the choice architect has designed. The possible design decisions you can make in the domain of financial planning explicitly need to consider the decision-makers you are serving, which makes feedback all the more critical—whether it be about the intent, experience, or outcomes. Consider making it a default part of your choice architecture to ask every client how you can make at least one improvement to the way that you work together—with the goal of enhancing their experience or outcomes. This one simple change can reinforce your value as an intentional choice architect who is focused on designing an environment that will get your clients to where they need to go.

While this chapter primarily focused on practitioners and their clients, it also cited perspectives from researchers in behavioral finance, economics, psychology, law, and more. My hope is that the information and ideas presented here inspire crosstalk between practitioners and academics to answer critical questions in financial planning choice architecture. One question that could benefit from extensive collaboration: What is the most effective marriage between technology and human beings in the financial planning process? This requires exploration and experimentation at the organizational, practice, and client levels. Identifying the choice architecture that optimally utilizes technology to improve experiences and outcomes for employees, advisors, and their clients is essential. It is also a place where various academic theories and research in areas from economics to psychology to computer science could yield ongoing insights as we continue to move into increasingly digital decision environments.

In what is being called the age of the client, intentional choice architects have an extraordinary opportunity. While there is much to evaluate and consider, remember that making slow, incremental changes—however small—can have a large and lasting impact on the outcomes of the decision-makers that you serve.

REFERENCES

Barber, B. M., & Odean, T. (2001). Boys will be boys: Gender, overconfidence, and common stock investment. *The Quarterly Journal of Economics, 116*(1), 261–292.

Baumeister, R. F. (2002). Ego depletion and self-control failure: An energy model of the self's executive function. *Self and Identity, 1*(2), 129–136.

Benartzi, S., & Levin, R. (2012). *Save more tomorrow: Practical behavioral finance solutions to improve 401(k) plans.* New York: Portfolio/Penguin.

Benartzi, S., & Thaler, R. H. (2001). Naive diversification strategies in defined contribution savings plans. *American Economic Review, 91*, 79–98.

Benartzi, S., & Thaler, R. H. (2013). Behavioral economics and the retirement savings crisis. *Science, 339*(6124), 1152–1153.

Beshears, J., Choi, J. J., Laibson, D., & Madrian, B. C. (2009). The importance of default options for retirement savings uutcomes. In J. Brown, J. Liebman, & D. A. Wise (Eds.), *Social Security policy in a changing environment* (pp. 167–195). Chicago: University of Chicago Press.

Brunel, J. L. P. (2015). *Goals-based wealth management: An integrated and practical approach to changing the structure of wealth advisory practices.* Hoboken, NJ: John Wiley & Sons.

Gigerenzer, G., & Selten, R. (2002). *Bounded rationality: The adaptive toolbox.* Cambridge, MA: MIT Press.

Hershfield, H. E., Goldstein, D. G., Sharpe, W. F., Fox, J., Yeykelis, L., Carstensen, L. L., & Bailenson, J. N. (2011). Increasing saving behavior through age-progressed renderings of the future self. *Journal of Marketing Research, 48*(SPL) S23–S37.

Iyengar, S. S., Huberman, G., & Jiang, G. (2004). How much choice is too much? Contributions to 401(k) retirement plans. In O. S. Mitchell (Ed.), *Pension design and structure: New lessons from behavioral finance* (pp. 83–95). Oxford, UK: Oxford University Press.

Iyengar, S. S., & Lepper, M. R. (2000). When choice is demotivating: Can one desire too much of a good thing? *Journal of Personality and Social Psychology, 79*(6), 995–1006.

Johnson, E. J., & Goldstein, D. (2003). Do defaults save lives? *Science, 302*(5649), 1338–1339.

Johnson, E. J., Hershey, J., Mezaros, J., & Kunreuther, H. (1993). Framing, probability distortions, and insurance decisions. *Journal of Risk and Uncertainty, 7*, 35–53.

Johnson, E. J., Shu, S. B., Dellaert, B. G. C., Fox, C. R., Goldstein, D. G., Haubel, G., et al. (2012). Beyond nudges: Tools of a choice architecture. *Marketing Letters, 23*, 487–504.

Kahneman, D. (2011). *Thinking, fast and slow*. New York: Farrar, Straus and Giroux.

Kahneman, D., Knetsch, J. L., & Thaler, R. H. (1991). Anomalies: The endowment effect, loss aversion, and status quo bias. *The Journal of Economic Perspectives, 5*(1), 193–206.

Lewis, M. (2012, September). Obama's way. *Vanity Fair.*

Lewis, M. (2016). *The undoing project: The friendship that changed our minds.* W. W. Norton: New York.

Liersch, M. J., & Etheridge, R. O. (2015). Behavioral insights: Risk tolerance and decision making. *Investments & Wealth Monitor, March/April,* 19–22.

Liersch, M. J., & McKenzie, C. R. M. (2009). Can we put our trust in defaults? *Defined Contribution Insights,* November/December, 10–12.

Liersch, M. J., & Suri, A. (2017). Making group decisions the behavioral finance way. *Investments & Wealth Monitor,* May/June, 20–25.

Madrian, B. C., & Shea, D. F. (2001). The power of suggestion: Inertia in 401(k) participation and savings behavior. *Quarterly Journal of Economics, 116,* 1149–1187.

Maymin, P., & Fisher, G. (2011). Preventing emotional investing: An added value of an investment advisor. *Journal of Wealth Management, 13*(4), 34–43.

McKenzie, C. R. M., & Liersch, M. J. (2011). Misunderstanding savings growth: Implications for retirement savings behavior. *Journal of Marketing Research, 48*(SPL), S1–S13.

McKenzie, C. R. M., Liersch, M. J., & Finkelstein, S. R. (2006). Recommendations implicit in policy defaults. *Psychological Science, 17*(5), 414–420.

Mischel, W., Shoda, Y., & Rodriguez, M. L. (1989). Delay of gratification in children. *Science, 244*(4907), 933–938.

Odean, T. (1998). Are investors reluctant to realize their losses? *The Journal of Finance, 53*(5), 1775–1798.

Shefrin, H., & Statman, M. (1985). The disposition to sell winners too early and ride losers too long: Theory and evidence. *The Journal of Finance, 40*(3), 777–790.

Sher, S., & McKenzie, C. R. M. (2006). Information leakage from logically equivalent frames. *Cognition, 101*, 467–494.

Thaler, R. H. (2016). *Misbehaving: The making of behavioral economics.* New York: W. W. Norton.

Thaler, R. H., & Sunstein, C. R. (2008). *Nudge: Improving decisions about health, wealth, and happiness.* New Haven, CT: Yale University Press.

Thaler, R. H., & Benartzi, S. (2004). Save more tomorrow: Using behavioral economics to increase employee saving. *Journal of Political Economy, 112*(1), 164–187.

Tversky, A., & Kahneman, D. (1974). Judgment under uncertainty: Heuristics and biases. *Science, 185*(4157), 1124–1131.

Tversky, A. & Kahneman, D. (1979). Prospect theory: An analysis of decision under risk. *Econometrica, 47*(2), 263-292.

Tversky, A., & Kahneman, D. (1981). The framing of decisions and the psychology of choice. *Science, 211*(4481), 453–458.

Tversky, A., & Kahneman, D. (1991). Loss aversion in riskless choice: A reference dependent model. *The Quarterly Journal of Economics, 106* (4), 1039–1061.

Vohs, K. D., Baumeister, R. F., Schmeichel, B. J., Twenge, J. M., Nelson, N. M., & Tice, D. M. (2008). Making choices impairs subsequent self-control: A limited-resource account of decision making, self-regulation, and active initiative. *Journal of Personality and Social Psychology, 94*(5), 883–898.

Wang, X. T. (1996). Framing effects: Dynamics and task domains. *Organizational Behavior and Human Decision Processes, 68* (2), 145–157.

Wansink, B., & Sobal, J. (2007). Mindless eating. *Environment and Behavior, 39*(1), 106–123.

Wesley, M., Liersch, M. J., & Cooper, S. (2017, April). A strategic approach to estate design. *Trusts & Estates*, 2–4.

CHAPTER 8

Cognition, Distraction, and the Financial Planning Client

Nils Olsen, Vanessa G. Perry, and Zhuo Jin
George Washington University

The profound role of emotions in financial planning and financial decision-making is well documented in the popular press, among scholars, policy makers, and certainly by financial planning professionals. For example, a recent article in *U.S. News and World Report* describes fear and risk avoidance among millennial investors resulting from their reactions to the most recent economic recession, and the costly effects of these emotional responses on their financial portfolios (Lake, 2017).

In one example, a financial planning blogger mentions the emotion of fear:

Not a single financial planner wants to scare his potential clients off when telling the story about their business. (Sier, August 17, 2017)

The author further describes apathy, or perhaps ambivalence, on the part of financial planning clients:

You see, people mostly don't care about financial planning. They mostly don't care about financial goals. And they certainly don't care about how much YOU care about it. (Sier, August 19, 2017)

According to Baker and Ricciardi (2014), fear, trepidation, and anxiety about consequences can result in avoidance of and increased subjectivity within the financial planning decision-making process (Taffler & Tuckett, 2010). Fisher (2014) argues that the financial planner's responsibility is to help establish controls to protect the client against emotional, as opposed to rational, reactions. Research in psychology and behavioral economics has found evidence of the effects of emotion on decision-quality

119

in many contexts, across cultures, demographic categories, and interestingly, across knowledge levels. In fact, both novices and experts are susceptible to the disruptive influence of emotions on financial decisions.

Drawing on prior research within the psychology of decision-making, this chapter will provide an overview of the impact of emotions, cognitive processing, and cognitive resource availability on financial planning clients' decision-making processes. What can be done to help financial planners identify and leverage the best circumstances for having these discussions with clients?

INFLUENCES ON THE FRAME OF MIND

The problem facing many financial planning professionals is that clients may not be in an optimal frame of mind to make long-term financial decisions when they meet with a financial planning professional. Frame of mind, as defined by Loewenstein (1988), refers to a psychological point of reference that affects intertemporal choice. To the extent that intertemporal choices characterize financial planning efforts, for example, a client is asked to consider long-term goals, evaluate alternatives, and consider consequences during a given time span, these processes can be affected by situational and enduring cognitive and emotional factors. These factors, including individual characteristics, such as the type of cognitive processing and emotions, and influences resulting from the context, such as information overload and cognitive resource depletion, are depicted in Figure 8.1.

Researchers have explored ways in which one can divide the cognitive processing of information into two systems—Systems 1 and 2 (Kahneman, 2011; Stanovich & West, 2000). System 1 thinking tends to be characterized

Psychological Influences on the Financial
Planning Client's Frame of Mind

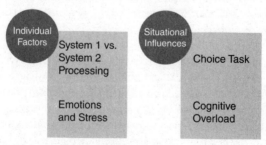

FIGURE 8.1   Cognitive Processing: Systems 1 and 2

as fast, automatic, innately programmed, and intuitive and is marked by low amounts of voluntary control, whereas System 2 tends to be rational, logic-based, effortful, controlled, and marked by complex calculations and deliberative processing (Kahneman, 2011). On a related note, when one is beginning to develop a set of financial planning skills, one might start out with an effortful (System 2) approach and—once the financial planning skill-set has been fine-tuned—evolve toward an automatic (System 1) version of that highly trained skill. As one progresses, it is likely that there may be a need to toggle between System 1 and System 2 to ensure that one is processing information at an optimal level.

Along these lines, and according to Schunk and Betsch (2006), when making decisions, intuitive and deliberative decision-makers access different sources of information. Specifically, intuitive (versus deliberative) individuals tend to be more impacted by biases associated with emotional information (Schunk & Betsch, 2006). Deliberative (as opposed to intuitive) decision-makers, on the other hand, tend to use more objective information while making decisions, and perform more time consuming cognitive tasks (Schunk & Betsch, 2006).

Based on an internet survey of 140 entrepreneurs and managing partners, the data show that exploration success (associated with experimentation, risk taking and innovation) is strongly associated with *intuitive* (System 1) decision-making, whereas exploitation success is associated with both *intuitive* (System 1) and *effort-based* (System 2) decision-making (Matzler, Uzelac, & Florian, 2014). All of this can have a great deal of implications for how much risk one maintains within a financial planning portfolio.

Intuitive Processing (System 1)

When it comes to financial planning, it stands to reason that a large portion of analysis and planning is directed toward future-oriented goals and data. With respect to forming decisions about future-oriented events, researchers suggest that, in some cases, it can be suboptimal to use quantitative (mathematical) methods and models, because of probabilistic challenges related to predicting future events (Gigerenzer, 2007; Gigerenzer & Gaissmaier, 2011). It is suggested, instead, that one consider using intuitive assessments when making predictions about future events, outcomes, and data (Gigerenzer, 2007; Gigerenzer & Gaissmaier, 2011); or, at the very least, adding intuitive assessments to the effort-based (quantitative) ones.

Gigerenzer, Hertwig, and Pachur (2011) found that fast and frugal heuristics are types of cognitive shortcuts where less information and computation can, in some cases, lead to greater accuracy and higher levels of performance.

Deliberative Processing (System 2)

When comparing highly trained professional traders (German bank) and relatively less trained undergraduate students (University of Bonn) in an option pricing experiment, it has been found that—compared to professional traders—students seemed to embrace a probability-driven option valuation the most (Abbink & Rockenbach, 2006). That is, experienced traders tended to rely more on intuition, all of which explains why they neglected a deliberate processing of the probability distribution (Abbink & Rockenbach, 2006). Students, on the other hand, tended to have lower levels of real world experience, and were—via their early stage of academic training—more likely to make deliberated decisions based on actual probabilistic details of financial data, as opposed to intuition (Abbink & Rockenbach, 2006).

This finding suggests that, perhaps, as one develops a true specialty and high level of expertise within the financial planning arena, one is more likely to take an intuitive (versus analytical) approach. This also may have implications for the different types of training one may pursue at various stages of one's career (e.g., Dreyfus, 2004).

EMOTION, STRESS, AND TOUCH

Emotion

The effects of emotions on financial decision-making have been well-documented by psychologists and behavioral economists. Intense emotions can dynamically change the way that people make decisions—sometimes leading to suboptimal cognitive processing and an overreliance on heuristics. For example, Andrade and Ho (2009) show that individuals can actually improve financial outcomes via a falsification of emotions (delivering the outward appearance of emotions that one is not necessarily experiencing). Andrade and Ho (2009) explored the intentional use of emotion within a series of dictator and ultimatum games. Typically, within these games, the proposer is a person who first receives a sum of money with the caveat that he or she must determine how to best divide that money with a receiver. The receiver in this case can either accept the offer (in which case the proposer and receiver each receive the amounts of money determined by the proposer's initial offer) or reject the offer (in which case the proposer and receiver each receive no money at all). Within the Andrade and Ho (2009) study, receivers deliberately conveyed angry responses to matched-proposers to maximize financial gains. When proposers believed the credibility of receivers' anger, they tended to offer higher financial payouts in line with receivers' anger. However, when proposers perceived that receivers might be insincerely expressing angry emotions, proposers tended to ignore matched receivers' displays of affect (Andrade & Ho, 2009). Moreover, those who displayed contrived levels of anger were more likely to influence their partner's behavior than those displaying contrived levels of expectation, because anger is thought to be associated with impulsive, irrational, and vindictive behavior (i.e., less amenable to falsification) (Andrade & Ho, 2009).

Andrade and Ariely (2009) explored the impact of transient emotions on decisions via ultimatum and dictator games. In the first ultimatum game, receivers were primed with either a happy or angry emotion before making decisions about rejecting or accepting an unfair offer. The results showed that angry (as opposed to happy) receivers were more likely to reject unfair offers—a finding consistent with expected effects of incidental emotions on immediate decisions (Andrade & Ariely, 2009). Further, once-angry (as opposed to once-happy) proposers made fairer offers (on average) to their paired receivers in a second ultimatum game—supporting the assertion that incidental emotions have a lasting impact on future decisions (Andrade & Ariely, 2009). This lasting impact of emotions finding tends to be most pronounced for those who rejected unfair offers in the first (ultimatum 1) incidental anger condition; and, when actual proposers and receivers are included, angry (versus happy) participants (who became fairer proposers over time) ended up making less money (Andrade & Ariely, 2009). All of this suggests that the type and consistency of one's emotions can impact one's behavior toward another person as well as that person's financial outcomes (Andrade & Ariely, 2009).

Lee and Andrade (2015) found that fear can significantly impact risk-taking behavior. Specifically, when a task is framed as a stock-investment decision, incidental fear (versus control) tends to increase risk-averse behavior (Lee & Andrade, 2015). Given that fear can be reinterpreted as a state of excitement (i.e., comparable heart-rate levels), when framing the decision-making task as an exciting casino game, fear tends to be associated with increased risk-taking behavior (Lee & Andrade, 2015).

Shiv, Loewenstein, Bechara, Damasio, and Damasio (2005) found that people with a dysfunction in the neural system underlying the emotion-centered areas of their brain (versus those without such a dysfunction), tended to optimize their decisions and achieve greater financial returns. Interestingly, people without an emotion-based neural dysfunction became more conservative (and reluctant to participate) in upcoming investment opportunities (Shiv, Loewenstein, Bechara, Damasio, & Damasio, 2005). It has also been suggested that self-expression can impact one's financial decisions (Apsara, Chakravarti, & Hoffmann, 2015). That is, people are in some cases motivated to forego financial outcomes (focal goals) for an opportunity to invest in stocks that can enhance their self-expression (e.g., the case of Apple). Curiously, when people are directly shown the effects of choosing background goals (e.g., self-expression), thereby making it more obvious to them, this can lead people to realign with their focal (financial) goals (Apsara, Chakravarti, & Hoffmann, 2015).

Usul, Ozdemir, and Kiessling (2017) discovered a significant relationship between novice investors' affective self-affinity (ASA) and their financial decision-making. Specifically, as investors leaned more toward identifying themselves within a specific category (i.e., nationality), ASA toward a specific category tended to likewise increase (Usul, Ozdemir, & Kiessling, 2017). That is, investors may be affectively motivated to invest in certain stocks with which they feel emotionally linked—at a rate above and beyond that of the classic financial investment markers (Usul, Ozdemir, & Kiessling, 2017). When investors identify with individuals, groups, companies, and even ideas, their emotion-based motivation (via ASA) can serve as a key driver for financial decisions (Usul, Ozdemir, & Kiessling, 2017).

When it comes to strategically using emotions to one's advantage within cognitive tasks (including those of the financial variety), Cohen and Andrade (2004) found that individuals can deliberately use emotion-regulation strategies to optimize performance. Specifically, people tend to seek out positive mood-congruent stimuli (e.g., happy songs) to buffer against negative emotions when presented with an impulse buying opportunity (Cohen & Andrade, 2004). When faced with an analytical task, people tend to seek out negative mood-congruent stimuli (e.g., sad songs); whereas, when people take on creative challenges they often avoid negative affect (Cohen & Andrade, 2004).

With respect to financial planning, and many other professional domains, one take-away from the research on emotions and performance is that—contrary to the suggestion that one must remove all emotional influences before making financial and other decisions—there are benefits to be enjoyed (in some cases) by *embracing* one's emotional reactions. In this way, and while technology can help human beings to not only survive but thrive in their lives, there are components of the emotional parts of the human brain that can help people perform in ways that cannot be anticipated by software, applications, and other technological advances.

Stress

Stress can significantly impact risk-taking and decisional biases, such that within gain-domain trials, individuals tend to make fewer risky decisions under acute stress; whereas, in loss-domain trials (and under acute stress), individuals tend to make riskier decisions (Porcelli & Delgado, 2009). Further, high levels of stress can lead to a cascading occurrence of risky decisional biases (Porcelli & Delgado, 2009). In this way, individuals tend to be risk averse within a context of gains and risk seeking within a context of losses (Kahneman & Tversky, 1979; Kahneman, 2011).

The application of prospect theory (Kahneman & Tversky, 1979)—that losses loom larger than their respective gains—is immediately evident in the way that individuals behave within the housing, corporate, and other financial markets. In spite of the fact that without risk, one will ironically risk having fewer large gains, many individuals steer clear of the potential for any type of loss.

Physical Touch

Levav and Argo (2010) presented data from three studies to show that even slight physical contact can have an impact on the riskiness of a person's financial behavior. Specifically, when presented with both simulated and real monetary rewards, a female experimenter's subtle touch on a person's shoulder was associated with those people taking more financial risks (Levav & Argo, 2010). The comforting touch effect diminished when delivered via handshake and when delivered by a male (Levav & Argo, 2010).

As we explore data related to the benefits of physical touch, one can start to see possible applications not only within financial investments, but also perhaps within fields such as healthcare. For example, there are data showing that physical touch can actual lead to improved physiological outcomes, such as reduced cortisol, anxiety, and blood pressure levels as well as increased endorphin and oxytocin—a hormone linked with feelings of security and trust (Dworkin-McDaniel, 2011).

CHOICE AND COGNITIVE OVERLOAD

Asymmetric Dominance

When it comes to making choices between various options, choice-context can play a major role in financial planning. Specifically, when one is presented with two options where there is a case of nondominance (indifference)—and one adds a third option (i.e., decoy) that is very similar (yet slightly inferior) to one of the initial two options—in this case, most individuals end up selecting the better of the two most similar options (e.g., Ariely, 2008; Ariely & Wallsten, 1995; Huber, Payne, & Puto, 1982, 2014; Sedikides, Ariely, & Olsen, 1999). This phenomenon violates the principle of regularity (e.g., Sedikides, Ariely, & Olsen, 1999) in that, traditionally, many would expect that as the number of options within a choice set increases, the probability of any option being selected should decrease; yet, when one option asymmetrically dominates another (i.e., it is similar and slightly superior to one option in a way that is not true for the other options), the probability of selecting the dominating option actually tends to increase (i.e., option A within the context of three options is more likely to be selected if it is similar, yet slightly superior, to option C, even in cases where B may be the optimal option).

With that said, one can see that there is a sweet spot when it comes to choice context within the financial planning world. That is, when financial planners are interacting with clients, it goes without saying that presenting one option is far too narrow (many clients might react against this lack of options). Also, presenting two fairly equivalent options may create unnecessary cognitive stress. The preferred context would be a trilogy of sorts— made up of two fairly equivalent options, with a third option that is highly similar (yet slightly inferior to) one of the original two options. By being highly similar, yet only slightly inferior, the perceiver will be most attracted to processing the pairwise comparison between the two most similar options (whereas two vastly different options would actually create a cognitively more complex environment that would, in itself, be unappealing (Sedikides, Ariely, & Olsen, 1999).

Less Is More

Iyengar and Lepper (2000) found that although participants appeared to enjoy the process of selecting a chocolate within a high-choice setting (n = 30 versus n = 6), the high-choice participants also communicated that they were less satisfied and had more regrets about the chocolate that they did select. Further, when testing the same effect with jams, and while clients in the high-choice context (24 jams) found the jams to be more *appealing* than in the low-choice context (6 jams), clients were actually much more likely to purchase a jam in the low-choice context (Iyengar & Lepper, 2000). It is posited that a higher volume of options can actually both attract and push away potential clients, and that—yes—one can have too much of a good thing (Iyengar, 2011; Iyengar & Lepper, 2000; Schwartz, 2004).

With respect to financial planning, the immediate application is to carefully consider one's choice-context when options are presented. That is, presenting a handful (as opposed to a seemingly endless array) of financial options may lead to optimal results for both the planner and client.

VISUAL PORTRAYAL OF DATA

Duclos (2015) has explored the ways in which individuals cognitively process visual displays of data to make predictions about financial trends (e.g., stock market). Eye-tracking technology helps to show the effect of stock prices closing on an upward trajectory leading to upward investments in the future (and smaller investments in the present)—a phenomenon known as *end anchoring* (Duclos, 2015). Interestingly when upward-trending stock activity was communicated visually (via graphs), as opposed to numerically, individuals were much more likely to invest in an organization about which they knew very little (Duclos, 2015).

LOSSES AND GAINS

Kahneman and Tversky (1979) addressed the value function associated with gains and losses (as opposed to overall assets), and presented data to support the idea that losses tend to loom larger than their respective gains (i.e., $100 lost is more debilitating than $100 gained is exhilarating). Further an overemphasis on low probability events could actually lead individuals to make less than optimal decisions within the realms of gambling and/or insurance (Kahneman & Tversky, 1979). The application to financial investments comes in the way that, when financial investments are increasing in value, people tend to sell off those investments too early (risk averse within a context of gains), whereas when investments are decreasing in value, people tend to hold on to those investments too long (risk seeking within a context of losses) (Kahneman, 2011; Kahneman & Tversky, 1979).

COGNITIVE RESOURCE DEPLETION

It has often been assumed that a sophisticated decision-maker will dedicate available time, attention, and energy to thoroughly researching and evaluating all possible options before making a decision—and particularly within the *financial planning* domain. There are data suggesting that when additional effort is expended—due to high levels of cognitive or emotional involvement associated with the processing of information (e.g., dread, uncertain information, psychological stress)—cognitive resource (ego) depletion can result. Ego depletion can lower one's cognitive capacity for making high-quality decisions—via one's construal, or processing, of events (Baumeister, Bratslavsky, Muraven, & Tice, 1998; Baumeister, Vohs, & Tice, 2007; Fujita & Han, 2009; Muraven, Baumeister, & Tice, 1999; Vohs et al., 2008). Much of the previous research on cognitive resource depletion suggests that self-control, a necessary feature for carefully deliberated decisions, is a limited resource that can be depleted over time, which can affect resource availability for cognitive processing—even within unrelated tasks. There have actually been relatively few studies demonstrating how to offset or reduce these deleterious (ego depletion) effects, to enhance the quality of one's cognitive processing and decision-making within the financial planning realm. Baumeister, Bratslavsky, Muraven, and Tice (1998) provide empirical support for the assertion that self-control is a perishable and limited resource. For example, when participants were told that they could eat only radishes (a relatively less desirable food option), the cognitive resources consumed by this self-control lead to earlier quitting times on a puzzle than for counterparts who were instructed to eat a relatively more desirable food (chocolate) (Baumeister et al., 1998).

In another study, participants making counterattitudinal speeches under high choice, relative to those making the same speech within a low-choice context, showed a subsequent drop in their persistence on a puzzle task (Baumeister et al., 1998). As it turns out, participants in the high-choice, proattitudinal condition also showed decreased performance on a puzzle (Baumeister et al., 1998). It is this very process of making volitional choices that can actually deplete one's self-control capacity (Baumeister et al., 1998). In a related study, the data showed that participants who were asked to conceal (actively suppress) their emotions performed worse on anagrams than those encouraged to let their emotions flow freely (Baumeister et al., 1998).

Mukhopadhyay and Johar (2005) showed how consumers' conceptions of self-control can shape their goal-directed behaviors. When participants were primed to believe that self-control is adjustable and unlimited, they tended to make more behavioral resolutions (Mukhopadhyay & Johar, 2005). When, on the other hand, participants were primed with the idea that self-control is a limited resource, those people made fewer resolutions and, if low in self-efficacy, were less likely to follow through on their resolutions (Mukhopadhyay & Johar, 2005).

Vohs and Faber (2007) investigated the relationship between self-control and impulse buying through three experiments, and found that participants who were cognitively depleted via various tasks—and particularly those with high baseline impulse-buying tendencies—tended to spend more money on impulsive purchases. It is also the case that as ego depletion occurs, one tends to rely more heavily on heuristics (cognitive shortcuts), thereby making one more susceptible to social influence attempts (Janssen, Fennis, Pruyn, & Vohs, 2008).

Vohs and colleagues (Vohs et al., 2008) demonstrated that making a series of choices (i.e., taxing one's self-regulatory [self-control] system) can impair a person's subsequent self-control. Relative to a no-choice condition, those given choice in a task tended to spend a smaller amount of time on both solvable and unsolvable tasks, and had much higher error rates on math problems (Vohs et al., 2008).

Further, when ostensible shoppers were given various levels of choice, the greater the choice array, the more mathematical errors they made, and the less persistent they were within those mathematical tasks (Vohs et al., 2008).

They also found that when participants were asked to complete a video-based task—and a technical (video equipment) issue was purposely introduced (as part of the script)—the more choices participants were given, the less likely they were to report that any of the video equipment malfunctions (Vohs et al., 2008).

Perry and Lee (2012) found that the cognitively taxing experience of shopping for a home can create a state of cognitive resource depletion—a state that ultimately affects one's choice of mortgage financing. That is, high-depletion individuals (relative to controls) were more likely to select high-risk mortgages, even when controlling for a priori financial knowledge (Perry & Lee, 2012). Ironically, the very behavior that is intended to sharpen one's skills for purchasing a home (doing the proper research, examining each option), can actually lead to suboptimal outcomes. Reassuringly, there are data (Alberts, Martijn, & de Vries, 2011) to support the idea that increasing one's self-awareness can help to reduce ego depletion, especially when the baseline depletion level is particularly high. There are also data supporting the notion that smart (strategically placed) breaks can actually help one replenish (reset) one's self-control capacity (Olsen, Lee, & Perry, 2013), and that self-regulation can be improved over time via practice (Baumeister, Gailliot, DeWall, & Oaten, 2006; Muraven, Baumeister, & Tice, 1999).

The upshot for financial planning here is that—while it is often advised that one prepares as much as possible and conducts a thorough analysis of one's financial options before launching into any financial decisions—there are data to suggest that some of these actions can actually reduce one's capacity for self-control in subsequent tasks, which could actually affect one's financial outcomes.

Thinking Slow in a Fast World

As financial management executives are often compensated on a quarterly basis, many tend to focus on short-range goals, as opposed to long-range returns—and this short-range thinking is particularly salient given the amount of technology that guides many of our financial decisions (Partnoy, 2011). Technology has taken a big role within the management of many of our decisions. The very algorithms, applications (apps), that help us to automate and visualize everything from what we eat to how we make business decisions can ironically make human beings less adept at doing their own cognitive heavy lifting for optimal decisions (Duus & Cooray, 2015). Specifically,

> When our ability to make independent decisions is taken away, we become easier to manipulate and influence. (Duus & Cooray, 2015, p. 4)

Given the trend toward short-range thinking, and an overreliance on heuristic-based (System 1) thinking, some are calling for strategic pauses within the financial world:

> ... it is also worth asking more generally if markets would benefit from the introduction of longer pauses, of breaks during the day designed to encourage thinking and deliberation before action. (Partnoy, 2011, p. 174)

By introducing strategically placed delays in financial markets (and presumably within one's own financial planning) one can engage in proper, deliberative thinking (Partnoy, 2011). An example of this purposeful pause occurred when a high-frequency trading firm, UNX (from 2005 to 2007), adopted an approach where "... its trading executive was slightly delayed, by a few dozen milliseconds" (Partnoy, 2011, p. 173).

Even longer pauses, known as circuit breakers, have been introduced within the financial market, specifically,

> ... the SEC adopted a pilot program to introduce a five-minute pause if the price of any stock in the S&P 500 Index fell by 10 percent or more during a five-minute period. (Partnoy, 2011, p. 173)

With that said, when it comes to examining the impact of heuristics and biases on the way that we process information, there are few who have contributed more to this realm than Nobel Prize–winning scholar Daniel Kahneman (Kahneman, 2011; Kahneman & Tversky, 1979). While it is not possible to altogether avoid heuristics and biases in the ways that one makes financial decisions, one point is clear—by investing time, energy, and other resources into an effortful processing of information, one takes a first step toward reducing the automaticity of engaging in heuristic-based thinking (Kahenman, 2011), and an oversimplification of what are actually highly dynamic financial data points.

IMPLICATIONS FOR FINANCIAL PLANNING PROFESSIONALS

One of the key challenges faced by financial planning professionals is how to advise and influence their clients' decisions when clients can engage in informed decision-making without interference from emotional or informational distractions. Evidence from prior research on cognitive psychology and behavioral decision-making has revealed a great deal about systematic limitations on financial decision-making, and effects resulting from individual and situational constraints. We know, for example, that financial planners would prefer to elicit System 2 processing to encourage clients to process information about investment alternatives and economy-related facts. At the same time, clients need to rely on both Systems (1 and 2) in order to evaluate and predict possible future scenarios, such as retirement, changes in family status, and so on. In this way, System 2 processes are informed by System 1, but also integrate emotions and depend on an individual's mechanisms for coping with uncertainty, anxiety, and stress. These systems are far more complex than conventional wisdom would suggest, namely that decisions are either rational or emotional. On the contrary, these processing systems require both cognitive and emotional inputs and are interdependent. In addition, these differences have implications for the types of information presented by financial planners, and particularly the language and framing used in communications, due to differences in interpretation for intuitive versus deliberative processors. A key part of overcoming the frame of mind challenge is to understand these effects.

We also know from previous research that incidental emotions have a lasting impact on future decisions, and that negative emotions, for example, anger or fear, and the consistency of emotional responses over time affect financial decisions, and risk-taking in particular (Ariely & Andrade, 2009; Kahneman & Tversky, 1979; Lee & Andrade, 2015). Thus, in order to overcome these biases, financial planners need to develop multiple approaches for framing the information that they convey to clients, depending on emotional variants. Financial planning professionals might consider using language that is associated with gambling versus investing, as an example (Lee & Andrade, 2015), and should recognize the negativity bias in decision-making when framing their messages to clients (Kahneman & Tversky, 1979); that is, losses loom larger than gains.

Prior research suggests that the number of options, the order of presentation of options, and the visual presentation of information affect processing and choice. These findings have important implications for financial planning. Clients expect to be given options, but too many options and options that are very similar may frustrate the decisional process. Evidence of asymmetric dominance effects has revealed that decision-makers expend cognitive resources evaluating differences between alternatives—at times at the expense of determining which option is optimal (Ariely & Olsen, 1999). In addition, because of System 1 versus System 2 processing differences, clients may respond differently to charts, graphs, and other visual displays of data. For example, in one study, investors who were presented with graphic representations of a company's stock trend relied less on other, seemingly relevant company information.

Perhaps the most cautionary evidence on the limitations of cognitive processing can be drawn from the literature on cognitive resource (also known as ego) depletion. Financial planning requires active, cognitively taxing, and often emotionally charged decision-making under risk and uncertainty. These activities require that clients expend limited cognitive resources, and often under time constraints. Research shows that under these decision conditions, once cognitive resources are depleted, they are no longer available for subsequent use. This suggests that sequential decisions, and particularly those decisions that become increasingly impactful, may result in suboptimal results, simply because the decision-maker is too drained mentally to focus as much attention on latter decisions as earlier ones.

Thus, given the evidence that is already available within this arena, financial planners have an opportunity to actively manage the array and timing of choices—along with the decisional environment itself—to maximize the planning experience and financial outcomes for their clients. Future research might embrace methodologies that are focused on simulated environments—which would give researchers both the experimental control (ruling out potential confounds, third-party variables) and realistic applications (considering the external validity found in many financial, aviation, and surgical simulators today). Additional research could tease out how decision-making is affected by cognitive versus emotional responses to the financial planner herself, as well as responses to her company. Further, it may be fruitful to examine the potential benefits of checklists and cognitive bundling of data. Finally, given the apparent benefits of both effortful (System 2) and intuitive (System 1) processing, future researchers might explore ways of measuring the potential cognitive and performance benefits of a blend of Systems 1 and 2.

A final factor for researchers to consider might be tracking the investment behavior of millennials. Within the context of a full technology boom, millennials have shown behavior that is marked by a compartmentalized culture (due to the fragmenting nature of the internet), high skepticism toward established organizations, a digital lifestyle, and somewhat conservative investment behavior (Knowledge@Wharton, 2017). Financial planners might explore whether this is a momentary trend or significant link between generational affiliation and financial health. It may in fact be the case that millennials are placing their own unique stamp on the financial world—or that perhaps many individuals in their early twenties have shown such qualities over time.

Whatever the case, it is extraordinarily important that financial planners gather as much data as they can about prospective clients. In this digital revolution, people have so many options for financial services (online, in-person, software) that service providers will need to continuously vie for their precious attention—and, of course, investments.

REFERENCES

Abbink, K., & Rockenbach, B. (2006). Option pricing by students and professional traders: A behavioural investigation, *Managerial and Decision Economics, 27*, 497–510. doi:10.1002/mde.1284.

Alberts, H. J. E. M., Martijn, C., & de Vries, N. K. (2011). Fighting self-control failure: Overcoming ego depletion by increasing self-awareness. *Journal of Experimental Social Psychology, 47*, 58–62. doi:10.1016/j.jesp.2010.08.004.

Andrade, E. B., & Ariely, D. (2009). The enduring impact of transient emotions on decision making. *Organizational Behavior and Human Decision Processes, 109*, 1–8. doi:10.1016/j.obhdp.2009.02.003.

Andrade, E. B., & Ho, T. H. (2009). Gaming emotions in social interactions. *Journal of Consumer Research, 36*, 539–552. doi:10.1086/599221.

Apsara, J., Chakravarti, A., & Hoffmann, A. O. I. (2015). Focal versus background goals in consumer financial decision-making: Trading off financial returns for self-expression? *European Journal of Marketing, 49*, 1114–1138. doi:10.1108/ EJM-04-2014-0244.

Ariely, D. (2008). *Predictably irrational: The hidden forces that shape our decisions.* New York: HarperCollins.

Ariely, D., & Wallsten, T. S. (1995). Seeking subjective dominance in multidimensional space: An explanation of the asymmetric dominance effect. *Organizational Behavior and Human Decision Processes, 63*, 223–232. doi:10.1006/ obhd.1995.1075.

Baker, H. K., & Ricciardi, V. (2014). *Investor behavior—The psychology of financial planning and investing.* Hoboken, NJ: John Wiley & Sons.

Baumeister, R. F., Bratslavsky, E., Muraven, M., & Tice, D. M. (1998). Ego depletion: Is the active self a limited resource? *Journal of Personality and Social Psychology, 74*, 1252–1265. doi:10.1037/0022-3514.74.5.1252.

Baumeister, R. F., Gailliot, M., DeWall, C. N., & Oaten, M. (2006). Self-regulation and personality: How interventions increase regulatory success, and how depletion moderates the effects of traits on behavior. *Journal of Personality, 74*, 1773–1802. doi:10.1111/j.1467-6494.2006.00428.x.

Baumeister, R. F., Vohs, K. D., & Tice, D. M. (2007). The strength model of self-control. *Current Directions in Psychological Science, 16*, 351–355. doi:10.1111/ j.1467-8721.2007.00534.x.

Cohen, J. B., & Andrade, E. B. (2004). Affective intuition and task-contingent affect regulation. *Journal of Consumer Research, 31*, 358–367. doi:10.1086/422114.

Dreyfus, S. E. (2004). The five-stage model of adult skill acquisition. *Bulletin of Science, Technology and Society, 24*, 177–181. doi:10.1177/0270467604264992.

Duclos, R. (2015). The psychology of investment behavior: (De)biasing financial decision-making one graph at a time. *Journal of Consumer Psychology, 25*, 317–325. doi:10.1016/j.jcps.2014.11.005.

Duus, R., & Cooray, M. (2015, July 15). Information overload is killing our ability to make decisions. *Business Insider: Strategy.* Retrieved from http://www .businessinsider.com/information-overload-is-killing-our-ability-to-make-decisions-2015-7.

Dworkin-McDaniel, N. (2011, January 5). Touching makes you healthier. *CNN/ Health.com* Retrieved from http://www.cnn.com/2011/HEALTH/01/05/touching.makes.you.healthier.health/index.html.

Fisher, G. S. (2014). Advising the behavioral investor: Lessons from the real world. In H. Kent Baker & Victor Ricciardi (Eds.), *Investor behavior—The psychology of financial planning and investing,* 265–283. Hoboken, NJ: John Wiley & Sons.

Fujita, K., & Han, H. A. (2009). Moving beyond deliberative control of impulses: The effect of construal levels on evaluative associations in self-control conflicts. *Psychological Science, 20,* 799–804. doi:10.1111/j.1467–9280.2009.02372.x.

Gigerenzer, G. (2007). *Gut feelings: The intelligence of the unconscious.* New York: Viking.

Gigerenzer, G., & Gaissmaier, W. (2011). Heuristic decision making. *Annual Review of Psychology, 62,* 451–482. doi:10.1146/annurev-psych-120709-145346.

Gigerenzer, G., Hertwig, R., & Pachur, T. (2011). *Heuristics: The foundations of adaptive behavior.* Oxford, UK: Oxford University Press.

Huber, J., Payne, J. W., & Puto, C. (1982). Adding asymmetrically dominated alternatives: Violations of regularity and the similarity hypothesis. *Journal of Consumer Research, 9,* 90–98. doi:10.1086/208899.

Huber, J., Payne, J. W., & Puto, C. (2014). Let's be honest about the attraction effect. *Journal of Marketing Research, 51,* 520–525. doi:10.1509/jmr.14.0208.

Iyengar, S. (2011). *The art of choosing.* New York: Hachette Book Group.

Iyengar, S. S., & Lepper, M. R. (2000). When choice is demotivating: Can one desire too much of a good thing? *Journal of Personality and Social Psychology, 79,* 995–1006. doi:10.1037//0022–3514.79.6.995.

Janssen, L., Fennis, B. M., Pruyn, A. T. H., & Vohs, K. D. (2008). The path of least resistance: Regulatory resource depletion and the effectiveness of social influence techniques. *Journal of Business Research, 61,* 1041–1045. doi:10.1016/j.jbusres.2007.09.013.

Kahneman, D. (2011). *Thinking, fast and slow.* New York: Farrar, Straus and Giroux.

Kahneman, D., & Tversky, A. (1979). Prospect theory: An analysis of decision under risk. *Econometrica, 47,* 263–291. doi:10.2307/1914185.

Knowledge@Wharton (2017, October 3). What defines millennials—and how marketers can reach them. Retrieved from http://knowledge.wharton.upenn.edu/article/marketing-to-millennials.

Lake, R. (2017, July 18). The mental mistake hurting millennial investors. *U.S. News and World Report.* Retrieved from https://money.usnews.com/investing/articles/2017–07–28/the-mental-mistake-hurting-millennial-investors.

Lee, C. J., & Andrade, E. B. (2015). Fear, excitement, and financial risk-taking. *Cognition and Emotion, 29,* 178–187. doi:10.1080/02699931.2014.898611.

Levav, J., & Argo, J. J. (2010). Physical contact and financial risk taking. *Psychological Science, 21,* 804–810. Retrieved from http://www.jstor.org.proxygw.wrlc.org/stable/41062294.

Loewenstein, G. F. (1988). Frames of mind in intertemporal choice. *Management Science, 34*(2), 200–214.

Matzler, K., Uzelac, B., & Florian, B. (2014). The role of intuition and deliberation of exploration and exploitation success. *Creativity and Innovation Management, 23,* 252–263. doi:10.1111/caim.12065.

Mukhopadhyay, A., & Johar, G. V. (2005). Where there is a will, is there a way? Effects of lay theories of self-control on setting and keeping resolutions. *Journal of Consumer Research, 31*, 779–786. doi:10.1086/426611.

Muraven, M., Baumeister, R. F., & Tice, D. M. (1999). Longitudinal improvement of self-regulation through practice: Building self-control through repeated exercise. *Journal of Social Psychology, 139*, 446–457. doi:10.1080/00224549909598404.

Olsen, N., Lee, J. D., & Perry, V. G. (2013). *Smart breaks and financial decision-making: in search of optimal cognitive replenishment.* Presented at the Association for Psychological Science Annual Convention, Washington, DC, May 24.

Partnoy, F. (2011). The Abraham L. Pomerantz lecture: Don't blink, snap decisions and securities regulation. *Brooklyn Law Review, 77*(1), 151–180. Retrieved from http://heinonline.org.ezproxy.uwc.ac.za/HOL/Page?handle=hein.journals/brklr77&id=153&div=&collection=journals.

Perry, V. G., & Lee, J. D. (2012). Shopping for a home vs. a loan: The role of cognitive resource depletion. *International Journal of Consumer Studies, 36*, 580–587. doi:10.1111/j.1470-6431.2012.01124.x.

Porcelli, J. P., & Delgado, M. R. (2009). Acute stress modulates risk taking in financial decision making. *Psychological Science, 20*, 278–283. doi:10.1111/j.1467-9280.2009.02288.x.

Schunk, D., & Betsch, C. (2006). Explaining the heterogeneity in utility functions by individual differences in decision modes. *Journal of Economic Psychology, 27*, 386–401. doi:10.1016/j.joep.2005.08.003.

Schwartz, B. (2004). *The paradox of choice: Why more is less.* New York: Harper Perennial.

Sedikides, C., Ariely, D., & Olsen, N. (1999). Contextual and procedural determinants of partner selection: Of asymmetric dominance and prominence. *Social Cognition, 17*, 118–139. doi:10.1521/soco.1999.17.2.118.

Shiv, B., Loewenstein, G., Bechara, A., Damasio, H., & Damasio, A. R. (2005). Investment behavior and the negative side of emotion. *Psychological Science, 16*, 435–439. doi:10.1111/j.0956-7976.2005.01553.x.

Sier, R. (2017, August 19). *How to engage people in financial planning by reversing the order of your story.* Retrieved from https://www.linkedin.com/pulse/how-engage-people-financial-planning-reversing-order-your-sier-cfp-?articleId=6304689087240642560#comments-6304689087240642560&trk=prof-post.

Sier, R. (2017, August 26). *Here's how your financial planning clients want to feel.* Retrieved from https://smartfinancialplanner.com/financial-planning-feeling/.

Stanovich, K. E., & West, R. F (2000). Individual differences in reasoning: Implications for the rationality debate? *Behavioral and Brain Science, 23*, 645–726. doi:10.1017/S0140525X00003435.

Taffler, R. J., & Tuckett, D. A. (2010). Emotional finance: The role of the unconscious in financial decisions. In H. Kent Baker & John R. Nofsinger (Eds.), *Behavioral finance—investors, corporations, and markets* (pp. 95–112). Hoboken, NJ: John Wiley & Sons.

Usul, N., Ozdemir, O., & Kiessling, T. (2017). Affect-based stock investment decision: The role of affective self-affinity. *Journal of Behavioral and Experimental Economics, 68*, 97–109. doi:10.1016/j.socec.2017.04.004.

Vohs, K. D., Baumeister, R. F., Schmeichel, B. J., Twenge, J. M., Nelson, N. M., & Tice, D. M. (2008). Making choices impairs subsequent self-control: A limited-resource account of decision making, self-regulation, and active initiative. *Journal of Personality and Social Psychology, 94,* 883–898. doi:10.1037/0022-3514.94.5.883.

Vohs, K. D., & Faber, R. J. (2007). Spent resources: Self-regulatory resource availability affects impulse buying. *Journal of Consumer Research, 33,* 537–547. doi:10.1086/510228.

CHAPTER 9

Personality and Financial Behavior

Sarah D. Asebedo, PhD, CFP®

Texas Tech University

In turbulent markets, practitioners know exactly which clients they expect to hear from as they tend to develop a sixth sense through experience as to who their clients are and how they might behave and respond to certain situations. A reaction to stock market volatility could be a function of the client's risk tolerance; however, behavioral patterns often emerge that suggest the root of client behavior runs much deeper. While understanding, managing, and responding to client behavior is often referred to as the art of financial planning that is learned and developed over time, there is a growing body of science that suggests people's behavioral tendencies can be accurately predicted by their basic personality characteristics. Understanding this research allows the practitioner to be more effective in predicting how their clients might behave, and how they as financial planners should respond to such behavior. Enduring stress and worry; frequent phone calls and emails from the same clients; overspending clients; underspending clients—these are all examples of client characteristics that can be explained by personality traits, which is the focus of this chapter.

Personality is broadly defined by the American Psychological Association (2017) as "individual differences in characteristic patterns of thinking, feeling and behaving." In other words, personality describes an individual's innate tendency to respond cognitively, affectively, and behaviorally to various situations and life events (Pytlik Zillig, Hemenover, & Dienstbier, 2002). Personality traits have been shown to accurately predict daily behaviors (e.g., social interaction, communication style, mood, location, and language use; Mehl, Gosling, & Pennebaker, 2006), with a growing body of research providing evidence that a variety of financial behaviors can be traced back to personality. Moreover, while personality traits are relatively stable across the life course, research has shown that personality traits can and do change gradually over time (Roberts & DelVecchio, 2000). Changes in personality tend to occur most during young adulthood, but still occur with middle-aged and older adults (Roberts & Mroczek, 2008). This suggests that certain aspects of an individual's personality may be altered (to some extent) to facilitate desired financial behavior. For example, it may be possible for clients to manage and reduce their negative emotions, enhance positive emotions, and improve self-control such that they can follow through with a savings plan.

The consistent (yet somewhat malleable) nature of personality provides a valuable area of study for research and practice in client psychology. Research has demonstrated that personality can explain financial behavior; the financial planner can use this knowledge to understand clients' behavioral tendencies. This understanding paves the way for tailored recommendations that accommodate potentially harmful personality characteristics (e.g., stress, worry, lack of self-control, etc.) that undermine clients' financial goals and objectives. The purpose of this chapter is to provide an overview of personality and how it can be used to inform research and practice in financial planning. This chapter will cover basic models of personality, theory, and research that provide evidence for the utility of incorporating personality into financial planning research and practice.

MODELS OF PERSONALITY

The Big Five

While several approaches to personality exist, the personality psychology field has reached a general consensus that five broad personality traits, commonly known as the Big Five, form the basic foundation of personality (John & Srivastava, 1999). The Big Five consists of five domains (Costa & McCrae, 1992): openness to experience, conscientiousness, extraversion, agreeableness, and neuroticism. Each domain encompasses more specific traits, known as facets. A summary of each of these domain specific facets is listed in Table 9.1.

Each domain and associated facet can also be described by a set of correlated adjectives (Costa & McCrae, 1992). For example, the anxiety facet of neuroticism was associated with these adjectives: anxious, fearful, worrying, tense, and nervous (Costa & McCrae, 1992). A full list of associated adjectives for each domain and facet can be found in the *Revised NEO Personality Inventory (NEO PI-R™)* and *NEO Five-Factor Inventory (NEO-FFI) Professional Manual* (Costa & McCrae, 1992).

TABLE 9.1   Big Five Personality Trait Facets

Domain	Facets
Openness to experience	Fantasy, aesthetics, feelings, actions, ideas, values
Conscientiousness	Competence, order, dutifulness, achievement striving, self-discipline, deliberation
Extraversion	Warmth, gregariousness, assertiveness, activity, excitement seeking, positive emotions
Agreeableness	Trust, straightforwardness, altruism, compliance, modesty, tender-mindedness
Neuroticism	Anxiety, angry, hostility, depression, self-consciousness, impulsiveness, vulnerability

Source: Adapted from Costa and McCrae (1992).

HEXACO

In addition to the Big Five Traits, honesty–humility has been proposed as a sixth personality factor under the HEXACO Personality Inventory. Ashton and Lee (2004) argued that honesty–humility is a unique personality trait that should be measured separately from the standard Big Five traits. Honesty–humility can be characterized by honesty, fairness, sincerity, modesty, and lack of greed (Lee & Ashton, 2004). Overall, the HEXACO model encompasses these six personality traits: honesty–humility (H), emotionality (E), extraversion (X), agreeableness (A), conscientiousness (C), and openness to experience (O) (Ashton & Lee, 2005; Lee & Ashton, 2004). The honesty–humility trait distinguishes the HEXACO model from the Big Five model.

THE RELATIONSHIP BETWEEN PERSONALITY AND FINANCIAL BEHAVIOR

The Big Five personality traits have been the predominant focus of financial behavior research as a model of personality. This growing body of literature provides evidence for significant connections between each of the Big Five personality traits and financial behavior. Thus, this section will provide a review of these relationships according to the Big Five traits.

OPENNESS TO EXPERIENCE

Costa and McCrae (1992) indicated that individuals with high levels of the openness trait have active imaginations, prefer variety, are intellectually curious, hold unconventional values, and pursue activities that lead to rich life experiences; open individuals are also in tune with their inner feelings and experience intense positive and negative emotions. Their less open counterparts tend to prefer familiarity, exhibit conventional behavior, hold a conservative outlook, and display a more subdued emotional response (Costa & McCrae, 1992).

The link between openness to experience and financial behavior is somewhat mixed, but points more strongly toward the damaging effects of this trait on financial behavior. Troisi, Christopher, and Marek (2006) suggested that those with high levels of openness value experiences (e.g., knowledge and memories) and are less materialistic; however, they are less prudent with their money management behavior. In support of this finding, research has shown the openness trait to be associated with impulsive buying behavior (Mowen, 2000; Shahjehan, Qureshi, Zeb, & Saifullah, 2012). Similarly, a greater openness trait was indirectly connected to a lower change in net worth due to lower financial self-efficacy beliefs (Asebedo, 2016a). Viinikainen and Kokko (2012) noted a concerning finding that links greater openness to more frequent periods of unemployment and a longer cumulative duration of unemployment. These results suggest that a greater openness trait might undermine desired financial behavior; however, research also suggests that this trait is associated with long-term saving and investing intentions (Mayfield, Perdue, & Wooten, 2008), and a greater likelihood of stock ownership (Nabeshima, 2014).

Working with Open Clients

Based upon Costa and McCrae's (1992) description of the openness trait, open individuals may find the goal-setting component of the financial planning process enjoyable and rewarding; they may also find a life-planning approach very natural as focusing on life experiences is an innate component of their personality. However, the combined research results suggest that open individuals may struggle significantly with the day-to-day management of their financial situation as they seek to enhance their life experiences. Consequently, they may have more difficulty in achieving their financial goals and objectives. From an investment perspective, however, open individuals have a long-term orientation toward their investment portfolio and a willingness to hold equities—which are necessary characteristics for most financial goals. Moreover, financial planners working with open clients will need to become skilled at managing the positive and negative emotional swings their open clients might experience. Research has shown that negative emotions, such as fear and worry, can undermine goals and financial behavior (e.g., see Neukam & Hershey, 2003), whereas positive emotions have been shown to facilitate actions conducive to financial success, such as saving (e.g., see Guven, 2012; Lyubomirsky, King, & Diener, 2005). However, extreme positive emotions, such as over-optimism, can result in risky financial decisions (e.g., see Puri & Robinson, 2007). Thus, it may be necessary to counsel open clients through the peaks and valleys of their emotional experience during the financial planning process for financial goal achievement. In summary, open individuals can benefit greatly from working with a financial planner; however, they may also prove to be challenging clients to serve.

CONSCIENTIOUSNESS

Costa and McCrae (1992) described conscientious individuals as purposeful, strong-willed, planning oriented, organized, task oriented, and determined. They are also very punctual, reliable, and meticulous. Conscientious individuals tend to be adept at exercising self-control by taking an active role are in the planning, organization, and task execution process. Costa and McCrae noted that conscientious individuals tend to experience high levels of academic and career success. While the conscientiousness trait has many positive characteristics, individuals who score high on this trait can exhibit workaholic, compulsive, and extreme meticulous behavior. Those who score lower on the conscientiousness trait tend to be more laid-back, less exact, and "more lackadaisical in working toward their goals" (Costa & McCrae, 1992, p. 16).

The link between conscientiousness and financial behavior is overwhelmingly positive. The conscientiousness trait is associated with higher lifetime earnings, greater financial wealth, and a higher net worth (Duckworth & Weir, 2010; Nabeshima & Seay, 2015). This link to greater financial resources may be in part due to more prudent financial behavior. Mowen (2000) found conscientious individuals to be value conscious; they seek out bargains, live modestly, and are thrifty when it comes to their money. In support of this finding, Verplanken and Herabadi (2001) found the conscientiousness trait to be negatively correlated with an impulse buying tendency; similarly, Mowen and Spears (1999) found that a higher conscientiousness score was associated with less compulsive buying behavior. Moreover, conscientiousness is associated with a longer future time perspective that supports retirement planning and saving behavior (Hershey & Mowen, 2000).

Asebedo (2016a) found conscientious individuals to have a greater change in net worth as a result of higher financial self-efficacy beliefs.

Working with Conscientious Clients

It is not hard to see that conscientious people likely make good financial planning clients. The conscientious client may be more likely to implement financial recommendations with little handholding, as they are naturally inclined to value planning, organizing, and following through with tasks. They also might be likely to take an active role in the financial planning process and provide the documents needed to conduct analyses and provide recommendations. Moreover, research indicates they are good at saving and accumulating wealth, thereby generating an investment portfolio that can be managed by a financial planner. Despite these positive characteristics, working with highly conscientious clients might pose nontraditional (yet still significant) challenges within the financial planning process. For example, conscientious clients may be extremely prudent with their money to the point they are unable to spend it effectively during their retirement years. Moreover, they may forego too many life experiences during their earning years for the sake of saving. It is important for financial planners to help highly conscientious clients strike a balance between saving and spending across the life course in a way that leads to a flourishing life. Overall, conscientious clients who are functioning well financially may benefit from a positive psychology approach to financial planning that facilitates the discovery of how to align their money with their well-being (Asebedo & Seay, 2015).

EXTROVERSION

Extroversion often gets equated to sociability, yet a preference for being with others is only one characteristic of an extroverted individual. Costa and McCrae (1992) suggested that extroverts are also assertive, active, talkative, optimistic, energetic, cheerful, and upbeat. Those who score low on the extroversion trait would be classified as introverts; however, introversion should be conceptualized as the absence of extroversion as opposed to the opposite of extroversion. For example, Costa and McCrae discuss that introverts are not unfriendly, but are more reserved; introverts are not shy, rather they prefer to be alone.

Overall, the link between extroversion and financial behavior is positive; however, contrary results have been noted. Nyhus and Webley (2001) found introversion (the absence of extroversion according to Costa and McCrae) to be associated with increased saving and reduced borrowing behavior. In other words, a higher extroversion score would be associated with less saving and more debt. In support of this notion, Verplanken and Herabadi (2001) found extroversion to be correlated with greater impulse buying tendencies. On the other hand, extroversion is positively related to higher annual labor market income, which may stem from extroverted individuals engaging in higher earning professions than introverts (Viinikainen, Kokko, Pulkkinen, & Pehkonen, 2010). Costa, McCrae, and Holland (1984) supported this notion with their finding that the extroversion trait is strongly correlated with enterprising occupations; Costa and McCrae noted that "salespeople [sales tends to be a higher earning occupation] are the prototypic extroverts in our culture" (p. 15). Moreover, extroversion is associated with a greater net worth level (Nabeshima & Seay, 2015). Similarly, Asebedo (2016a) found extroversion to be associated with a greater change in net worth due to higher financial self-efficacy beliefs. Finally, Viinikainen and Kokko (2012) found extroversion to be associated with reduced cumulative unemployment and fewer unemployment periods.

Working with Extroverted Clients

Overall, research suggests that extroverted clients may exhibit somewhat impulsive and imprudent financial behavior. This behavior may be partially due to the extrovert's natural desire to be with people, possibly making it more difficult to control expenditures. Despite these less prudent money-management characteristics, it appears that extroverts can recover from this behavior through earning higher incomes and translating income into an increased net worth over time through saving and/or a higher risk tolerance and allocation to equities. Although Filbeck, Hatfield, and Horvath (2005) did not find a significant relationship between extroversion and individual risk tolerance, Harlow and Brown (1990) provided evidence that extroverted individuals were more willing to accept financial risk. Thus, risk tolerance and portfolio allocation could play roles in the financial success of the extrovert. Moreover, it could also be due to the strong presence of positive emotions found in extroverted individuals: Positive emotions have been found to precede positive financial outcomes (Guven, 2012; Lyubomirsky, King, & Diener, 2005). The financial planner may find it challenging to work with extroverted clients when it comes to managing their day-to-day finances; however, the financial planner can play a significant role in helping higher-earning extroverted clients translate their earnings into long-term wealth.

AGREEABLENESS

The agreeableness trait is associated with altruism, sympathy, and helpfulness (Costa & McCrae, 1992). Agreeable individuals believe that others will equally reciprocate their goodwill and are less likely to protect their own interests and goals. Costa and McCrae described the agreeableness trait as one that is generally seen as socially and psychologically preferable; however, high agreeableness is associated with the Dependent Personality Disorder (Costa & MacCrae, 1990). Individuals who score lower on the agreeableness trait tend to be more antagonistic, egocentric, skeptical, and competitive. Extremely low agreeableness is associated with narcissistic, antisocial, and paranoid personality disorders (Costa & McCrae, 1990). Overall, agreeable individuals tend to be socially popular, yet are more likely to sacrifice their own goals and objectives for the sake of others and relationships.

Unfortunately, agreeableness has been linked to less desirable financial behaviors and outcomes. Agreeableness is associated with lower levels of net worth and financial wealth (Duckworth & Weir, 2010; Nabeshima & Seay, 2015; Nyhus & Webley, 2001), low risk/return investments (Jadlow & Mowen, 2010), and high levels of compulsive buying behavior (Mowen & Spears, 1999). Agreeable individuals were also more likely to borrow money (Nyhus & Webley, 2001). Similarly, Asebedo (2016) found agreeable individuals to have a lower change in net worth due to lower financial self-efficacy beliefs. These results could be due in part to a lower probability of stock ownership for highly agreeable individuals (Nabeshima, 2014). On the positive side, however, Viinikainen and Kokko (2012) found agreeableness to be associated with reduced cumulative unemployment. In line with the benevolent nature of an agreeable individual, Sikkel and Schoenmakers (2012) found characteristics associated with the agreeableness trait to be related to increased bequest motives.

Working with Agreeable Clients

Agreeable clients present a unique set of challenges for the financial planner. The research suggests that the natural tendency for an agreeable individual to be helpful, sympathetic, and altruistic can translate into negative financial consequences. Agreeable clients may be tempted to spend their financial resources on others while sacrificing their own financial goals. For example, agreeable individuals may have a difficult time declining requests for financial assistance from friends, family, or charitable organizations. If the high level of gifting is unsustainable, negative financial outcomes may result. Consequently, agreeable clients may be more likely to have difficulties following through with a savings plan or managing their portfolio withdrawals.

Moreover, Asebedo (2016) found the agreeableness trait to be associated with lower levels of positive affect and elevated levels of negative affect. Thus, agreeable clients may be susceptible to feelings of stress and failure throughout the financial planning process because of the competing desire to help others while simultaneously accomplishing their own financial goals and objectives. As previously discussed, negative emotions can hinder financial goals and objectives (Neukam & Hershey, 2003), whereas positive emotions can promote a greater sense of self-efficacy and prudent financial behavior (Asebedo, 2016a; Bandura, 1997; Guven, 2012; Lyubomirsky, King, & Diener, 2005). Consequently, agreeable clients may benefit from a positive psychology approach to financial planning to help manage and cultivate their sense of well-being (Asebedo & Seay, 2015). Moreover, it may be useful for the financial planner to focus on the financial planning basics when it comes to agreeable clients. For example, having a budget that provides clear boundaries around spending, saving, and giving may help the agreeable client exert control over requests from family, friends, or charitable organizations. In extreme situations, the financial planner may act as an intermediary for the client. For example, the client may direct a friend or family member to talk with their financial planner when requesting money.

Overall, working with agreeable clients requires the financial planner to be skilled in their communication techniques and ability to manage clients' emotional states. Moreover, the financial planner may need to facilitate the resolution of money arguments between their client and family members or friends; if the client is a couple, then conflict resolution may be needed to resolve money arguments within the relationship. Asebedo (2016b) provided a conflict resolution framework from the mediation profession, based on principled negotiation techniques and conflict theory, that financial planners can use to facilitate the resolution of client money arguments. Lastly, while the agreeableness trait may present obstacles for the client and financial planner, it has also been shown to have utility in the retirement phase: Agreeableness has been found to predict life satisfaction and positive experiences in retirement (Robinson, Demetre, & Corney, 2010). Thus, agreeableness may offer an increased ability to adjust and transition to life circumstances.

NEUROTICISM

Costa and McCrae (1992) described neuroticism as the most pervasive of the Big Five traits. The enduring disposition to experience negative affects (e.g., fear, sadness, embarrassment, anger, guilt, frustration, envy, jealousy, depressed moods, loneliness, and disgust) is the hallmark of the neuroticism trait (Costa & McCrae, 1992). Those who score low on the neuroticism trait tend to be emotionally stable, whereas high neuroticism scores indicate emotional instability. Costa and McCrae also emphasized that neuroticism encompasses adaptation and adjustment, with low neuroticism associated with the ability to adapt or adjust, and high neuroticism associated with maladjustment and a lack of adaptability. Costa and McCrae attribute this feature to the presence of negative emotions that can thwart the adaptation and adjustment process. Moreover, there is a tendency for high "N" individuals to have irrational ideas, to lack self-control, and to cope less effectively with stress. Those with low neuroticism scores tend to be relaxed, even-tempered, and calm—even when facing stressful situations.

It is not surprising that neuroticism is associated with poor financial behavior and outcomes. As previously described, negative emotions are central to the neuroticism trait, which have been shown to harm financial goal achievement, financial behavior, and financial self-efficacy beliefs (Asebedo, 2016a; Bandura, 1997; Neukam & Hershey, 2003). Neuroticism has also been directly linked to longer durations of single unemployment spells (Viinikainen & Kokko, 2012), and compulsive and impulsive buying behavior (Shahjehan, Qureshi, Zeb, & Saifullah, 2012). While neurotic individuals have a greater likelihood of stock ownership (Nabeshima, 2014), they have a lower change in net worth over time (Asebedo, 2016a). Moreover, emotionally stable individuals (the opposite of neuroticism) demonstrate less compulsive buying behavior (Mowen & Spears, 1999), and have higher levels of lifetime earnings (Duckworth & Weir, 2010).

Working with Neurotic Clients

Neurotic clients pose a significant challenge to the financial planner. This challenge is due to the pervasive impact of negative emotions and the difficulties they may have with adjustment and adaptability. Financial planning is a dynamic process that is shaped over the life course as clients experience change and transition. Costa and McCrae's description of neuroticism suggests that neurotic clients will have a challenging time adjusting and adapting over time. Thus, the financial planner must be adept at coaching and counseling their neurotic clients through change and transition. Again, a positive psychology approach to financial planning can be effective at helping neurotic clients manage their negative emotions such that they can better adjust and adapt to life changes throughout the financial planning process (Asebedo & Seay, 2015). It is important to note that if clients appear stuck in their negative emotional states and the financial planner is unable to move them forward, then a referral to a mental health professional (such as a financial therapist, psychologist, or marriage and family therapist) may be necessary.

CONNECTING PERSONALITY TO FINANCIAL BEHAVIOR THROUGH THEORY

Personality traits can be theoretically connected to financial behavior (also referred to as consumer behavior in this section) through a relatively new and innovative framework called the Meta-Theoretic Model of Motivation and Personality (Mowen, 2000)—the 3M. The 3M was developed by John C. Mowen to unite personality psychology and consumer behavior research with a testable meta-theory that combined control theory, evolutionary psychology, and a hierarchical approach to personality to explain consumer motivation and behavior. Mowen (2000) observed a departure from investigating broad personality traits within the consumer behavior literature given the weak direct relationships often found between broad personality traits (e.g., Big Five personality traits) and behavior. Mowen argued that consumer behavior can be more fully understood by investigating the combination of broad and narrow traits simultaneously. Thus, he developed the 3M model to explain how different layers of personality traits combine to explain consumer behavior.

Mowen (2000) defines personality as the "hierarchically related set of intrapsychic constructs that reveal consistency across time and that combines with situations to influence the feelings, thoughts, intentions, and behavior of individuals." (p. 2). The 3M posits that a four-level hierarchy of traits explains consumer behavior: elemental traits, compound traits, situational traits, and surface traits. Elemental traits form the foundation of the 3M and are defined as the basic, "underlying predispositions of individuals that arise from genetics and early learning history" (Mowen, 2000, p. 21). The Big Five personality traits are among eight elemental traits proposed by Mowen. Every individual possesses a unique combination of these elemental traits; these unique combinations at the elemental level interact with an individual's cultural background and learning history to produce compound traits.

Numerous compound traits exist and the researcher must use existing literature and theory to determine which compound traits are relevant to their research question. Compound traits should meet certain psychometric properties to function effectively within the 3M framework, including (a) the measurement scales are unidimensional, (b) the scales demonstrate strong internal reliability (i.e., Cronbach's alpha of .75 or higher), (c) they can be significantly explained with an r-squared of .25 or more by at least two of the elemental traits, and (d) they can account for variance in situational traits above and beyond that of the elemental traits in a hierarchical model. Mowen provided examples of compound traits that meet these criteria, including general self-efficacy beliefs, competitiveness, and task orientation (among others).

Elemental and compound traits combine with situational forces to produce situational traits such as domain specific self-efficacy (e.g., financial self-efficacy, relationship self-efficacy, health self-efficacy, etc.), value consciousness, and health motivation (among others). Finally, elemental, compound, and situational traits interact together to produce surface traits. Surface traits are specific and concrete behaviors that can be measured and observed. Mowen provided evidence for the effectiveness of the 3M in explaining five surface traits: compulsive buying, sports participation, healthy diet lifestyles, proneness to bargaining, and frugality.

Despite the utility of the 3M model, it has yet to be widely used within financial planning research and practice to connect personality traits and other psychological characteristics to financial behavior; however, several relevant research studies have been completed using the 3M. For example, the 3M has been used to explain online shopping (Bosnjak, Galesic, & Tuten, 2007; Kang & Johnson, 2015), financial self-efficacy and saving behavior (Asebedo, 2016a), financial satisfaction (Davis & Runyan, 2016), gambling propensity (Mowen, Fang, & Scott, 2009), compulsive buying (Mowen & Spears, 1999), a comparison of stock market investors and gamblers (Jadlow & Mowen, 2010), and financial preparedness for retirement (Hershey & Mowen, 2000). Researchers should consider utilizing the 3M model as it provides a theoretical integration of psychology and financial attributes that facilitates the discovery of the underlying psychological factors that motivate and shape client behavior.

PERSONALITY MEASUREMENT

There are several Big Five personality assessments available online that financial planners can employ to measure their client's personality traits. For example, *Psychology Today* (https://www.psychologytoday.com/test/1297) has a publicly available Big Five personality test that provides a free personality summary with the option to purchase full results. For researchers, larger secondary data sets may include the Big Five personality traits. For example, the Psychosocial and Lifestyle Questionnaire from the Health and Retirement Study includes variables measuring each of the Big Five traits (Smith, Ryan, Sonnega, & Weir, 2017); the National Longitudinal Survey of Youth (NLSY) also includes measures of the Big Five traits. For a thorough discussion of personality measurement according to the Big Five traits, see the *Revised NEO Personality Inventory (NEO PI-R) and NEO Five-Factor Inventory (NEO-FFI) Professional Manual* (Costa & McCrae, 1992). Moreover, Srivastava (2017) provides an overview of the Big Five traits in conjunction with several links to resources and publicly available measurement tools.

IMPLICATIONS FOR RESEARCH AND PRACTICE

Overall, the personality and financial behavior literature reveal relevant implications for financial planners and researchers. First, themes have begun to emerge from the literature that suggest personality can predict financial behavior. Conscientiousness and extroversion are generally associated with financial behavior that is conducive to goal achievement and asset accumulation, whereas openness, agreeableness, and neuroticism tend to undermine judicious financial behavior and present unique challenges that must be overcome throughout the financial planning process. It is important to note that each personality trait is neither good nor bad; each simply represents one's natural patterns of thinking, feeling, and behaving that tend to be consistent across time and situations (American Psychological Association, 2017; Mowen, 2000). What the research has shown is that certain personality patterns may result in less desirable financial outcomes.

For the financial planner, understanding their clients' personality characteristics can help them predict possible challenges their clients might face when implementing recommendations; financial planners will also be able to effectively tailor recommendations to meet their clients' behavioral and psychological needs from the beginning of the financial planning process. Understanding where challenges might arise and tailoring recommendations accordingly can facilitate a more enjoyable and fruitful relationship for both the financial planner and the client. Moreover, while dramatic changes to personality cannot be expected in the short term, research suggests that personality can shift over time (Roberts & Mroczek, 2008). Thus, it is possible for a client to adjust certain aspects of his or her personality such that his or her financial behavior can improve (e.g., reduce negative affect, improve self-control, or increase task follow-through, etc.). For example, a less conscientious client may slowly become more conscientious over time. Fortunately, as people age they tend to exhibit increased self-confidence, warmth, self-control, and emotional stability (Roberts & Mroczek, 2008), which are characteristics that primarily support financial behavior. While personality can change, Roberts and DelVecchio (2000) note that personality trait consistency reaches a peak and plateaus between ages 50 and 70. This suggests that personality changes for older adults are less likely to occur.

From a research perspective, personality provides an effective framework from which to explore a variety of financial behavior to continue to build the body of knowledge that informs practice. The Big Five personality traits have been widely documented in the literature as the foundation of personality. The Personality Psychology field is very active in furthering our understanding of personality and how these traits manifest within individuals over the life course.

Second, existing research and the 3M model suggest that a complex network of psychological characteristics explain financial behavior. Specifically, financial behavior can be traced back to broader personality dispositions, but are more directly explained through narrow traits influenced by situational forces. Personality origins can provide insight into clients' general tendencies to exhibit more specific traits and thus provide a foundation from which to explore financial behavior. Financial planners can utilize this framework (3M) to provide holistic financial planning recommendations that acknowledge the psychological roots of behavior. Understanding these psychological origins can help financial planners more effectively tailor advice to help individuals overcome adversity and manage stress associated with failures during the financial planning process. For example, an agreeable individual may be more susceptible to negative emotions associated with managing and succumbing to the financial expectations of others. Through gaining an understanding of these psychological origins, a financial planner might adopt a strategy to specifically counteract these negative attributes. In summary, by adapting and integrating an understanding of clients' personality into financial planning recommendations, financial planners can provide more comprehensive advice and support by accounting for clients' psychological characteristics that manifest through behavioral tendencies, which can affect the successful implementation of recommendations.

FUTURE DIRECTION

In summary, personality describes our innate cognitive, affective, and behavioral responses to life events and circumstances (Pytlik Zillig et al., 2002), thereby forming a basic explanation for the root of client behavior. The financial planning profession would benefit from future research that expands our knowledge of the relationship between personality and financial behaviors, such as investing, debt choices, retirement timing, portfolio withdrawal rates, and behavior among couples, and so on. It is possible that the combination of basic personality factors and narrower psychological characteristics may further explain why observed client behaviors deviate from rational expectations. Future research should also investigate how personality traits interact together to influence behavior, as each individual possesses a combination of traits. For example, it is possible for a highly neurotic client to also be highly conscientious; perhaps this client's conscientiousness trait promotes action and follow through, which can help them overcome their tendencies to experience high levels of stress and worry. Moreover, the unit of measurement should be expanded from individual to coupled clients to investigate how the personality traits of each spouse interact to produce financial decisions and behavior of the household. Lastly, advanced statistical methods are needed to understand the causal relationship between variables and to account for measurement errors associated with psychological constructs, such as personality. These research objectives can be accomplished by employing structural equation modeling and longitudinal techniques that are frequently used within psychology (Little, 2013).

REFERENCES

American Psychological Association. (2017). *Personality*. Retrieved August 29, 2017 from http://www.apa.org/topics/personality.

Asebedo, S. D. (2016a). *Three essays on financial self-efficacy beliefs and the saving behavior of older pre-retirees*. Kansas State University.

Asebedo, S. D. (2016b). Building financial peace: A conflict resolution framework for money arguments. *Journal of Financial Therapy, (7)*2, 1–15.

Asebedo, S. D., & Seay, M. C. (2015). From functioning to flourishing: Applying positive psychology to financial planning. *Journal of Financial Planning, 28*(11), 50–58.

Ashton, M. C., & Lee, K. (2005). Honesty–humility, the big five, and the five-factor model. *Journal of Personality, 73*(5), 1321–1354.

Bandura, A. (1997). *Self-efficacy: The exercise of control*. New York: W.H. Freeman.

Bosnjak, M., Galesic, M., & Tuten, T. (2007). Personality determinants of online shopping: Explaining online purchase intentions using a hierarchical approach. *Journal of Business Research, 60*(6), 597–605.

Costa, P. T., Jr., & McCrae, R. R. (1990). Personality disorders and the five-factor model of personality. *Journal of Personality Disorders, 4*(4), 362–371.

Costa, P. T., Jr., & McCrae, R. R. (1992). *NEO-PI-R: Professional manual*. Odessa, FL: Psychological Assessment Resources.

Costa, P. T., McCrae, R. R., & Holland, J. L. (1984). Personality and vocational interests in an adult sample. *Journal of Applied Psychology, 69*(3), 390.

Davis, K., & Runyan, R. C. (2016). Personality traits and financial satisfaction: Investigation of a hierarchical approach. *Journal of Financial Counseling and Planning, 27*(1), 47–60.

Duckworth, A. L., & Weir, D. R. (2010). *Personality, lifetime earnings, and retirement wealth*. Working paper, WP 2010–235, Ann Arbor: University of Michigan Retirement Research Center.

Filbeck, G., Hatfield, P., & Horvath, P. (2005). Risk aversion and personality type. *Journal of Behavioral Finance, 6*(4), 170–180.

Guven, C. (2012). Reversing the question: Does happiness affect consumption and savings behavior? *Journal of Economic Psychology, 33*(4), 701–717.

Harlow, W. V., & Brown, K. C. (1990). Understanding and assessing financial risk tolerance: a biological perspective. *Financial Analysts Journal, 46*(6), 50–62.

Hershey, D. A., & Mowen, J. C. (2000). Psychological determinants of financial preparedness for retirement. *The Gerontologist, 40*(6), 687–697.

Jadlow, J. W., & Mowen, J. C. (2010). Comparing the traits of stock market investors and gamblers. *Journal of Behavioral Finance, 11*(2), 67–81.

John, O. P., and Srivastava, S. (1999). The big five trait taxonomy: History, measurement, and theoretical perspectives. In L. A. Pervin & O. P. John (Eds.), *Handbook of Personality: Theory and research*, 2nd ed. (pp. 102–138). New York: Guilford Press.

Kang, J. M., & Johnson, K. K. P. (2015). F-commerce platform for apparel online social shopping: Testing Mowen's 3M model. *International Journal of Information Management, 35*(6), 691–701.

Lee, K., & Ashton, M. C. (2004). Psychometric properties of the HEXACO Personality Inventory. *Multivariate Behavioral Research, 39*(2), 329–358.

Little, T. D. (2013). *Longitudinal structural equation modeling.* New York: Guilford Press.

Lyubomirsky, S., King, L., & Diener, E. (2005). The benefits of frequent positive affect: Does happiness lead to success? *Psychological Bulletin, 131*(6), 803–855.

Mayfield, C., Perdue, G., & Wooten, K. (2008). Investment management and personality type. *Financial Services Review, 17*, 219–236.

Mehl, M. R., Gosling, S. D., & Pennebaker, J. W. (2006). Personality in its natural habitat: Manifestations and implicit folk theories of personality in daily life. *Journal of Personality and Social Psychology, 90*(5), 862–877.

Mowen, J. C. (2000). *The 3M model of motivation and personality: Theory and empirical applications to consumer behavior.* Norwell, MA: Kluwer Academic Publishers.

Mowen, J. C., Fang, X., & Scott, K. (2009). A hierarchical model approach for identifying the trait antecedents of general gambling propensity and of four gambling-related genres. *Journal of Business Research, 62*(12), 1262–1268.

Mowen, J. C., & Spears, N. (1999). Understanding compulsive buying among college students: A hierarchical approach. *Journal of Consumer Psychology, 8*(4), 407–430.

Nabeshima, G. (2014). *Three essays on personality and net worth.* Kansas State University.

Nabeshima, G., & Seay, M. C. (2015). Wealth and personality: Can personality traits make your clients rich? *Journal of Financial Planning, 28*(7), 50–57.

Neukam, K. A., & Hershey, D. A. (2003). Financial inhibition, financial activation, and saving for retirement. *Financial Services Review, 12*(1), 19–37.

Nyhus, E. K., & Webley, P. (2001). The role of personality in household savings and borrowing behavior. *European Journal of Personality, 15*, S85–S103.

Puri, M., & Robinson, D. T. (2007). Optimism and economic choice. *Journal of Financial Economics, 86*, 71–99.

Pytlik Zillig, L. M., Hemenover, S. H., & Dienstbier, R. A. (2002). What do we assess when we assess a big 5 trait? A content analysis of the affective, behavioral, and cognitive processes represented in big 5 personality inventories. *Personality and Social Psychology Bulletin, 28*(6), 847–858.

Roberts, B. W., & DelVecchio, W. F. (2000). The rank-order consistency of personality traits from childhood to old age: A quantitative review of longitudinal studies. *Psychological Bulletin, 126*(1), 3–25.

Roberts, B. W., & Mroczek, D. (2008). Personality trait change in adulthood. *Current directions in psychological science, 17*(1), 31–35.

Robinson, O. C., Demetre, J. D., & Corney, R. (2010). Personality and retirement: Exploring the links between the big five personality traits, reasons for retirement and the experience of being retired. *Personality and Individual Differences, 48*(7), 792–797.

Shahjehan, A., Qureshi, J. A., Zeb, F., & Saifullah, K. (2012). The effect of personality on impulsive and compulsive buying behaviors. *African Journal of Business Management, 6*(6), 2187–2194.

Sikkel, D., & Schoenmakers, E. (2012). Bequests to health-related charitable organizations: A structural model. *International Journal of Nonprofit and Voluntary Sector Marketing, 17*(3), 183–197.

Smith, J., Ryan, L., Sonnega, A., & Weir, D. (2017). *Psychosocial and Lifestyle Questionnaire 2006–2016.* The HRS Psychosocial Working Group. Ann Arbor: University of Michigan Institute for Social Research, Survey Research Center.

Srivastava, S. (2017). *Measuring the big five personality factors.* Retrieved from http://pages.uoregon.edu/sanjay/bigfive.html.

Verplanken, B., & Herabadi, A. (2001). Individual differences in impulse buying tendency: Feeling and no thinking. *European Journal of Personality, 15*, S71-S83.

Viinikainen, J., & Kokko, K. (2012). Personality traits and unemployment: Evidence from longitudinal data. *Journal of Economic Psychology, 33*(6), 1204–1222.

Viinikainen, J., Kokko, K., Pulkkinen, L., & Pehkonen, J. (2010). Personality and labor market income: Evidence from longitudinal data. *Labor, 24*(2), 201–220.

CHAPTER 10

Risk Literacy

Meghaan R. Lurtz, MS, and Stuart J. Heckman, PhD, CFP®

Kansas State University

Risk can be defined as "any situation in which some events are not known with certainty" (Chavas, 2004, p. 5) and it is, therefore, ubiquitous. Risk is especially present in the personal financial planning context—nearly all financial decisions involve risk, and financial planners know that clients' willingness to take risks (i.e., risk tolerance) varies across individuals. Measuring risk tolerance and understanding how risk tolerance influences behavior has been a key focus in financial planning research and a critical component of the investment management process. Although there are a number of studies that examine risk tolerance measurement issues and applications (for a review, see Finke & Guillemette, 2016), the financial planning profession has much to learn from other fields regarding how individuals perceive and use information when making risky choices. Certainly within the context of this book, examining client psychology—the biases, behaviors, and perceptions that impact client decision-making and financial well-being—risk literacy has an important place in helping the profession better serve its clients.

Understanding how individuals make decisions involving risk or uncertainty has a rich academic history in several disciplines including statistics, psychology, and economics. Recent advances in decision-making sciences[1] have furthered our understanding of how people make decisions in a variety of contexts, including the criminal justice system, public safety,

---

[1] The term *decision-making sciences* is being used somewhat informally to refer to a variety of interdisciplinary disciplines focused on how people make decisions, which includes but is not limited to the following: judgment and decision-making, economic psychology/behavioral economics, and behavioral finance.

health, and finances. One advancement in particular that is of value to the financial planning profession is the measurement of a concept known as risk literacy. The purpose of this chapter is to introduce the growing literature on risk literacy and to discuss applications to the financial planning profession.

Risk literacy is defined as "the ability to interpret and act on information about risk" (Cokely, Galesic, Schulz, Ghazal, & Garcia-Retamero, 2012, p. 26). Objective numeracy, the underlying operator of risk literacy, has been established as an independent and unique predictor of the ability to make risky decisions, controlling for subjective numeracy, need for cognition, worry, and intellectual ability (Låg, Bauger, Lindberg, & Friborg, 2014). Cokely et al. (2012) sought to improve previous work on measuring numeracy and developed the Berlin Numeracy Test (BNT). Their results showed that the BNT is a strong predictor of an individual's numeracy, which aids in understanding and assessing risk across a variety of contexts, even after controlling for cognitive ability. Their findings have been recently confirmed and elaborated upon—numeracy outpredicts fluid intelligence tests when considering risky tradeoffs. Numeracy can be improved upon, unlike intelligence that is more stable, through graph literacy training and or numeracy skill building (Cokely et al., in press). This review discusses (1) Cokely et al.'s (2012) measure of risk literacy, (2) risk literacy applications in health contexts, and (3) risk literacy applications in financial contexts.

BERLIN NUMERACY TEST

Since the Berlin Numeracy test (BNT) was originally developed and validated at the Max Planck Institute for Human Development, the BNT has been used worldwide and across diverse backgrounds in 21 studies (n = 5,336) where the BNT's convergent validity, discriminant validity, as well as criterion validity have all been supported (Cokely et al., 2012). The BNT comes in two forms based on the population to be examined. For individuals with moderate-to-high numeracy, the four-item test presented in Cokely et al. (2012) is best. Most of the literature has treated college-educated populations as individuals with moderate-to-high numeracy. The high-numerate version is also available in a computer adaptive version (see www.riskliteracy.org); questions become easier or harder based on correctness of previous answers provided. The computer adaptive version only requires answering two to three questions and generally takes less than three minutes to complete. The second version of the test is for low-numerate individuals; it includes four items. This test has also been found to have high validity (Cokely et al., 2012). Both versions of the BNT are included in the appendix at the end of this chapter.

Healthcare Applications

The majority of researchers using the BNT have focused on applications in the healthcare field. Many of these findings were recently summarized in a systematic review of articles published from 1995 to 2016, and concluded with an introduction of a conceptual framework (Garcia-Retamero & Cokely, 2017). The framework focused on the power of transparent visual aides. The literature review examined how visual aids lend themselves to encouraging a wide range of individuals to deliberate on their decisions. As such, visual aids through mediation of the deliberation process, according to the framework, not only reduced errors and biases, they improved self-assessment of information (Garcia-Retamero & Cokely, 2017). People improved their decision-making abilities and felt better about the decisions that they made. These findings have been further developed and the framework is now referred to as the skilled decision theory (Cokely et al., in press).

Cardiovascular disease is the leading cause of death, and acute coronary syndrome (ACS) has been responsible for nearly half of those deaths (Petrova et al., 2017). Timely treatment of ACS has significantly increased survival rates (Petrova et al., 2017) so there have been numerous educational campaigns designed to promote quicker reaction times. These programs have had marginal, if any, ability to speed patient reaction (Petrova et al., 2017). Petrova et al. (2017) examined patient reaction times and the importance of numeracy. Results from their study follow previous studies of numeracy and medical decision-making: "A patient with high (vs. low) objective numeracy was four times more likely to seek medical attention within the first 50 minutes of symptom onset" (Petrova et al., 2017, p. 299).

In a study using a highly educated population from the Netherlands (between 30% and 50% of the population held graduate degrees), individuals with higher numeracy spent more time deliberating and did better on financial and medical tasks when compared to lower numerate individuals (Ghazal, Cokely, & Garcia-Retamero, 2014). Numeracy has also been found to predict the way individuals want or desire to interact with a healthcare professional. Low numeracy individuals prefer paternalistic relationships, whereas highly numerate individuals prefer a shared relationship (Galesic & Garcia-Retamero, 2011). These findings held even when controlling for age; literacy predicted the type of relationship individuals wanted from their healthcare provider (Rodriguez et al., 2013).

Researchers have also examined the numeracy levels of profession-als. Surgeons and senior-level police officers with graduate degrees are two special populations that regularly review and interact with risk informa-tion, such as risks involved with a particular surgical procedure or risks of terrorism. Surgeons' numeracy has been reviewed for connections to both communication style and improvements (Garcia-Retamero, Cokely, Wicki, & Joeris, 2016; Garcia-Retamero & Hoffrage, 2013). More numerate surgeons utilize collaborative decision-making (Garcia-Retamero, Wicki, Cokely & Hanson, 2014).

More numerate police officers were better able to estimate the accuracy of counterterrorism techniques and were more likely to recommend the tech-niques to policymakers (Garcia-Retamero & Dhami, 2013). Although surgeons and police officers who had higher levels of numeracy were better at under-standing and interpreting risk information, both groups contained low numer-ate individuals (Garcia-Retamero et al., 2016; Garcia-Retamero & Dhami, 2013). Furthermore, both high- and low-numerate surgeons and police officers improved their decision-making abilities through the use of graphical informa-tion (Garcia-Retamero et al., 2016; Garcia-Retamero & Dhami, 2013).

The importance of the use of graphs and icon arrays in communicat-ing risk cannot be overstated. The literature shows that certain types of graphs and icon arrays greatly improve decision-making ability and the abil-ity to communicate information. Graphs help individuals to avoid fram-ing effects[2] and denominator neglect[3] (Garcia-Retamero & Hoffrage, 2013; Garcia-Retamero, Okan, & Cokely, 2012; Okan, Garcia-Retamero, Cokely, & Maldonado, 2012). These findings have even been further explored and supported by frequency hypothesis (Brase, 2014) and spatial-to-conceptual mapping (Okan et al., 2012), which says graphical information needs to mirror what we would expect in life, namely, a larger bar in the bar graph represents more.

---

[2] Framing effects are cognitive biases where individuals become risk seeking when the certain choice is presented in a negative frame and will avoid risk in the exact same scenario if the certain choice is presented in a positive frame. The classic exam-ple is the Asian disease problem in which the certain choice frame changed from 200 out of 600 people will be saved to 400 out of 600 people will die—people sought risk when the frame was negative and preferred certainty when the frame was posi-tive (Tversky & Kahneman, 1981).

[3] Denominator neglect refers to a tendency for individuals to focus on ratio numera-tors while neglecting the denominator. For example, if you win a drawing by having a red marble drawn out of a jar filled with other marbles, people tend to judge the likelihood of winning based on the number of red marbles rather than the overall proportion of red marbles in the jar (for a review, see Kahneman, 2011).

Researchers have also found that appropriate risk presentation (i.e., risk presentations that account for individual's numeracy) can significantly alter behavior. For example, in analyzing health behaviors and sexually transmitted diseases (STDs), visual representations helped to facilitate an understanding of the risk of STDs, which led to changes in attitudes and behavior (Garcia-Retamero & Cokely, 2014, 2015). Attitudes about condom use changed as young adults understood the information (Garcia-Retamero & Cokely, 2014, 2015). In follow-up surveys, a statistically significant number of students reported a change in behavior; they started using condoms to protect themselves from the high risk of STDs (Garcia-Retamero & Cokely, 2014, 2015).

Financial Applications

The connections that can be drawn from the findings in the medical field to personal financial planning and the financial planning industry are numerous. Downside financial risk (i.e., the risk of financial loss) is a major concern in economic and financial literature. Like many other probabilistic trade-offs, understanding and calculating downside risk is often misunderstood (Newall, 2016). Clients with low to even moderate numeracy may not understand that it takes more than a 20% gain to recover from a 20% loss. The misunderstanding of downside risk may have previously been thought of as an issue of financial literacy. Financial literacy's impact on financial behavior has been widely studied along with programs and interventions aimed at improving literacy in order to improve behavior, but these interventions have had little, if any, impact (Fernandes, Lynch, & Netemeyer, 2014). Given that numeracy has outperformed health literacy in medical research (Låg, Bauger, Lindberg, & Friborg, 2014), numeracy may be more important than financial literacy in determining personal finance behavior.

In a study by Campara, Paraboni, da Costa, Saurin, and Lopes (2017) on Brazilian university students, lower levels of numeracy were linked to higher risk tolerance, and higher numeracy levels were linked to lower risk tolerance. The higher numerate university students understood the risk and were less likely to want to take that risk. This study was conducted with students, but those students will one day be deciding on portfolio allocations. This same phenomenon was previously identified by Petrova, van der Pligt, and Garcia-Retamero (2014), who stated individuals with higher numeracy, "seemed to have a clearer idea of how bad, a bad choice is" (p. 197).

Although low-numeracy individuals differ from high-numeracy individuals in their preference for decision-making in the healthcare context, younger individuals have been found to prefer a collaborative or shared decision-making relationship in career and financial domains regardless of numeracy level (Garcia-Retamero & Galesic, 2013). Young persons also desired a financial professional who employed transformational leadership versus laissez-faire or transactional leadership. Transformational leadership "involves establishing oneself as a role model by gaining trust and confidence of followers. Transformational leaders motivate their followers by exhibiting a deep sense of enjoyment and purpose" (Garcia-Reatamero & Galesic, 2013 p. 494). Petrova et al. (2017) had given students one of three descriptions about a camera they hypothetically owned: neutral, affect-rich, affect-rich with reappraisal. Students were then given probabilities of loss and asked to make insurance decisions. Higher-numerate students, especially those who went through the reappraisal, made better decisions and were less influenced by their emotions (Petrova et al., 2017).

RISK LITERACY AND FINANCIAL PLANNING

Risk management plays a critical role in the development of financial plans and recommendations; communication about risk is entirely unavoidable in the financial planning process. If the client is to understand and act on the information about risk being present, financial planners have a responsibility to be sure they are communicating at a level that is appropriate based on the client's risk literacy. While acting as fiduciaries, Certified Financial Planner professionals in particular have a duty to be sure to only implement plans that are suitable for their clients and to be sure they are communicating risk in a way that can be understood by the client. Therefore, as suggested by Cokely et al. (2012) in the health context, it may be appropriate to assess each client's level of risk literacy before engaging in discussions about risks in the financial plan and calibrating the conversation to the appropriate level. This is especially true when determining an appropriate level of risk for client portfolios.

Although there are numerous risk-tolerance questionnaires available, some of these questionnaires may be inappropriate depending on a client's risk literacy. Analyzing client risk literacy is not only practical with tools like the BNT, but it is also prudent given previous findings on the relationship between numeracy and risk tolerance (Campara Paraboni, da Costa, Saurin, & Lopez, 2017). Current measures of risk tolerance may be conflating risk tolerance and risk literacy. Given the significant emphasis throughout the industry on designing portfolios that are consistent with client risk tolerance, the extent to which risk literacy is influencing the measurement of risk tolerance may lead to inappropriate risk taking.

Trevena et al. (2013) found "patient decision aids can be an effective strategy for integrating research evidence with patient values and other factors to facilitate greater patient involvement, improve decision quality and increase knowledge about decision options" (p. 2). In a similar way, client decision aids may be useful in helping clients to understand risks and the strategies being recommended to manage that risk. Financial planners can also benefit from research about how to effectively communicate risk. Bruine de Bruin and Bostrom (2013) identified four steps for designing useful scientific presentations for lay audiences. First, identify what needs to be known or what point needs to be made. Second, determine what the client or audience already knows. Third, based on the professional point that needs to be made and what the clients or audience knows, design a communication piece. Last, test the effectiveness of the communication. Effectiveness may be measured and remeasured as adjustments are made to the communication. As an example, consider developing portfolio recommendations for a new client.

In designing the communication piece, Trevena et al. (2013) presented a useful review of risk communication issues and guidelines—some of these recommendations are reviewed here, but interested readers are referred to the full article for a more complete discussion. When presenting the chance of a single event or changes in rates, Trevena et al. (2013) recommend using a percent or simple frequency; equal denominators are key if using frequencies. Natural frequencies are also recommended over conditional probabilities when presenting information about connected events. Providing risk in context is also helpful; in health research, this is done by "provid[ing] the chance of death over the next 10 years from the disease under consideration, as well as the chance of dying from other major causes" (p. 5). Visual and personalized messages can also make communication about risk more tangible.

Finally, and most important, advisors need to realize that employing effective graphical information, measuring numeracy, and presenting risk in specific ways may change clients' behaviors. This is incredible news when one considers the less-than-dramatic findings that financial education programs have had on increasing financial literacy, and therefore influencing behavior (Fernandes et al., 2014), or that health literacy programs have had on health behaviors.

CONCLUSION

Measuring and addressing risk tolerance and financial literacy are just the tip of the iceberg. Financial advisors may be better able to serve clients by implementing practices that also address numeracy and risk literacy. Simple, easy-to-use tools exist, such as the BNT, that financial advisory firms can take advantage quickly and with ease in serving their clients. As mentioned above, numeracy and graph literacy are skills that can be improved upon. As such, even if advisors find that many of their clients or they themselves are less numerate than they would have imagined, simple changes to information presentation and skill building can improve numeracy and risk literacy. Numeracy improves communication between practitioners and clients, and has the potential to improve attitudes and change behavior. Financial advisors who want to deliver exceptional service to clients should aim to elevate numeracy and risk literacy in their practice.

REFERENCES

Brase, G. L. (2014). The power of representation and interpretation: Doubling statistical reasoning performance with icons and frequentist interpretations of ambiguous numbers. *Journal of Cognitive Psychology, 26*(1), 81–97. doi:10.1080/20445911.2013.861840.

Bruine de Bruin, W., & Bostrom, A. (2013). Assessing what to address in science communication. *Proceedings of the National Academy of Sciences, USA, 110*(Suppl. 3), 14062–14068. doi:10.1073/pnas.1212729110.

Campara, J. P., Paraboni, A. L., da Costa, N., Saurin, V., & Lopes, A. (2017). Subjective risk tolerance and numeracy skills: A study in Brazil. *Journal of Behavioral and Experimental Finance, 14*, 39–46. doi: 10.1016/j.jbef.2017.04.001.

Chavas, J.-P. (2004). *Risk analysis in theory and practice.* San Diego: Elsevier Academic Press.

Cokely, E. T., Feltz, A., Ghazal, S., Allan, J. N., Petrova, D., & Garcia-Retamero, R. (in press). Decision making skill: From intelligence to numeracy and expertise. In K. A. Ericsson, R. R. Hoffman, A. Kozbelt, & A. M. Williams (Eds.), *Cambridge handbook of expertise and expert performance.* New York: Cambridge University Press. Retrieved from http://www.riskliteracy.org/files/1414/8312/0711/2016_Cokely_et_al_Decision_Making_Skill_CamHandbook_Final_Pre-Print.pdf.

Cokely, E. T., Galesic, M., Schulz, E., Ghazal, S., & Garcia-Retamero, R. (2012). Measuring risk literacy: The Berlin numeracy test. *Judgment and Decision Making, 7*(1), 25.

Fernandes, D., Lynch, J. G., Jr., & Netemeyer, R. G. (2014). Financial literacy, financial education, and downstream financial behaviors. *Management Science, 60*(8), 1861–1883. doi:10.1287/mnsc.2013.1849.

Finke, M. S., & Guillemette, M. A. (2016). Measuring risk tolerance: A review of literature. *Journal of Personal Finance, 15*(1), 63–76.

Galesic, M., & Garcia-Retamero, R. (2011). Do low-numeracy people avoid shared decision making? *Health Psychology, 30*(3), 336–341. doi:10.1037/a0022723.

Garcia-Retamero, R., & Cokely, E. T. (2014). The influence of skills, message frame, and visual aids on prevention of sexually transmitted diseases. *Journal of Behavioral Decision Making, 27*(2), 179–189. doi:10.1002/bdm.1797.

Garcia-Retamero, R., & Cokely, E. T. (2015). Simple but powerful health messages for increasing condom use in young adults. *The Journal of Sex Research, 52*(1), 30–42. doi:10.1080/00224499.2013.806647.

Garcia-Retamero, R., & Cokely, E. T. (2017). Designing visual aids that promote risk literacy: A systematic review of health research and evidence-based design heuristics. *Human Factors, 59*(4), 582–627. doi:10.1177/0018720817690634.

Garcia-Retamero, R., Cokely, E. T., Wicki, B., & Joeris, A. (2016). Improving risk literacy in surgeons. *Patient Education and Counseling, 99*(7), 1156–1161. doi: 10.1016/j.pec.2016.01.013.

Garcia-Retamero, R., & Dhami, M. K. (2013). On avoiding framing effects in experienced decision makers. *The Quarterly Journal of Experimental Psychology, 66*(4), 829–842. doi:10.1080/17470218.2012.727836.

Garcia-Retamero, R., & Galesic, M. (2013). Does young adults' preferred role in decision making about health, money, and career depend on their advisors' leadership skills? *International Journal of Psychology, 48*(4), 492–501. doi:10.1080/00207594.2012.688135.

Garcia-Retamero, R., & Hoffrage, U. (2013). Visual representation of statistical information improves diagnostic inferences in doctors and their patients. *Social Science & Medicine, 83*, 27–33. doi: 10.1016/j.socscimed.2013.01.034.

Garcia-Retamero, R., Okan, Y., & Cokely, E. T. (2012). Using visual aids to improve communication of risks about health: A review. *The Scientific World Journal, 2012*, 10. doi:10.1100/2012/562637.

Ghazal, S., Cokely, E. T., & Garcia-Retamero, R. (2014). Predicting biases in very highly educated samples: Numeracy and metacognition. *Judgment and Decision Making, 9*(1), 15.

Kahneman, D. (2011). *Thinking, fast and slow*. New York: Farrar, Straus and Giroux.

Låg, T., Bauger, L., Lindberg, M., & Friborg, O. (2014). The role of numeracy and intelligence in health-risk estimation and medical data interpretation. *Journal of Behavioral Decision Making, 27*(2), 95–108. doi:10.1002/bdm.1788.

Newall, P. W. S. (2016). Downside financial risk is misunderstood. *Judgment and Decision Making, 11*(5), 416–423.

Okan, Y., Garcia-Retamero, R., Cokely, E. T., & Maldonado, A. (2012). Individual differences in graph literacy: Overcoming denominator neglect in risk comprehension. *Journal of Behavioral Decision Making, 25*(4), 390–401. doi:10.1002/bdm.751.

Okan, Y., Garcia-Retamero, R., Galesic, M., & Cokely, E. T. (2012). When higher bars are not larger quantities: On individual differences in the use of spatial information in graph comprehension. *Spatial Cognition & Computation, 12* (2–3), 195–218. doi:10.1080/13875868.2012.659302.

Petrova, D. G., Garcia-Retamero, R., Catena, A., Cokely, E., Heredia Carrasco, A., Arrebola Moreno, A., & Ramirez Hernandez, J. A. (2017). Numeracy predicts risk of pre-hospital decision delay: A retrospective study of acute coronary syndrome survival. *Annals of Behavioral Medicine, 51*(2), 292–306. doi:10.1007/s12160–016–9853–1.

Petrova, D. G., van der Pligt, J., & Garcia-Retamero, R. (2014). Feeling the numbers: On the interplay between risk, affect, and numeracy. *Journal of Behavioral Decision Making, 27*(3), 191–199. doi:10.1002/bdm.1803.

Rodriguez, V., Andrade, A. D., Garcia-Retamero, R., Anam, R., Rodriguez, R., Lisigurski, M., Sharit, J., & Ruiz, J. G. (2013). Health literacy, numeracy, and graphical literacy among veterans in primary care and their effect on shared decision making and trust in physicians. *Journal of Health Communication, 18* (Suppl. 1), 273–289. doi:10.1080/10810730.2013.829137.

Trevena, L. J., Zikmund-Fisher, B. J., Edwards, A., Gaissmaier, W., Galesic, M., Han, P. K., et al. (2013). Presenting quantitative information about decision outcomes: A risk communication primer for patient decision aid developers. *BMC Medical Informatics and Decision Making, 13*(2), S7. doi:10.1186/1472–6947–13-s2-s7.

Tversky, A., & Kahneman, D. (1981). The framing of decisions and the psychology of choice. *Science, 211*(4481), 453–458. doi:10.1126/science.7455683.

APPENDIX

Although there are computer-adaptive and multiple choice formats for the Berlin Numeracy Test, only the traditional format is included here (see Cokely et al., 2012). Scoring is done by adding up the "correct numbers and treating them as internal scaled scores" (Cokely et al., 2012).

BERLIN NUMERACY TEST FOR GENERAL POPULATION

1. Imagine that we flip a fair coin 1,000 times. What is your best guess about how many times the coin would come up head in 1,000 flips? *500*

2. Imagine we are throwing a five-sided die 50 times. On average, out of these 50 throws how many times would this five-sided die show an odd number (1, 3, or 5)? *30*

3. In the BIG BUCKS LOTTERY, the chance of winning a $10 prize is 1%. What is your best guess about how many people would win a $10 prize if 1,000 people buy a single ticket to BIG BUCKS? *10*

4. In ACME PUBLISHING SWEEPSTAKES, the chance of winning a car is 1 in 1,000. What percent of tickets to ACME PUBLISHING SWEEPSTAKES win a car? *10%*

BERLIN NUMERACY TEST FOR EDUCATED POPULATION

1. Imagine we are throwing a five-sided die 50 times. On average, out of these 50 throws how many times would this five-sided die show an odd number (1, 3, or 5)? *30*
2. Out of 1,000 people in a small town 500 are members of a choir. Out of these 500 members in a choir 100 are men. Out of the 500 inhabitants that are not in a choir 300 are men. What is the probability that a randomly drawn man is a member of the choir? *25%*
3. Imagine we are throwing a loaded die (six sides). The probability that the die shows a 6 is twice as high as the probability of each of the other numbers. On average, out of 70 throws how many times would the die show the number 6? *20*
4. In a forest, 30% of mushrooms are red, 50% brown, and 30% white. A red mushroom is poisonous with a probability of 20%. A mushroom that is not red is poisonous with a probability of 5%. What is the probability that a poisonous mushroom in the forest is red? *50%*

CHAPTER 11

Automated Decision Aids

Understanding Disuse and Designing for Trust, with Implications for Financial Planning

Jason S. McCarley, PhD
Oregon State University

By the mid-1700s, the emerging discipline of statistics had much to offer the insurance industry (Howie, 2002). Putting the theory of probability to use, thinkers had created tables of mortality risk and, based on those, had produced mathematically informed pricing schemes for annuities and insurance. But the insurers were not convinced. Among other objections, they believed that judgments about a customer's health and life expectancy required insight and sophisticated analysis that only they could provide (Daston, 1988).

> The broad experience and fine judgment of the professional, they argued, could not be replaced by equations and numerical prescriptions. The decision, on the basis of health, age, and occupation, whether or not a particular individual was appropriate for coverage required nice judgments that could not be supplanted by the blind average of a demographic table. (Howie, 2002, p. 18)

With hindsight, the notion that anyone in the business of insurance would scorn actuarial data is preposterous. The ethos of the early insurers' discomfort with statistical tables, however, persists. Decades of empirical research have confirmed the twin lessons inherent in the insurers' story: Human decision-makers often underperform statistical aids or rules. But human decision-makers often trust themselves more, nonetheless.

One modern manifestation of this phenomenon comes in the domain of human–automation interaction (Parasuraman & Riley, 1997; Wickens &

Dixon, 2007), and in particular, human interaction with automated or computerized decision aids. Improvements in sensory technology and data-processing algorithms have made computer systems into sophisticated assistants in domains such as air traffic control (Wickens, Mavor, Parasuraman, & McGee, 1998), combat identification (Wang, Jamieson, & Hollands, 2009), and forensic accounting (Dowling & Leech, 2007). Very frequently, though, the benefits that such aids present are disappointing: Mistrust causes users to disregard or downplay the automated aid's advice, and the resulting performance is suboptimal. As automated advising services—*robo-advisors*—become more sophisticated and widespread (Kitces, 2016; Wessel, 2015), financial planning may be the next domain in which this decision-making bias manifests.

MECHANICAL VERSUS HOLISTIC JUDGMENT

Much of our decision-making, big and small, is probabilistic: The information we have is incomplete or imperfect, and the outcome of the decision is uncertain. Statistical data on reliability and resale value may tell us that the car we are buying is good, for example, but if our luck is bad, we can end up with a lemon nonetheless. Making probabilistic decisions, our success rate is limited by the quality of information on which we base our judgment. In the worst cases—predicting coin flips or picking lottery numbers, for instance—our decisions are guesses. In better cases—selecting job applicants or predicting the weekend weather, perhaps—our decisions can be better than chance even if they are not 100% accurate. Because we cannot usually achieve perfect accuracy, our goal instead is just to do the best we can. The measure by which we judge performance will depend on the context. In some cases, our goal will be to maximize the long-run average payoff, or expected value, of our decisions. In other cases, the goal may be to be minimize the risk of a major loss (Berger, 1985; Wald, 1950). In other cases, we may be guided by other goals still.

Psychologists studying decision-making have contrasted two approaches to making probabilistic decisions (Dawes, Faust, & Meehl, 1989; Meehl, 1954). One of these is called *clinical* or *holistic*, and the other *actuarial*, *statistical*, or *mechanical*. (For consistency, we will stick with the labels *holistic* and *mechanical*.) A decision-maker using the holistic approach "combines or processes information in his or her head" (Dawes et al., 1989, p. 1668), "using informal, subjective methods" (Grove, Zald, Lebow, Snitz, & Nelson, 2000, p. 19). In other words, holistic decisions are made with "the gut." Mechanical decisions are formalized, and "the human judge is eliminated" (Dawes et al., 1989, p. 1668). Mechanical decision methods include "statistical prediction . . .

actuarial prediction . . . and what we may call algorithmic prediction" (Grove et al., 2000, p. 19).

Which method is to be preferred? Meehl (1954) tallied results from roughly two dozen studies that, at the time, had addressed this question by comparing the accuracy of human, holistic decision-makers to the accuracy of statistical techniques. One study, he concluded, favored holistic judgment (though not very convincingly). Of the rest, half were indifferent between holistic and mechanical methods, and half favored mechanical methods. Later meta-analyses, mathematically summarizing several decades' worth of subsequent research, reached similar conclusions (Ægisdóttir et al., 2006; Grove et al., 2000). About half of the studies reviewed favored mechanical prediction methods, almost half showed similar performance between mechanical and holistic methods, and only a few favored holistic methods. On average, the advantage for mechanical methods was modest but statistically significant (Spengler, 2013), though it may be much larger in particular contexts, for example, in personnel selection and academic admissions (Kuncel, Klieger, Connelly, & Ones, 2013).

More important, the reviews by Meehl and colleagues (Dawes et al., 1989; Meehl, 1954), Grove et al. (2000), and Ægisdóttir et al. (2006) considered only studies in which the human decision-makers were provided at least as much information as the statistical method. In fact, the human decision-makers' relative performance declined when the humans were provided more information than the mechanical techniques (Ægisdóttir et al., 2006; Grove et al., 2000). This means that the advantage for the mechanical techniques comes from the manner in which they use or combine informational cues. Holistic decisions tend to be highly inconsistent (Dawes & Corrigan, 1974), and are subject to a variety of cognitive biases (Dawes et al., 1989). Once they have been developed and validated, in contrast, mechanical techniques treat data with perfect consistency, "and conclusions rest solely on empirically established relations between data and the condition or event of interest" (Dawes et al., 1989, p. 1668).

Meehl (1996) acknowledged that the overall advantage for mechanical decision strategies over holistic strategies does not imply that mechanical strategies are superior in every context. He also pointed out that a mechanical strategy that is reliable on average may fail under outlier circumstances, when the conditions under which the strategy was developed are violated in an unexpected way. Others have noted that even where mechanical decision methods are available, a human might be needed to help implement them. For example, a person may be needed to conduct interviews and code the results for input to a statistical procedure (Dawes et al., 1989), or to choose and operationalize the criterion variable that the mechanical decision strategy is meant to predict (Spengler, 2013). Such constraints mean that in many contexts, it may be impossible to take the human decision-maker completely out of the decision-making loop. But, where practicable, mechanical decision strategies seem generally preferable to holistic strategies.

ALGORITHM AVERSION AND AUTOMATION DISUSE

Thus, mechanical decision strategies match or outperform human decision-makers' holistic strategies, but the human decision-maker nonetheless needs to remain in the decision-making loop. A seemingly obvious solution to this conflict is to provide the human with a mechanical procedure or system to assist her. The assistant can be as simple as a rule or arithmetic formula (e.g., Åstebro & Elhedhli, 2006), but often takes the form of an electronic or automated decision aid, such as a computer-aided medical diagnostic system (e.g., Eadie, Taylor, & Gibson, 2012) or a machine learning algorithm for detecting financial statement fraud (Perols, 2011). A familiar example is the spellcheck function that is common in word processing software.

Parasuraman, Sheridan, and Wickens (2000) proposed a taxonomy of ways in which an automated aid might assist a human operator. For present purposes, we can reduce their taxonomy to three broad categories of function:

1. The aid informs when it draws attention to potentially important information, or when it summarizes, integrates, or analyzes information for the user. Spellcheck informs a writer, for instance, when it underlines unrecognized words.
2. The aid counsels when it recommends a course of action. Spellcheck counsels a writer, for example, when it recommends a different spelling for an unrecognized word.
3. The aid acts when it selects and carries out an action by itself; the aid's choice of action is implemented unless the user intercedes to override or reverse it. Spellcheck acts when it automatically changes the spelling of a word it does not recognize.

Respectively, these three categories of function entail increasing levels of information processing and responsibility for the aid.

Intuitively, the benefits of a decision-making aid seem obvious. In practice, unfortunately, decision-making aids often do the human decision-maker little good. Why? The problem is simply that, upon learning that the aid is good but not perfect, the human user abandons it or begins to downplay its advice. Parasuraman and Riley (1997) named this pattern of behavior *disuse*, and Dietvorst and colleagues (Dietvorst, Simmons, & Massey, 2015) describe it as *algorithm aversion*.

The phenomenon of decision-aid disuse has long been recognized (e.g., Arkes, Dawes, & Christensen, 1986; Goldberg, 1968), but data from Dietvorst et al. (2015) illustrate the effect dramatically. Participants were asked to imagine themselves as admissions officers for an MBA program. Their task was to predict each applicant's success (percentile ranking within his or her cohort) in the program based on a set of variables including test scores, undergraduate GPA, and work experience. Participants were also informed that a statistical model, "put together by thoughtful analysis" (p. 11), was available to rank the graduates, as well.

Next, participants in different experimental groups completed a series of practice trials that provided them with different levels of exposure to the statistical model. In one condition, the participants performed 15 practice rankings by themselves, receiving feedback after each one. In another condition, the participants saw the aid make 15 practice rankings, again with feedback. In a third condition, the participants and the model both made the practice rankings, allowing the participants a direct comparison between their own performance and the model's. In a fourth condition, the control, practice trials were omitted entirely.

After the practice trials, participants each made "official" rankings for each of 10 new applicants, performing the task by themselves. In this phase of the experiment, the participants were informed that they would be rewarded for their accuracy, earning $1 for each ranking that fell within 5 points of the applicant's true score.

Finally, the participants were offered a surprise choice: They could receive their financial compensation either based on their own performance, or based on the performance of the statistical model. Their choices served as the measure of disuse.

As expected, the model outperformed the human judges, meaning that on average the participants would have earned more money by relying on the model's predictions instead of their own. What did they do? Of those participants who had not seen the model perform during the practice trials—that is, those in the control group and those who had practiced the task by themselves—roughly two-thirds (wisely) deferred to the model to determine their rewards. But of those who had seen the model in the practice trials, only one-quarter deferred to the model. In other words, the majority of participants who had seen that the model was imperfect opted not to rely on it, even when they knew its judgments were more accurate than their own, and even when the decision to disuse the model cost them money. These effects imply that participants approach a decision aid with a "perfect automation" or "perfect algorithm" schema (Dzindolet, Pierce, Beck, & Dawe, 2003), whereby they assume a priori that the aid's judgments will be near 100% accurate. When their expectations of a perfect algorithm are violated, they abandon the aid.

In Dietvorst et al. (2015), notably, participants were faced with an all-or-nothing choice, to rely on themselves or rely on the model. In other scenarios, human judges may be allowed to combine their judgments with the decision aid's in a more collaborative manner. In these cases, too, disuse is evident. For example, one experiment (Bartlett & McCarley, 2017) asked participants to perform a visual judgment task with or without the assistance of an automated aid. A cover story asked participants to imagine they were scientists sorting geological samples into categories based on appearance. The stimuli were random patterns of orange and blue dots, and the participants' task in each trial was to judge which color was dominant. On some blocks of trials, the participants were assisted by a 93% reliable computerized aid that assessed the most likely color. On average, the human judges were 86% reliable by themselves, and had they used the aid in a statistically optimal way, they would have achieved an accuracy rate of over 97%. Instead, they appeared to disuse the aid's advice, and achieved a mean assisted accuracy of only 90%. The human judges combined with the aid performed worse than the aid by itself (Bartlett & McCarley, 2017).

Other studies have reported similar results (e.g., Mayer, 2001). As one particularly shocking example, several studies have found that employee and student selection committees are no better, and can even be worse, at assessing candidates based on unstructured interviews than based on a statistical formulas alone (Dana, Dawes, & Peterson, 2013; DeVaul et al., 1987). Unstructured interviews, that is, can actually make it more difficult for assessors to distinguish good applicants from bad ones. But assessors imagine the interviews to be highly informative and insist on them, nonetheless (Dana et al., 2013).

Researchers have suggested a number of reasons that decision-makers might opt to disuse an aid even if it could improve their performance (Dietvorst et al., 2015, p. 290). Among these are the notion that statistical models ignore qualitative data and case-by-case context (Grove & Meehl, 1996), and the idea that the human operator has an ethical responsibility for self-reliance (an idea that is particularly ironic; ethical considerations in medicine, business, and other high-consequence domains surely place a higher value on making good decisions than on making bad decisions in a self-reliant manner) (Dawes, 1979). Research on human interaction with automated aids, though, has focused much of its attention on the role of trust in explaining automation disuse.

TRUST IN AUTOMATED SYSTEMS

Users often treat computers as social agents, inferring personality characteristics from their behaviors, treating them with politeness, demonstrating and expecting reciprocity in interactions (Nass & Moon, 2000). Recognizing this tendency to humanize technology, researchers have adopted the construct of trust to understand human users' willingness to depend on automated decision aids (Lee & See, 2004). A central aspect of interpersonal interactions, trust "may be the single most important ingredient for the development and maintenance of happy, well-functioning relationships" between people (Simpson, 2007, p. 264), and it appears to play a similar role in regulating users' interactions with electronic assistants, including, presumably, automated financial advisors.

Summarizing the views of other theorists, Lee and See (2004, p. 54) define trust as "the attitude that an agent will help achieve an individual's goals in a situation characterized by uncertainty and vulnerability." The opportunity for trust thus exists when one agent is dependent on another to avoid loss or achieve something of value (Deutsch, 1958; Mayer, Davis, & Schoorman, 1995; Simpson, 2007), circumstances that most certainly characterize the nonexpert seeking financial planning advice. Terming trust an attitude implies that it is a psychological disposition or orientation, rather than a form of behavior in and of itself. In the context of human–automation interaction, this distinction implies that users may sometimes choose not to use a decision aid even if they trust it, or may choose to use it despite mistrust (Parasuraman & Riley, 1997). On average, though, automation use will increase with trust (Lee & Moray, 1992, 1994; Muir, 1987; Muir & Moray, 1996), and trust should therefore be calibrated accurately against the automated aid's true reliability; misuse results when trust underestimates reliability (Lee & See, 2004). As the findings discussed earlier indicate, unfortunately, errors from an automated aid seem to reduce trust far out of proportion to their true frequency.

Organizational theorists have proposed three factors underlying interpersonal trust, which Mayer et al. (1995) label ability, benevolence, and integrity. Here, ability is the trusted person's capacity to aid the trustor, benevolence is the trusted person's good will toward the trustor, and integrity is the trusted person's commitment to behave in a way that the trustor finds ethical. Adapting this tripartite model, Lee and Moray (1992; Lee & See, 2004) posit three analogous factors to explain trust in an automated aid: performance, process, and purpose. Performance, akin to ability, refers to the aid's reliability. Simply, how accurate are its judgments and behaviors? An aid that is more reliable, of course, is more likely to be trusted. Process refers to the aid's operations. How does it work? Trust tends to be higher when operators understand how an aid works, and why it might occasionally make errors (Dzindolet, Peterson, Pomranky, Pierce, & Beck, 2003). Purpose, akin to benevolence and integrity, refers the aid's intended use. What was it designed to do? Trust is higher when the user knows the aid is being deployed in a way consistent with the designer's intent.

DEVELOPING TRUST

The inclination to trust is in part a trait, an enduring personal characteristic that differs among individuals (Rotter, 1980) and manifests in peoples' willingness to use an automated decision aid (Merritt & Ilgen, 2008). Individual differences in propensity to trust, however, are of the most consequence at the outset of a user's interactions with an aid. Thereafter, the user's trust is gradually shaped by experience with and of the aid itself. Trust in an automated aid thus shifts from being dominated by the user's generalized propensity to trust to being dominated by the user's history with that particular aid (Merrit & Ilgen, 2008).

Not surprisingly, the aid's reliability has a strong influence on the user's trust (Lee & Moray, 1992; Muir & Moray, 1996). Trust appears to grow slowly (Lee & Moray, 1992; Masalonis & Parasuraman, 1999; Muir & Moray, 1996), an effect that suggests people may come to the automated aid with the expectation it will perform perfectly (Dzindolet et al., 2003), but that they reserve trust while they test that expectation over time. In contrast, trust drops steeply following a misjudgment from aid (Lee & Moray, 1992), in particular if that misjudgment induces the operator to commit an error. A misjudgment from the aid has a smaller effect on trust if the operator is able to detect and compensate for it without committing an error (Lee & Moray, 1994; Masalonis & Parasuraman, 1999). This implies, for instance, that an automated financial planning advisor that makes an unsound recommendation may retain trust so long as a human advisor, or the clients themselves, intervene to keep the recommendation from being put into action.

However, there is reason to wonder if the normal process by which trust develops through gradual interactions with an aid will manifest in people's interactions with an automated financial planner. In experiments that have studied the development of trust, participants have generally received performance feedback within the course of a few minutes (e.g., Lee & Moray, 1992; Muir & Moray, 1996), allowing them to know quickly whether they have been led by the aid into committing an error. In financial planning, clients and planners may wait months, years, or even decades before knowing whether their judgments were sound or not. Along the way, moreover, probabilistic fluctuations in outcomes may provide spurious or misleading feedback. A financial plan that is sound in the long run may sometimes look ill-considered on a day-to-day or month-to-month basis. All of this means that users may not have opportunity to develop trust in an automated financial planner by observing its performance over the short term, the way they might with other sorts of automated decision aids.

In cases like this, trust may be determined less by direct observation of the system's reliability than by other aspects of context and system design. In contrast to the rational or analytic processes that determine trust based on an understanding of system reliability and the costs versus benefits of potential decision outcomes, these alternative influences are cognitive, social, or affective (Kramer, 1999; Lee & See, 2004). They include the following:

Transparency: As discussed, process has been identified as a basis of trust. Accordingly, decision-makers are more likely to trust and depend on an automated decision aid if they are given an explanation of how it works, and why it might occasionally err in its judgments (Dzindolet et al., 2003). This explanation does not have to be detailed or highly technical, just informative enough to let the user understand that occasional errors from the aid are not blunders or breakdowns, but are expected and have predictable causes. Trust may likewise improve if the aid briefly explains its decisions as it renders them (Muir, 1987), again keeping the user apprised that occasional misjudgments are not gross failures. An aid that operates in a way that is open and understandable to the user is said to be transparent (Hoff & Bashir, 2015).

Interface: Although the influence of interface design on trust has not been well-studied in the domain of automation use, studies of online retailing and banking have found that users express more trust in sites that are usable and aesthetically appealing (Beldad, de Jong, & Steehouder, 2010; Kim & Moon, 1998; Koufaris & Hampton-Sosa, 2004; Wang & Emurian, 2004). For instance, users in one study (Kim & Moon, 1998) perceived a website as more trustworthy if its interface used cool, dim colors than if it used warm or bright colors. Some research has suggested that cosmetic characteristics and convenience of an online retail site may have a larger influence on purchase intentions than do statements assuring privacy and security (Belanger, Hiller, & Smith, 2002). It seems likely that interface characteristics will also shade users' trust in an automated aid. An interface design that is confusing or difficult to use might be especially degrading to user trust, as it can cause the user to commit technical errors (Flavián, Guinalíu, & Gurrea, 2006). The inconvenience of navigating the interface can therefore be compounded by the costs of making and recovering from mistakes.

It is important to remember that the aesthetic characteristics that encourage trust may vary across cultures or contexts. The intensity of responses to aesthetic qualities of an interface can differ as well across demographic groups, with older and higher income users reporting less concern with ornamental visual aspects of interface design than other do users of other demographics (Lightner, 2003). Age-related sensory losses, however, may make older users more sensitive to functional sensory characteristics of the interface, such as a high-contrast, legible font.

Reputation: Trust in people and organizations is sensitive to second-hand knowledge shared by third parties (Burt & Knez, 1996). A customer's initial trust in an online retailer, for example, is correlated with the company's reputation (Koufaris & Hampton-Sosa, 2004; Kuan & Bock, 2007). Trust in the online component of a bricks-and-clicks retailer is determined in part by the reputation of its bricks-and-mortar counterpart (Kuan & Bock, 2007). It seems probable, analogously, that the reputation of the financial planning firm or individual within the firm will help determine a client's initial trust in an online or robo-advisor.

COMPLACENCY

Our attention so far has been on the phenomenon of disuse, the tendency to ignore or downplay advice from an algorithm or automated aid. The converse problem is also possible, though. When an algorithm or decision-aid performs without mistakes for a long time, users can come to overestimate its true reliability and accept its judgments complacently. If and when the aid eventually makes a misjudgment, then the user can be easily led into committing an error (Bahner, Hüper, & Manzey, 2008; Molloy & Parasuraman, 1996; Parasuraman & Manzey, 2010; Parasuraman, Molloy, & Singh, 1993; Wickens, Clegg, Vieane, & Sebok, 2015).

To counteract complacency, system designers can introduce occasional automation errors during training, when users are learning to interact with the aid (Bahner et al., 2008). Having been exposed to errors from the automation during the training period, users will be more vigilant monitoring for misjudgments thereafter. (Occasional bouts of re-training may be needed to maintain vigilance; cf. Wolfe et al., 2007.) Of course, exposure to errors from the aid during trying risks the possibility of mistrust and disuse. Systems developers and policymakers must decide how best to balance the risk of complacency against the costs of disuse.

CONCLUSION

Like the insurers of the 18th century, modern decision-makers overestimate our capacity for thoughtful, holistic judgments. What feels like nuance and expert insight is often inconsistency and caprice. Mechanical decision systems, from simple rules to sophisticated electronic aids, can push our decision-making closer to optimal, but only if we calibrate trust in them appropriately.

Automated advisors are unlikely to ever take humans out of the loop in a domain such as financial planning (Kitces, 2016), but designed and implemented with the psychology of trust in mind, they may make human planners more valuable to clients than ever. Future research exploring the partnership between human and robot in the domain of financial planning could enable practitioners to make financial planning services accessible to a broader segment of the market. Using experimental methods within contextual robo-advising sites and applications will help both practitioners and researchers better understand client behavior.

REFERENCES

Ægisdóttir, S., White, M. J., Spengler, P. M., Maugherman, A. S., Anderson, L. A., Cook, R. S., et al. (2006). The meta-analysis of clinical judgment project: Fifty-six years of accumulated research on clinical versus statistical prediction. *The Counseling Psychologist, 34*, 341–382.

Arkes, H. R., Dawes, R. M., & Christensen, C. (1986). Factors influencing the use of a decision rule in a probabilistic task. *Organizational Behavior and Human Decision Processes, 37*, 93–110.

Åstebro, T., & Elhedhli, S. (2006). The effectiveness of simple decision heuristics: Forecasting commercial success for early-stage ventures. *Management Science, 52*, 395–409.

Bahner, J. E., Hüber, A.-D., & Manzey, D. (2008). Misuse of automated decision aids: Complacency, automation bias and the impact of training experience. *International Journal of Human-Computer Studies, 66*, 688–699.

Bartlett, M. L., & McCarley, J. S. (2017). Benchmarking aided decision making in a signal detection task. *Human Factors, 59*, 881–900.

Belanger, F., Hiller, J. S., & Smith, W. J. (2002). Truthworthiness in electronic commerce: The role of privacy, security, and site attributes. *Journal of Strategic Information Systems, 11*, 245–270.

Beldad, A., de Jong, M., & Steelhouder, M. (2016). How shall I trust the faceless and the intangible? A literature review on the antecedents of online trust. *Computers in Human Behavior, 26*, 857–869.

Berger, J. O. (1985). *Statistical decision theory: Foundations, concepts, and methods* (2nd ed.). New York: Springer-Verlag.

Burt, R. S., & Knez, M. (1996). Trust and third-party gossip. In R. M. Kramer & T. R. Tyler (Eds.), *Trust in organizations: Frontiers of theory and research* (pp. 68–89). Thousand Oaks, CA: Sage.

Dana, J., Dawes, R., & Peterson, N. (2013). Belief in the unstructured interview: The persistence of an illusion. *Judgment and Decision Making, 8*(5), 512.

Daston, L. J. (1988). Fitting numbers to the world: The case of probability theory. In W. Aspray & P. Kitcher (Eds.), *History and philosophy of modern mathematics*. Minneapolis: University of Minnesota Press.

Dawes, R. M. (1979). The robust beauty of improper linear models in decision making. *American Psychologist, 34*, 571–582.

Dawes, R. M., & Corrigan, B. (1974). Linear models in decision making. *Psychological Bulletin, 81*, 95–106.

Dawes, R. M., Faust, D., & Meehl, P. E. (1989). Clinical versus actuarial judgment. *Science, 243,* 1668–1674.

Deutsch, M. (1958). Trust and suspicion. *Journal of Conflict Resolution, 2,* 265–279.

DeVaul, R. A., Jervey, F., Chappell, J. A., Caver, P., Short, B., & O'Keefe, S. (1987). Medical school performance of initially rejected students. *JAMA, 257,* 47–51.

Dietvorst, B. J., Simmons, J. P., & Massey, C. (2015). Algorithm aversion: People erroneously avoid algorithms after seeing them err. *Journal of Experimental Psychology: General, 144,* 114–126.

Dowling, C., & Leech, S. (2007). Audit support systems and decision aids: Current practice and opportunities for future research. *International Journal of Accounting Information Systems, 8,* 92–116.

Dzindolet, M. T., Peterson, S. A., Pomranky, R. A., Pierce, L. G., & Beck, H. P. (2003). The role of trust in automation reliance. *International Journal of Human-Computer Studies, 58,* 697–718.

Eadie, L. H., Taylor, P., & Gibson, A. P. (2012). A systematic review of computer-assisted diagnosis in diagnostic cancer imaging. *European Journal of Radiology, 81,* e70–e76.

Flavián, C., Guinalíu, M., & Gurrea, R. (2006). The role played by perceived usability, satisfaction, and consumer trust on website loyalty. *Information & Management, 43,* 1–14.

Goldberg, L. R. (1968). Simple models or simple processes: Some research on clinical judgments. *American Psychologist, 23,* 483–496.

Grove, W. M., Zald, D. H., Lebow, B. S., Snitz, B. E., & Nelson, C. (2000). Clinical versus mechanical prediction: A meta-analysis. *Psychological Assessment, 12,* 19–30.

Hoff, K. A., & Bashir, M. (2015). Trust in automation: Integrating empirical evidence on factors that influence trust. *Human Factors, 57,* 407–434.

Howie, D. (2002). *Interpreting probability: Controversy and developments n the early twentieth century.* Cambridge, UK: Cambridge University Press.

Kim, J., & Moon, J. Y. (1998). Designing towards emotional usability in customer interfaces—trustworthiness of cyber-banking system interfaces. *Interacting with Computers, 10,* 1–29.

Kitces, M. E. (2016). The future of financial planning in the digital age. *CFA Institute Conference Proceedings Quarterly, 33,* 17–22.

Koufaris, M., & Hampton-Sosa, W. (2004). The development of initial trust in an online company by new customers. *Information & Management, 41,* 377–397.

Kuan, H.-H., & Bock, G.-W. (2007). Trust transference in brick and click retailers: An investigation of the before-online-visit phase. *Information & Management, 44,* 175–187.

Kuncel, N. R., Klieger, D. M., Connelly, B. S., & Ones, D. S. (2013). Mechanical versus clinical data combination in selection and admissions decisions: A meta-analysis. *Journal of Applied Psychology, 98,* 1060–1072.

Lee, J. D., & Moray, N. (1992). Trust, control strategies and allocation of function in human-machine systems. *Ergonomics, 35,* 1243–1270.

Lee, J. D., & Moray, N. (1994). Trust, self-confidence, and operators' adaptation to automation. *International Journal of Human-Computer Studies, 40,* 153–184.

Lee, J. D., & See, K. A. (2004). Trust in automation: Designing for appropriate reliance. *Human Factors, 46,* 50–80.

Lightner, N. J. (2003). What users want in e-commerce deisgn: Effects of age, education, and income. *Ergonomics, 46,* 153–168.

Masalonis, A. J., & Parasuraman, R. (1999). Trust as a construct for evaluation of automated aids: Past and future theory and research. *Proceedings of the Human Factors and Ergonomics Society Annual Meeting, 43,* 184–188.

Mayer, R. C., Davis, J. H., & Schoorman, F. D. (1995). An integrative model of organizational trust. *Academy of Management Review, 30,* 709–734.

McKnight, D. H., Cummings, L. L., & Chervany, N. L. (1998). Initial trust formation in new organizational relationships. *Academy of Management Review, 23,* 473–490.

Meehl, P. E. (1954). *Clinical vs. statistical prediction: A theoretical analysis and a review of the evidence.* Minneapolis: University of Minnesota Press.

Meehl, P. E. (1997). Preface to the 1996 printing. In P. E. Meehl, *Clinical vs. statistical prediction: A theoretical analysis and a review of the evidence* (pp. v–xii). Minneapolis: University of Minnesota Press.

Merritt, S. M., & Ilgen, D. R. (2008). Not all trust is created equal: Dispositional and history-based trust in human-automation interactions. *Human Factors, 50,* 194–210.

Molloy, R., & Parasuraman, R. (1996). Monitoring an automated system for a single failure: Vigilance and task complexity effects. *Human Factors, 38,* 311–322.

Muir, B. M. (1987). Trust between humans and machines, and the design of decision aids. *International Journal of Man-Machine Studies, 27,* 527–539.

Muir, B. M. (1994). Trust in automation: Part I: Theoretical issues in the study of trust and human intervention in automated systems. *Ergonomics, 37,* 1905–1922.

Muir, B. M., & Moray, N. (1996). Trust in automation. Part II: Experimental studies of trust and human intervention in a process control simulation. *Ergonomics, 39,* 429–460.

Nass, C., & Moon, Y. (2000). Machines and mindlessness: Social responses to computers. *Journal of Social Issues, 56,* 81–103.

Parasuraman, R., & Manzey, D. H. (2010). Complacency and bias in human use of automation: An attentional integration. *Human Factors, 52,* 381–410.

Parasuraman, R., Molloy, R., & Singh, J. (1993). Performance consequences of automation-induced "complacency". *International Journal of Aviation Psychology, 3,* 1–23.

Parasuraman, R., & Riley, V. (1997). Humans and automation: Use, misuse, disuse, abuse. *Human Factors, 39,* 230–253.

Parasuraman, R., Sheridan, T. B., & Wickens, C. D. (2000). A model of types and levels of human interaction with automation. *IEEE Transactions on Systems, Man, and Cybernetics—Part A: Systems and Humans, 30,* 286–297.

Perols, J. (2011). Financial statement fraud detection: An analysis of statistical and machine learning algorithms. *Auditing: A Journal of Practice & Theory, 30,* 19–50.

Rotter, J. B. (1980). Interpersonal trust, trustworthiness, and gullibility. *American Psychologist, 35,* 1–7.

Seong, Y., & Bisantz, A. M. (2008). The impact of cognitive feedback on judgment performance and trust with decision aids. *International Journal of Industrial Ergonomics, 38,* 608–625.

Simpson, J. A. (2007). Psychological foundations of trust. *Current Directions in Psychological Science, 16,* 264–268.

Spengler, P. M. (2013). Clinical versus mechanical prediction. In J. R. Graham, J. A. Naglieri, & I. B. Weiner (Eds.) *Handbook of psychology: Assessment psychology* (pp. 26–49). Hoboken, NJ: John Wiley & Sons.

Wald, A. (1950). *Statistical decision functions.* New York: John Wiley & Sons.

Wang, L., Jamieson, G. A., & Hollands, J. G. (2009). Trust and reliance on an automated combat identification system. *Human Factors: The Journal of the Human Factors and Ergonomics Society, 51*(3), 281–291. https://doi .org/10.1177/0018720809338842.

Wang, Y. D., & Emurian, H. H. (2005). An overview of online trust: Concepts, elements, and implications. *Computers in Human Behavior, 21,* 105–125.

Wessel, R. (2015, March/April). The algorithm who advised me. *CFA Institute Magazine, 26,* 37–38.

Wickens, C. D., Clegg, B., Vieane, A. Z., & Sebok, A. (2015). Complacency and automation bias in the use of imperfect automation. *Human Factors, 57,* 728–739.

Wickens, C. D., & Dixon, S. R. (2007). The benefits of imperfect diagnostic automation: A synthesis of the literature. *Theoretical Issues in Ergonomics Science, 8,* 201–212.

Wickens, C. D., Mavor, M., Parasuraman, R., & McGee, J. (1998). *The future of air traffic control: Human operators and automation.* Washington, DC: National Academies Press.

Wolfe, J. M., Horowitz, T. S., Van Wert, M. J., Kenner, N. M., Place, S. S., & Kibbi, N. (2007). Low target prevalence is a stubborn source of errors in visual search tasks. *Journal of Experimental Psychology: General, 136,* 623–638. doi:10.1037/0096-3445.136.4.623.

Self-Determination Theory and Self-Efficacy in Financial Planning

Charles R. Chaffin, EdD
CFP Board Center for Financial Planning

The motivation that we have to do something can have a great impact on our desire and resolve to do it. If your motivation to enroll in a course at a local community college is driven purely by your own curiosity and enjoyment, it will be a different experience than if someone required you to enroll. Your motivation does not change the professor or content of the course, but it can alter your level of engagement and even your resolve when challenges arise. Intrinsic motivation, your innate desire to accomplish a task, can fuel your willingness and attention throughout each stage of the process. Extrinsic motivation, motivation driven by external factors usually from some form of an award, can be useful to encourage someone to complete a task initially, but has many more limitations than intrinsic motivation. Related, if one perceives that she is successful at performing a certain task, she is more likely to not only elect to perform the same task in the future, but will likely persevere if challenges arise. We tend to choose tasks and challenges that we think we can complete.

This chapter focuses on two important elements associated with personal motivation: self-determination theory and self-efficacy. Although these psychological constructs emanate from different fields of study, they are rooted in the discovery of how and why people take on different tasks and can have some element of prediction on the individual's success in completing that task in the future. We will also explore the implications of both of these phenomena for financial planning research and practice.

SELF-DETERMINATION THEORY

Self-determination theory is a theory of motivation that focuses on our innate psychological needs, specifically our motivation without external influences (Ryan & Deci, 1999). Inherent within the context of self-determination theory is intrinsic motivation, our innate desire to complete a given task. According to Ryan and Deci (2000), all of us have innate psychological needs relative to competence, relatedness, and autonomy. Competence is defined as our desire to control the outcome as well as experience mastery of a given task. Relatedness is our desire to interact with, as well as be connected to and care for, others. Autonomy is the desire to be the causal agent of one's own life. Each of these three traits, all considered vital to health and well-being, are not acquired or learned, but are innate and universal to all human kind. In many cases, extrinsic motivation to perform a given task can actually undermine one's intrinsic motivation (Deci, 1971). Relative to financial planning, it can be that clients want to achieve competence through control and mastery over their financial well-being; relatedness by caring for others through preparing for the financial future of their parents and children; and autonomy in controlling their own life goals that are consistent with their long-term dreams.

Within healthcare, self-determination theory has broad applications in helping patients meet short- and long-term goals. Williams, Grow, Freedman, Ryan, and Deci (1996) examined the success of individuals enrolled in a weight-loss program for morbidly obese patients. They found that individuals who had a higher level of autonomy, and thus a higher level of intrinsic motivation, led to a lower body-mass index and long-term success in losing and keeping weight off. The resolve of the patients was likely higher because the individuals sensed a higher level of control over their lives relative to weight loss.

Within education, much research has espoused the importance of intrinsic motivation and the innate desire for students to explore and learn on their own. Extrinsic motivation, or a controlled motivation, can harm the student's long-term interest in a given subject or exercise. As Alfie Kohn (1993) writes: ". . . rewards and punishments are not opposites at all; they are two sides of the same coin. And it is a coin that does not buy very much" (p. 50). It is therefore, the role of the educator to facilitate intrinsic motivation through the creation of an environment that allows for competence, relatedness, and autonomy. It is not necessarily that students will be intrinsically motivated to complete each and every assignment, but the teacher can provide an environment that feeds these three innate psychological needs in order for the student to be successful.

Why do financial planning clients seek a practitioner's services? If intrinsic motivation can lead to better decision-making on the part of the client, then it is likely not enough for the planner to merely ask in an initial discovery session with a client about their goals. Within these three psychological constructs, the planner may want to consider the following:

Competence: Relative to self-determination theory, competence can take the form of the planner constantly reminding the client that she or he can achieve mastery over her financial well-being, perhaps when there is some challenging life event that may threaten the long-term financial goals of the client. Any action that the planner can take to assist the client with the perception of confidence that she is making decisions that are congruent with accomplishing her long-term financial goals. This could include charts and data that indicate how her decisions have achieved progress toward her financial success.

Relatedness: Continually remind the client that their financial plan, and the decisions they make that impact the financial plan, impact their ability to care for the people closest to them. The spending habits and debt are not just numbers on the page and impact the client, but all of the people's futures that they have identified as important in their lives. It may be that as years go by, clients begin to separate the financial plan from their ultimate goals, leading to decisions that are inconsistent with the long-term approach established years ago. Reminding the client that these decisions will affect their grandson Jeffrey's college education is a great way to bring relatedness to the quantitative element of the financial plan.

Autonomy: Financial planners may want to continually remind the client that all aspects of the financial planning process facilitate the client being in control of their financial futures. Having choices, but not too many, as discussed in earlier chapters, can help the client feel as if she is free to choose her own goals. This notion of autonomy is a powerful tool for the profession of financial planning, providing intrinsic motivation for clients to work with financial planners. Essentially, the outcome of financial planning can be a feeling of competence, relatedness, and autonomy as the financial planner provides an environment that fuels this intrinsic motivation and thus enables the client to make better decisions that are consistent with the long-term financial plan.

The examples provided above about how the three basic psychological needs could exist in financial planning focus solely on verbal reminders. Financial planners are encouraged to consider other avenues for enabling clients to achieve these three needs beyond verbal feedback. Given the incorporation of technology into financial planning, are there ways to produce images and illustrations that help guide the client's behaviors to be consistent with their long-term financial goals? Practitioners may also want to consider ways to record the discovery sessions with their clients, where they learn about a client's financial situation and their goals and dreams, so to revisit those during challenging times in the client's financial life.

Future research relative to self-determination theory in financial planning should explore the impact of financial planning on the three intrinsic needs (competence, relatedness, autonomy) of the client. Does the perception of the value of a financial planner in the client's eyes rise or fall based upon satisfaction of these three, basic psychological needs? Experimental research could focus on the impacts of different verbal encouragements from the financial planner to the client as defined earlier in this chapter.

SELF-EFFICACY

We are motivated by a number of factors, certainly based upon our goals and interests, but also by our belief in how good we are at performing a certain task. Your belief in your own ability to be successful in a given task or task-setting is known as self-efficacy. Bandura (1994) defines self-efficacy as "people's beliefs about their capabilities to produce designated levels of performance that exercise influence over events that affect their lives" (p. 1). Self-efficacy is task-specific and not generalizable across multiple contexts. We can elect to complete a task where we have a high level of self-efficacy and conversely, we can elect not to perform a task where we have a low sense of self-efficacy. Self-efficacy is, to simplify, self-confidence within a given task environment (Kanter, 2006).

We have four main sources of self-efficacy (Bandura, 1994): First are mastery experiences, where past performance impacts one's beliefs regarding her or his effectiveness in a given task. If the past performance is viewed as poor, it can undermine self-efficacy. If someone sang karaoke for the first time at a local bar and it was perceived to have been a huge success, then the individual may be more likely to sing karaoke on a future occasion. Second, viewing others perform a task can lead to an individual's feeling that they, too, can perform that same task. If a student observes her peer successfully completing a difficult passage on the piano, she is more likely to try that passage herself. Third is social persuasion, where individuals are persuaded verbally by someone from within their social circle that they can successfully perform a given task. This notion is the element of encouragement to an individual from those closest to him that he has the ability to be successful at a given task or challenge. Family members might encourage a student to enroll in an advanced placement math course in high school, reminding her that she has the ability to be successful in the course. Finally, individuals rely upon their emotional and physical states during a given performance of a task, as they view reactions such as stress and fatigue as a negative representation of their ability to perform a task, lowering their self-efficacy. If one has sweaty palms and a high heart rate during a public speech, he might ascertain that he is not an effective public speaker and may perceive low self-efficacy relative to public speaking.

As Bandura (1982) notes, self-efficacy impacts performance in three ways: (1) the goals that individuals choose; (2) the amount of effort that individuals place into a given task; and (3) persistence in a given task when challenges or complexity arises.

There are essentially four different sources of self-efficacy: (1) actual performance of a given task; (2) the observation of others performing a given task; (3) verbal and nonverbal persuasion; and (4) emotional response and physiological responses to the performance of a given task. One who is experiencing anxiety may see himself as vulnerable and therefore experience a lower sense of self-efficacy. Obviously, the most powerful of the four is the actual performance of a given task. If one has past experience being successful at a given task, then they have a higher level of self-efficacy. If one has a history of trying and failing, then she will likely have a lower sense of self-efficacy.

The implications for financial planning clients with regard to self-efficacy are quite broad. Individuals within a variety of contexts set higher goals for themselves if they have a higher sense of self-efficacy. Therefore, it may be that clients with a higher sense of self-efficacy relative to their future financial well-being are more likely to set more ambitious retirement goals or perhaps learn more about options to provide more for their families. This high level of self-efficacy could lead to a higher level of engagement with their planner along with a higher vigilance of the factors that impact the factors that will affect their financial well-being.

Heckman and Grable (2011) suggest that there is a positive relationship between financial education and financial self-efficacy. Therefore, it is imperative for the profession to develop avenues to educate future generations of clients within both secondary and post-secondary education regarding basic elements of financial literacy. Further, self-efficacy may play a role for practitioners in working with current and prospective clients. How can the practitioner educate the client to take control of their financial well-being so that when challenges arise, they do not abandon the long-term financial plan? The implications of this work may be significant as the client's perceptions regarding the effectiveness of their financial planner may be impacted by their staying resolute regarding their actions and behaviors, particularly during difficult times.

Self-efficacy can predict the likelihood of an individual seeking a financial planner. Letkiewicz, Domian, Robinson, and Uborceva (2014) found that individuals with a high level of self-efficacy were more likely to seek a financial planner. The authors suggested that a society with a high level of self-efficacy may use financial planners more regularly. Related, Heckman and

Grable (2011) found that financial knowledge had a positive relationship with financial self-efficacy. Given the construct of self-efficacy where past performance plays an integral role, it seems plausible that financial literacy and financial planning client self-efficacy are interrelated. Education, whether during high school or undergraduate courses, could play a major part in helping build financial planning self-efficacy on the part of the future generation of financial planning clients. Regardless of method, from the perspective of self-efficacy research, the profession of financial planning has a vested interest in raising the level of financial self-efficacy of the general population.

Future research could help develop effective ways to measure financial self-efficacy, which could be used during client–planner interaction, as well as with the general population. Having this client data available could be useful in predicting whether clients are susceptible to decision-making that could negatively impact their long-term financial future.

Future research could also identify avenues for increasing the financial self-efficacy of the general population, particularly during both early education as well as during aspects of the client–planner engagement. Future research could also explore whether an increased level of financial self-efficacy does in fact assist clients during challenging life events that might negatively affect client decision-making.

The motivation of a client to both seek a financial planner as well as make decisions that are consistent with the long-term financial plan may be seriously impacted by intrinsic motivation. Our profession has a vested interest in providing an environment for current clients to feel a sense of competence, relatedness, and autonomy so that they can feel empowered both during client–planner meetings as well as during all of the time that they are away from the planner, when the life decisions occur that likely have the highest impact on meeting long-term financial goals. Having a population that has a high level of financial self-efficacy can not only provide for a better society with more financial literacy, it can also bring more clients to financial planning, as individuals view their long-term financial goals as accessible and want to better understand their options for the future.

REFERENCES

Bandura, A (1977). Self-efficacy: Toward a unifying theory of behavioral change. *Psychological Review, 84(2)*, 191–215. doi:10.1037/0033–295x.84.2.191.

Bandura, A. (1982). Self-efficacy mechanism in human agency. *American Psychologist, 37*, 122–147.

Bandura A. (1986). *Social foundations of thought and action: A social cognitive theory*. Englewood Cliffs, NJ: Prentice Hall.

Bandura, A. (1997). *Self-efficacy: The exercise of control*. New York: W. H. Freeman.

Deci, E. L. (1971). Effects of externally mediated rewards on intrinsic motivation. *Journal of Personality and Social Psychology, 18*, 105–115.

Heckman, S. J., & Grable, J. E. (2011). Testing the role of parental debt attitudes, student income, dependency status, and financial knowledge have in shaping financial self-efficacy among college students. *College Student Journal, 45*(1), 51–64.

Kanter, R. M. (2006). *Confidence: How winning and losing streaks begin and end.* New York: Crown Publishing.

Kohn, A. (1993). *Punished by rewards.* New York: Houghton Mifflin.

Letkiewicz, J. C., Domian, D. L., Robinson, C., & Uborceva, N. (2014). *Self-efficacy, financial stress, and the decision to seek professional financial planning help.* Presented at the Academy of Financial Services Meeting. Nashville, October.

Ryan, R. M., & Deci, E. L. (1999). Intrinsic and extrinsic motivations: Classic definitions and new directions. *Contemporary Education Psychology, 25*(1), 54–67.

Ryan, R. M., & Deci, E. L. (Eds.). (2000). Self-determination theory and the facilitation of intrinsic motivation, social development, and well-being. *American Psychologist, 55*, 68–78. doi: 10.1037/0003–066X.55.1.68.

Williams, G. C., Grow, V. M., Freedman, Z. R., Ryan, R. M., & Deci, E. L. (1996). Motivational predictors of weight loss and weight-loss maintenance. *Journal of Personality and Social Psychology, 70*, 115–126.

CHAPTER 13

Marriage and Family Therapy, Financial Therapy, and Client Psychology

Kristy Archuleta, PhD, and Sonya Britt-Lutter, PhD

Kansas State University

Have you ever felt like you heard what your partner said, but somehow still ended up in an argument about some financial manner? Or, maybe you have found yourself doing the exact opposite of your parents when it comes to spending versus savings. Maybe you have witnessed what seems like strange client behavior when discussing altering spending patterns in order to achieve retirement goals. Better yet, maybe you witnessed a client couple arguing about money in front of you. The emotions in the room became so intense that you did not know what to do. These are common occurrences that happen to most everyone and especially to financial professionals. When these situations happen, you have experienced the psychological and relational dimensions of money. To grasp the intersection of the psychological and relational aspects of money, this chapter introduces readers to marriage and family therapy, family systems theory, and financial therapy and extends the systemic focus of client psychology through application of financial therapy techniques. If you are a financial practitioner, these phenomena are probably familiar to you. However, helpful ways to understand the causes and ways to address these behaviors come out of the marriage and family therapy literature, which may be a new approach to you.

MARRIAGE AND FAMILY THERAPY

To understand the relational aspects of behavior, we look to the discipline of marriage and family therapy. Marriage and family therapy helps to describe client behavior from a family systems or relational perspective. It differs from other aspects of client psychology because the focus is on the influence of relational interactions in the development of behavior. Marriage and family therapy (MFT)—also known as couples and family therapy—is a discipline that grew out of psychiatry as early as the 1940s through the understanding that relational interactions among family members have an impact on individuals' mental health and well-being. Over the course of time, empirical evidence has supported the use of marriage and family therapy as effective treatment for a variety of mental health disorders and family functioning (Sprenkle, 2012) and as cost-effective (Crane & Christenson, 2012).

The American Association of Marriage and Family Therapy (AAMFT) described a "family's patterns of behavior as influences for individuals and therefore the family may need to be a part of the treatment plan. In marriage and family therapy, the unit of treatment isn't just the person—even if only a single person is interviewed—it is the set of relationships in which the person is imbedded" (http://www.aamft.org/iMIS15/AAMFT/Content/About_AAMFT/About_Marriage_and_Family_Therapists.aspx). In other words, marriage and family therapists focus on the interactions of the broader family system in order to explain individual behavior and treat presenting issues. Family is defined broadly to include long-term relationships that have an impact on an individual and may or may not be blood related.

Treatment Issues

According to the AAMFT, the federal government identifies MFT as a "core mental health profession." Other designated professions are psychiatry, psychology, social work, and psychiatric nursing. MFT therapists are trained to diagnose and treat a variety of issues from schizophrenia to generalized anxiety disorder to major depressive disorder to relational problems. While MFT therapists can diagnose mental disorders, their approach to treatment is different, including having an end in mind and utilizing family systems theory as a lens to view clients and how the relational dynamics are affecting them. Unlike some disciplines, MFT therapists have a goal that they should work themselves out of a job by helping the client(s) become self-sustaining without the constant dependence of a mental health professional.

MFT therapists utilize various therapeutic and theoretically grounded modalities in their work with clients. Examples of these therapy modalities include Bowenian family therapy, strategic family therapy, structural family therapy, collaborative language systems therapy, solution focused therapy, cognitive behavioral family therapy, Milan family systems therapy, MRI brief therapy, experiential family therapy, and emotion focused family therapy. It is beyond the scope of this chapter to describe each of these therapy modalities; however, at the center of each of these approaches is either family systems theory or the theory of cybernetics. While working with money is not a focus of MFT training, MFT therapists see financial problems and how money affects clients' behavior and interactions with one another all of the time in their work with clients. Unfortunately, MFT therapists are often considered to be money avoiders (Britt, Klontz, Tibbetts, & Leitz, 2015) and are afraid to talk about money specifically because they either do not feel comfortable or do not feel like they are knowledgeable enough about money to be helpful to their clients. As a result, the topic of money is treated as any other mental health issue or swept aside and not dealt with in the therapeutic process. Regardless, MFT therapists utilize a powerful lens (i.e., family systems theory) in which they seem to understand client behavior and modalities with which to change behavior.

FAMILY SYSTEMS THEORY

To understand marriage and family therapy or what is more commonly being referred to as couples and family therapy, a strong understanding of family systems theory is required. To grasp family systems theory, it is helpful to understand some of its theoretical underpinnings, most notably general systems theory (GST), developed by Ludwig von Bertalanffy. Von Bertalanffy initially developed GST to combine systems thinking and biology to understand living systems (Nichols, 2008). He then began applying GST to social systems and coined the the idea that the whole system is more than the sum of its parts, meaning that the family is greater than any one individual and that each individual has an impact on each other and the overall family dynamics.

Major Theoretical Assumptions and Concepts

Pioneers in family therapy took these principles, combined them with principles from cybernetics, and applied them to understanding family systems where individual behavior could, in part, be understood by the relational interactions among family members. Cybernetics is the study of feedback mechanisms in self-regulating systems. A central concept of cybernetics is the feedback loop, which refers to the process in which information flows in and out of the system to remain steady. Feedback loops, a concept derived from cybernetics, is the process in which systems receive information (i.e., input) and sends out information (i.e., output) to maintain stability (Nichols, 2008). Feedback loops can be either positive or negative. Positive feedback loops refer to a system adapting and changing to accommodate a change from the homeostasis or a "balanced state of equilibrium" (Nichols, 2008, p. 492). Homeostasis is maintained when change does not occur. When information brought into the system is met with resistance and corrects itself to maintain homeostasis, negative feedback loops have occurred.

Jurich and Myers-Bowman (1998) summarized family systems theory assumptions as: (1) holism; (2) systems are hierarchically organized; (3) living systems are open, nondetermined, and active; (4) human systems are self-reflexive; and (5) reality is constructed. Holism refers to the whole being larger than the sum of its parts. Applied to families, holism means that individuals cannot be understood in isolation, rather they are part of a larger system. It is the interactions among the system's parts that can help to understand the individual.

To help explain the concept of family systems, wealth transfer agreements from one generation to the next are typically good illustrations of how relational aspects of money can interfere with otherwise simplistic planning. When viewed from a family system's perspective, it is much easier to understand the logic behind dividing a family business into five-and-three-quarter shares rather than passing it on to the one person responsible for daily management. When wealth transfers or any other family decision is made by one member of the family, change automatically trickles to the other family members.

The assumption that systems are hierarchically organized assumes that systems are nested. In other words, there are multiple forms of systems within a larger system. Consider that a children system and parent system (i.e., subsystems) are part of a larger family system. The family system can also be seen as part of a community system, a religious system, and a cultural system (i.e., suprasystems). All of these systems interact with one another. For example, culture is especially relevant to a couple's money management. The intricacies of decisions within one family system is doubled when accounting for two different sets of cultural, religious, and other family beliefs. There are also individual personality characteristics of the partners that influence beliefs and behaviors.

The belief that systems interact with one another leads to another assumption that living systems are open, nondetermined, and active. Open systems refers to exchanges that happen among systems. Systems can exchange resources with their environment to help it adapt to its environment. Rather than thinking of livings systems as being mechanistic, where X causes Y, von Bertalanffy believed that livings systems (i.e., people) can achieve their objectives in different ways (Nichols, 2008). This concept is referred to as equifinality. Not only can systems react and adapt to exchanges made, they can initiate exchanges as well. Therefore, systems can be seen to be both active and reactive.

Wealth transfers demonstrate the systemic nature of families in another way. It is commonly observed that wealth skips generations. Generation A accumulates wealth and leaves it to Generation B. Generation B spends the wealth down and then Generation C builds it back up again. Generation B observed family characteristics that were either desirable or undesirable and attempted to dissociate by giving or spending all of the wealth to avoid certain stigmas they felt. Alternatively, Generation B observed family characteristics of living carefree and taking frequent vacations and failed to observe the hard work or budgeting that went on to ensure that too much wealth was not spent. In either case, what is happening is the push to remain at homeostasis. The family (take Generation B, for example) gathered information, processed the information in a way that made sense to them, and took action to remain at or return to the perceived homeostatic level, an example of how feedback loops impact the system.

Human beings are self-reflexive refers to people being able to reflect upon their own actions and interaction. In other words, people can recognize what they are doing. Reality is constructed means that people's "knowledge of the world can never be fully objective because what we see is through a particular perspective" (Jurich & Myers-Bowman, 1998, p. 75). Our interactions with others help to shape to how we view the world.

Important concepts in addition to those already mentioned (i.e., systems, subsystems, suprasystems, equifinality, open and closed systems, and feedback loops) that are helpful to understand systems thinking are interdependence and boundaries (Jurich & Myers-Bowman, 1998). Interdependence refers to systems having influence on one another. The way one system or individual in the system acts has an effect on other subsystems and individuals in the system. Boundaries mark what is part of the system, subsystem, or suprasystem and what is not. Boundaries can range from open to closed, in regard to how much or how often information is let in or out of the system.

Family Systems and Client Psychology

How can family systems theory and marriage and family therapists help to inform client psychology? If the working definition of client psychology is behaviors, biases, perceptions, and other variables that impact a client's decision-making and overall financial well-being, then family systems theory provides a way to understand clients beyond an individualistic perspective. The majority of financial conflict can be tied back to differences in behaviors, biases, perceptions, and values and it is known that financial conflict is a leading cause of marital conflict and dissatisfaction (Britt, Huston, & Durband, 2010; Dew, Britt, & Huston, 2012). Financial practitioners have undoubtedly sat across the table from a couple (not unlike Ben and Colleen from the opening case) involved in an intimate discussion of whether to plan for the family vacation or save a little extra in their retirement account. Differences in values are the most common culprit of money arguments between partners. Financial practitioners can diffuse the tension by helping to find common ground. Couples often need help understanding why their partner wants to do a certain thing (e.g., the family vs. the retirement savings). Creating a value's assessment for couples to independently rank what is important to them will help start the conversation. Then, encourage the couples to use the language of "I feel . . . when . . . because . . . " to help the conversation focus on feelings instead of blaming and criticizing their partner.

Marriage and family therapists have a toolkit of varying modalities that utilize a family systems lens that can be used to intervene in order to change behaviors, attitudes, biases, and perceptions to improve client decision-making and financial well-being. "Individual clients cannot be understood without understanding the client's environment and their relationship with family members" (Archuleta & Ross, 2015, p. 765) and others who are a part of their system. Marriage and family therapists focus on process or the dynamics and relational aspects that occur among family members rather than the content or what is being said. MFT therapists who focus on process look for how one communicates with others rather than the content of what is communicated. Process-focused therapists also observe what one is doing when they talk to or about someone or something and what a person does when it is their turn to be quiet or to listen to another person.

Education

To become an MFT therapist, graduate-level training is required. Three options are available: master's degree, doctoral degree, or post-graduate clinical training program. Marriage and family therapy programs that are accredited by the Commission on Accreditation for Marriage and Family Therapy Education (COAMFTE) help to ensure quality education that meets state licensing requirements.

All 50 states support licensing of MFT therapists; however, the licensing requirements vary among states. In general, a master's-level graduate will have completed not only coursework in marriage and family therapy including psychopathology, but also will have completed 500 clinical hours working face-to-face with clients, with at least 250 being relational contact hours (i.e., working with more than one person in the room) at the time of graduation. One hundred of these hours must be supervised by an approved supervisor. While licensure among states varies, marriage and family therapists, in general, must have least two years of supervised clinical experience in the field to receive licensure. For example, in Kansas, to become fully clinically licensed, MFT therapists must have engaged in 4,000 clinical hours with 1,500 hours being client-contact hours. In addition, 150 hours of supervision hours are required with 50 hours supervision being individual supervision (not group supervision) post-graduation to earn full clinical licensure. Full clinical licensure allows MFT therapists to practice independently without supervision.

FINANCIAL THERAPY

Financial therapy integrates cognitive, emotional, relational, and financial aspects of one's overall well-being. Financial therapy is essentially a way of practicing client psychology. Both consider the emotions, behaviors, and perceptions that influence overall financial well-being. Although a few scholars and practitioners have worked in this area for decades, financial therapy as a field of study did not become formalized until 2009 when the Financial Therapy Association (FTA) was established. Comprised of scholars and practitioners from a wide range of disciplines, including marriage and family therapy, psychology, social work, financial planning, and financial counseling, the organization is dedicated to developing the field by promoting the integration of research, theory, and practice (Financial Therapy Association, 2017). A financial therapist helps a person think, feel, and behave differently with money to improve overall well-being through evidence-based practices and interventions that aim to resolve underlying issues limiting self-growth and well-being (informed by the mental health profession). One way a financial therapist might help a client is by using a family therapy approach. Regardless, financial therapists

> *employ evidence-based assessments to measure both characteristics of mental health (i.e., depression, anxiety) and financial characteristics (i.e., money scripts, risk tolerance, financial stress/anxiety, financial knowledge) that affect well-being. The combined approach allows financial therapists to help clients meet their financial goals by addressing financial challenges as well as emotional, psychological, behavioral, and relational hurdles (Financial Therapy Association, 2017).*

At the time of this writing, the FTA announced the eight core competency domains for financial therapists. The domains include:

1. Theory-based practices applied to financial therapy
2. General counseling skills and techniques
3. Basic financial knowledge and skills
4. Ethics and standards in financial therapy
5. Money and relationships: Working with complex systems in financial therapy
6. Understanding diversity and culture in financial therapy
7. Mental health diagnoses and financial therapy
8. Evaluation of research in financial therapy

These eight competencies are to serve as the foundational core skills for certification. Certification as a financial therapist is expected to be a tiered process, with the first level of certification expected to be available in 2018.

BUILDING ALLIANCES WITH FAMILIES AND COUPLES

Addressing the values, beliefs, and biases of an individual can be challenging enough, but when you add people to the physical space or at a minimum discuss their perceived impact on the discussion-making process, there are additional factors to consider. Oftentimes, perceptions are more informative and important to clients than reality. As mentioned previously, perceptions are shaped by interactions with others and because of this there is no objective reality, only perceptions (Jurich & Myers-Bowman, 1998). For instance, perceptions of a wife who spends so much money that it puts a strain on household finances (i.e., she's a spender) is most predictive of financial conflict for both spouses (Britt, Hill, LeBaron, Lawson, & Bean, 2017). In other words, husbands who think their wife is a spender report increased conflict and wives who report that their husband thinks they are a spender report increased conflict. Perceptions of husbands being spenders is also predictive of financial conflict, but to a lesser degree. More important in predicting conflict according to husbands is having financial worries and low income. When wives rate their husbands as spenders, husband are three times more likely to report financial conflict, as compared to the nine times more likely a husband is to report conflict when he views his wife as a spender. The odds of having financial conflict for women is 11 times as likely when her husband views her as a spender. Also important in predicting financial conflict according to the wife is having financial worries, husband's low income, not talking about money with her husband, and having a spendy husband (Britt et al., 2017).

Common Factors

In thinking about how change occurs for clients, therapeutic approaches or modalities are not effective alone. Common factors exist across psychotherapy modalities, including client/extratherapeutic change factors, therapist factors, therapeutic alliance, and hope and expectancy (Asay & Lambert, 2003). Client/extratherapeutic change factors consist of events that happen outside of the therapeutic relationship that have an impact on client change (Asay & Lambert, 2003), such as inheritance, job loss, or finding a new job. In addition, client factors include the resources and characteristics the client has for making change successful separate from the therapy process, like family support, personality trait characteristics, and readiness for change (Asay & Lambert, 2003; Karam, Blow, Sprenkle & Davis, 2015). Therapist factors refer to the characteristics that the therapist brings to the alliance. Wampold (2001) suggested that therapists may have larger effects on the change process than the treatment itself. For change to occur, therapists must "provide trust, acceptance, acknowledgement, collaboration, and respect for the client in an environment that supports risk and maximizes safety" (Karam et al., 2015, p. 141). For MFTs, common factors are expanded and include conceptualizing difficulties in relational terms, interrupting dysfunctional relational patterns, expanding the direct treatment system, and expanding the therapeutic alliance (Karam et al., 2015; Sprenkle, Davis, & Lebow, 2009).

We have already discussed the importance of the relational interactions among systems. The goal of marriage and family therapy is to interrupt dysfunctional relational patterns, utilizing a modality steeped in family systems theory. However, when working with couples and families, the treatment system expands beyond an individual client. One of the reasons that couples and families are more difficult to work with than individual clients is the focus on process and the interactions among and between the clients and facilitator of the session. For the facilitator, the challenge is not only to listen to the content but to pay attention to how the husband reacts to the wife talking about her spending, while at the same time observing how the wife responds nonverbally while talking. When the husband responds verbally, the facilitator observes the husband's nonverbals and the wife's reaction.

None of the modalities nor the observations of process versus content can occur without the facilitator building a strong alliance with the couple or family. The most common definition of the therapeutic alliance is comprised of three aspects: (1) bonds, (2) tasks, and (3) goals (Bordin, 1979). Bonds refer to trust, care, and involvement that make up the affective quality of the client–therapist relationship (Karam et al., 2015). Tasks refer to how comfortable the client is with the major activities used in the therapy process.

Goals indicate agreeableness between the client and therapist as to the direction and expected outcomes of the therapy. When working with more than one person, like the couple mentioned previously or the family intergenerational wealth transfer, the alliance must be formed with multiple systems.

REFERRALS AND COLLABORATIONS

Financial therapy and client psychology may reveal bigger concerns for the client. Mental health concerns may be so severe that a clinical diagnosis with empirically supported treatments and/or medication is recommended. This requires the services of a psychiatrist (if medication are prescribed) or other mental health professional trained in diagnosing and treatment of mental health disorders. The *Diagnostic and Statistical Manual for Mental Health Disorders*, fifth edition (*DSM-V*; American Psychiatric Association, 2013) used by psychologists, marriage and family therapists, and other mental professionals who are licensed to make mental health diagnoses, specifically references two money disorders: gambling disorder and hoarding (Canale, Archuleta, & Klontz, 2015), along with other general disorders of anxiety, depressive, obsessive–compulsive, and sleep–wake disorders that could be initiated due to financial issues. It would be ill-advised and unethical for financial planners to do more than acknowledge that potential issues may be present and make appropriate referrals. Utilizing MFT therapists and financial therapists as resources in financial planning can be an excellent way to tap into address the client psychological aspects driving financial behavior and impacting well-being.

Assessment

To address client psychological issues and bridge the gap between financial planning and therapy, assessment tools and techniques may provide a starting point (Archuleta & Grable, 2010). Initial screening could be handled by a financial planner. There are several screening tools available online that could be incorporated into the data gathering phase of the relationship. The PHQ-9, a nine-item depression inventory, or the Outcome Questionnaire–45, a 45-item measure that assesses clinical outcomes and can identify red flag issues like thoughts of suicide or alcoholism, are measures that could be used to assess for issues that are out of the scope of practice for most financial planners. Concerns noted on the screening do not necessitate immediate dismissal and loss of a client. Rather, it presents the opportunity for collaborative work with a professional trained in the area collaborative services are required.

Other assessments can be used to screen for beliefs or behaviors that may interfere with progress with the client, but do not necessarily necessitate referral to another professional. Oftentimes, acknowledgement of biases and open communication is all the client needs to continue to make progress toward their goals. The Klontz Money Script Inventory (Klontz & Britt, 2012; Klontz, Britt, Mentzer, & Klontz, 2011) and the Klontz Money Behavior Inventory (Klontz, Britt, Archuleta, & Klontz, 2012) are two examples of assessments that can be used to screen for problematic beliefs or behaviors around money. Some of the behaviors, such as pathological gambling, may require additional help from a trained professional, yet many of the items are simply useful in opening a conversation with the clients about the multidimensional aspects of money in their relationships.

According to the American Psychological Association (2017), money has been the number one stressor for Americans for the past decade. Assessment such as the Financial Anxiety scale (Archuleta, Dale, & Spann, 2013) can be used to assess how anxious one is feeling in regard to their financial situation. If high anxiety is exhibited, it may be an indicator that a marriage and family therapist may be helpful in reducing anxiety behaviors. The Personal Finance Employee Education Foundation's Personal Financial Wellness scale, originally called the InCharge Financial Distress/Financial Well-being Scale (Prawitz, Garman, Sorhaindo, O'Neill, Kim, & Drentea, 2006) measures financial distress and financial well-being. The Consumer Financial Protection Bureau's Financial Well-being Scale assesses one's financial situation and their capability to address their financial situation (https://www.consumerfinance.gov/data-research/research-reports/financial-well-being-scale/).

For couples, the Shared Goals and Values scale (Archuleta, 2013; Archuleta, Grable, & Britt, 2013) assesses common life goals and values that can be helpful conversation starters, especially if couples disagree. Discussing individual differences and then looking at what the couple does have in common can help couples refocus their attention on what is important for partners as a couple unit. Grable, Archuleta, and Nazarinia (2010) edited a book of existing scales and measurements designed to use in financial planning and counseling. Sages, Griesdorn, Gudmunson, and Archuleta (2015) identified additional scales and measurements that could also be useful in initial screenings or client assessment when appropriate.

The focus on initial screening sets up the opportunity for collaborative work with a financial therapist or mental health professional. Surveying professionals in the financial planner's area will be beneficial in identifying several options available for clients who may want a referral to someone aware of the multidimensional aspect of money and who is willing to provide services in this area. Teaming with a financial therapist or mental health professional to provide joint data gathering sessions is often seen as a nonthreatening way of introducing a referral. In this way, the mental health professional is seen as part of the team. Older research suggests that one-third of clients who seek mental health/relational counseling have a concurring financial concern and one-third of clients who seek financial counseling have a concurring mental health/relational concern (Aniol & Synder, 1997). It is likely that the percentage of desire or need for overlapping services is growing with the increased stress of money on individuals and relationships.

CONCLUSION

Without an understanding of family systems theory, practitioners may be missing key elements that inform what they observe in their office. Financial stress, attitudes, perceptions, and behaviors cannot be understood without knowing an individual's story. That story of how a person perceives what is real is developed by how their own systems interacted and currently interact with one another. Marriage and family therapy is one information point of financial therapy, where family systems theory and financial practices merge to treat underlying issues that may be limiting or inhibiting self-growth. Utilizing appropriate assessment tools and evidence-based practices, financial therapists can help to alter cognitions, emotions, relationships, and behavior related to money.

Marriage and family therapy, financial therapy, and client psychology work hand in hand. Additional research is needed to further connect theory and practice. Family systems theory poses that interactions are circular rather than linear. However, the majority of research conducted aligns with linear thinking. Researchers should further explore the circular nature of how money impacts individual, couple, and family relationship dynamics and how these relationship dynamics impact financial behaviors and decision-making. Researchers from diverse disciplines (e.g., marriage and family therapy and personal finance) should work together to further understand these phenomena and test approaches that work in order to help clients achieve successful outcomes and reach their financial goals.

REFERENCES

American Psychiatric Association. (2013). *Diagnostic and statistical manual of mental disorders* (5th ed.). Washington, DC: Author.

Aniol, J. C., & Snyder, D. K. (1997). Differential assessment of financial and relationship distress: Implications for couples therapy. *Journal of Marital and Family Therapy, 23*(3), 347–353.

Archuleta, K. L. (2013). Couples, money, and expectations: Negotiating financial management roles to increase relationship satisfaction. *Marriage & Family Review, 49*(5), 391–411.

Archuleta, K. L., Dale, A., & Spann, S. M. (2013). College students and financial distress: Exploring debt, financial satisfaction, and financial anxiety. *Journal of Financial Counseling and Planning, 24*(2), 50–62.

Archuleta, K. L., & Grable, J. E. (2010). The future of financial planning and counseling: An introduction to financial therapy. In J. E. Grable, K. L. Archuleta, & R. Nazarinia Roy (Eds.), *Financial planning and counseling scales* (pp. 33–59). New York: Springer.

Archuleta, K. L., Grable, J. E., & Britt, S. L. (2013). Financial and relationship satisfaction as a function of harsh start-up and shared goals and values. *Journal of Financial Counseling and Planning, 24*(1), 3–14.

Archuleta, K. L., & Ross, D. B., III. (2015). Marriage and family therapy: Applications to financial planning. In C. Chaffin (Ed.), *Financial planning competency handbook* (2nd ed., pp. 763–777). Hoboken, NJ: John Wiley & Sons.

Asay, T. P., & Lambert, M. J. (2003). The empirical case for the common factors in therapy: Quantitative findings. In M. A. Hubble, B. L. Duncan, & S. D. Miller (Eds.), *The heart & soul of change: What works in therapy*. Washington, DC: American Psychological Association.

Britt, S. L., Hill, J. E., LeBaron, A., Lawson, D., & Bean, R. (2017, May). Savers and spenders: Predicting financial conflict in couple relationships. *Journal of Financial Planning, 36*–42.

Britt, S. L., Huston, S. J., & Durband, D. B. (2010). The determinants of money arguments between spouses. *Journal of Financial Therapy, 1*(1), 41–59.

Britt, S. L., Klontz, B., Tibbetts, R., & Leitz, L. (2015). The financial health of mental health professionals. *Journal of Financial Therapy, 6*(1), 17–32.

Canale, A., Archuleta, K. L., & Klontz, B. T. (2015). Money disorders. In B. T. Klontz, S. L. Britt, & K. L. Archuleta (Eds.), *Financial therapy: Theory, research & practice* (pp. 35–67). New York: Springer.

Crane, D. R., & Christenson, J. D. (2012). A summary report of the cost-effectiveness of the profession and practice of marriage and family therapy. *Contemporary Family Therapy, 34*(2), 204–216.

Dew, J., Britt, S. L., & Huston, S. J. (2012). Examining the relationship between financial issues and divorce. *Family Relations, 61*(4), 615–628. doi:10.1111/j.1741-3729.2012.00715.x.

Grable, J. E., Archuleta, K. L., & Nazarinia, R. R. (2010). *Financial planning and counseling scales*. New York: Springer.

Jurich, J. A., & Myers-Bowman, K. S. (1998). Systems theory and its application to research on human sexuality. *Journal of Sex Research, 35*(1), 72–87. doi:10.1080/00224499809551918.

Karam, E. A., Blow, A. J., Sprenkle, D. H., & Davis, S. D. (2015). Strengthening the systemic ties that bind: Integrating common factors into marriage and family therapy curricula. *Journal of Marital and Family Therapy, 41*, 136–149. doi:10.1111/jmft.12096.

Klontz, B. T., & Britt, S. L. (2012). How clients' money scripts predict their financial behaviors. *Journal of Financial Planning, 25*(11), 33–43.

Klontz, B. T., Britt, S. L., Archuleta, K. L., & Klontz, T. (2012). Disordered money behaviors: Development of the Klontz money behavior inventory. *Journal of Financial Therapy, 3*(1), 17–42.

Klontz, B. T., Britt, S. L., Mentzer, J., & Klontz, T. (2011). Money beliefs and financial behaviors: Development of the Klontz money script inventory. *Journal of Financial Therapy, 2*(1), 1–22.

Nichols, M. P. (2008). *Family therapy: Concepts and methods.* New York: Pearson Education.

Prawitz, A. D., Garman, E. T., Sorhaindo, B., O'Neill, B., Kim, J., & Drentea, P. (2006). InCharge financial distress/financial well-being scale: Development, administration, and score interpretation. *Financial Counseling and Planning, 17*(1), 34–50.

Sages, R. A., Griesdorn, T. S., Gudmunson, C. G., & Archuleta, K. L. (2015). Assessment in financial therapy. In B. T. Klontz, S. L. Britt, & K. L. Archuleta (Eds.), *Financial therapy: Theory, research, and practice* (pp. 69–86). New York: Springer.

Sprenkle, D. H. (2012). Intervention research in couple and family therapy: A methodological and substantive review and an introduction to the special issue. *Journal of Marital and Family Therapy, 38*(1), 3–29.

Sprenkle, D. H., Davis, S., & Lebow, J. (2009). *Common factors in couple and family therapy: The overlooked foundation for effective practice.* New York: Guilford Press.

Wampold, B. E. (2001). *The great psychotherapy debate: Models, methods, and findings.* Mahwah, NJ: Erlbaum.

CHAPTER 14

Client Diversity

Understanding and Leveraging Difference to Enhance Financial Planning Practice

Quinetta Roberson, PhD
Villanova University

Following federal equal employment opportunity laws, which prohibit discrimination based on a person's race, color, religion, sex, national origin, age, or disability (https://www.eeoc.gov/eeoc/), the term *diversity* emerged in the early 1990s. As forecasted in the Hudson Institute's report on the changing workforce (Johnston & Packer, 1987), employee demographics would become more diverse along several dimensions. Specifically, the report forecasted that white males would, for the first time, become the numerical minority in the workforce and that by the year 2000, women, immigrants, and people of color would represent a larger share of new entrants into the U.S. workforce. Consistent with such predictions, the 21st-century workforce is typified by more women and employees of different ethnic backgrounds and origins. However, with blurred geographic boundaries and changing socioeconomic trends, stakeholder groups are composed of people of varied backgrounds, cultures, and lifestyles (Mor Barak & Travis, 2013).

Along with greater stakeholder diversity, the business landscape has changed. Increased competition has decreased businesses' market power, while shrinking resource bases have increased their need for sources of organic growth, such as innovation and economies of scale. Operating environments characterized by velocity, uncertainty, complexity, and ambiguity have underscored a need for strategic flexibility and agility. Further, the transition to a service economy has reconfigured value chains in ways that start with the development of niche markets as well as business processes that depend upon human capital, such as service design and customer engagement. Further, given the ease with which physical assets and other resources can be obtained and/or duplicated, organizations are attempting to leverage intangibles and other nonphysical assets that are likely to contribute to the achievement of competitive advantage and the sustainability of such performance gains.

Yet, while approximately 30 years have elapsed since the advent of diversity as a business concern, leaders still struggle to understand its meaning and import in organizations. What employee differences matter? How do such differences relate to differences in consumer preferences, values, and needs? What are the potential performance gains or losses from diversity? Can diversity be leveraged to improve effectiveness? Such questions echo in firms across regions, sizes, and industries, and the financial planning sector is no different. Clients' needs are influenced by their unique backgrounds and experiences, which highlight the importance of understanding diversity and how it operates in a financial planning context. Further, as client psychology, or biases, behaviors, and perceptions that impact their decision-making and financial well-being are also impacted by individuals' characteristics and circumstances, diversity plays a critical role in financial planning practice.

This chapter discusses the concept of diversity and how financial planners can understand and leverage it to improve practice. I begin by reviewing theory and research on the conceptualization of diversity and the mechanisms through which it influences interpersonal interactions and intergroup relations. To determine how the process outcomes of diversity translate to business contexts, I articulate the business value of diversity in organizations—specifically, the ways in which diversity serves as a source of competitive advantage. I conclude with practice perspectives on how to leverage client diversity. In particular, I highlight different organizational approaches for diversity and discuss practices and strategies for diversifying client bases, managing client relationships more inclusively, and developing and leveraging diverse networks.

UNDERSTANDING THE CONCEPT OF DIVERSITY

What Is Diversity?

Since its inception, a range of definitions of diversity have emerged. To adequately capture the range of difference among stakeholder groups, practitioners have adopted broad definitions of diversity that incorporate "people with distinctly different group affiliations of cultural significance" (Cox, 1993) or are inclusive of all differences (Thomas, 1991). However, diversity researchers have utilized more nuanced approaches to the conceptualization of diversity. One such approach categorizes diversity attributes based on the degree to which they are visible or readily detected (Jackson, May, & Whitney, 1995). Surface-level diversity, or readily observed personal attributes, such as gender, race, and age, is distinguished from deep-level diversity, or less apparent characteristics, such as personality, education, and experience (Harrison, Price, & Bell, 1998; Harrison, Price, Gavin, & Florey, 2002). Related to classes protected by federal discrimination laws, surface-level diversity is speculated to be reflective of many of the biological or innate characteristics protected by such legislation and to be more easily assessed. In comparison, deep-level diversity is considered to be more reflective of people's belief systems and attitudes and, therefore, expressed through interpersonal interactions with others (Harrison et al., 1998; Harrison et al., 2002).

Researchers have also conceptualized diversity as a structural characteristic of groups that is reflected in the distribution of specific attributes among members of the group. Inspired by sociological work on the influence of proportions on interactions between demographically dissimilar groups (Blau, 1977; Kanter, 1977), the thesis of such research is that the percentage of any minority within a group will influence the quality of relations between group members. Representing a more compositional approach to diversity, the distribution of member attributes within the group determines whether they are part of the majority versus minority or their status as members of the in-group versus out-group, subsequently impacting intergroup relations. More recent work has expanded this compositional view by integrating categorical and compositional perspectives, and proposing three forms of diversity based on the type of differences between people. Specifically, researchers have proposed: (1) diversity as separation, which represents perceptual disagreement between people, such as values and beliefs; (2) diversity as variety, which captures differences in sources of information, such as knowledge and networks; and (3) diversity as disparity, which reflects differences in access to, or ownership of, valued resources, such as privilege and status (Harrison & Klein, 2007).

Other diversity research that conceptualizes diversity as a structural characteristic of groups has moved beyond a focus on diversity as a single characteristic, and instead explores diversity in terms of the alignment of attributes. Termed faultlines (Lau & Murnighan, 1998), such research explores hypothetical dividing lines in a group that split it into subgroups based on one or more demographic attributes. For example, consider two groups—one that consists of two women who are married and three men who are unmarried, and one that consists of one woman who is married, one woman who is married with two children, one man who is unmarried, one man who is unmarried with one child, and one man who is unmarried with two children. From a single-attribute diversity perspective, the two groups are identical in terms of gender. However, from a faultline perspective, these groups are very different as their attributes (gender, marital status, parental status) are not aligned. As faultline strength is determined by the extent to which the subgroups are homogeneous, the first group would have a stronger faultline because the subgroups (gender and marital status) are homogeneous (Lau & Murnighan, 1998, 2005). Further, as demographic faultlines have been found to influence group processes and outcomes (see Thatcher, 2013), understanding nuances in the composition of groups is important for understanding diversity.

Regardless of the specific conceptualization of diversity, clients may have different experiences (e.g., perceptions, expectations, reactions) based on their specific group memberships and the salience of such memberships in different contexts. While it may seem like a challenge to do relationship-building with, and provide personalized service to, every client, the practice of aggregating groups under umbrella classifications (e.g., minorities, older Americans, etc.) fosters inaccurate assumptions about individuals and groups, limits our development, and fails to uncover clients' unique needs and challenges. For example, a financial planner may choose to specialize in working with older clients, focusing on insurance, estate, and/or long-term care planning. However, variability in age, years to retirement, existing savings, and other circumstances gives rise to different planning needs. Clients who have not planned for retirement may require budgeting or late-stage planning strategies, while those who have may require planning that shifts from wealth accumulation to retaining or drawing down assets. Similarly, older clients' marital or parental status may determine whether planning for new family dynamics, such as supporting spouses or adult children, is needed. As all individuals belong to multiple social categories, focusing on one category or viewing them independently constrains our understanding of the meaning, consequences, and unique experiences at the intersections of various identities. As clients' advice and planning needs derive from their unique backgrounds and experiences, practices and approaches that account for such diversity in client bases are paramount.

How Does Diversity Work?

The operation of diversity has been understood through social–psychological theories of intergroup relations, such as social identity and categorization theories (Tajfel, 1978; Turner, 1985), which articulate processes through which individuals make sense of, and locate, themselves within their social environments. They also help to explain the processes through which individuals relate to others via their group memberships. The theories propose that because individuals' self-concepts are shaped by their group memberships, they are motivated to positively distinguish their group from others.

To do so, they compare their in-groups to relevant out-groups to emphasize similarities to those with whom they share group memberships and differences from those who belong to different identity groups. Social categorization theory further suggests that demographic characteristics may serve as a basis by which individuals classify themselves and others into social categories (Turner, Hogg, Oakes, Reicher, & Wetherell, 1987). As a result, individuals tend to view themselves and others as representatives of social categories rather than as unique individuals. Such categorizations are important given that people tend to exhibit higher levels of trust for, and affective reactions to, members of their in-groups, consequently developing biases in favor of members of one's in-groups and against members of one's out-groups (Tajfel & Turner, 1986; Turner et al., 1987). Further, such biases are likely to inhibit interpersonal processes, such as cohesion and communication, among dissimilar others (Williams & O'Reilly, 1998). A similar theoretical foundation for the effects of diversity derives from the similarity-attraction paradigm (Byrne, 1971), which assumes that people are more attracted to those with whom they perceive to have similar characteristics (Berscheid & Walster, 1978). Consistent with the predictions of social identity and categorization theories, such attraction is likely to produce in-group/out-group distinctions and to influence social interactions and intergroup relations.

Sociological theories also hypothesize the effects of diversity on interpersonal relations. For example, Blau's (1977) theory of intergroup relations suggests that group functioning is influenced by the opportunity for, and quality of, social interaction between diverse individuals. Based on the logic of the social-contact hypothesis, which suggests that interaction between individuals will increase attraction, liking, and understanding (Pettigrew, 1982), the theory suggests that diversity will facilitate increased contact between dissimilar individuals. It also suggests that representation of different demographic groups will influence the quality of social contact, such that groups with skewed demographies will have qualitatively worse interactions, while greater demographic balance will give rise to increased contact and cooperation between individuals. Following this logic, it is suggested that meaningful representation of people from a range of group memberships can positively impact the quality of intergroup relations (Blau, 1977; Kanter, 1977).

Social categorization and comparison processes can become manifested in several ways, including stereotyping and ideology emergence. Early psychology research shows how placing individuals into groups leads to depersonalization, such that out-group members are perceived as representatives of their group rather than as individuals with unique characteristics (see Tajfel, 1982). In addition, out-group members are viewed as having increased amounts of similarity between them and exaggerated differences from in-group members. This perceptual process further distinguishes in-group and out-group identities, which becomes the lens through which individuals' behaviors are interpreted. For example, members of in-groups will typically interpret out-group behaviors more negatively and/or consistent with stereotypes associated with their group while in-group behaviors will be viewed more positively and consistent with self-enhancement attributes (Ferguson & Porter, 2013). Ideologies are similar systems of beliefs that depict the nature of the social world and how it operates (see Jost, Federico, & Napier, 2009). Such belief systems can be prescriptive, expressing how people believe the social world should operate, or descriptive, expressing how the social world does operate. Most ideologies can be categorized as hierarchy-enhancing, which justify some groups having greater access to resources and status-related outcomes, or hierarchy-attenuating, which justify social equality (Sidanius & Pratto, 1999). For example, beliefs in a meritocratic world, or that outcomes are (or should be) distributed according to one's deservingness, which is a function of effort and ability (Major, Kaiser, O'Brien & McCoy, 2007), and colorblindness, or beliefs that racial and ethnic differences should be disregarded in favor of treating everyone as unique individuals, are often used to justify the status quo and existing social hierarchies (O'Brien & Gilbert, 2013). In contrast, egalitarianism and multiculturalism, which correspondingly emphasize social justice and that all groups be treated equally with respect, are used to delegitimize social hierarchies and foster the even distribution of social goods and resources. On balance, ideologies are used to support a particular worldview as reasonable and accurate, and to filter the way people perceive the world.

In contrast to identity-related theories of diversity, researchers have postulated that diversity operates through information exchange processes. Referred to as the informational/decision-making perspective (Williams & O'Reilly, 1998), this idea proposes that because diversity brings about a range of knowledge, perspectives, and other cognitive resources, it facilitates greater access to information and expertise. Accordingly, diverse groups have a greater capacity for engaging in problem-solving and decision-making (Williams & O'Reilly, 1998). Research also suggests that dissimilarity exposes people to minority opinions and more creative alternatives and solutions, while providing access to a larger and more varied social network (see Mannix & Neale, 2005). Thus, the informational perspective reasons that diversity serves as an informational resource that benefits both individuals and groups.

While the social categorization and information-processing perspectives on diversity have traditionally been considered mutually exclusive, the categorization-elaboration model (CEM) of diversity (van Knippenberg, De Dreu, & Homan, 2004) offers an approach for reconciling their divergent influences. Specifically, the model considers how intergroup biases engendered by diversity may disrupt information exchange and integration processes that are core to realizing the synergetic benefits of diversity as an informational resource. As such, the model assumes that while reducing bias is important to realizing the potential benefits of diversity, doing so is not enough to stimulate the processes that require active engagement with diversity. Instead, the critical role of exchanging and integrating perspectives and cognitive resources within groups to experience the positive effects of diversity is also acknowledged. Accordingly, the CEM offers a means of integrating the positive and negative effects of diversity.

In considering the role of diversity in financial planning, diversity's potential benefits as well as its potentially disruptive effects must be taken into account. On one hand, diversity may offer access to informational resources and networks typically not available from more homogeneous clientele. On the other hand, it may foster intergroup biases and other mindsets that hinder social interaction and cooperation. As the planning process is dependent upon planner–client communication and collaboration, strategies for harnessing the potential of diversity while reducing interpersonal obstacles that may impact the process must be considered.

THE BUSINESS VALUE OF DIVERSITY

Given that the unique knowledge, skills, and abilities of an organization's workforce cannot be perfectly duplicated by competitors, an organization's human capital can be considered a strategic resource (Wright & McMahan, 1992). Further, as knowledge and firm capabilities may be generated through employee social relationships (Barney, 1991), an organization's human capital may serve as a source of sustained competitive advantage. In general, knowledge and its exchange and application are typically considered to be an organization's most strategically significant resource to enable a competitive advantage (Grant, 1996). More specifically, because knowledge-based capabilities are socially complex, and thus difficult to imitate, diverse knowledge resources are key determinants of sustainable competitive advantage and superior firm performance. It follows, then, that diversity as a unique compilation of competencies and talent that adds value, yet is difficult to capture and transfer across organizations, is also considered a source of competitive advantage (Richard, 2000).

Cox and Blake (1991) propose several ways through which a competitive advantage can accrue from diversity in organizations. From a recruitment perspective, they suggest that those organizations with reputations for having diverse workforces and/or inclusive environments will be able to attract the best talent. As potential employees seek organizations in which they will have a sense of belonging, be fairly treated, and have an opportunity to meaningfully contribute to the mission, employers recognized for diversity and inclusion will have a brand advantage over their competitors. Relative to the work of organizations, Cox and Blake (1991) suggest that diversity will also enhance decision-making capabilities. Particularly, the unique perspectives afforded by diversity as well as operating norms that value such perspectives will drive higher levels of creativity and innovation. Further, such variability in perspective will facilitate more critical analysis of problems and issues, thus leading to improved problem solving in the organization. The range of employee backgrounds and experiences may also offer insight into the breadth of customer needs. Diversity inside organizations is believed to enable greater cultural competence, which may translate outside of the organization in the form of greater understanding of customer needs and expectations, enhancing organizational marketing efforts, and quality of service. Diversity may also enhance organizational flexibility, as it engenders less standardization and greater agility. Consistent with the prior arguments, diverse perspectives may provide organizations with greater awareness of customer and environmental trends. In addition, with increased operational fluidity, organizations may be more adaptable and able to more quickly respond to changes in the marketplace. Overall, Cox and Blake (1991) posit that these benefits, along with reduced costs associated with absenteeism, turnover, and low productivity will contribute net-added value to organizations, thus serving as a source of competitive advantage.

More recent research articulates the mechanisms through which diversity at different levels of organizations (e.g., leadership, managers, employees) may affect performance outcomes. Roberson, Holmes, and Perry (2017) offer a capabilities model of diversity that articulates the ways in which organizations may deploy their diversity resources to adapt to evolving markets and achieve sustainable advantages in dynamic business markets. Building upon Cox and Blake (1991), they identify six organizational capabilities resulting from the coordination and integration of diversity resources and knowledge into organizational routines: market access, research and development, efficiency, knowledge management, alliancing/brokerage, and system flexibility. Specifically, they argue that in addition to enhancing an organization's ability to enter and compete in specific markets, diversity will strengthen its capability for engaging in activities to discover and create new and/or better products and services. The authors also speculate that diversity may be useful for developing firm capabilities for forming and managing strategic alliances as well as to sense and respond to environmental changes. However, from an operational perspective, Roberson and colleagues (2017) propose that diversity may give rise to coordination challenges that diminish an organization's capability for knowledge management and subsequently, efficiency. Thus, at an organizational level of analysis, the potential benefits and disruptive effects of must also be considered.

LEVERAGING CLIENT DIVERSITY

Approaches to Diversity

Research shows that organizations differ in their approaches to diversity management (Thomas & Ely, 1996). Based on an assumption that prejudice has excluded members of historically disadvantaged groups from access and opportunity, some organizations approach diversity with a focus on equal opportunity and fair treatment. With the goal of changing the composition of organizational workforces to more closely reflect the composition of society, this approach concentrates on compliance with federal legislation to facilitate equal employment opportunity and affirmative action. Referred to as the *discrimination-and-fairness diversity paradigm* (Thomas & Ely, 1996), this approach also involves policies and programs to increase the diversity of workforces through the recruitment and retention of women and unrepresented minorities. However, the downside of this approach is its primary focus on diversity for the sake of diversity itself. With an overarching focus on the composition of the workforce (e.g., percentage of women in the workforce, percentage of ethnic minorities in management, total number of people with disabilities hired, etc.), rather than the unique skills and capabilities resulting from such diversity, there is little consideration of the potential benefits of diversity to organizations. In addition, the emphasis on equal treatment often engenders an identity-blind perspective that seeks to suppress the effects of difference. As such, diversity initiatives in such organizations tend to be relatively superficial.

In comparison to the discrimination-and-fairness paradigm, other organizations approach diversity using an *access-and-legitimacy paradigm* with a goal of changing the composition of their workforces to more closely reflect the composition of key consumer groups (Thomas & Ely, 1996). Identified as the most common approach to diversity management, such organizations view diversity as a business opportunity to expand into new markets and service specialized consumer segments as markets become more diverse and minority purchasing power increases. Differences are believed to enhance an organization's ability to gain access to, and credibility in, differentiated markets, as well as to understand and develop products and services that meet the needs of such market segments. As such, diversity is accepted and valued as a source of niche competencies. The limitation of this approach, however, is an assumption that such competencies are a necessary condition of diversity. For example, organizations following an access-and-legitimacy paradigm assumes Hispanic employees will have the knowledge and language skills to better serve Hispanic market segments without giving consideration to how such skills can be specifically integrated into organizational work processes and/or help to improve customer service. Accordingly, employees become pigeonholed or valued for their group membership rather than the unique knowledge, skills, and abilities they contribute to organizations.

Rather than focus on changing the composition of workforces to match that of other stakeholder groups, some organizations value diversity for its contribution to business processes. Termed the *learning-and-effectiveness paradigm* (Thomas & Ely, 1996), this approach incorporates diversity into organizational strategy, markets, processes, and culture in the interest of organizational learning and growth. As such, it has elements of the discrimination-and-fairness paradigm in that legal compliance is monitored, although methods of compliance beyond those mandated by law are undertaken. It also has elements of the access-and-legitimacy paradigm, as there are efforts to gain access to, and legitimacy among, diverse customer groups, although an understanding of such groups is viewed as a learning opportunity rather than a business one. However, diversity is conceptualized as differences in employee perspectives that, when incorporated into business processes, foster the achievement of strategic objectives, such as innovation, efficiency, customer satisfaction, or social responsibility. Further, employees are valued for their knowledge, skills and abilities, and the ways in which such resources are used to enhance job and organizational performance. Still, organizations following this approach tend to understand the potential advantages and disadvantages of diversity and, therefore, leaders view it as an opportunity for continuous learning and cultural transformation that drives growth and enhances long-term performance.

While Thomas and Ely (1996) offer three distinct paradigms, they may be viewed on a continuum of strategic diversity management. On one end, organizations strive to diversify their workforces to offer and respect differences between employees. On the other end, organizations strive to diversify their workforces and integrate differences in employee perspectives into work processes to improve effectiveness. As such, organizational approaches to diversity can be distinguished according to how diversity is defined, how it is valued, and how it is managed. The following sections offer guidance on ways in which financial planners can define, value, and manage diversity to enhance practice effectiveness.

PRACTICE PERSPECTIVES

Building a Diverse Clientele

As financial planning is dependent upon individuals' financial situations in terms of income, spending, saving, and their personal financial goals, there is diversity inherent in client bases. However, since planners will often rely on the same strategies to make initial contact with potential clients, to develop those leads into planning opportunities, and to convert those opportunities into client relationships, the actual diversity of clienteles may be limited. For example, some financial planners may advertise on specific radio shows or podcasts, which may be useful for targeting certain prospects, but may also limit access to those niche markets. Similarly, some planners may leverage their current clientele to market themselves via referrals and word of mouth, which may expedite the prospecting process while creating homogeneity in client bases. While broader marketing strategies, such as direct mailing or advertising on a personal website, may broaden the pool of potential clients, such strategies do not target specific audiences, which may result in a lower conversion rate. Therefore, financial planners should employ more focused approaches to developing diverse client bases.

A key consideration in generating a diverse pool of leads is how you define diversity. As an individual's financial situation and goals are typically correlated with his/her personal characteristics, such as age or marital and/or parental status, such characteristics will often be used as a proxy for a potential client's situation and goals. However, individual priorities, risk tolerance, and motivational factors influenced by these characteristics are what drive financial planning decisions. For example, a person's time horizon rather than age is important for determining the degree to which investments can be growth-oriented. Similarly, the type and amount of familial financial assistance needed is more pertinent to one's financial goals than is the nature of the dependent relationship (i.e., child entering college, grown child, aging parent, etc.). Therefore, financial planners would be well-served by understanding the deep-level diversity characteristics that influence a potential client's financial situation and goals rather than his/her demographic memberships to better understand (and subsequently, address) client needs.

While increasing client diversity may allow a planner further access and legitimacy into differentiated market segments, there are other benefits of diversity. Variability in client objectives and circumstances may facilitate greater learning of the range of products and services available to address their needs. However, such diversity may also help to strengthen planners' capabilities for identifying financial strategies and investment mixes for clients to achieve their unique goals. Financial planning professionals may also find themselves innovating to develop plans and advice that help clients to reach their goals as efficiently and effectively as possible. Thus, while the value in client diversity may be in increased fees, commissions, and/or market share, it may also be in the cultivation of a broader variety of skills and capabilities to better serve clients overall.

To increase client diversity, financial planners should give attention to diversifying the client pipeline. More specifically, they should seek to identify sources of clients with differentiated financial needs, goals, and situations. For example, planners can use social media platforms to filter and sort contacts to prospect potential clients based on their content or career achievements, or to use mutual connections to garner introductions. Another might be to hold informational workshops at private and public colleges and universities to begin the relationship-building process with potential future clients. Planners might also consider writing a blog or article for media sources with specific readerships to build and communicate their brand more widely. While a host of other strategies may be employed, financial planners may be more likely to experience the value of client diversity by identifying meaningful differences in client objectives, expectations, and circumstances, and expanding the breadth of sources used to build their book of business.

Inclusive Relationship Management

As financial planning is dependent upon developing and maintaining relationships with clients, there is a need to foster engagement among individuals with diverse financial situations. However, as some planners will employ an across-the-board approach to managing their client bases, achieving such engagement may be difficult. For example, when planners attempt to sell specific products without first getting to know their clients' goals and develop a financial plan, clients may feel ignored or simply like a source of revenue. Similarly, not tailoring financial strategies and advice to clients' unique needs may be demotivating, such that they do not consider the achievement of their financial goals likely and therefore may fail to see the value in financial planning services. While credentials and certifications are useful for conveying a certain level of expertise and accountability, such background information is not a direct indicator of the quality of service that can be expected. Therefore, financial planners should explore approaches for engaging their total clientele and managing client relationships more inclusively.

Inclusion is defined as the degree to which an employee views himself or herself as a valued member of a work group (Shore et al., 2011). Such value derives from the extent that individuals are acknowledged for their unique characteristics and are involved in critical work processes through access to information, connectedness to supervisors and coworkers and the ability to influence decision-making processes (Mor Barak & Cherin, 1998; Shore et al., 2011). In addition, it represents organizational efforts to engage individuals' whole selves at work, and to integrate and learn from their diverse perspectives (Roberson, 2006; Nishii, 2013). Thus, rather than emphasizing diversity as an organizational commodity that has value in terms of economic performance, the value in inclusion stems from individuals feeling like full contributors in important organizational processes. It follows, then, that inclusive relationship management, or treating each person (regardless of financial goals and situation) as a valued client, would create value for a financial planning practice.

Because inclusive relationship management will enhance the overall level of service provided, there are several benefits to the financial planner. Accounting for the time and effort to generate leads, understanding their unique financial situations and generating plans tailored to them, developing deeper, longer-term relationships with clients increases the return on the investment of a planner's resources. Understanding clients' unique situations and working in tandem to address their needs helps to create a partnership for moving toward client goals, which can also enhance client engagement and loyalty. As a result, clients are likely to feel more satisfied with the planning relationship. Further, as the tenets of marketing suggest that satisfied customers, based on quality of service (Rucci, Kim, & Quinn, 1998) and perceived value, tend to make repeat purchases and at larger amounts, inclusive relationship management may help to ensure that clients retain their relationship with a specific planner for the long term. Assuming clients' asset bases are likely to increase over time, this means increasingly higher fees and commissions. In addition, as client needs change with their financial situations, their portfolio of services and subsequently the relationship, may broaden. Inclusive relationship management may also enhance the likelihood that clients will refer the planner to others.

To manage clients more inclusively, financial planners should give attention to developing and demonstrating inclusive behaviors. At a general level, inclusive relationship management means appreciating and seeking to understand the uniqueness of each client's situation, as well as treating everyone with the same level of respect and interest in their business. It involves maintaining open lines of communication with all clients to keep them informed of trends and issues and allow them input into their financial plan. It also entails interacting authentically with clients to build trust and a stronger personal relationship. While these things may sound straightforward, they are by no means easy. Therefore, taking steps to enhance one's cultural competence may be useful. For example, presentations or seminars to understand new consumer trends, niche markets, and other changes in the market may be useful for keeping informed of the diversity in the market. Coursework or seminars may be helpful for learning and practicing inclusive behaviors, while developmental activities such as discussion groups, peer mentoring, or professional coaching may help to supplement what has been learned by strengthening the transfer of such behaviors into financial planning practice. Of course, more uncomplicated strategies, such as soliciting client feedback on their experiences and satisfaction with service, may help to identify best practices as well as areas of improvement. Overall, while a range of developmental strategies can be used, financial planners may be more likely to experience the value of client diversity by appreciating the variability in client needs, goals, and situations, yet working to ensure that a consistent level of service is provided to all clients regardless of such factors.

Developing and Leveraging Diverse Networks

For financial planners, personal networks are a critical resource. Referrals can be an effective way of obtaining new clients given that satisfied clients are often willing to refer others to their planner, and even make introductions. As people tend to have networks consisting of similar others, referrals can be useful for connecting with potential clients within a certain niche or target market. While relying on personal networks helps planners to develop their prospect pipeline and grow their business, there is a downside. Given the typically homogeneous nature of personal networks, referrals limit a planner's ability to identify and take advantage of opportunities in emergent markets. For example, a focus on C-suite executives or high net-worth individuals may ignore the market potential of traditionally underserved groups, such as recent college graduates or veterans, or those with significant purchasing power, such as religious or lesbian, gay, bisexual, and transgender communities. It also constrains a planner's capacity for keeping pace with the changing demographics of society. Therefore, financial planners should explore approaches for developing and leveraging more diverse networks.

Beyond the potential for generating new clients, there are other benefits of diverse networks. As networks are a source of professional resources and support (Ibarra, 1995; Ibarra & Andrews, 1993), they may be leveraged to enhance the financial planning process. For example, planners may gain work-related resources, such as information about new products or insight into new available technologies, which may help to enhance the value provided to clients. Similarly, planners may gain professional advice and support from mentors or peers that may help them to better manage their careers. The may also identify other professionals within the financial services industry with whom they could partner to develop more full-service offerings for clients. In general, research suggests that diversity in networks increases a person's network reach, or access to knowledge and resources in the network (Reagans, 2013). Therefore, financial planners would be well-served by taking steps to increase the breadth and depth of their personal networks to create value for their clients as well as for their practice.

As suggested earlier, there is the potential for greater market access associated with developing more diverse networks. However, there is also the potential for strengthening a range of capabilities. With greater access to knowledge and information, planners are better equipped to conduct more critical analyses of a client's financial situation, thus improving their ability to meet clients' financial goals. With greater access to professional resources, planners have a larger pool of potential partners with whom they can innovate new client offerings and/or collaborate to create economies of scale, thereby adding value to their services. Finally, with greater access to professional and personal resources, planners have increased adaptability and operational flexibility, enhancing their ability to respond to changes in the industry. Overall, diverse networks may provide financial planners with a variety of resources that, if leveraged, may be useful for enhancing their practice effectiveness and creating a competitive advantage in the market.

To develop and leverage diverse networks, financial planners should consider strategies for connecting and building relationships while inter-acting with people outside of their existing networks. While professional networking may be useful for making such connections, more authentic engagement across stakeholder groups helps to establish relationships and build trust. For example, rather than just host events in the local community, financial planners who get involved in community events are able to expose others to their brand as well as get to know them as people, which is the foundation for developing an effective client relationship. Planners can share articles, write blogs, host educational workshops, or engage in other forms of knowledge exchange to give people insight into their expertise as well as create meaningful dialogue to better inform the field of financial planning. Planners can form partnerships with organizations or professional societies to get access to a large pool of potential clients or to engage in their own professional development. Planners can attend tax, estate, philanthropy, or other planning seminars to connect with potential industry partners, recognize areas for adding value to their current service portfolio, and innovate wealth management services overall. While a range of approaches can be employed, the true value of diverse networks will be realized through those approaches that both expand personal networks and use such diversity to enhance financial planning practice.

CONCLUSION

As interest and demand for personal financial advice has increased, so has the diversity of client pools. Characterized by a wide range of backgrounds, cultures, and lifestyles, financial planners must understand and address an assortment of goals and financial situations. While a one-size-fits-all approach may be effective for managing a large book of clients, it neglects the opportunities and challenges associated with diversity, and more importantly, the diversity itself, thus inhibiting the progress of the profession. To address market changes as well as challenges facing the profession, culturally competent financial planning that moves beyond diversity as numbers and instead focuses on diversity as needs is critical. Further, to realize the true value in diversity, the role of diversity in financial planning processes or its effects on advising and financial services offered must be considered. As the composition of client pools change, the profession must also evolve to incorporate such changes into financial planning practice with the goal of enhancing client service. It is through such efforts to understand and leverage difference that financial planners can be reflective on, rather than of, the public it serves.

REFERENCES

Barney, J. (1991). Firm resources and sustained competitive advantage. *Journal of Management, 17*(1), 99–120.

Berscheid, E., & Walster, E. H. (1978). *Interpersonal attraction*. Reading, MA: Addison-Wesley.

Blau, P. M. (1977). *Inequality and heterogeneity*. New York: Free Press.

Byrne, D. (1971). *The attraction paradigm*. New York: Academic.

Cox, T. H., Jr. (1993). *Cultural diversity in organizations: Theory, research and practice*. San Francisco, CA: Berrett-Koehler.

Cox, T. H., Jr., & Blake, S. (1991). Managing cultural diversity: Implications for organizational competitiveness. *Academy of Management Executive, 5*, 45–56.

Ferguson, M., & Porter, S. C. (2013). An examination of categorization processes in organizations: The root of intergroup bias and a route to prejudice reduction. In Q. Roberson (Ed.), *The Oxford handbook of diversity and work* (pp. 98–114). Oxford, UK: Oxford University Press.

Grant, R. M. (1996). Toward a knowledge-based theory of the firm. *Strategic Management Journal, 17*(10), 109–122.

Harrison, D. A., & Klein, K. J. (2007). What's the difference? Diversity constructs as separation, variety, or disparity in organizations. *Academy of Management Review, 32*, 1199–1228.

Harrison, D. A., Price, K. H., & Bell, M. P. (1998). Beyond relational demography: Time and the effects of surface- and deep-level diversity on work group cohesion. *Academy of Management Journal, 41*, 96–107.

Harrison, D. A., Price, K. H., Gavin, J. H., & Florey, A. T. (2002). Time, teams, and task performance: Changing effects of surface- and deep-level diversity on group functioning. *Academy of Management Journal, 45*(5), 1029–1045.

Ibarra, H. (1995). Race, opportunity and diversity of social circles in managerial networks. *Academy of Management Journal, 38,* 673–703.

Ibarra, H., & Andrews, S. B. (1993). Power, social influence, and sense making: Effects of network centrality and proximity on employee perceptions. *Administrative Science Quarterly, 38,* 277–303.

Jackson, S. E., May, K. A., & Whitney, K. (1995). Understanding the dynamics of diversity in decision making teams. In R. A. Guzzo & E. Salas (Eds.), *Team decision making effectiveness in organizations* (pp. 204–261). San Francisco: Jossey-Bass.

Johnston, W. B., & Packer, A. E. (1987). *Workforce 2000: Work and workers for the 21st century.* Indianapolis, IN: Hudson Institute.

Jost, J. T., Federico, C. M., & Napier, J. L. (2009). Political ideology: Its structure, functions, and elective affinities. *Annual Review of Psychology, 60,* 307–337.

Kanter, R. (1977). *Men and women of the organization.* New York: Basic Books.

Lau, D. C., & Murnighan, J. K. (1998). Demographic diversity and faultlines: The compositional dynamics of organizational groups. *Academy of Management Review, 23,* 325–340.

Mannix, E., & Neale, M. A. (2005). What differences make a difference? The promise and reality of diverse teams in organizations. *Psychological Science in the Public Interest, 6*(2), 31–55.

Major, B., Kaiser, C. R., O'Brien, L. T., & McCoy, S. K. (2007). Perceived discrimination as worldview threat or worldview confirmation: Implications for self-esteem. *Journal of Personality and Social Psychology, 92,* 1068–1086.

Mor Barak, M. E., & Cherin, D. (1998). A tool to expand organizational understanding of workforce diversity. *Administration in Social Work, 22,* 47–64.

Mor Barak, M. E., & Travis, D. J. (2013). Socioeconomic trends: Broadening the diversity ecosystem. In Q. Roberson (Ed.), *The Oxford handbook of diversity and work* (pp. 393–418). Oxford, UK: Oxford University Press.

Nishii, L. H. (2013). The benefits of climate for inclusion for gender-diverse groups. *Academy of Management Journal, 56*(6), 1754–1774.

O'Brien, L. T., & Gilbert, P. N. (2013). Ideology: An invisible yet potent dimension of diversity. In Q. Roberson (Ed.), *The Oxford handbook of diversity and work* (pp. 132–153). Oxford, UK: Oxford University Press.

Pettigrew, T. (1982). *Prejudice.* Cambridge, MA: Belknap Press.

Reagans, R. (2013). Demographic diversity as network connections: Homophily and the diversity-performance debate. In Q. Roberson (Ed.), *The Oxford handbook of diversity and work* (pp. 192–206). Oxford, UK: Oxford University Press.

Richard, O. C. (2000). Racial diversity, business strategy, and firm performance: A resource based view. *Academy of Management Journal, 43,* 164–177.

Roberson, Q. M. (2006). Disentangling the meanings of diversity and inclusion in organizations. *Group & Organization Management, 31,* 212–236.

Roberson, Q. M., Holmes, O. H. & Perry, J. L. (2017). Transforming research on diversity and firm performance: A dynamic capabilities perspective. *Academy of Management Annals, 11*(1), 189–216.

Rucci, A. J., Kim, S. P., & Quinn, R. T. The employee-customer-profit chair at Sears. *Harvard Business Review, 76,* 82–97.

Shore, L. M., Randel, A. E., Chung, B. G., Dean, M. A., Ehrhart, K. H., & Singh, G. (2011). Inclusion and diversity in work groups: A review and model for future research. *Journal of Management, 37,* 1262–1289.

Sidanius, J., & Pratto, F. (1999). *Social dominance: An intergroup theory of social hierarchy and oppression.* New York: Cambridge University Press.

Tajfel, H. (1978). *Differentiation between social groups: Studies in the social psychology of intergroup relations.* London: Academic Press.

Tajfel, H. (1982). *Social identity and intergroup relations.* Cambridge, UK: Cambridge University Press.

Tajfel, H., & Turner, J. C. (1986). The social identity theory of intergroup behavior. In S. Worchel & W. G. Austin (Eds.), *The psychology of intergroup relations* (pp. 7–24). Chicago: Nelson-Hall.

Thatcher, S. M. B. (2013). Moving beyond a categorical approach to diversity: The role of demographic faultlines. In Q. Roberson (Ed.), *The Oxford handbook of diversity and work* (pp. 52–70). Oxford, UK: Oxford University Press.

Thomas, D. A., & Ely, R. J. 1996. Making differences matter: A new paradigm for managing diversity. *Harvard Business Review, 74,* 79–90.

Thomas, R. R., Jr. (1991). *Beyond race and gender: Unleashing the power of your total workforce by managing diversity.* New York: AMACOM Books.

Turner, J. C. (1985). Social categorization and the self-concept: A social cognitive theory of group behavior. In E. E. Lawler, III (Ed.), *Advances in group processes* (Vol. 2, pp. 77–121). Greenwich, CT: JAI Press.

Turner, J. C., Hogg, M. A., Oakes, P. J., Reicher, S. D., & Wetherell, M. S. (1987). *Rediscovering the social group: A self-categorization theory.* Oxford, UK: Blackwell.

van Knippenberg, D., De Dreu, C. K. W., & Homan, A. C. (2004). Work group diversity and group performance: An integrative model and research agenda. *Journal of Applied Psychology, 89,* 1008–1022.

Williams, K., & O'Reilly, C. A. (1998). Demography and diversity in organizations: A review of 40 years of research. In B. M. Staw & L. L. Cummings (Eds.), *Research in organizational behavior* (pp. 77–140). Greenwich, CT: JAI Press.

Wright, P. M., & McMahan, G.C. (1992). Theoretical perspectives for strategic human resource management. *Journal of Management, 18*(2), 295–320.

CHAPTER 15

Client Psychology

The Older Client

Deanna L. Sharpe, PhD, CFP®, CRPS®, CRPC®
University of Missouri

INTRODUCTION

Financial planning is an interactive and facilitative process. Through skillful professional conversations, planners help clients identify value-based goals, assess financial resources, and develop a mutually agreed upon process to achieve those goals. Implicit in this process is the assumption that the client is a capable, rational decision-maker, able to fully understand and carefully evaluate alternatives and make satisfaction-maximizing choices. But, as noted throughout this volume, the rational model may not always accurately represent the client decision-making process.

Client psychology offers an alternative perspective of client thought and action. By applying the science of mind and behavior to the financial planning environment and explicitly considering the behavioral aspects of decision-making, client psychology generates a more richly textured and nuanced understanding of factors influencing client perceptions, understanding, decisions, and actions.

When working with older clients, the psychological and behavioral aspects of the financial planning process discussed in other chapters remain important. But, the biological and cognitive aspects of the aging process and their effects on decision-making capacity must be considered as well. Although research on later life cognitive change clearly refutes the idea that the years past midlife offer only mental decline and eventual senility, it remains true that mental capacity and function can change and deteriorate with aging, especially in the advanced years.

As the U.S. population ages, the number of older financial planning clients will certainly increase. To ensure these clients' needs are met and fiduciary standards are upheld, financial planners will need to be able to distinguish normal age-related cognitive changes from onset of debilitating decline in mental function. Further, an understanding of normal age-related cognitive and physical changes can facilitate structuring client meetings in ways that help preserve autonomy and build on the strengths and capacities of older clients. This chapter will preview significant demographic changes in the older population, discuss key insights from current research on age-related cognitive change, distinguish normal cognitive decline from concerning behavior, offer suggestions for best practice when working with older clients, and propose directions for future research.

Waves of Gray

The United States is in the midst of a seismic demographic shift. By 2030, the last baby boomers will have celebrated their 65th birthday, boosting the number of older adults by 18 million. Between 2014 and 2060, the size of the age 65 and older population is expected to more than double, rising from 46.2 million to 98.2 million. (Mather, Jacobsen, & Pollard, 2015). In 2014, the ratio of 65 and older to under 65 was about 1 in 7. By 2030, this ratio will be 1 in 5 and by 2060, it will be 1 in 4 (Federal Interagency Forum on Aging-Related Statistics, 2016; Ortman, Velkoff, & Hogan, 2014).

Not only is the older adult population growing in size, those reaching age 65 can expect to live longer than past generations. Current life expectancy of someone age 65 is almost 20 years, as compared with less than 14 years in 1950. Some older individuals will exceed that life expectancy. At age 75, life expectancy is 12 years; at age 85, it is a little over 6.5 years. Even those reaching 100 can expect to live 2 additional years (Arias, 2006). This greater longevity will increase the proportion of the population of advanced age. By 2050, 4.8% of the population is expected to be age 85 or older, up from 1.9% in 2014 (Federal Interagency Forum on Aging-Related Statistics, 2016).

Women currently comprise 58% of those age 65 and older and 68% of those 85 and older, due to differential survival rates (Seltzer & Yahirun, 2013). This differential is likely to persist. But, in contrast to past trends, the older population is projected to become more racially and ethnically diverse. Demographers expect by 2060 the older population will be about 9% Asian, 12% black, 22% Hispanic, and 55% white versus the current distribution of 4% Asian, 9% black, 8% Hispanic, and 78% white (Federal Interagency Forum on Aging-Related Statistics, 2016; Mather et al., 2015).

These demographic trends will certainly affect the characteristics and needs of those seeking financial services. The rising number of older adults potentially living to an advanced age provokes critical questions about sustainability of cognitive function and decision-making ability though later life. There is good reason for concern. Incidence of dementia is higher with age, affecting 3% of persons age 65 to 74, 17% of persons age 75 to 84, and 32% of those aged 85 and older. Projections are by 2025 there will be 7.1 million persons in the United States with Alzheimer's dementia, an almost 35% increase from 2017 (Alzheimer Association, 2017).

Yet, at the same time, current research indicates that the brain is more responsive to growth and development than once thought. Neuroscience and psychology researchers affirm that learning can occur into advanced age and that lifestyle choices can help prevent or slow mental decline (Cabeza, Anderson, Nicole, Locantore, & McIntosh, 2002; Raz & Rodrigue, 2006). There is optimism that most older adults will be able to live in community without major illness or debility into their 70s and 80s (Hess, Strough, & Lockenhoff, 2015).

Researchers are also recognizing that aging is not solely a biological process. Life is lived in the context of culture, which deeply shapes both the content and process of perception, thought, roles, and expectations of self and others, as well as views of aging as a positive culmination of life or a negative descent into decline (Kitayama, 2000). Crosscultural studies have identified cultural variation among older adults in several cognitive aspects of aging, including focus, attention, inference, comprehension, judgment, communication, reasoning, and memory (Kitayama, 2000; Park & Huang, 2010; Park, Nisbett, & Hedden, 1999; Peng & Nisbett, 1999). Recognizing cultural variation in the aging process will be important when serving an increasingly racially and ethnically diverse older population.

Effective financial planning with older clients requires a broad understanding of aging as a psychological and physical process. As will be discussed in this chapter, aging is a complex process that has different meanings, depending on context. Neurological and physical change occurs in the brain with aging. But, the amount and rate of change as well as the effect of this change on cognitive performance is not uniform and can vary greatly among older adults, challenging efforts to characterize the aging process in general terms. In part due to later-life neurological changes, older adult decision-making does not always align with the classic economic rational model. Context, emotion, and culture can also have significant effects on thought, judgment, and decisions in later life as well. Viewing the effects of cognitive aging through the lens of client psychology can broaden understanding of contextual and behavioral influences on later-life decision-making. It can also highlight potential vulnerabilities in the decision-making process of older adults and help enhance the quality and productivity of the financial planning process with and for older clients.

What Is Aging?

"What is aging?" is a surprisingly challenging question to answer. Aging is far from just simply accumulating birthdays. Rather, current research indicates aging is a complex process resulting from interactions among biochemical, neurological, and physical systems, which are mediated to some extent by culture, environment, personal history, and lifestyle (Carstensen & Hartel, 2006; Hess et al., 2015; Pinto da Costa et al., 2016; Stern & Carstensen, 2000). Exactly how these interactions bring about the mental and physical changes observed in later life is the central focus of much current biological and behavioral science research. Although theories and scientific discussions about that process abound, researchers agree that aging, per se, does not generate inevitable cognitive decline. Further, cognitive change, when it occurs, is not evenly distributed. Some cognitive functions remain relatively stable throughout life. Other cognitive functions begin life-long decline as early as the second or third decade of life, whereas still other cognitive functions decline only late in life (Hedden & Gabrieli, 2004).

Arking (2006), a respected scholar on the biological aspects of aging, defines aging as "the time-independent series of cumulative, progressive, intrinsic, and deleterious functional and structural changes that usually begin to manifest themselves at reproductive maturity and eventually culminate in death" (p. 11). Though this is an apt description of the underlying biological processes in humans, aging has significant psychological and sociocultural dimensions as well.

Researchers view age from several perspectives. These perspectives not only capture different facets of growing older but also apply to various aspects of financial planning with older clients. *Chronological age* is simply the number of years from birth (Cannon, 2015). Relevant to financial planning, chronological age determines eligibility for certain programs or benefits such as social security, Medicare, senior discounts offered by retail establishments, or the start of mandated withdrawals from retirement accounts. A somewhat related concept is *biological age*, defined as the number of years lived relative to potential years remaining (Birren, 1968). This view of aging implicitly underlies retirement income need calculations, especially when such things as a client's current health status and longevity of family members are considered in that calculation. The awareness that years lived is finite may explain why even across different cultures, older adults see future time and opportunity as limited (Lockenhoff & Rutt, 2015).

Age also has social and psychological meaning. *Social age* relates to the roles one has in life as well as to the cultural expectations regarding the mental performance and behavior of persons of different ages (Birren, 1968; Kitayama, 2000). A number of roles change in later life. For example, individuals cease to be employees and become retirees. Some individuals become a grandparent, a caregiver for a loved one, or a widow(er).

In a financial planning context, role changes can affect financial demands, resources, goals, and plans. Some obvious examples would be that income sources change and spending on transportation and clothing may decline following the transition from worker to retiree. Or, after the birth of a grandchild or death of a spouse, a client may change life insurance beneficiary designations.

It is important for financial planners to recognize that role changes, even when anticipated and positive, may be stressful for clients. Some role changes may contribute to depression, especially if unwanted or burdensome. For some clients, exiting the workplace at retirement will mean losing the sense of belonging, purpose, and worth that work provided. About 1 in 5 family caregivers experience depression, a rate twice that of the general population (Family Caregiver Alliance, 2002). Of course, the loss of a spouse or partner is a major role change from life shared intimately with another to life alone. Nearly a third of those losing a spouse experience a major episode of depression within the first month of the loss. About half of these individuals meet the criteria for clinical depression a year later. Among former caregivers of a spouse with dementia, close to 2 in 5 experienced mild to severe depression as long as 3 years after their spouse died (Family Caregiver Alliance, 2002). Having multiple illnesses or taking medication, events common among older individuals, also increases risk of depression (Centers for Disease Control, 2013; National Institute of Mental Health, 2005). Left unaddressed, depression can be a contributing factor to poor decision-making, even in an otherwise healthy older adult.

A person's view of their own age is *subjective age*. Those having a relatively higher level of health and activity as compared with age peers may perceive themselves as younger than their chronological age (Quadagno, 2011). Financial planning clients who view themselves as "younger than their years" could be the adventure seekers, active and engaged in life, enjoying travel and new experiences. But, this type of client might also be apt to put off or avoid important conversations about such things as moderating retirement distributions or funding long-term care, deeming those issues for someone older and not yet relevant to their lives.

Neurobiological changes that negatively affect client judgment, decision-making, and completion of financial tasks are of particular concern when working with older clients. Laboratory assessments of later life cognitive function use two definitions of age. *Psychological age* refers to the level of ability to adapt to one's environment and depends on such things as perception speed, learning, reasoning, and memory (Birren, 1968). *Functional age* is the ability to perform specific tasks, functions, or roles. Decline in ability to function, although it typically occurs over time, has been linked to neurobiological changes in the brain rather than to chronological age (Ferrucci, Hesdorffer, Bandinelli, & Simonsick, 2010), affirming the perspective that functional decline in later life is not an inevitable aspect of growing older.

Normal Cognitive Aging

In initial studies of cognitive aging, researchers utilized discipline specific theories and methods in psychology, behavioral economics, and neuroscience, essentially working in separate worlds. Recently, however, development of brain imagery technology has fostered interdisciplinary research. From this collaboration, neuroeconomics, where researchers track brain activity as study participants complete structured economic decision-making tasks in an experimental setting, has emerged as a new field of study (Brown & Ridderinkhof, 2009).

Interdisciplinary work over the past two decades has greatly expanded knowledge of which aspects of cognition tend to be sustained or degenerate over time and of age-related differences in cognitive performance. Although scientists have not yet determined a precise description of normal cognitive aging, some patterns are beginning to become clear. In this section, what is known about age-related physical and neurological change in the brain will be reviewed. Then, potential links between these changes and age-related differences in the context of economic and financial decision-making will be examined.

AGE-RELATED CHANGES IN BRAIN STRUCTURE AND FUNCTION

Scientific research has established that normal aging does not mean absence of either physical change in the brain or decline in brain function. Nor does cognitive decline occur only in later life. In fact, neurological studies indicate some aspects of cognitive decline may begin even in highly educated healthy adults as early as the second or third decade of life (Salthouse, 2009).

Postmortem studies of brain structure reveal that, with aging, brain volume decreases, gray and white brain matter atrophies, blood flow decreases, nerve synapses degenerate, and neurochemical changes occur (Cabeza et al., 2002; Raz & Rodrigue, 2006). Scientists hypothesized these physical changes in the brain would underlie change in cognitive function. But, postmortem studies cannot provide insight into physical–mental connections or onset of decline. Nor can anything be learned about the lifestyle or the behavioral or medical history of the person whose brain is being examined (Raz & Rodrigue, 2006).

Using brain imagery technology such as positron emission tomography and functional magnetic resonance imaging with living older adults, neuroscientists have been able to measure brain activity, associate brain structure and activity with various cognitive functions, and make cross-age comparisons. After completing an extensive review of 229 postmortem and brain-imaging studies, Raz and Rodrique (2006) drew these tentative broad conclusions about the aging brain: The decline in brain volume that occurs with age does not affect all parts of the brain equally. Decreased brain volume in specific sections of the brain has been associated with poor performance on executive tasks, skill acquisition, and spatial memory tasks. Decline in neuron size or density may be a contributing factor in the decrease in the size of the area of the brain involved in decision-making. Interestingly, Raz and Roderique noted that areas in the brain associated with sensory function are less affected by aging.

In general, the interdisciplinary research of brain and behavioral scientists conducted to date suggests that normal cognitive aging is characterized by gradual change in the structure and function of the underlying bioneural circuitry of thought and decision-making, though specifics of that process are still under investigation. These changes in the brain do not occur in the same way or at the same rate across all older individuals, nor do these changes appear to cause the same level of debility. Consequently, ability to predict the type, timing, and severity of cognitive and functional changes that are observed to occur in later life is still limited.

Approaching the question of normal cognitive aging from a somewhat different perspective, psychologists have investigated various aspects of intelligence, typically by having community-dwelling older adults complete standardized cognitive tests in structured lab experiments. Most of these tests have been performed at a point in time although a few have followed the same adults over time. Some studies have gathered comparison data from younger individuals (Christensen, 2001; Harada, Natelson-Love, & Triebel, 2013; Raz & Rodrigue, 2006).

From this work, psychologists have classified different types of intelligence and distinguished the aspects of intelligence that tend to change with aging from those that do not. Rate of change in intelligence components varies across older individuals. Some older adults maintain cognitive performance equal to that of younger adults, whereas others experience significant cognitive decline (Cabeza et al., 2002). This variation makes it difficult to identify a common measure of normal level and change in later life cognitive function. Some general observations regarding age-related cognitive change from a psychological perspective can be made, however.

Psychologists broadly categorize intelligence as crystalized or fluid (Horn & Cattell, 1966). Crystalized intelligence refers to accumulated knowledge as well as numeric and verbal skills gained through formal education and life experience. Because it develops over time in the context of life as it is lived, crystalized intelligence reflects the norms of a given culture or society (Dima, 2009). This type of knowledge is used when solving routine or familiar problems and is typically measured by assessing a person's vocabulary and general knowledge (Lezak, Howieson, Bigler, & Tranel, 2012). Crystalized intelligence remains constant or improves slightly over time (at a rate of 0.02 to 0.003 standard deviations per year) until around age 60 or 70. Since it reflects accumulated knowledge, older persons tend to outperform younger persons on tasks utilizing this type of intelligence (Harada et al., 2013; Salthouse, 2012).

Fluid intelligence is the ability to use logic and reason to solve novel or abstract problems with little to no prior instruction or examples. It includes a person's innate ability to quickly attend to and process new information (Elias & Saucier, 2006). Several components of fluid intelligence relate to the ability to think quickly on your feet, including executive function, processing speed, memory, and psychomotor ability. Research indicates processing speed and psychomotor ability peaks near age 30, then gradually declines (at a rate of −0.02 standard deviations per year) (Harada et al., 2013; Salthouse, 2012). Fluid intelligence seems particularly susceptible to physiological and neurological change in brain structure. David Laibson (2011) notes that over a lifespan, overall intellectual performance is curvilinear, rising until around a person's early 50s, then declining, with lifetime gains in crystalized intelligence tending to offset losses in fluid intelligence. Harada, Natelson-Love, and Triebel (2013) review research on six specific aspects of cognitive ability in later life that are linked to crystalized and fluid intelligence. A summary of what is known about age-related change in these abilities is listed in Table 15.1. Language and visuospatial ability have aspects of both crystalized and fluid intelligence. In contrast, attention, processing speed, memory, and executive function are all aspects of fluid intelligence. A review of research findings on age-related change in these aspects of cognitive ability follows.

Language

Language includes one's current stock of words, as well as ability to access, use, and add to that stock. Research indicates that vocabulary, an aspect of crystalized intelligence, remains intact over time and can even improve (et al., 2013; Park & Reuter-Lorenz, 2009). Ability to see and name a common item (visual confrontation naming) remains relatively stable over time,

TABLE 15.1. Components of Crystalized and Fluid Intelligence

Crystalized Intelligence: Mental Functions That Tend to Remain Stable with Age
Vocabulary Retrieval
General Knowledge Retrieval
Memory Function
Recognition Memory—information retrieval when given a cue
Temporal Order Memory
Procedural Memory
Memory Type
Nondeclarative (implicit) Memory

Fluid Intelligence: Mental Functions That Tend to Decline with Age
Executive Function
Processing Speed (including Psychomotor)
Memory Functions
Short-term recall
Delayed free recall—information retrieval without a cue
Source memory—recall of source of information
Prospective memory—remembering to do intended action in future
Memory Types
Declarative (explicit) Memory
Semantic Memory (late life decline)
Episodic Memory (lifelong decline)

Source: Christensen, 2001; Harada et al., 2013; Morgan 2006.

declining only after age 70 (Harada et al., 2013; Zec, Markwekk, Burkett, & Larsen, 2005). Verbal fluency is closely aligned with fluid intelligence (Roca, et al, 2012). In assessments that required older adults to complete a word search and produce words that exemplified a certain category in a timed test (e.g. names of animals), performance declined with age (Harada et al., 2013). However, this measured decline could also have reflected the need for more time to process and perform the request rather than a loss in fluid intelligence, per se.

Visuospatial Ability

Processing, interpreting, and using information about the location of objects in three-dimensional space is critical for moving safely within one's environment, judging distance to objects, and orienting oneself within space. Absent failing sight or dementia, recognition of familiar items or people (object perception) or of the physical location of objects (spatial perception) remains intact with aging. This aspect of visuospatial ability relates to crystalized intelligence. In contrast, the ability to assemble parts to make a correct or logical whole either mentally, on paper, or physically in three-dimensional space (visual construction) declines with age (Harada et al., 2013; Howieson, Holm, Kaye, Oken, & Howieson, 1993). Use of current level of skill and ability to solve a novel problem relates this aspect of visuospatial ability to fluid intelligence.

Attention

Attention is the "ability to concentrate and focus on specific stimuli" (Harada et al., 2013, p. 3). Differences between older and younger adults depend on the type of attention required. Ability to attend to simple verbal instructions (immediate memory), as assessed by repeating a list of numbers immediately after hearing them, appears to decline only by a small amount for older adults (Lezak et al., 2012). Larger differences by age have been found for the more complex attention tasks requiring selective or divided attention, with older individuals performing less well than younger individuals (Carlson, Hasher, Zacks, & Connelly, 1995; Salthouse, Fristoe, Lineweaver, & Coon, 1995). Selective attention is required to center on what is relevant and block out what is not relevant to a given task. An example would be listening to a friend in a noisy restaurant. Divided attention is ability to attend to more than one task at a time. Carrying on a conversation while cooking is an example (Harada et al., 2013).

Processing Speed

When responding to a specific stimulus, whether in an experimental setting in a lab or in daily life, four things must happen: attention given to the stimulus, sensory transmission of data regarding the stimulus, data processing, and resulting motor activity (Morgan, 2006). These four steps taken together comprise response time. Research indicates that although aging is associated with a decline in speed in all four components of response time, most of the decline is due to a decline in data-processing speed (Morgan, 2006). Scientific evaluation of processing speed indicates that a slowing of this ability begins around age 30 and continues through remaining life (Carlson et al., 1995; Salthouse, 2010; Salthouse et al., 1995).

Older adults appear to trade-off speed for accuracy. To avoid costly errors in judgment, older adults "monitor their activities more closely, preferring slower but more accurate performance" (Morgan, 2006, p. 81). This compensation helps explain why drivers over age 65 tend to drive slower. Morgan (2006) notes that lower processing speed and reaction time places older people at a disadvantage when similar performance speed is expected of all ages such as when entering or leaving an escalator or elevator. Pressure to perform faster can increase stress, deteriorating performance even more.

Memory

Forgetfulness is a common frustration and complaint of older individuals, often giving rise to the fear that descent into dementia or Alzheimer's has begun. Research on memory in older individuals offers some reassurance and hope, however. Currently, only about 1 in 10 individuals age 65 and older has Alzheimer's (Alzheimer's Association, 2017). For the majority of older adults, although some types of memory slow or decline in productivity with age, other types of memory stay the same or can improve.

Memory involves the acquisition, retention, and use of information. Research indicates the rate at which individuals acquire information declines rather steadily with age, starting as early as the second decade of life (Haaland, Price, & Larue, 2003). Age-related differences in the retention and use of information depend on the type of memory considered.

Short-term memory is maintaining information for about a minute, such as remembering the dollar amount of a check received to write on a bank deposit slip. In a common test of short-term memory, older adults are able to repeat a string of about 7 digits with minimal deficits as compared with younger adults (Glisky, 2007).

Working memory is the ability to temporarily store and use information needed to complete complex mental tasks. Psychologists see this type of memory as a determining factor in other important cognitive functions, including language comprehension, reasoning, and problem solving (Brehmer, Westerberg, & Bäckman, 2012). Results from experimental studies indicate working memory performance is worse in older adults as compared with younger adults (Nilsson et al., 2004; Salthouse, 2004).

Long-term memory has several aspects. *Declarative (explicit) memory* is recall of facts and events. It has two parts, semantic and episodic memory. *Semantic memory* is one's general knowledge of the world gained from formal education, interaction in society, and life experience. It includes language use and practical knowledge. Normal older adults typically have a much larger store of this type of knowledge than younger adults. Retrieval of this type of information in later life may take a little longer, but the organization of and access to this type of memory seems little changed with age (Glisky, 2007; Light, 1992). *Episodic (autobiographical) memory* is recall of one's own past. Research indicates it is typically easier to retrieve recent experience than early childhood experiences. An interesting exception is that events between age 15 and 25 can typically be retrieved at a higher rate, a fact usually explained by the relatively high emotions and importance of these coming-of-age years (Glisky, 2007). Some researchers have noted that although older adults retain memories of their own past over time, they report fewer details of that past as compared with younger adults (Levine, Svoboda, Hay, Winocur, & Moscovitch, 2002). There is little difference by age in recall of details of highly emotional public events such as the 2001 attack on the World Trade Center (Davidson & Glisky, 2002).

Nondeclarative (implicit) memory is knowledge acquired and used without conscious thought. A common form of this type of memory is procedural memory, the knowledge of how to do a skilled activity such as reading a book. This type of memory is acquired over time through extensive practice and, once acquired, is used automatically or by rote. Older individuals can acquire procedural skills that involve mind or body and retain these skills over time. There is evidence that among those older individuals with high levels of expertise, even though some components of a skill may decline with age (e.g. movement becomes slower), use of compensating mental or physical actions leads to little overall degrading of performance with time (Glisky, 2007).

Prospective memory deals with remembering to do things at a future time such as paying a bill, keeping a dentist appointment, or returning a borrowed item. Older adults who rely on external memory aids such as a calendar or a reminder posted in a visible place can do well accomplishing these types of tasks. Recalling the need to complete habitual tasks such as taking medication can be difficult, though, as there are fewer environmental cues (Glisky, 2007).

Executive Function

Executive function encompasses several cognitive processes including capacity to self-monitor, reason, be mentally flexible, problem solve, organize, coordinate, plan, implement, and evaluate (Glisky, 2007; Harada et al., 2013). Glisky (2007) notes that executive control:

> *Plays a key role in virtually all aspects of cognition, allocating attentional resources among stimuli or tasks, inhibiting distracting or irrelevant information in working memory, formulating strategies*

> *for encoding and retrieval, and directing all manner of problem-solving, decision-making, and other goal-directed activities. Executive control is particularly important for novel tasks for which a set of habitual processes is not readily available (p. 9).*

Neuroimaging studies indicate a possible physical basis for cognitive decline in older adults is loss of volume and function of the prefrontal regions of the brain (West, 1996). As compared with younger individuals, older adults tend to think concretely. The ability to form concepts, think abstractly, reason using unfamiliar material, and be mentally flexible declines with age, especially beyond age 70 (Lezak et al., 2012). Verbal and math reasoning ability begins to decline around age 45 (Singh-Manoux et al., 2011). Some executive functions, however, seem to change little over life. These include the ability to note similarity, to explain the meaning of a proverb, or to reason using familiar material (Harada et al., 2013).

AGING AND ECONOMIC DECISION-MAKING

Rational economic theory, which provided the initial basis for scientific study of decision-making, casts decision-making process as cognitive, calculated, and deliberative, unaffected by context. Cognitive psychologists David Kahneman and Amos Tversky questioned this perspective, recognizing the role that emotion, subjective valuation, and intuition have in decision-making. Their challenge to conventional economic theory, published in the now seminal 1979 article *Prospect Theory: An Analysis of Decision Under Risk,* spurred development of behavioral economics.

Behavioral economics examines the influence of cognitive, emotional, social, and psychological factors on economic decisions, typically by assessing study participant response to specific tasks structured as lab experiments. Initial research in behavioral economics focused on young adults. Recent research efforts have turned attention to older adults and to incorporating simultaneous brain imaging into the experimental setting. Although this work is at a relatively early stage, several interesting age-related differences have been identified.

Learning

Learning is a complex cognitive task that requires recognizing the outcome of a choice, contrasting actual versus expected outcome, determining whether or not to change actions for similar future situations, and recalling and implementing that determination as needed. Older adults require more time to learn, but can make gains with repetition and experience (Samanez-Larkin, 2015; Samanez-Larkin, Worthy, Mata, McClure, & Knutson, 2014). Some researchers attribute this age difference to the difficulty older adults have with calculating prediction errors in new settings (Chowdhury et al., 2013). Neuroimaging shows lower brain activity in older adults in the learning process as compared with younger adults (Mell et al., 2009). Neurological studies also indicate older adults struggle more with learning when rewards are probabilistic (uncertain) versus when reward information is reliable (Pietschmann, Endrass, Czerwon, & Kathmann, 2017).

Whether the type of feedback makes a difference has been debated. Some studies suggest older adults respond more to negative feedback (Denburg, Recknor, Bechara, & Tranel, 2006; Wood, Busemeyer, Koling, Cox, & Davis, 2005), whereas other studies found greater response to positive feedback (Eppinger, Schuck, Nystrom, & Cohen, 2013). Still other research found no age difference in type of feedback (Lighthall, Gorlick, Schoeke, Frank, & Mather, 2012).

Reaction to Gains and Losses.

Behavioral and neural research indicate there is no difference between younger and older adults in self-reported positive responses to the anticipation or receipt of monetary gains (Nielsen, Knutson, & Carstensen, 2008; Samanez-Larkin et al., 2007). Interestingly, results differ for anticipated losses but not actual losses. Older adults report lower levels of negative response in anticipation of monetary losses. Neural assessment confirms reduced brain activity in this situation for older versus younger adults (Samanez-Larkin et al., 2007). But, with actual loss of money, there is no difference in the reactions of older and younger adults (Samanez-Larkin et al., 2007).

Intertemporal Decision-Making

Intertemporal decisions are complex. Options differ in time of receipt and in size. Rewards can be immediate or delayed. Waiting usually gains a larger reward, but self-control and patience must be exercised. Trade-offs must be evaluated. Interestingly, in behavior studies with rodent models and with humans, there is a section of the brain that, when activated, predicts choice of a delayed reward. This section of the brain appears to play a role in both self-control and lower preference for a smaller, immediate reward (Beas, Setlow, Samanez-Larkin, & Bizon, 2015).

In a number of studies, older adults have demonstrated a relatively greater willingness to wait as compared with younger adults. Scientists have viewed this willingness of older adults in two ways. It could be a happy accident of age-related neural decline that reduces impulsivity and immediacy (Eppinger, Nystrom, & Cohen, 2012). Alternatively, older adults may be relying more on previous life experience with delayed rewards (Li, Baldassi, Johnson, & Weber, 2013).

Recent neuroimaging studies of older adults who were deciding between an immediate or delayed reward have found that those adults with neurological dysfunction in the section of the brain related to the transfer of emotion-related signals were more likely to select an immediate reward. The adults for whom this section of the brain was intact were more likely to pick a higher, delayed reward. Both groups were otherwise healthy (Denburg & Hedgcock, 2015).

Probabilistic (Risky) Decision-Making

Results of behavioral economics experiments designed to assess age difference in risky decision-making have yielded mixed results. Some studies indicate older adults are relatively more risk averse (Deakin, Aitken, Robbins, & Sahakian, 2004; Kumar, 2007). Other studies have failed to find a significant difference between the two age groups. Still other studies have found that under some conditions, older adults were more likely than younger adult to pick a high-risk option (Deakin et al., 2004; Denburg, Tranel, & Bechara, 2005; Henninger, Madden, & Huettel, 2010; Kumar, 2007).

One of the few neuroimaging studies of choice between high- and low-risk options by age included a series of choices between risky stocks and safe bonds (Kuhnen & Knutson, 2005) In this experiment, feedback from one trial regarding which assets had better returns had to be used on a subsequent trial to maximize returns. No age difference was found for risk aversion. There were age differences in choice of risky stock options, not related to over-investment in bonds (suggesting risk aversion), but to mistiming stock selection. Brain imagery results pointed to greater difficulty in processing information during the task for older adults, suggesting observed differences were not due to risk aversion but to differences in cognitive function (Beas et al., 2015). In a related study, Weller, Levin, & Denburg (2011) determined that compared with younger adults, older adults responded less to expected value when making risky decisions.

Framing Effects

Framing effects occur when change in the way information is presented can influence preference even though the same facts have been given. An example would be to describe ground beef as 90% lean versus 10% fat. Usually, one frame has a positive connotation, the other a negative, engaging an emotional response in the choice making process. Neuroimaging studies have found older adults who have lost efficiency in transmitting emotional information are less responsive to framing effects (Denburg & Hedgcock, 2015).

Overconfidence

Overconfidence is present when one's expected performance level exceeds measured performance. Research involving those age 60 and older has found that, although financial literacy scores decline steadily across age, confidence in one's ability to make financial decisions does not drop with age (Finke, Howe, & Huston, 2016). Research indicates that men are more susceptible to being overconfident than women, particularly regarding the ability to realize gains from stock trading (Barber & Odean, 2001).

Compensation and Adaptation

To compensate for a decline in short-term memory, older adults often use external memory supports, such as putting keys in the same place, writing appointments on a calendar, or using a pill dispenser marked with days of the week (Alzheimer's Association, 2017). To cope with decline in areas of mental function related to fluid intelligence, older adults tend to compensate by drawing on their accumulated knowledge and life experience (Christensen, 2001; Morgan, 2006). As processing speed slows, older adults tend to adapt by becoming more cautious and deliberative in thought and action (Morgan, 2006).

In a review of decision strategies, Mata, Josef, & Lemaire (2015) note that as compared with younger adults, older adults tend to rely more on recognition, take-the-best, and tallying as decision-making strategies. Recognition means selecting the more recognized option in a set of alternatives, inferring the recognized option has a higher value. In take-the-best, the decision-maker searches through options, looking for a discriminating factor, then selecting on the basis of this factor. Tallying is used when a decision-maker counts the number of positive attributes each alternative has and then selects the one with the highest count. Each of these strategies is some form of a rule of thumb, relying more on affect (i.e., which alternative is appealing) and salient visual clues than on a conscious, rational, deliberative process.

In summary, research on cognitive aging indicates that the physical and neurological structure of the brain and cognitive function declines with age. Rate of change and the specific areas of brain form and function that decline vary across individuals, making descriptions of normal cognitive aging challenging. Comparisons of older adults to younger adults indicate that older adults do better on mental tasks that rely on general knowledge and experience (using crystalized intelligence) but less well on novel tasks that require complex mental processes (relying on fluid intelligence) to complete. Older adults appear favor rules of thumb for decision-making over conscious, deliberative processes. Ability to effectively engage in a number of aspects of economic decisions declines over time for many older adults. Researchers point to both changes in brain structure and neuro-connections and slowed processing speed as reasons for that decline.

CONCERNING SIGNS

Findings from recent research on the financial knowledge and ability of older adults are concerning. Lusardi & Mitchell (2011) evaluated levels of financial literacy of community-living adults aged 50 and over by asking them three basic questions about interest rate calculations, effect of inflation, and diversification of investment risk. Survey answers indicate the older U.S. population has a very low level of financial knowledge. Only about half of respondents could correctly complete a simple percentage calculation to show understanding of the effects of inflation. Two-thirds of the respondents missed at least one of the questions. The questions were incorporated into another national survey of the U.S. adult population. Results from that survey indicated that older individuals had fewer correct answers than younger individuals. In addition, for each question, older women had fewer correct answers and selected do not know as the response more frequently as compared with older men.

In an effort to identify when and how financial ability begins to fail in older adults, Daniel Marson and colleagues at the University of Alabama at Birmingham integrated concepts and research methods from psychology and neurological science to develop the Financial Capacity Instrument (FCI; Marson et al., 2000). The research team was multidisciplinary. Marson is an attorney and professor with a joint appointment in psychology and neurology. His colleagues were engaged in research or clinical practice with individuals diagnosed with Alzheimer's disease. Their affiliations included the Department of Neurology, the Alzheimer's Disease Research Center, the School of Education, and the Birmingham Veterans Administration Medical Center. The research team's varied backgrounds uniquely positioned them to gauge decline in financial ability not just from a theoretical perspective, but from a clinical, legal, and practical perspective as well.

The FCI is a standardized psychometric instrument that evaluates six types of financial abilities, ranging from simple to complex. Selection of abilities was based on relevance of ability to independent life as a community-dwelling adult, clinical work with older adults in a healthcare setting, and legal assessment of financial competence. The abilities and assessment measures are:

1. Demonstrate basic money skills.
   a. Name coins and currency.
   b. Indicate relative value of coins and currency.
   c. Correctly count coins and currency.
2. Demonstrate financial knowledge.
   a. Define various simple financial concepts.
   b. Apply or calculate financial concepts.
3. Complete simulated purchase transactions.
   a. One item, verify change.
   b. Three items, verify change.
   c. Obtain exact change to use in vending machine.
4. Manage checkbook.
   a. Identify and explain parts of check and checkbook register.
   b. Simulate transaction with payment by check.
5. Manage bank statement.
   a. Identify and explain parts of a bank statement.
   b. Identify parts of a specific transaction on a bank statement.
6. Demonstrate financial judgment.
   a. Detect and explain fraud in fraudulent mail solicitation.
   b. Explain investment options and make an investment decision.

In a clinical trial that used the FCI to compare performance of older adults diagnosed with mild or moderate Alzheimer's disease (AD) with that of a healthy control group, Marson and colleagues (2000) determined that there were differences in financial ability by stage of dementia. Results were consistent with the idea that loss of financial abilities accompanies the progressive loss of cognitive function characteristic of AD. Decline in ability to perform complex financial tasks appeared to precede decline in ability to perform simple financial tasks. About half of the patients diagnosed with mild AD measured as capable on basic money skills, description and application of simple financial concepts, and cash transactions. But, less than a third demonstrated ability to manage a checkbook or a bank statement, and less than one in seven could demonstrate sound financial judgment. In contrast, performance of virtually all patients with moderate AD was at the incapable level for all tasks.

Discussion of the work of Marson and his colleagues (2000) is not meant to imply that financial planners should use psychometric instruments when working with older clients. Financial planners are not diagnosticians and clearly could not ethically take on that role. But, research based on the FCI does provide several important insights for financial planners. First, cognitive decline and loss of financial skills are linked. Second, this loss appears to be progressive, with deterioration in ability to complete more complex skills occurring before loss of simple skills. Consequently, the inability to correctly perform basic financial tasks might actually be a late rather than early warning signal of cognitive decline as has commonly been thought. Finally, basic financial skills are essential for independent community living. Decline in these skills can foreshadow a client's need for financial oversight by family members or other designees and, perhaps, eventual custodial care.

SUPPORTING OLDER CLIENTS

Current science indicates that cognitive abilities of clients will change as they grow older, but the timing, specific form, and extent of that change cannot be predicted. Consequently, being watchful for signs of change and being prepared and proactive is becoming part of providing excellent client service when working with older adults. Of course, judgment will be needed to recognize signs of change, determine appropriate adaptations to make, and decide when an older client needs additional help or support beyond what a financial planning professional can provide. Knowledge of typical later-life cognitive changes provides a basis for some practical suggestions for financial planning practice with older clients:

1. Type and timing of cognitive change in older adults vary across individuals.

   Avoid assuming that aging leads to inevitable cognitive decline or that all older clients will have the same cognitive issues. At the same time watch for signs of change in older clients' abilities to understand, reason, or make judgments and decisions.

2. Change in mental function is gradual.

   Passage of time between meetings may make decline in an older client's mental status more noticeable to a financial planner than to those interacting with the client on a daily basis. As an aid in identifying cognitive change in an older client, add to the usual meeting notes regarding what was discussed and what decisions were made some brief comments regarding client's ability to be an engaged partner in the meeting. Was there an unexpected memory lapse, a seeming overreliance on rule-of-thumb decision rules, or trouble understanding complex concepts?

Refer to notes prior to subsequent client meetings to facilitate recognizing an increase in frequency or intensity of markers of cognitive decline.

3. Decline in short-term memory.

Provide older clients tangible memory aids—for example, mail a postcard meeting reminder prior to a meeting. Or, hand the client a page at the start of a face-to-face meeting that briefly lists key data, questions, or other items that will be the focus of that meeting. When talking with older clients, check understanding of items discussed and realize information may need to be patiently restated or explained more than once.

4. Decline in cognitive function.

Recognize that age-related change in brain function may adversely affect an older client's reaction to gain and loss as well as ability to engage in probabilistic (risky) decision-making. Clients experiencing difficulty in processing abstract ideas may need concrete examples instead. Watch for signs of overconfidence or overreliance on heuristics in client's decision-making process. When possible in client interaction, use approaches, explanations, or examples that allow a client to draw on general knowledge and life experience (i.e., favor use of crystalized knowledge over fluid knowledge).

5. Decline in computational ability.

In client meetings, consider using graphs or visuals to help communicate mathematical concepts such as portfolio allocation, rebalance, or returns in addition to or instead of numerical tables or calculations.

6. Slowing of processing speed.

Be thoughtful about speed of conversations with older clients. Pace communication to match client response. It may be helpful to slow rate of speech and use brief, clear statements rather than lengthy descriptions or discussions. Verify that client has understood one point before moving to another.

7. Decline in ability to manage complex tasks.

Break complex tasks down to smaller components. When feasible, simplify descriptions and explanations. Focus on a few key points or issues at a time.

8. Change in preference for short term over long term.

Recognize that what may seem like a change in preference for short-term versus long-term rewards or a change in risk preference may actually reflect a decline in mental process.

Distinguishing Normal from Concerning Cognitive Change

The ability of older adults to manage their financial affairs given the potential for cognitive slowdown and the possibility for serious cognitive decline is a serious concern. The Alzheimer's Association (2017) provides excellent resources to help one distinguish between typical and concerning cognitive changes that occur in later life. In general, distinctions between the types of behaviors that do and do not suggest onset of dementia focus on frequency, duration, and ability to recover. For example, occasionally forgetting a name or a bill payment, but remembering later is not a concern. The inability to recall names of family members on a consistent basis or having bills pile up unpaid are concerns.

The client–planner relationship in financial planning is ongoing, but it is not daily and it is on a professional versus a personal level. Consequently, some early signs of cognitive decline such as difficulty completing familiar tasks at home might not be evident in the financial planning process. On the other hand, as previously noted, a gradual change in cognitive function that a family member might miss could be noticeable in periodic client meetings.

Adams & Lichtenberg (2014) provide a list of warning signs that a client may be in early stages of dementia:

- Missed office appointments.
- Confusion about instructions.
- Frequent calls to office.
- Repetitive speech or questions.
- Missed paying bills.
- Difficulty following directions.
- Trouble handling paperwork.
- Difficulty recalling past decisions or actions.

Also, Adams and Lichtenberg (2014) encourage financial planners to take these four steps to improve service to vulnerable older clients:

1. Learn to recognize neurocognitive disorders such as Alzheimer's disease.
2. Understand the basic tenets of decisional abilities for a financial judgment or decision.
3. Establish professional relationships with experts in geriatric health care and financial capacity who could provide guidance or a professional assessment if a client's financial capacity is in question.
4. Establish a relationship with the local adult protecting services agency to facilitate report of cases of financial exploitation.

When working with older clients, it is important to prepare a plan of action well before signs of cognitive decline become evident. As part of that preparation, frank and open discussions with clients regarding their risk of declining cognitive ability and financial literacy as they age should be part of financial planning meetings. Knowledge of that risk can help motivate clients to take steps to ensure their wishes are honored if cognitive decline occurs (Guillemette, 2017). Encourage clients to work with an attorney to establish a living will, healthcare directives, and springing or durable powers of attorney for care of themselves and their material resources should they become unable to care for themselves. Discuss with clients how they would like to proceed should cognitive decline occur. For instance, what specific behaviors would the client want used as a trigger to permit help to be sought on his or her behalf? Which person or persons would the client wish to be involved in making a determination of his or her functional incapacity? Under what conditions would the client want a family member to join his or her financial planning meetings?

RESEARCH CHALLENGES

There are a number of research challenges related to aging clients' cognitive processes, factors associated with later-life financial and overall well-being, and financial planning best practices. Research on links between the aging brain and observed choice and behavior is still a young science. It is clear that brain physiology and thought processes are inextricably linked. Interdisciplinary work is needed to continue to map relationships among the neurobiological, psychological, and emotional aspects of financial decisions and actions. More remains to be learned about the specific biological and behavioral underpinnings of such things as risk-tolerance level or the ability to delay gratification, evaluate options, weigh costs and benefits, or imagine future outcome of a present choice. What changes in which brain sectors or what other factors affect these dispositions or abilities? Where do and should the boundary of ethical financial planning practice lie if manipulation of one or more of these factors could guide a client to a particular outcome? What if the outcome is deemed to be in the client's best interest? Age-related cognitive decline may make older individuals more susceptible to such things as framing effects or overuse of rules of thumb. A better understanding of this susceptibility would be important to help prevent fraud and deceptive practices among older consumers as well as to inform best practice when presenting information to older clients in a financial planning setting.

Although scientists currently struggle to describe a path of normal cognitive aging, as the science of cognitive aging advances, might it become possible to identify a number of relatively common trajectories of cognitive change through later life? Rise in longevity will enable research of cognitive processes in those of very advanced age. How do the cognitive processes of these survivors compare with those of younger individuals who have otherwise similar characteristics?

Early research on the behavioral aspects of decision-making was often conducted in a controlled experimental setting with college-aged individuals. Less is known about whether mid- or later-life individuals exhibit the same behavioral biases in their decision-making processes. Experimental design needs careful structure to identify age effects. Cross-sectional studies of age and intelligence conducted in the 1950s implied mental performance dropped sharply between ages 40 and 60. Subsequent research revealed this age difference was overstated, and due instead to cohort differences in such things in education, life experience, cultural background, and skill sets rather than the aging process (Hedden & Gabrieli, 2004; Williams & Klug, 1996). Longitudinal research following the same individuals over time found intelligence test scores remained relatively stable until about age 60 and then declined somewhat after that (Morgan, 2006). But, longitudinal research also has limitations. Over time, study participants drop out due to choice, declining health, or death. Those remaining often have relatively better health, education, economic resources, and baseline scores (Harada et al., 2013; Van Beijsterveldt et al., 2002). Also, when tests are repeated over time, scores can maintain or increase due to practice, despite cognitive decline (Abner et al., 2012; Harada et al., 2013; Hedden & Gabrieli, 2004). Consequently, the effect of age can be understated in longitudinal research.

Another challenge to clearly identifying the effects of age on cognitive function is that everyone experiences some degree of physical change in the brain over time. Bioneurological processes in the brain form the elemental and initiating constructs of thought and action. So, as these physical changes occur, cognitive function changes as well. Since age cannot be altered in experiments, any determination regarding the effects of aging will necessarily correlate with age (Hedden & Gabrieli, 2004). Although brain imaging methods provide a remarkable real-time view of the physical and neurological correlates of various types of task performance in the living brain, a direct process of causation cannot be inferred from simple correlation. Identifying exactly how changes in brain biochemistry and neural pathways leads to specific changes in thought and behavior will require considerably more research to disentangle age from cohort effects.

As the aging population becomes more racially and culturally diverse, it will be helpful to conduct further research on the ways that culture shapes crystalized intelligence and the effect that shaping has on decision-making in later life. Researchers comparing European-American culture with Asian culture have found "considerable cultural variation in inference, memory, reasoning, and attention"(Kitayama, 2000, p. 224). Kitayama (2000) notes this variation "raises significant doubt about the universalistic assumption that cognition is the hard-wired machinery of the psyche that exists independent of the cultural milieu" (p. 224). Differences in the concept of human agency were also noted. European Americans typically think in terms of cause and effect, centering on objects more than context, whereas Asians tend to think in more holistic and inclusive terms, centering on context and situation. Kitayama (2000) argues these differences are fundamental and pervasive, deeply shaping what psychologists call crystalized intelligence. Would similar differences be found in comparison between other cultures outside the United States or between subcultures within the United States? Would culturally shaped views of self, others, and norms of interpersonal interaction affect susceptibility to framing effects, risk tolerance, or other behavioral aspects of decision-making? Crosscultural comparisons could enrich understanding of the aspects of cognition and age-related cognitive change that are inherent in individuals across culture versus the factors that are shaped by culture.

Choice management is another important issue. Many of today's retirees have used an employer sponsored 401(k) defined contribution plan to save for retirement. Initially, these plans offered participants a large number of investment choices on the premise more is better. But, when research revealed abundant choice led to information overload and inaction, choices were streamlined, participation ticked up, and the lesson learned was less is more (Iyengar, Jiang, & Huberman, 2003). Similarly, retired individuals now face a daunting amount of options and choices related to postretirement finances. For example, Brian Alleva, a researcher at the Social Security Administration's Office of Policy Analysis, explains that married couples with a lower-earning spouse who is entitled to an own-record benefit and a spousal benefit face nearly 40,000 possible claiming-age combinations, depending on the birth year of each spouse (Alleva, 2017)! Add to Social Security claiming-age choice another myriad of choices regarding such things as retirement account disbursements, Medicare supplements, consumption patterns, housing, and lifestyle, and the postretirement choice burdens quickly become immense.

Helping older clients navigate the maze of options that exist for a number of significant financial decisions can be an important value added that financial planners provide. Indeed, as the size of the aged population grows, the complexity of later life financial decisions as well as the framing of the options presented to older adults will likely become an increasingly important focus of research and public policy discussion. For example, is there a way to streamline the number of Social Security retirement benefit claim options while preserving equity in benefit payments? What are the most important factors to consider when deciding postretirement housing type, location, and cost? Can the market offer innovative strategies of information management to help reduce decision complexity or are changes in public policy needed? What can be learned from behavioral research regarding the ways that the framing of options may influence choice? Similar to prior research on ways to decrease information overload and choice paralysis with 401(k) investment options, research-based guidance on ways to effectively manage, sort, and select utility-enhancing post-retirement financial choices could be of great benefit to public policy, provision of financial services, and individual well-being.

Currently, smartphone applications are available that help individuals build budgets, track spending, and conduct financial transactions. Little is known about the use of such aids among older individuals. As technology advances, it is an open question as to whether electronic tools or applications could be developed that would compensate for at least some types of later-life cognitive decline.

As the number of older individuals increases, research is needed to evaluate which financial planning business models best meet the unique needs of this age group. For example, it is typical for family members to provide care and oversight of an older person's financial affairs when that person experiences cognitive decline. Given this fact, would a family-centric model work better than a client-centric model for older clients? Or, would an integrated practice model that placed the client as the hub of a wheel of support services from a number of professionals (e.g. financial planner, medical provider, lawyer, geriatric-care manager) and family prove better for meeting older clients' needs? In what situations would it be more cost-effective for a financial planning firm to reach out to other professionals (e.g., lawyer, geriatric care manager, or social worker) on an as-needed basis versus having an in-house service team of several relevant professionals?

FINAL THOUGHTS

In conclusion, it is clear that the needs of older clients and the cognitive challenges facing them in later life are quite different from those of other age groups. With the U.S. population aging, it is certain that adults aged 65 and older will form an increasing proportion of the client base in financial planning. Being familiar with the ways that cognitive abilities change with age, adapting client service to build on client strengths, and being alert to signs of onset of dementia will become important aspects in serving older clients right and serving them well.

REFERENCES

Abner, E. L., Dennis, B. C., Mathews, M. J., Mendiondo, M. S., Caban-Holt, A., Kryscio, R. J., Schmitt, F. A., & Crowley, J. J. (2012). Practice effects in a longitudinal, multi-center Alzheimer's disease prevention clinical trial. *Trials*, *13*, 217. doi:10.1186/1745-6215-13-217.

Adams, S. D., & Lichtenberg, P. A. (2014). How to protect and help clients with diminished capacity. *Journal of Financial Planning*, *27*(4), 22–28.

Alleva, B. (2017). Social security retirement benefit claiming-age combinations available to married couples. Research and Statistics Note No. 2017-01. Office of Policy Analysis, Office of Retirement Policy, Office of Retirement and Disability Policy, Social Security Administration. Retrieved from https://www.ssa.gov/policy/docs/rsnotes/rsn2017-01.html.

Alzheimer's Association. (2017). 2017 Alzheimer's disease facts and figures. doi:10.1016/j.jalz.2017.02.001.

Arias, E. (2006). United States life tables. *National Vital Statistics Reports*, *65*(8). Retrieved from https://www.cdc.gov/nchs/data/nvsr/nvsr65/nvsr65_08.pdf.

Arking, R. (2006). *The biology of aging: Observations and principles*. Oxford, UK: Oxford University Press.

Barber, B. M., & Odean, T. (2001). Boys will be boys: Gender, overconfidence, and common stock investment. *The Quarterly Journal of Economics*, *116*(1), 261–292.

Beas, B. S., Setlow, B., Samanez-Larkin, G. R., & Bizon, J. L. (2015). Modeling cost-benefit decision making in aged rodents. In *Aging and decision making: Empirical and applied perspectives*. San Diego: Elsevier.

Birren, J. (1968). Psychological aspects of aging: Intellectual functioning. *The Gerontologist*, *8*(1, Part 2), 16–19.

Brehmer, Y., Westerberg, H., & Backman, L. (2012). Working-memory training in younger and older adults: Training gains, transfer, and maintenance. *Frontiers in Human Neuroscience*, *6*, 1–7.

Brown, S. B. R. E., & Ridderinkhof, K. R. (2009). Aging and the neuroeconomics of decision making: A review. *Cognitive, Affective, & Behavioral Neuroscience*, *9*(4), 365–379. doi:10.3758/CABN.9.4.365.

Cabeza, R., Anderson, N. D., Locantore, J. K., & McIntosh, A. R. (2002). Aging gracefully: Compensatory brain activity in high-performing older adults. *NeuroImage*, *17*, 1394–1402.

Cannon, M. L. (2015). What is aging? Disease-a-Month, *61*, 454–459.

Carlson, M. C., Hasher, L., Zacks, R. T., & Connelly, S. L. (1995). Aging, distraction, and the benefits of predictable location. *Psychology and Aging*, *10*, 427–436.

Carstensen, L. L., & Hartel, C. R. (Eds.). (2006). *When I'm 64*. Washington, DC: National Academies Press. Retrieved from https://www.ncbi.nlm.nih.gov/books/NBK83776/pdf/Bookshelf_NBK83776.pdf.

Centers for Disease Control. (2013). The state of aging and health in America 2013. Retrieved from https://www.cdc.gov/aging/pdf/State-Aging-Health-in-America-2013.pdf.

Chowdhury, R., Guitart-Masip, M., Lambert, C., Dayan, P., Huys, Q., Düzel, E., & Dolan, R. J. (2013). Dopamine restores reward prediction errors in old age. *Nature Neuroscience, 16*(5), 648–653.

Christensen, H. (2001). What cognitive changes can be expected with normal ageing? *Australian and New Zealand Journal of Psychiatry, 35*(6), 768–775. doi:10.1046/j.1440-1614.2001.00966.x.

Davidson, P. S. R., & Glisky, E. L. (2002). Is flashbulb memory a special instance of source memory? Evidence from older adults. *Memory, 10*, 99.

Deakin, J., Aitken, M., Robbins, T., & Sahakian, B. J. (2004). Risk taking during decision-making in normal volunteers changes with age. *Journal of the International Neurophychological Society, 10*(4), 590–598.

Denburg, N. L., & Hedgcock, W. M. (2015). Age-associated executive dysfunction, the prefrontal cortex, and complex decision making. In T. M. Hess, J. Strough, & C. E. Lockenhoff (Eds.), *Aging and decision making: Empirical and applied perspectives*. San Diego: Elsevier.

Denburg, N. L., Recknor, E. C., Bechara, A., & Tranel, D. (2006). Psychophysiological anticipation of positive outcomes promotes advantageous decision-making in normal older persons. *International Journal of Psychophysiology, 61*(1), 19–25.

Denburg, N. L., Tranel, D., & Bechara, A. (2005). The ability to decide advantageously declines prematurely in some normal older persons. *Neuropsychologia, 43*(7), 1099–1106.

Dima. (2009). Fluid and crystallized intelligence. *Mind Forums*. Retrieved from http://mindforums.com/fluid-and-crystallized-intelligence.

Elias, L., & Saucier, D. (2006). Neuropsychology: Clinical and experimental foundations. Boston: Pearson Education.

Eppinger, B., Nystrom, L. E., & Cohen, J. D. (2012). Reduced sensitivity to immediate reward during decison-making in older than younger adults. *PLoS ONE, 7*(5), e36953.

Eppinger, B., Schuck, N. W., Nystrom, L. E., & Cohen, J. D. (2013). Reduced striatal responses to reward prediction errors in older compared with younger adults. *The Journal of Neuroscience, 33*(24), 9905–9912.

Family Caregiver Alliance. (2002). Caregiver depression: A silent health crisis. Retrieved July 26, 2017, from https://www.caregiver.org/caregiver-depression-silent-health-crisis.

Federal Interagency Forum on Aging-Related Statistics. (2016). Older Americans 2016: Key indicators of well-being. U.S. Government Printing Office, August.

Ferrucci, L., Hesdorffer, C., Bandinelli, S., & Simonsick, E. M. (2010). Frailty as a nexus between the biology of aging, environmental conditions and clinical geriatrics. *Public Health Review, 32*(2), 475–488.

Finke, M. J., Howe, J. S., & Huston, S. J. (2016). Old age and the decline in financial literacy. *Management Science, 63*(1), 213–230.

Glisky, E. L. (2007). Changes in cognitive function in human aging. In D. R. Riddle (Ed.), *Brain aging: Models, methods, and mechanisms* (pp. 1–11). Boca Raton, FL: CRC Press, Taylor & Francis.

Guillemette, M. A. (2017). Risks in advanced age. *Journal of Financial Planning, forthcoming*. Available at SSRN: https://ssrn.com/abstract=2932336.

Haaland, K. Y., Price, L., & Larue, A. (2003). What does the WMS-III tell us about memory changes with normal aging? *Journal of The International Neuropsychological Society, 9*, 89–96.

Harada, C. N., Natelson-Love, M. C., & Triebel, K. L. (2013). Normal cognitive aging. *Clinics in Geriatric Medicine, 29*(4), 737–752. doi:10.1016/j.cger.2013.07.002.

Hedden, T., & Gabrieli, J. D. E. (2004). Insights into the ageing mind: A view from cognitive neuroscience. *Nature Reviews Neuroscience, 5*(2), 87–96. doi:10.1038/nrn1323.

Henninger, D. E., Madden, D. J., & Huettel, S. A. (2010). Processing speed and memory mediate age-related differences in decision making. *Psychology and Aging, 25*(2), 262–270.

Hess, T. M., Strough, J., & Lockenhoff, C. E. (Eds.). (2015). *Aging and decision making: empirical and applied perspectives*. San Diego: Elsevier.

Horn, L., & Cattell, R. B. (1966). Refinement and test of the theory of fluid and crystallized intelligence. *Journal of Educational Psychology, 57*, 253–270.

Howieson, D. B., Holm, L. A., Kaye, J. A., Oken, B. S., & Howieson, J. (1993). Neurologic function in the optimally healthy oldest old. *Neuropsyscholgical Evaluation Neurology, 43*, 1882–1886.

Iyengar, S. S., Jiang, W., & Huberman, G. (2003). How much choice is too much?: Contributions to 401(k) retirement plans. Pension Research Council Working Paper 2003-10. The Wharton School, University of Pennsylvania. Retrieved from https://pensionresearchcouncil.wharton.upenn.edu/ publications/papers/how-much-choice-is-too-much-contributions-to-401k-retirement-plans/.

Kahneman, D., & Tversky, A. (1979). Prospect theory: An analysis of decision under risk. *Econometrica, 47*(2), 263–292.

Kitayama, S. (2000). Cultural variations in cognition: Implications for aging research. In P. D. Stern & L. L. Carstensen (Eds.), *The aging mind: Opportunities in cognitive research*. Washington, DC: National Academies Press.

Kuhnen, C. M., & Knutson, B. (2005). The neural basis of financial risk taking. *Neuron, 47*(5), 763–770.

Kumar, A. (2007). Who gambles in the stock market. Austin: University of Texas Press. Retrieved from http://www.econ.yale.edu/~shiller/behfin/2005-04/kumar.pdf.

Laibson, D. (2011) Aging and investing: The risk of cognitive impairment. *AAII Journal*. Retrieved from http://www.aaii.com/journal/article/aging-and-investing-the-risk-of-cognitive-impairment.touch.

Levine, B., Svoboda, E., Hay, J. F., Winocur, G., & Moscovitch, M. (2002). Aging and autobiographical memory: Dissociating episodic from semantic retrieval aging and autobiographical memory. *Psychology and Aging, 17*(4), 677–689. doi:10.1037//0882-7974.17.4.677.

Lezak, M. D., Howieson, D. B., Bigler, E. D., & Tranel, D. (2012). *Neuropsychological assessment*. New York: Oxford University Press.

Li, Y., Baldassi, M., Johnson, E. J., & Weber, E. U. (2013). Complementary cognitive capabilities, economic decision making, and aging. *Psychology and Aging, 28*(3), 595–613. doi:10.1037/a0034172.

Light, L. L. (1992). The organization of memory in old age. In F. I. M. Craik & T. A. Salthouse (Eds.), *The handbook of aging and cognition* (p. 111). Hillsdale, NJ: Erlbaum.

Lighthall, N. R., Gorlick, M. A., Schoeke, A., Frank, M. J., & Mather, M. (2012). Stress modulates reinforcement learning in younger and older adults. *Psychology and Aging, 28*(1), 35–46.

Lockenhoff, C. E., & Rutt, J. L. (2015). Age differences in time perception and their implications for decision making across the life span. In T. M. Hess, J. Strough, & C. E. Lockenhoff (Eds.), *Aging and decision making: Empirical and applied perspectives* (pp. 213–233). San Diego: Elsevier.

Lusardi, A., & Mitchell, O. S. (2011). NBER Working Paper Series financial literacy and retirement planning in the United States. *Journal of Pension Economics & Finance, 10*(4), 509–525. https://doi.org/10.1017/CBO9781107415324.004.

Marson, D. C., Sawrie, S. M., Snyder, S., McInturff, B., Stalvey, T., Boothe, A., et al. (2000). Assessing financial capacity in patients with alzheimer disease. *Archives of Neurology, 57*(6), 877. doi:10.1001/archneur.57.6.877.

Mata, R., Josef, A. K., & Lemaire, P. (2015). Adaptive decision making and aging. In T. M. Hess, J. Strough, & C. E. Loeckenhoff (Eds.), *Aging and decision making: Empirical and applied perspectives* (pp. 105–122). San Diego: Elsevier.

Mather, M., Jacobsen, L. A., & Pollard, K. M. (2015). Aging in the United States (Vol. 70). Retrieved from http://www.prb.org/pdf16/aging-us-population-bulletin.pdf.

Mell, T., Wartenburger, I., Marschner, A., Villringer, A., Reischies, F. M., & Heekeren, H. R. (2009). Altered function of ventral striatum during reward-based decision making in old age. *Frontiers in Human Neuroscience, 3*, 34.

Morgan, K. (2006). Psychological aspects of ageing. *Women's Health Medicine, 3*(2), 81–83.

National Institute of Mental Health. (2005). The many dimensions of depression in women. Retrieved from https://www.mentalhelp.net/articles/depression-and-women-dimensions/.

Nielsen, L., Knutson, B., & Carstensen, L. L. (2008). Affect dynamics, affective forecasting and aging. *Emotion, 8*(3), 318–330.

Nilsson, L., Adolfsson, R., Backman, L., DeFrias, C. J., Molander, B., & Nyberg, L. (2004). Betula: A prospective cohort study on memory, health and aging. *Aging, Neuriphyshology, and Cognition, 11*, 134–148.

Ortman, J. J., Velkoff, V. A., & Hogan, H. (2014). *An aging nation: The older population in the United States.* U.S. Census Bureau Publication No. P25-1140. Washington, DC: U.S. Census Bureau.

Park, D. C., & Huang, C.-M. (2010). Culture wires the brain: A cognitive neuroscience perspective. *Perspectives on Psychological Science, 5*(4), 391–400. https://doi.org/10.1177/1745691610374591.

Park, D. C., Nisbett, R. E., & Hedden, T. (1999). Aging, culture, and cognition. *Journal of Gerontology: Psychological Sciences, 54B*, 75–84.

Park, D. C., & Reuter-Lorenz, P. A. (2009). The adaptive brain: Aging and neurocognitive scaffolding. *Annual Review of Psychology, 60*, 173–196.

Peng, K., & Nisbett, R. E. (1999). Culture, dialectics, and reasoning about contradiction. *American Psychologist, 54*, 741–754.

Pietschmann, M., Endrass, T., Czerwon, B., & Kathmann, N. (2011). Aging, probabilistic learning and performance monitoring. *Biological Psychology, 86*, 74–82.

Pinto da Costa, J., Vitorino, R., Silva, G. M., Cogel, C., Duarte, A. C., & Rocha-Santos, T. (2016). A synopsis on aging—Theories, mechanisms and future prospects. *Ageing Research Reviews, 29*, 90–112.

Quadagno, J. (2011). *Aging and the life course: An introduction to social gerontology* (2nd ed.). New York: McGraw-Hill.

Raz, N., & Rodrigue, K. M. (2006). Differential aging of the brain: Patterns, cognitive correlates and modifiers. *Neuroscience and Biobehavioral Reviews.* doi:j.neubiorev.2006.07.001.

Roca, M., Manes, F., Chade, A., Gleichgerrcht, E., Gershanik, O., Arévalo, G. G., et al. (2012). The relationship between executive functions and fluid intelligence in Parkinson's disease. *Psychological Medicine, 42*(11), 2445–52.

Salthouse, T. A. (2004). What and when of cognitive aging. *Current Directions in Psychological Science.* doi:10.1111/j.0963-7214.2004.00293.x.

Salthouse, T. A. (2009). When does age-related cogntive decline begin? Neurobiological Aging, *30*(4), 507–514. doi:10.1016/j.neruobiolaging.2008.09.023.

Salthouse, T. A. (2010). Selective review of cognitive aging. *Journal of the International Neuropsychological Society. JINS, 16*(5), 754–60. doi:10.1017/S1355617710000706.

Salthouse, T. A. (2012). Consequences of age-related cognitive decline. *Annual Review of Psychology, 63*, 201–226.

Salthouse, T. A., Fristoe, N. M., Lineweaver, T. T., & Coon, V. E. (1995). Aging of attention: Does the ability to divide decline? *Memory and Cognition, 23*, 59–71.

Samanez-Larkin, G. R. (2015). Decision neuroscience and aging. In T. M. Hess, J. Strough, & C. E. Löckenhoff (Eds.), *Aging and decision making: Empirical and applied perspectives* (pp. 41–61). San Diego: Elsevier.

Samanez-Larkin, G. R., Gibbs, S. E. B., Khanna, K., Nielsen, L., Carstensen, L. L., & Knutson, B. (2007). Anticiation of monetary gain but not loss in healthy older adults. *Nature Neuroscience, 10*(6), 787–791.

Samanez-Larkin, G. R., Worthy, D. A., Mata, R., McClure, S. M., & Knutson, B. (2014). Adult age differences in frontostriatal representation of prediction error but not reward outcome. *Cognitive, Affective, and Behavioral Neuroscience, 14*(2), 672–682.

Seltzer, J. A., & Yahirun, J. J. (2013). Diversity in old age. In J. R. Logan (Ed.), *The lost decade? Social change in the U.S. after 2000.* New York: Russell Sage Foundation. Retrieved from https://s4.ad.brown.edu/Projects/Diversity/Data/Report/report11062013.pdf.

Singh-Manoux, A., Kivimaki, M., Glymour, M. M., Elbaz, A., Berr, C., Ebmeier, K. P., Ferrie, J. E., & Dugravot, A. (2011). Timing of onset of cognitive decline: Results from Whitehall II prospective cohort study. *BMJ, 344*(January), d7622. doi:10.1136/bmj.d7622.

Stern, P. C., & Carstensen, L. L. (Eds.). (2000). *The aging mind: Opportunities in cognitive research* (Vol. *288*). Washington, DC: National Academies Press. Retrieved from http://www.nap.edu/catalog/9783.html.

Van Beijsterveldt, C. E. M., Van Boxtel, M. P. J., Bosma, H., Houx, P. J., Buntinx, F., & Jolles, J. (2002). Predictors of attrition in a longitudinal cognitive aging study: The Maastricht Aging Study (MAAS). *Journal of Clinical Epidemiology, 55*(3), 216–223. doi:10.1016/S0895-4356(01)00473-5.

Weller, J. A., Levin, I. P., & Denburg, N. L. (2011). Trajectory of risky decision making for potential gains and losses from ages 5 to 85. *Journal of Behavioral Decison Making, 24*(4), 331–344.

West, R. L. (1996). An application of prefrontal cortex function theory to cognitive aging. *Psychological Bulletin, 120*(2), 272–292.

Williams, J. D., & Klug, M. G. (1996). Aging and cognition: Methodological difference in outcome. *Experimental Aging Research, 22,* 219–244.

Wood, S., Busemeyer, J., Koling, A., Cox, C. R., & Davis, H. (2005). Older adults as adaptive decision makers: Evidence from the Iowa gambling task. *Psychology and Aging, 20*(2), 220–225.

Zec, R. F., Markwekk, S. J., Burkett, N. R., & Larsen, D. L. (2005). A longitudinal study of confrontation naming in the "normal" elderly. *Journal of the International Neruopsychological Society, 11,* 716–726.

CHAPTER 16

Financial Psychology

Bradley T. Klontz, PsyD, CFP®
Creighton University

Faith Zabek, MEd
Georgia State University

Edward Horwitz, PhD, CFP®
Creighton University

There is growing interest among financial planning professionals in the blending of psychological theories and techniques with financial planning. The most recent edition of the *CFP Planning Competency Handbook* (CFP Board, 2016), as well as this text, illustrates this integration. While behavioral finance has been described as the application of psychology to finance, we argue that it is more accurately described as the application of *cognitive psychology* to finance (Klontz & Horwitz, 2017; Klontz, Kahler, & Klontz, 2016). Viewing the totality of financial behaviors exclusively through the lens of cognitive psychology, which is a laboratory versus applied science, has resulted in limited practical applications for financial planners working with clients. In contrast to behavioral finance, financial psychology applies findings from a diverse body of research across many subspecialties of psychology and draws from elements of clinical psychology to help improve a client's financial well-being.

Key theories from many disciplines of psychology are of direct relevance and benefit to financial planners and their clients. Research findings from fields such as social psychology, personality psychology, multicultural psychology, positive psychology, humanistic psychology, and developmental psychology can be applied to financial planning. Tools and techniques from many of these fields have already been adapted for use with clients. In addition, strategies from various modalities of psychotherapy, including cognitive–behavioral, motivational interviewing, solution-focused, and positive psychology strategies, can be used to improve rapport with clients and increase the success of financial planning.

This chapter explores the link between behavioral finance and cognitive psychology, as well as the practical limitations of behavioral finance to the practice of financial planning. This chapter follows with a discussion of what financial planners need and how the field of financial psychology can assist. The chapter concludes with a brief introduction to several fields of psychology and psychotherapy. It discusses how psychological theory and technique can help financial planners better understand their clients' psychology and provide better service, and improve client satisfaction and client retention.

FINANCIAL PSYCHOLOGY

Although it is a large portion of this book and an important component of a working definition of client psychology, behavioral finance only scratches the surface of what psychology has to offer the financial planning profession. The broader integration of psychology into the world of personal finance has been termed *financial psychology* (Klontz et al., 2016). Financial psychology can be seen as akin to clinical psychology, which "integrates science, theory, and practice to understand, predict, and alleviate maladjustment, disability, and discomfort as well as promote human adaptation, adjustment, and personality development" (American Psychological Association, 2017b). Applied clinical psychology draws from the entire body of psychological theory and research to apply findings to alleviate maladjustment and promote adaptation in individuals and groups. Similarly, financial psychology draws from behavioral finance and other areas of psychology to help alleviate financial stress and promote healthy financial behaviors.

Financial psychology focuses on using psychological research and theory to create microbased techniques to help shape idiosyncratic financial beliefs and behaviors to improve financial health. These efforts go beyond cognitive biases and into the realm of a client's idiosyncratic beliefs (e.g., money scripts) and financial behaviors (e.g., resisting financial advice, overspending, financial enabling, financial anxiety, etc.). Many of the numerous fields of psychology are of direct benefit to the financial planning profession. While we are unable to explore them all in this chapter, some examples of application to financial planning will be discussed as they relate to the fields of social psychology, developmental psychology, personality psychology, multicultural psychology, and positive psychology.

Social Psychology

According to the American Psychological Association (2017c), social psychology is defined as "the study of how individuals affect and are affected by other people and by their social and physical environments." There are many aspects of social psychology that can be and are being applied to financial planning. For example, it is important for financial planners to be aware of how their gender may affect the decisions of their client. The gender of the financial planner appears to have a significant impact on the risk tolerance reported by clients (Grable & Britt, 2011). Specifically, men and women both report higher levels of risk tolerance when they are working with a financial planner of the opposite sex. Financial planners can also harness research from social psychology to improve their relationships with clients. Research shows that younger-looking faces are associated with a perceived lack of responsibility and immaturity (Zebrowitz & Montepare, 1992). However, younger financial planners can use aspects of social psychology to influence client perceptions (Klontz, 2014). One study found that wearing glasses can increase the degree to which others see someone as more trustworthy and intelligent, and if they are rimless glasses, they do not decrease the person's attractiveness (Leder, Forster, & Gerger, 2011).

With regard to the physical environment, research has found that how a financial planner arranges furniture and the nature of that furniture can have a direct impact on a client's level of stress (Britt & Grable, 2012). Additionally, the type of news programs being played in the financial planner's lobby may influence their level of financial stress (Grable & Britt, 2012). These findings are important because client-stress level has been found to be associated with their readiness to take action towards changing their financial behaviors and, subsequently, the success of financial planning (Britt, Lawson, & Haselwood, 2016). Implementing strategies to optimize the office environment, such as rearranging the furniture to create a living-room feel and turning off televisions playing financial news may reduce client stress (Britt et al., 2016). If a financial planner's office is optimized, the planner can expect that a client's experience of stress will be lower and the effectiveness of financial planning enhanced.

Developmental Psychology

Developmental psychology studies "human growth and development over the lifespan, including physical, cognitive, social, intellectual, perceptual, personality and emotional growth" (American Psychological Association, 2017d). Whereas cognitive psychology looks at universal aspects of human cognition such as cognitive biases in behavioral finance (nature), developmental psychology takes into account the growth and development of the individual (nurture). For example, financial behaviors may change throughout one's lifespan. As individuals get older, they may be more tolerant of risk within a financial planning context (Grable, 2000). Recently, aspects of developmental psychology and their relationship to financial planning have received increased attention. This includes the intergenerational transfer of money beliefs (e.g., Britt, 2016; Klontz et al., 2016) and the impact of financial events (Klontz & Britt, 2012) on the development of money beliefs and financial behaviors.

Money attitudes and values are formed early in life and affect financial health. Klontz and Britt (2012) found that attitudes such as money avoidance ("money is bad"), money worship ("more money will make things better"), and money status ("net worth equals self-worth") are associated with disordered financial behaviors, whereas money vigilance ("money should be saved not spent") acts as a protective factor and is linked to lower levels of credit card debt. The development of such money attitudes and related financial behaviors are based on observations of and interactions with caregivers during childhood (Britt, 2016). For example, involvement in savings and budgeting discussions with parents during childhood is associated with higher financial knowledge and well-being in adulthood (Shim, Xiao, Barber, & Lyons, 2009).

The manner in which one's parents discuss money during childhood may also influence their financial decisions as an adult. Individuals who witnessed their parents arguing about money during childhood report higher levels of financial stress and higher credit card debt as adults, regardless of parental socioeconomic status (Allen, Edwards, Hayhoe, & Leach, 2007; Britt, 2016; Hancock, Jorgensen, & Swanson, 2013). To understand the financial behavior of a client, a financial planner may look to the financial behaviors of that client's parents (Britt, 2016; Garrison & Gutter, 2010).

Psychology of Personality

As discussed in previous chapters, personality refers to "individual differences in characteristic patterns of thinking, feeling and behaving" (American Psychological Association, 2017e). The psychological study of personality focuses on "understanding individual differences in particular personality characteristics . . ." and "how the various parts of a person come together as a whole" (American Psychological Association, 2017e). Many theories of personality psychology have been applied to personal finances. These include personality as it relates to the psychodynamic perspective (Baker & Lyons, 2015; Trachtman, 2015), humanistic perspective

(Johnson & Takasawa, 2015), dispositional/trait perspective such as the Big Five personality theory (Viinikainen, Kokko, Pulkkinen, & Pehkonen, 2010), and social learning perspective, including Albert Bandura's social learning theory (Carrier & Maurice, 1998; Steed & Symes, 2009).

Various aspects of personality have been associated with a variety of financial behaviors as well as socioeconomic outcomes, including occupation, job performance, higher income, and higher net worth (e.g. Heckman et al., 2006; Mueller & Plug, 2006: Zagorsky, 2007). For example, conscientiousness—the personality trait of being careful or vigilant—has been found to have a direct influence on risk aversion (Nga & Ken Yien, 2013). Locus of control is another personality trait that has been shown to be related to a variety of financial behaviors and outcome of interest to planners. Locus of control refers to the amount of control an individual believes they have over the outcome of events in their lives, and it has been found to be associated with income and net worth (Klontz, Seay, Sullivan, & Canale, 2014; Klontz, Sullivan, Seay, & Canale, 2015; Zagorsky, 2007) and a variety of money disorders (Britt, Cumbie, & Bell, 2013; Taylor, Klontz, & Lawson, 2017). It has been suggested that financial planners might benefit from assessing a client's locus of control to see if the client might be at higher risk for problematic financial behaviors (Taylor et al., 2017).

Awareness of the influence of various personality traits on financial beliefs and behaviors can help financial planners tailor their approach to meet the needs of individual clients. It is also important to consider differences in personality predispositions within the client–planner relationship to avoid misunderstandings (Nabeshima & Seay, 2015). In addition, since personality traits can be altered through interventions (Borghans, Duckworth, Heckman, & Weel, 2008), it has been argued that "a deeper understanding of the financial psychology of high earners can help financial planners better serve this population and better help individuals aspiring to increase their income and net worth" (Klontz et al., 2014, p. 52).

Multicultural Psychology

Multicultural psychology has been defined as "the systematic study of how culture influences affect, cognition, and behavior . . . [it] is about how culture influences the way people feel, think, and act" (University of Rhode Island Department of Psychology, 2015). Culture is nuanced and includes the influence of "ethnicity, gender, age, nationality, language, religion, sexual orientation, socioeconomic status (SES), and disability status," among other factors (Hays, Klontz, & Kemnitz, 2015, p.88). There is enormous diversity in beliefs, values, experiences, and norms across various cultures, and it is critical that financial planners are aware of how these cultural differences may shape their own and their clients' decisions and the financial planning process as a whole.

Culture may affect the financial values and behaviors of individuals in many ways. In the United States, the financial planning profession is overwhelmingly comprised of European Americans, who tend to value personal independence (Falicov, 2001; Hays et al., 2015; U.S. Bureau of Labor Statistics, 2012). However, the United States is becoming increasingly ethnically diverse and the largest ethnic minority group, Latinos, tend to more strongly value "interdependence and shared financial responsibility among family members" (Hays et al., 2015, p. 89; Falicov, 2001; U.S. Census Bureau, 2015). Similarly, the European American culture tends to value assertiveness and verbal facility in professional interactions, whereas many American Indian and Alaska Native cultures often more strongly value subtle communication and listening skills (Hays, 2006; Hays et al., 2015). Other aspects of culture are important to consider as well. For example, individuals with disabilities face much more constraint in terms of financial security and planning than others due to less access to jobs and higher costs of living (Quilgars, Jones, & Abbott, 2008). In addition, individuals with a strong sense of faith may be more inclined to resist debt and "live within ones means" (Quilgars et al., 2008, p. 588). It is important for financial planners to be aware of how culture may influence their own financial values and beliefs as well as their clients.

Positive Psychology

Positive psychology emphasizes the study and promotion of constructs that do not just ameliorate problems, but promote thriving and enhance "what goes right in life" (Peterson, 2006, p.4). Findings from the study of positive psychology may assist financial planners in identifying the factors that promote the financial health of their clients. For example, a strong, positive relationship between one's self-esteem and their decision to engage in financial planning has been demonstrated in research (Neymotin, 2010). Guven (2012) demonstrated a causal relationship between happiness and consumption and savings behavior. Happier people save more, spend less, and "seem more concerned about the future than the present" (p. 703). Positive psychology may also provide a framework from which to study the efficacy of financial planning. Irving (2012) suggests that the process of financial planning is potentially supportive of individual well-being. Financial planning involves assessing one's values and setting goals for the future. Both the progression toward and attainment of goals is linked to improved self-concept, life attitude, and mood (Irving, 2012; MacLeod, Coates, & Hetherton, 2008; Sheldon, Kasser, Smith, & Share, 2002).

Humanistic Psychology

Humanistic psychology highlights the importance of the subjective human being with a focus on themes such as "self, self-actualization, health, creativity, intrinsic nature, being, becoming, individuality, and meaning" (The Association for Humanistic Psychology, 2017). Some of the basic tenets of Humanistic Psychology are that humans are inherently good, have a natural propensity toward growth in even the most adverse situations, and can thrive when a therapist provides an environment of authenticity, empathic understanding, and unconditional positive regard (Johnson & Takasawa, 2015).

A focus on client communication and active listening is a primary intervention in Humanistic Psychology, which has been applied to the planner–client relationship in a growing body of financial planning books and articles (e.g., Bowen, 2011; Daniel, 2015; Klontz et al., 2016; Klontz & Klontz, 2016; Pullen, 2000). Motivational interviewing and experiential therapy techniques have also emerged from Humanistic Psychology, and have been applied for use in the planner–client relationship as techniques to help facilitate client behavioral change (Horwitz & Klontz, 2017; Klontz, Bivens, Klontz, Wada, & Kahler, 2008; Klontz et al., 2016).

FINANCIAL PSYCHOLOGY FOR FINANCIAL PLANNERS

To make behavioral finance relevant to planners, an expansion into applied, practice-oriented psychology is needed. In the previous sections, findings from various disciplines of psychology have been briefly summarized and their relevance to financial planning has been demonstrated. For example, the impact of a client's development and culture on their financial beliefs and behaviors has been explored. However, how can a planner use this information to help a client? Applied techniques adapted from schools of psychotherapy, such as cognitive behavioral therapy, motivational interviewing, solution-focused therapy, or positive psychology, can assist planners in maximizing the financial planning process. These areas of psychology are perhaps the most useful for financial planners who want to take behavioral finance further and help individual clients identify, challenge, and change self-limiting beliefs and behaviors.

Cognitive Behavioral Techniques

Cognitive behavioral therapy (CBT) is based on the theory that dysfunctional thinking—that which is inaccurate or unproductive—is the source of self-defeating behaviors (Beck, 2011). That is, "the way that individuals perceive a situation is more closely connected to their reaction than the situation itself" (Beck Institute for Cognitive Behavior Therapy, n.d.). CBT treatment is based on "a conceptualization, or understanding, of individual patients (their specific beliefs and patterns of behaviors)" (Beck, 2011, p. 2). As described in the previous section, an individual's beliefs about money may be shaped by a variety of individual, developmental, and cultural factors, and specific money beliefs (e.g., money avoidance, money worship, and money status) are related to disordered financial behaviors. With an understanding of where unproductive beliefs and behaviors may have stemmed, financial planners can use CBT strategies to help clients change their unhelpful financial thoughts and behaviors and promote enduring improvement in their financial functioning and progress toward their goals.

Financial planners can apply CBT techniques to assist clients in identifying and reassessing "self-defeating beliefs that hinder or impede positive financial behaviors" (Nabeshima & Klontz, 2015, p. 145). Nabeshima and Klontz (2015) describe a scenario in which a client's belief that she is "too dumb" to understand retirement planning is impeding her savings behavior. The process of restructuring irrational beliefs such as this one is typically completed in a series of steps: (1) identify irrational beliefs, (2) challenge irrational beliefs, (3) test the validity of irrational beliefs, (4) create replacement beliefs, and (5) modify behavior (Beck, 2011; Nabeshima & Klontz, 2015). This process is generally a present-focused and collaborative experience that assists clients in developing coping strategies to deal with dysfunctional beliefs and implementing proactive behaviors to improve their circumstances.

To identify, challenge, and change problematic money scripts, financial planners may encourage their clients to keep an automatic thought record to track both their good and bad thoughts throughout the day. Referred to as a *money script log* (Klontz et al., 2008; Klontz et al., 2016; Klontz, Britt, Mentzer, & Klontz, 2011), this technique can be used as "a tool to help clients examine their thoughts, feelings, and unconscious thinking patterns around money" (Nabeshima & Klontz, 2015, p. 146). Clients are instructed to think about a financial situation that caused distress and record the emotion associated with the distress. They are then directed to identify the money-related thought, or money script, underlying that emotion and are asked to develop an alternative money script that will promote positive financial behaviors. CBT techniques have been shown to be effective in improving problematic money behaviors, including hoarding (Tolin, Frost, & Steketee, 2007), gambling (Toneatto & Gunaratne, 2009), and compulsive buying (Kellett & Bolton, 2009) disorders.

MOTIVATIONAL INTERVIEWING TECHNIQUES

Motivational interviewing (MI) refers to strategies that people in the helping professions can use to increase a client's motivation for change (Miller & Rollnick, 2012). It builds on Carl Rogers' humanistic theories of individual's capabilities for change and is "a way of being with a client, not just a set of techniques for doing counseling" (Miller & Rollnick, 1991, p. 62). Specifically, MI is about "arranging conversations so that people talk themselves into change, based on their own values and interests" (Miller & Rollnick, 2012, p. 4). Financial planners often encounter clients who express resistance to change. In those instances, it is often the planner's natural response to "provide more information, be encouraging, provide warnings, or confront the client" (Klontz, Horwitz, & Klontz, 2015, p. 347). However, research suggests that, when faced with resistance, this tactic often backfires and results in the client being less likely to change. Financial planners can utilize the key aspects of MI—partnership, acceptance, compassion, and evocation—to recognize client resistance and implement more productive behavior change tactics (Klontz, Horwitz, et al., 2015; Miller & Rollnick, 2012).

MI theory and techniques suggest that the financial planning process should begin with establishing trust. Britt et al. (2016) suggest noticing the temperature of your clients' hands when greeting them. A cold or clammy hand may indicate stress, whereas a warm hand may indicate a more relaxed state. For clients experiencing stress, it may be particularly important to join them in conversation before beginning the financial planning process. Spending time in congenial conversation before diving into the subject of finances establishes rapport and increases trust, creating a foundation for change that can increase the efficacy of financial planning. When working with clients, it is also important to offer encouragement and support with regard to what the client has been doing well so as to increase "the likelihood that clients continue the relationship and follow through on the strategies recommended during the meeting" (Britt et al., 2016, p. 50; Miller & Rollnick, 2012).

Financial planners can also engage in *reflective listening* to overcome client resistance and increase motivation for change (Klontz et al., 2016). Reflective listening is an active listening technique that involves a concerted effort to understand what someone is trying to say, even if he is not fully articulating it (Britt et al., 2016; Klontz, Horwitz, et al., 2015; Miller & Rollnick, 2012). When engaging in reflective listening, financial planners should avoid asking questions, as they can be perceived as confrontational. Instead, financial planners should interpret and summarize what their client is trying to say, "then reflect it back to them in the form of a statement" (Klontz, Horwitz, & Klontz, 2015, p. 351). A skilled reflective response confirms to the client that you understand them and that you are on the same page. It allows clients to continue talking, build on their thoughts, and develop possible solutions in line with their personal values (Britt et al., 2016; Klontz, Horwitz, et al., 2015; Miller & Rollnick, 2012).

Solution-Focused Techniques

Solution-focused therapy (SFT) "is a future-focused, goal-directed approach to brief therapy" (de Shazer & Dolan, 2012, p. 1) that is based on the perspective that it is most helpful to focus on "client strengths, skills, and attributes rather than past and current problems (Archuleta, Grable, & Burr, 2015, p. 121). Its developers observed hundreds of hours of therapy and noted the questions, behaviors, and emotions that were most successful in facilitating client conceptualization and solutions. Financial planners can apply key SFT techniques to help clients reduce financial stress and make progress toward their goals. SFT techniques include: (1) recognizing and affirming presession change, (2) developing solution-focused goals, (3) asking the miracle question, (4) asking scaling questions, and (5) complimenting clients (Archuleta et al., 2015; de Shazer & Dolan, 2012).

Identifying presession change occurs at the beginning of each financial planning session. The planner simply asks the client what changes she has noticed have happened or have started to happen since the last session or since she called to make the appointment for the session (de Shazer & Dolan, 2012). Recognizing and affirming presession change, even if it is small, increases the client's belief that change is possible (Archuleta et al., 2015; Lethem, 2002). Financial planners should work with their clients to develop concrete, achievable, measurable, and solution-focused goals. That is, clients should be encouraged to frame goals as a solution, rather than the absence of a problem (Archuleta et al., 2015; de Shazer & Dolan, 2012). Planners can use the *miracle question* to assist clients who struggle to articulate a goal. The miracle question asks the client to imagine what life would be like if, in the middle of the night, all of her problems were solved. The client's response can guide the planner's follow-up questions, which serve to understand the client's values and identify small, manageable goals.

After the client has developed goals, financial planners can use scaling questions "to establish the relevancy of goals and to gauge progress toward goals through the client's eyes" (Archuleta et al., 2015). Scaling questions are popular in SFT due to their versatility. A financial planner can use scaling questions to measure a client's progress toward or feelings about a variety of goals, events, or topics (de Shazer & Dolan, 2012). For example, a financial planner may ask the client to rate, on a scale from 0 (low/terrible/not at all) to 10 (high/exceptional/goal is met), how well they are managing their money, how confident they are in their retirement plan, or how much financial anxiety they feel in various real or hypothetical situations (Archuleta et al., 2015; Britt et al., 2016). Financial planners can follow up by asking clients where they would like to be on that scale and what they have already done to help them move up the scale. Financial planners should offer affirmation of productive behaviors by complimenting clients on their progress toward goals, even if it is minor progress.

Positive Psychology Techniques

A positive psychology framework focuses on not just how to alleviate or minimize problems, but how to promote and maximize thriving. It provides the opportunity for financial planners to move beyond maximizing returns and toward assisting clients in "maximizing the quality of their life as they define it" (Weber, 2012, p. 22). Positive psychology theory and technique has been adapted for use with financial planning clients. Asebedo and Seay (2015) make an argument for the overlapping goals of positive psychology and financial planning. They suggest planners might assess a client's overall well-being in addition to their financial health and promote client well-being through the use of positive psychology exercises.

Applying positive psychology techniques to the financial planning process may start with asking, "How do we help our clients move beyond this basic financial security to accomplish those personal goals that make life worth living?" (Weber, 2012, p. 22). As such, rather than an exclusive focus on the external aspects of money, clients would benefit from an exploration of the underlying goals and values that motivate them to seek financial planning in the first place. One of these motivating influences is a desire to increase happiness. Positive psychology theory suggests that there are three levels of authentic happiness: positive emotions, engagement, and meaning (Seligman, 2012). Weber (2012) describes how financial planners can facilitate a process that works toward achieving each of these levels of happiness. First, planners may work with clients to create a financial plan that promotes positive emotions by ensuring income is set aside for activities the client enjoys, such as hiking, fishing, gardening, or going to concerts. Next, financial planners can encourage clients to be engaged with the present instead of focused exclusively on the future goal (e.g., a comfortable retirement). Planners can assist clients in doing this by using the techniques described above to assist clients in setting small, manageable, value-based goals along the way to their final goals. Research suggests that the process of goal setting, in addition to making progress toward and attaining goals, increases individual well-being (Irving, 2012). The final level of happiness, meaning, can also be promoted through the financial planning process. Meaning requires active engagement in serving a higher purpose. Financial planners may educate their clients on the levels of happiness and encourage them to not just set aside a portion of their income to charitable giving but also, or instead, actively participate in organizations that support their values.

Experiential Techniques

Similar to motivational interviewing, experiential therapy grew from the theories of humanistic psychology. Experiential therapy aims to balance the trust and relationship building of motivational interviewing with a more active, task-focused process of reflection on aroused emotions and promotes new and deeper meaning (Greenberg, Elliot, & Lietaer, 1994). The "most central characteristic of experiential psychotherapy is its focus on promoting in-therapy experiencing" (Greenberg et al., 1994, p. 493). Klontz, Klontz, and Tharp (2015) describe "Experiential Financial Therapy (EFT), an integration of experiential therapy and financial planning" (2015). The application of EFT techniques has been shown to reduce psychological distress, anxiety, and worry about finance-related issues and increase financial health—improvements that were found to persist over time (Klontz et al., 2008).

EFT is grounded in the theory and techniques of psychodrama. It "has a strong emotional component and offers clients the opportunity to increase awareness of their feelings and sensations" (Klontz, Klontz, et al., 2015, p. 104). This is achieved through techniques, including and employing the use of role-playing, art therapy, music therapy, family sculpting, and mindfulness exercises. Financial planners can apply EFT techniques to their sessions by actively engaging their clients in these activities. The application of such techniques has been shown to increase the success of financial planning above and beyond traditional strategies. For example, a recent double-blind, randomized, controlled study investigated the effectiveness of two approaches aimed to increase the savings of 102 participants (Klontz et al., 2017). One applied a traditional, financial education–style approach (the control condition), while the other engaged the participants in experiential activities, such as guided imagery and the creation of vision boards. Results showed that at a 3-week follow-up, participants in the experimental group had significantly greater increases in their proportional savings (an increase of 73%) when compared to participants in the control group (an increase of 22%). In another study, using a 60-minute financial psychology intervention with experiential methods in retirement planning, meeting with three companies and a total of 198 employees, 401(k) contributions rates increased 39% (Horwitz & Klontz, 2017).

Financial planners may consider applying these experiential techniques to their own practice to maximize the efficacy of sessions. Planners can facilitate mindfulness activities, such as guided imagery, by asking clients to picture their goal, perhaps a beach vacation with their family. With a calm voice, instruct the clients to close their eyes and imagine the beach. What do they see? Hear? Smell? Feel? Who is with them? What are they doing? What emotions does this evoke? Financial planners may also facilitate art therapy strategies, such as vision boards, with their clients. More specifically, savings boards can help clients conceptualize how their future goals connect with their past experiences and present feelings and values. Planners may provide the client with materials and ask them to create a board, divided in three sections. The Past section should contain the people, things, and events in their life that give their life meaning. Perhaps significant individuals, activities, or heirlooms. In the Present section, clients should be encouraged to get in touch with the feelings and values that are associated with what gives their life meaning. What do these feelings and values represent? Perhaps they represent the importance of family, security, safety, adventure, or excitement. Lastly, clients should be instructed to create the Future section of the board. The Future section should contain their financial goals and how they are in line with their values and fit into their optimal future. EFT techniques such as these can assist clients in identifying what is important to them at a deep and fundamental level, linking these motivations and values to present goals and encouraging goal-directed behaviors.

CONCLUSION

To be useful to financial planners, the findings of behavioral finance need to be viewed from the broader context of financial psychology. Behavioral finance has identified our common, inborn cognitive biases, which when left unhindered can have a detrimental impact on our financial outcomes. In addition to knowing how our cognitive processes and perceptions impact our financial decisions, it is important to take into account a client's unique personality, developmental history, social, cultural, and gender influences, as well as family dynamics, and how these aspects of clients' financial psychology have shaped their beliefs and behaviors. With a broadening understanding of client psychology, the financial planning field continues to benefit from practice-oriented solutions to equip planners to better understand, assess, intervene, and shape clients' financial beliefs and behaviors to improve their financial health and overall well-being.

Practitioners would benefit from research efforts expanding our knowledge of what the various fields of psychology can tell us about the financial beliefs, behaviors, and outcomes of financial planning clients. While there is a growing body of literature integrating psychology with personal finances, until recently, the field of psychology has all but ignored the area of money (Klontz, et al., 2008; Trachtman, 1999). This book and the work of many of its authors is a clear demonstration that the field of financial planning has taken the lead in championing these efforts. That said, with regard to research in financial psychology, we are indeed just getting started.

Perhaps of most interest to financial planners, research is desperately needed to examine the effectiveness of techniques drawn from psychology for use in financial planning. Ideally, these will include "practice-oriented solutions to equip planners to better understand, assess, intervene, and shape clients' financial beliefs and behaviors to improve their financial health and overall well-being" (Klontz & Horwitz, 2017). While a growing body of articles are discussing this integration, few studies of their effectiveness exist. Studies are needed that will further examine aspects of financial psychology, including: (a) the nature of effective planner–client relationships, (b) the effectiveness of client communication techniques, (c) the financial planning environment and its impact on clients, (d) multicultural factors and their impact on financial planning, (e) the effectiveness of techniques drawn from various schools of psychotherapy in optimizing a client's financial health, and (f) the effectiveness of psychological techniques that help planners identify, challenge, and change clients' limiting or destructive financial beliefs and behaviors.

REFERENCES

Allen, M. W., Edwards, R., Hayhoe, C. R., & Leach, L. (2007). Imagined interactions, family money management patterns and coalitions, and attitudes toward money and credit. *Journal of Family Economic Issues*, 28, 3–22.

American Psychological Association. (2017a). *Careers in psychology*. Retrieved from http://www.apa.org/careers/resources/guides/careers.aspx.

American Psychological Association. (2017b). *Clinical psychology*. Retrieved from: www.apa.org/about/division/div12.aspx.

American Psychological Association. (2017c). *Pursuing a career in social psychology*. Retrieved from http://www.apa.org/action/science/social/education-training.aspx.

American Psychological Association. (2017d). *Understanding development psychology*. Retrieved from http://www.apa.org/action/science/developmental/index.aspx.

American Psychological Association. (2017e). *Psychology topics: Personality*. Retrieved from http://www.apa.org/topics/personality/.

Archuleta, K. L., Grable, J. E., & Burr, E. (2015). Solution-focused financial therapy. In B. T. Klontz, S. L. Britt, & K. L. Archuleta (Eds.), *Financial therapy: Theory, research & practice* (pp. 121–141). New York: Springer.

Asebedo, S. D., & Seay, M. C. (2015). From functioning to flourishing: Applying positive psychology to financial planning. *Journal of Financial Planning, 28*(11), 50–58.

Baker, M. N., & Lyons, C. P. (2015). Financial therapy from a self-psychological perspective. In B. T. Klontz, S. L. Britt, & K. L. Archuleta (Eds.), *Financial therapy: Theory, research & practice (pp.* 303–323). New York: Springer.

Beck, J. S. (2011). *Cognitive behavior therapy: Basics and beyond* (2nd ed.). New York: Guilford Press.

Beck Institute for Cognitive Behavior Therapy. (n.d.). *What is Cognitive Behavior Therapy (CBT)?* Retrieved from https://www.beckinstitute.org/get-informed/what-is-cognitive-therapy/.

Borghans, L., Duckworth, A. L., Heckman, J. J., & Weel, B. T. (2008). The economics of psychology and personality traits. *Journal of Human Resources, 43*(4), 972–1059.

Bowen, J. J. (2011). Listen up! Are you asking your clients the right probing questions and then listening thoughtfully to their answers? *Financial Planning, 41*(4), 27.

Britt, S. L. (2016). The intergenerational transference of money attitudes and behaviors. *Journal of Consumer Affairs, 50*(3), 539–556.

Britt, S. L., Cumbie, J. A., & Bell, M. M. (2013). The influence of locus of control on student financial behavior. *College Student Journal, 47*(1), 178–184.

Britt, S. L., & Grable, J. E. (2012). Your office may be a stressor: Understand how the physical environment of your office affects financial counseling clients. *The Standard, 30*(2), 5 & 13.

Britt, S. L., Lawson, D. R., & Haselwood, C. A. (2016). A descriptive analysis of physiological stress and readiness to change. *Journal of Financial Planning, 29*(12), 45–51.

Carrier, L., & Maurice, D. (1998). Beneath the surface: The psychological side of spending behaviors. *Journal of Financial Planning, 11*(1), 94–98.

de Shazer, S., & Dolan, Y. (2012). *More than miracles: The state of the art of solution-focused brief therapy.* New York: Routledge.

Falicov, C. J. (2001). The cultural meanings of money: The case of Latinos and Anglo-Americans. *The American Behavioral Scientist, 45*(2), 313–328.

Garrison, S. T., & Gutter, M. S. (2010). Gender differences in financial socialization and willingness to take financial risks. *Journal of Financial Counseling and Planning, 21*(2), 60–72.

Grable, J. E. (2000). Financial risk tolerance and additional factors that affect risk taking in everyday money matters. *Journal of Business and Psychology, 14*(4), 625–630.

Grable, J. E., & Britt, S. L. (2012). Financial news and client stress: Understanding the association from a financial planning perspective. *Financial Planning Review, 5*(3), 23–36.

Grable, J. E., & Britt, S. L. (2011, January). A test of the video narration effect on financial risk- tolerance assessment. *Journal of Financial Planning: Between the Issues*.

Greenberg, L., Elliot, R., & Lietaer, G. (1994). Research on experiential psychotherapies. In A. E. Bergin & S. L. Garfield (Eds.), *Handbook of psychotherapy and behavior change* (4th ed., pp. 509–539). New York: John Wiley & Sons.

Guven, C. (2012). Reversing the question: Does happiness affect consumption and savings behavior? *Journal Of Economic Psychology, 33,* 701–717.

Hancock, A. M., Jorgensen, B. L., & Swanson, M. S. (2013). College students and credit card use: The role of parents, work experience, financial knowledge, and credit card attitudes. *Journal of Family and Economic Issues, 34,* 369–381.

Hays, P., Klontz, B. T., & Kemnitz, R. (2015). Seven steps to culturally responsive financial therapy. In *Financial Therapy* (pp. 87–99). New York: Springer.

Heckman, J. J., Stixrud, J., & Urzua, S. (2006). *The effects of cognitive and noncognitive abilities on labor market outcomes and social behavior.* Working Paper No. w12006. Cambridge, MA: National Bureau of Economic Research.

Horwitz, E. J., & Klontz, B. T. (2017). *A financial psychology intervention for increasing employee engagement in a retirement plan meeting: Results of three studies.* Manuscript under review.

Johnson, L. M., & Takasawa, K. H. (2015). Humanistic psychotherapy for money disorders: Wholistic approaches to financial therapy. In B. T. Klontz, S. L. Britt, & K. L. Archuleta (Eds.), *Financial therapy: Theory, research, and practice* (pp. 325–345). New York: Springer.

Kellett, S., & Bolton, J. V. (2009). Compulsive buying: A cognitive-behavioural model. *Clinical Psychological and Psychotherapy, 16,* 83–99.

Klontz, B. T. (2014, January). Junior achievement: Clients are wary of working with young advisors. Here's how to win them over. *On Wall Street,* 29–30.

Klontz, B. T. (2016). Why financial planning research doesn't matter (and what to do about it). *Journal of Financial Planning, 29*(10), 42–44.

Klontz, B. T., Bivens, A., Klontz, P. T., & Wada, J., Kahler, R. (2008). The treatment of disordered money behaviors: Results of an open clinical trial. *Psychological Services, 5*(3), 295–308.

Klontz, B. T., & Britt, S. L. (2012). Financial trauma: Why the abandonment of buy-and-hold in favor of tactical asset management may be a symptom of post-traumatic stress. *Journal of Financial Therapy, 3*(2), 14–27.

Klontz, B. T., Britt, S. L., Mentzer, K., & Klontz, P. T. (2011). Money beliefs and financial behaviors: Development of the Klontz Money Script Inventory. *Journal of Financial Therapy, 2*(1), 1–22.

Klontz, B. T., & Horwitz, E. (2017). Behavioral finance 2.0: Financial psychology. *Journal of Financial Planning, 30*(5), 28–29.

Klontz, B. T., Horwitz, E. J., & Klontz, P. T. (2015). Stages of change and motivational interviewing in financial therapy. In *Financial Therapy* (pp. 347–362). New York: Springer.

Klontz, B. T., Kahler, R., & Klontz, P. T. (2016). *Facilitating financial health: Tools for financial planners, coaches, and therapists* (2nd ed.). Cincinnati: National Underwriters Company.

Klontz, P. T., Kahler, R., & Klontz, B. T. (2006). *The financial wisdom of Ebenezer Scrooge: 5 principles to transform your relationship with money*. Deerfield Beach, FL: Health Communications.

Klontz, B. T., & Klontz, P. T. (2016). 7 steps to facilitate exquisite listening. *Journal of Financial Planning, 29*(11), 24–26.

Klontz, B. T., Klontz, P. T., & Tharp, D. (2015). Experiential financial therapy. In B. T. Klontz, S. L. Britt, & K. L. Archuleta (Eds.), *Financial therapy: Theory, research, and practice* (pp. 103–120). New York: Springer.

Klontz, B. T., Seay, M. C., Sullivan, P., & Canale, A. (2014). The psychology of wealth: Psychological factors associated with high income. *Journal of Financial Planning, 27*(12), 46–53.

Klontz, B. T., Sullivan, P., Seay, M. C., & Canale, A. (2015). The wealthy: A financial psychological profile. *Consulting Psychology Journal: Practice and Research, 67*(2), 127–143.

Klontz, B. T., Zabek, F., Taylor, C., Bivens, A., Horwitz, E., Klontz, P. T., et al. (2018). The sentimental savings study: Results of a double-blind, randomized control experiment to increase personal savings. In progress.

Leder, H., Forster, M., & Gerger, G. (2011). The glasses stereotype revisited: Effects of eyeglasses on perception, recognition, and impression of faces. *Swiss Journal of Psychology, 70*(4), 211–222.

Lethem, J. (2002). Brief solution focused therapy. *Child and Adolescent Mental Health, 7*(4), 189–192.

MacLeod, A. K., Coates, E., & Hetherton, J. (2008). Increasing well-being through teaching goal- setting and planning skills: Results of a brief intervention. *Journal of Happiness Studies, 9*, 185–196.

Miller, W. R., & Rollnick, S. (1991). *Motivational interviewing: Preparing people to change addictive behavior*. New York: Guilford Press.

Miller, W. R., & Rollnick, S. (2012). *Motivational interviewing: Helping people change*. (3rd ed.) New York: Guilford Press.

Mueller, G., & Plug, E. (2006). Estimating the effect of personality on male and female earnings. *Industrial and Labor Relations Review, 60*(1), 3–22.

Nabeshima, G., & Klontz, B. T. (2015). Cognitive-behavioral financial therapy. In B. T. Klontz, S. L. Britt, & K. L. Archuleta (Eds.), *Financial therapy: Theory, research, and practice* (pp. 143–159). New York: Springer.

Nabeshima, G., & Seay, M. (2015). Wealth and personality: Can personality traits make your clients rich? *Journal of Financial Planning, 28*(7), 50–57.

Neymotin, F. (2010). Linking self-esteem with the tendency to engage in financial planning. *Journal of Economic Psychology, 31*(6), 996–1007.

Nga, J. K., & Ken Yien, L. (2013). The influence of personality trait and demographics on financial decision making among Generation Y. *Young Consumers, 14*(3), 230–243.

Peterson, C. (2006). *A primer in positive psychology*. Oxford, UK: Oxford University Press.

Pullen, C. (2000). Listening to retirement. *Journal of Financial Planning, 13*(4), 50–51.

Quilgars, D., Jones, A., & Abbott, D. (2008). Does difference make a difference in financial planning for risk? *Social Policy & Administration, 42*(6), 576–592.

Seligman, M. E. (2012). *Flourish: A visionary new understanding of happiness and well-being.* New York: Simon & Schuster.

Sheldon, K. M., Kasser, T., Smith, K., & Share, T. (2002). Personal goals and psychological growth: Testing an intervention to enhance goal attainment and personality integration. *Journal of Personality, 70*(1), 5–31.

Shim, S., Xiao, J. J., Barber, B. L., & Lyons, A. C. (2009). Pathways to life success: A conceptual model of financial well-being for young adults. *Journal of Applied Developmental Psychology, 30*, 708–723.

Steed, L., & Symes, M. (2009). The role of perceived wealth competence, wealth values, and internal wealth locus of control in predicting wealth creation behavior. *Journal of Applied Social Psychology, 39*(10), 2525–2540.

Taylor, C. D., Klontz, B. T., & Lawson, D. R. (2017). Money disorders and locus of control: Implications for assessment and treatment. *Journal of Financial Therapy 8*(1), 124–137.

The Association of Humanistic Psychology. (2017). Historic review of humanistic psychology. Retrieved from https://www.ahpweb.org/about/what-is-humanistic-psychology.html.

Tolin, D. F., Frost, R. O., & Steketee, G. (2007). An open trial of cognitive-behavioral therapy for compulsive hoarding. *Behavior Research and Therapy, 45*, 1461–1470.

Toneatto, T., & Gunaratne, M. (2009). Does the treatment of cognitive distortions improve clinical outcomes for problem gambling? *Journal of Contemporary Psychotherapy, 39*, 221–229.

Trachtman, R. (1999). The money taboo: Its effects in everyday life and in the practice of psychotherapy. *Clinical Social Work Journal, 27*, 275–288.

Trachtman, R. (2015). Psychodynamic financial therapy. In B. T. Klontz, S. L. Britt, & K. L. Archuleta (Eds.). *Financial therapy: Theory, research, and practice* (pp. 285–301). New York: Springer

University of Rhode Island Department of Psychology (2015). *Multicultural psychology definition.* Retrieved from http://web.uri.edu/psychology/files/Multicultural-Psychology-Definition-3.19.15.pdf.

U.S. Bureau of Labor Statistics. (2012). *Household data annual percentages: Employed persons by detailed occupation, sex, race, and Latino or Latino ethnicity.* Retrieved from http://www.bls.gov/cps/cpsaat11.pdf.

U.S. Census Bureau. (2015). *FFF: Hispanic heritage month 2015.* Retrieved from https://www.census.gov/newsroom/facts-for-features/2015/cb15-ff18.html.

Viinikainen, J., Kokko, K., Pulkkinen, L., & Pehkonen, J. (2010). Personality and labour market income: Evidence from longitudinal data. *Labour, 24*(2), 201–220.

Weber, K. (2012). Planning parallels with positive psychology. *Bank Investment Consultant, 20*(1), 21–23.

Zagorsky, J. L. (2007). Do you have to be smart to be rich? The impact of IQ on wealth, income, and financial distress. *Intelligence, 35*(5), 489–501.

Zebrowitz, L. A., & Montepare, J. M. (1992). Impressions of babyfaced individuals across the life-span. *Developmental Psychology, 28*, 1143–1152.

CHAPTER 17

Money Disorders and Other Problematic Financial Behaviors

Edward Horwitz, PhD, CFP®
Creighton University

Bradley T. Klontz, PsyD, CFP®
Creighton University

Meghaan Lurtz, MS
Kansas State University

While it would be ideal if our clients' financial decisions were made logically using financial best practices, extensive empirical and anecdotal evidence indicate that that is just not the case. Clients' psychology has a significant impact on their financial behaviors. Their financial beliefs, biases, and perceptions drive much of their financial decision-making. As a result, clients often make financial decisions that are incongruent with their stated financial desires and goals. When clients engage in patterns of chronic self-destructive financial behaviors they may be exhibiting symptoms of a money disorder. Contrary to popular belief, money disorders are not caused by a lack of money (Klontz, Bivens, Klontz, Wada, & Kahler, 2008). Money disorders are not punctuated by a single bout of overspending nor a single, poor financial choice. Money disorders, instead, manifest as ongoing and "persistent, predictable, often rigid, patters of self-destructive financial behaviors that cause significant stress, anxiety, emotional distress, and impairment in major areas of one's life" (Klontz & Klontz, 2009, p. 129). When not properly understood and addressed, these beliefs and resulting behaviors undermine clients' abilities to achieve financial goals and decrease their overall financial health and wellness.

Financial planners and the client–planner relationship offer powerful mediums through which money disorders can be identified and acted upon. For example, tools exist for the assessment of money beliefs and behaviors, which can be given as part of the data-gathering step of the financial planning process. There are also established techniques to discuss, challenge, and repair maladaptive financial behaviors (Klontz, Britt, Archuleta, & Klontz, 2012). Common money disorders include: overspending and compulsive buying disorder, gambling disorder, financial enabling, financial dependence, hoarding disorder, and financial denial and avoidance. Money disorders range in severity. More severe and diagnosable disorders according to the *Diagnostic and Statistical Manual of Mental Disorders*, 5th edition *DSM-5*®; American Psychiatric Association [APA], 2013), such as hoarding and pathological gambling, should be referred to a trained mental health professional.

Despite the best efforts and practice engaged by financial planners, clients exhibit financial behaviors that run contrary to the achievement of their identified financial goals. It is assumed in standard finance theory that we assume a logical individual, unlike in behavioral finance, where there is an understanding that individuals act irrationally at times. Financial planners commonly observe client behaviors that defy what planners believe is a logical decision or action. To a highly trained financial expert who thinks in a logical and quantitative manner, our clients' decisions can be very puzzling and frustrating. However, psychological research informs us that many of our decisions are made emotionally and at our subconscious level of thinking. In other words, when our clients are making financial decisions, they are probably not always using logical thought processes to reach these decisions, but rather reacting emotionally based on cognitive biases and subconscious money beliefs.

This leads the financial planner to the most important questions: (1) How can I better recognize and understand these financial beliefs that inform my client's decision-making?, (2) How can I better communicate with my clients to help make them aware of these beliefs and behaviors?, and (3) What, if anything, can I do in my role of financial planner to help them change? This chapter will explain the different types of money disorders and related financial behaviors. There will be a more detailed review of several commonly encountered disordered money behaviors by financial planners. Lastly, we will present several case studies for examples of how planners can identify money disorders and techniques they can use to raise client awareness.

Before moving forward, it is important to discuss money disorders within the context of the role of the financial planner. As in other specialized and licensed professional disciplines that financial planners encounter through the course of best practice (e.g. estate planning attorneys or tax professionals), referrals are often needed when the situation demands. By definition, money disorders cause significant impairment in one's functioning. In some cases, they exist alongside other psychological disorders (comorbidity) such as depression or anxiety. In these situations, a referral to a licensed and trained mental health professional is necessary. While a financial planner can assist with making the referral and with helping the client examine the financial impact of these behaviors, financial planners should not attempt to treat a diagnosable mental disorder, such as hoarding disorder, gambling disorder, or compulsive buying disorder.

Therefore, the role of the financial planning professional related to money disorders and their related financial behaviors exists within the domains of: (1) assessment, (2) awareness, (3) education, and (4) communication of the disordered money behaviors as integrated within the overall financial planning process. Without specialized and professional training, actions to address or treat these behavioral disorders should be referred to a mental health provider. Some financial planners who gain a graduate level of education and training within the field of financial psychology or financial therapy, and have earned an FBS designation (certified financial behavioral specialist), may be qualified to engage in client interventions to address some aspects of disordered money behaviors, such as financial enabling or financial dependence. These individuals should be part of the financial planner's extended team, much as an estate attorney or CPA might be, to help clients understand and address their financial behavioral issues or concerns. As the field of financial psychology continues to grow and evolve, so will the desire for education, information, and application of these skills by financial planners to more actively and deeply help their clients achieve their financial goals.

LITERATURE ON MONEY DISORDERS AND RELATED FINANCIAL BEHAVIORS

Money disorders and related disordered money beliefs are different from biases and predictable heuristic mistakes. Biases and heuristics often describe common computing errors that can be treated in the moment with brief education or a change in how risky information is presented (Baker & Ricciardi, 2014). A common example of this can be seen when clients buy high and sell low, the opposite of what investment theory would dictate. Conversely, money disorders are emotional and pervasive. Their impacts may subconsciously affect a client throughout his or her daily life. Money disorders are described as "emotional and spiritual imbalances that express themselves as continuing problems with money and work" (Gallen, 2002). Money disorders are said to be the results of emotional difficulties, where individuals engage in self-defeating financial behavior to avoid feeling intense and unresolved emotions (Gallen, 2002). For example, financial planners frequently encounter grief-stricken clients who may spend excessively or give money away irrationally, trying to cope with underlying emotional pain.

Research has found that money disorders are associated with stress, financial difficulties, income, net worth, credit card debt, job performance, and financial health (Klontz et al., 2008; Klontz et al., 2012). Disordered money behaviors have been defined as "maladaptive patterns of financial beliefs and behaviors that lead to clinically significant distress, impairment in social or occupational functioning, undue financial strain or an inability to appropriately enjoy one's financial resources" (Klontz et al., 2008; Klontz, Britt, & Archuleta, 2015). Further, despite the emotional and financial consequences, maladaptive patterns of money beliefs and behaviors persist (Klontz et al., 2008).

Research has also found that money disorders are associated with money beliefs. Money scripts are patterns of financial beliefs, which can be assessed to understand and predict financial behaviors. Consistent with social learning theory, money scripts are often passed down from parent to child and can be conscious or unconscious. The messages, once the child has reached adulthood, manifest as privately held beliefs (Furnham, von Strumm, & Milner, 2014). Money scripts have been associated with negative financial health indicators across multiple populations (Archuleta, Dale, Spann, 2013; Klontz, Britt, Mentzer, & Klontz, 2011). Assessing money scripts has been established as an appropriate practice in financial planning to understand and gather information on resulting disordered money behaviors (Klontz & Britt, 2012; Lawson & Klontz, 2017). Within the context of the six-stage financial planning process, questions related to money scripts can be integrated into the client data-gathering phase and assessed under the analysis and evaluation of client data. The following section summarizes several money disorders and problematic financial behaviors that have been identified in the financial planning literature.

Compulsive Buying Disorder (CBD)

The *DSM-5®* is the fifth edition of the *Diagnostic and Statistical Manual of Mental Health Disorders*, which is used as the American Psychiatric Association's official diagnostic and classification tool for mental disorders (APA, 2013). CBD was not included in the *DSM-5®* as there were debates on how it should be classified. CBD could have been classified as: (1) obsessive–compulsive disorder, (2) addiction, or (3) mood disorder (Black, Shaw, & Allen, 2016). Regardless, CBD has remained in the spotlight for consumer researchers, and can be diagnosed and treated as a mental disorder under the diagnoses of "Other Specified Disruptive, Impulse-Control, and Conduct

Disorder" or "Unspecified Disruptive, Impulse-Control, and Conduct Disorder" (Klontz, Kahler, & Klontz, 2016). CBD is characterized by "obsessive, irresistible, out of control buying urges that lead to financial difficulties, feelings of guilt and/or shame, and interference with ones work or close relationships" (Klontz et al., 2012). In a 5-year follow-up report on individuals with CBD, Black et al. (2016) found that some individuals were able to quit (18%), but most were not (65%). Other studies have found that cognitive-behavioral therapy interventions can help (Aboujaoude, Gamel, & Koran, 2003; Mueller et al., 2008). CBD primarily impacts women and begins to manifest in the teenage years (Black et al., 2016).

Gambling Disorder

Gambling disorder is included in the *DSM-5®* and is described as "persistent and recurrent problematic gambling behavior leading to clinically significant impairment or distress" (APA, 2013, p. 585). Addressing and being aware of gambling issues has been a topic in financial planning literature. For example, in 2000, the *Journal of Financial Planning* dedicated an entire issue to the disorder and implications for financial planners. Gambling disorder has been found in a wide variety of populations and differences in prevalence by gender, age of onset, types of gambling, attitudes toward gambling, and treatment outcomes have been well researched (Blanco et al., 2015).

Hoarding Disorder

Hoarding disorder is also included in the *DSM-5®*. It has been described as "accumulation and having great difficulty discarding objects that most other people would consider useless or of limited value; having clutter so severe that it prevents or seriously limits the use of living spaces for which the space was intended; and cluttering, acquiring, or difficulty discarding causes significant impairment or distress" (Tolin, Frost, & Steketee, 2007, p. 11–12). Research on hoarding disorders has begun to tease apart hoarding disorder as an issue of obsessive compulsion and perhaps turn more to an etiology of environmental factors (Iervolino et al., 2009). This is an interesting advancement as, for example, Benson-Townsend (2015) has focused on compulsive hoarding as a function of money attitudes. There is some evidence to suggest that hoarding behaviors are often modeled by parents (Tolin, 2011) and that for some, money can be the primary object that is hoarded, which could lead to financial planning clients being unable to enjoy the financial success they may have been able to achieve (Canale & Klontz, 2013).

Workaholism

Workaholsim has not been formally established as a disorder in the *DSM-5*®; however, it is an addiction similar to alcoholism (Oates, 1971). Workaholism has been defined as "an addiction wherein the workaholic is highly involved in work, feels driven to work because of inner pressures that make the person feel guilty or depressed when not working, and in which the person has low levels of work enjoyment" (Spence & Robbins, 1992, p. 161). Workaholism has been described both negatively and positively in literature. In some cases there is a focus on motivation while other times the focus is on compulsion and or rigidness (Andreassen, Griffiths, Hetland, & Pallesen, 2012). While there can be financial and professional benefits to workaholism, it is a serious problem associated with low self-esteem, anxiety, depression, family conflict, stress, and lower job satisfaction (Klontz et al., 2016). Planners will often encounter workaholics and be in a position to recommend that they set aside time and resources to pursue non-work-related relationships and activities.

Financial Dependence

Financial dependence, or affluenza as it has been referred to in the popular media, has become a hot topic in both financial planning and economic literature as culture and financial trends shift work motivation and social norms. It is defined as "the reliance on others for non-work income that creates fear or anxiety of being cut-off, feelings of anger or resentment related to the non-work income, and a stifling of one's motivation, passion, and/or drive to achieve" (Klontz et al., 2012, p. 21). Recent work in financial planning has detailed some of the dangers and difficulties in working with clients and their families who are struggling with financial dependent/enabling relationships (Klontz & Canale, 2016). Women from wealthier families are more likely to endorse comfort with financial dependence (Newcomb & Rabow, 1999). Financial dependence has also been associated with lower income, higher socioeconomic status in childhood, singlehood, and lower levels of education (Klontz et al., 2012).

Financial Enabling

Financial enabling, the other side of the financial dependence equation, has often been associated with stress and depression as either a result of exceeding one's financial constraints and/or a strained personal relationship (Canale, Archuleta, & Klontz, 2015). Financial enabling is "the inability to say 'no' when someone, such as a family member, continues to ask for money" (Klontz et al., 2012, p. 21). Financial enabling has been found to be associated with lower income and higher revolving credit card debt and often involves sacrificing one's financial well-being for the sake of others and feeling resentment or anger after giving money to others (Klontz et al., 2012). In working with financial enablers in a financial planning role, Klontz and Canale (2016) suggest that planners help clients: (1) recognize that financial help can hurt, (2) recognize the psychological value in the need for someone to generate their own income stream, (3) acknowledge the curse of unstructured free time on the mental health of the financial dependent, and (4) help the enabler develop, implement, and stick to a plan to stop the financial aid.

Financial Denial

Denial is common in finance. When individuals regret or ignore selling losing stock options, they are possibly denying to themselves that they have made a mistake (Odean & Barber, 1999). Financial denial has been defined as an "attempt to cope by simply not thinking about money or trying not to deal with it" (Klontz et al., 2016, p. 121). Individuals avoid thinking about money in order to avoid feelings of distress (Canale et al., 2015); in financial planning literature, it has been described as a natural defense mechanism used to avoid feeling stress (Klontz & Klontz, 2009).

Financial Enmeshment

Different from all of the previously mentioned disorders, which can manifest and exhibit within a single individual, financial enmeshment is specifically about inappropriate relationships between two or more people. Financial enmeshment is "when family systems operate in a state of increased fluidity wherein the boundaries and roles are no longer clear or appropriate, resulting in the inducement of stress" (Kemnitz, Klontz, & Archuleta, 2016, p. 32). Research shows that financial enmeshments tend to occur more commonly with higher income males (Klontz et al., 2012).

It is important to be aware that many of these disordered money behaviors overlap with one another. It is not uncommon, for example, for individuals with one disorder to exhibit difficulties in another or to experience anxiety and depression as a result of the consequences of their money disorder(s). Financial planners may be in a great place to help clients consider buying behaviors and budgets, but are not necessarily trained to work with clients experiencing a money disorder or depression. The next two sections provide examples of ways that financial planners can assist clients who are manifesting disordered money behaviors and some case studies that illustrate how some of these disorders may be present in financial planning practice.

ADDRESSING MONEY DISORDERS AND RELATED FINANCIAL BEHAVIORS

Financial planners can assist in the identification of potential disordered money behaviors and can help a client move toward increasing awareness around their behaviors and their readiness to change. This can be done through several methods, including assessment and motivational interviewing. Each of these components and some related tools are presented below.

Assessment

In order to assist the planner with assessing overall financial wellness, a number of quantitative tools have been developed. Most recently, the Consumer Financial Protection Bureau (2017) released a Financial Well-Being scale. Their scale was developed to measure the impact of financial education and financial literacy, but has applicability within a financial planning practice.

Tools for the assessment of money disorders, specifically, have also been developed and researched. For instance, Klontz Money Script Inventory–Revised (KMSI–R) has been used in several studies and was recently found to have acceptable reliability and validity (Taylor, Klontz, & Britt, 2016). The Klontz Money Behaviors Inventory (KMBI) has also been researched and validated (Klontz et al., 2012). These tools can be used during the data-gathering and analysis steps of the financial planning process. The Financial Anxiety scale as well as the Klontz-Britt Financial Health scale (K-BFHS) are also useful tools for establishing the client-planner relationship. These two scales assist the financial planner in understanding and assessing the severity of financial and emotional distress. Development of the Financial Anxiety scale was based on diagnostic criteria for generalized anxiety disorder (APA, 2013; Archuleta, Dale, & Spann, 2013). The K-BFHS has been used in financial planning practices and has been validated by previous research (Britt, Klontz, Tibbetts, & Leitz, 2015; Klontz et al., 2016).

Please note that several of the assessment tools mentioned require specialized education and skills to interpret the results and address the underlying problems. As mentioned previously, receiving education in financial behavior and/or working with an expert can be useful in interpreting the results of these assessments so that you can make proper referrals when needed.

Motivational Interviewing

Often, the simple act of becoming aware of a problematic money belief or behavior allows the client to make immediate changes to their financial behaviors. Awareness can be powerful. However, at other times the support of a planner is needed. For financial planners who are interested in helping a client increase her readiness to change their behaviors, motivational interviewing is an extremely useful tool, and has been applied to the financial planner–client relationship (e.g., Horwitz & Klontz, 2013; Klontz et al., 2015; Klontz et al., 2016).

Motivational interviewing (MI) is a therapeutic communication technique with four stages: (1) engaging, (2) focusing, (3) evoking, and (4) planning. Each stage builds on a "collaborative conversation style for strengthening a person's own motivation and commitment to change" (Miller & Rollnick, 2013, p. 12). MI focuses on guiding the client to his or her own strengths and abilities related to change. MI's focus on guiding versus directing or following may be very different for financial planners who are often seen as the professional in an advice-giving role. Clients may even want the planner to provide an answer once a money disorder has been uncovered, but it is best to resist this temptation and request.

Instead MI focuses on three main techniques for working with clients: (1) change talk, (2) listening techniques, and (3) facilitation of behavioral change. Change talk is when the client expresses his or her desire and argument for change. Change talk typically happens during the evoking stage of MI. It is important for the planner to acknowledge and support the change talk when he or she hears it from the client. As such, the listening techniques utilized in MI happen throughout the four stages of MI. The most basic, yet most powerful, listening technique is active listening.

Active listening involves body language and reflection. Body language begins even before the client has entered the meeting room. The planner should be prepared, relaxed, and ready to concentrate on the client. Once together the planner can actively demonstrate to the client he or she is interested by sitting forward, making eye contact, and mirroring the client's own expressions (Miller & Rollnick, 2013). Reflective listening is a skill financial planners can learn and practice. Reflective listening uses the OARS system: open-ended questions, affirming, reflecting, and summarizing (Miller & Rollnick, 2013).

Facilitating behavioral change can actually begin before the client has awareness of the need to change. The decision to change may take many meetings, many months, and many conversations. In fact, clinical research has determined that only about 20% of individuals are willing and ready to make change at any given time, even if they have stated that they want change (Prochaska & Velicer, 1997). The main point here is that facilitating change will often be a slow process when clients aren't ready. With MI techniques, the focus is being with the client as they change—not trying to pull them along or push them from behind. Moreover, once the client has decided they are ready for change, the planner has many tools available to them. Planners interested in learning more about change theory, listening skills, and applying MI to the planner-client relationship are referred to the book *Facilitating Financial Health: Tools for Financial Planners Coaches, and Therapists*, 2nd edition (2016).

CASE STUDIES

The process for integrating financial psychology into financial planning is growing in popularity. Practitioners have called for outlines and strategies to better understand client behaviors, and a cross-section of academics have begun to answer these needs. For example, Britt (2016) published a report on intergenerational transference of money behaviors and concluded with practical suggestions. Lawson and Klontz (2017) expanded on the connection between financial planning, behavioral finance, financial psychology, and financial therapy, by integrating these concepts into the six stages of financial planning. The following section takes a similar approach and will illustrate how the process of financial planning can identify and address common examples of problematic financial beliefs and behaviors.

OVERSPENDING AND COMPULSIVE BUYING DISORDER

Case Overview

A couple has come to their CFP® professional and wants to begin saving for retirement and their child's education. Both spouses are working, homeowners, and seem to be interested in making better financial decisions. After reviewing bank and credit card statements, though, the conversation begins to get a bit more heated. One of the spouses comments on how difficult it is to keep up with credit card payments. The other spouse is now upset and begins to shut down. In reviewing their financial statements, the financial planner also notices that their monthly spending is exceeding their income, and they have less than $50,000 of total net worth mostly due to excessive credit card debt, even though both have well-paying jobs. In the assessment of the clients' money scripts, the planner identifies money worship status (e.g., your self-worth equals your net worth) and money worship beliefs (e.g., more money will make you happier) within both spouses. How can the practitioner get her clients to see their current patterns of overspending and what changes need to be made without alienating them, causing them to become defensive, or taking sides?

Financial and Psychological Symptoms

Chronic overspending has been described as the persistent inability to control one's spending (Faber & O'Guinn, 1992), and can be the result of a compulsive buying disorder. Individuals who exhibit beliefs associated with money worship, money status, and money avoidance scripts are significantly more likely to engage in compulsive buying behavior and have lower levels of net worth and income (Klontz & Britt, 2012).

These disorders create problems for clients in that needed cash flow for savings and attainment of financial goals are being consumed on items of lower priority and of a nonessential nature. Furthermore, when spending goes beyond the established budgets or income, interest and debt payments create on ongoing drag on savings ability. Clients who display these disordered money behaviors can prove to be a real challenge for financial planners. These individuals may fight among themselves and may ultimately fight against the planner if they begin to feel judged. Clients with CBD may also lose interest and become stagnant. Clients may be fearful of disclosing financial information, which can result in incorrect assumptions and render a financial plan useless.

Possible Actions

Working with and understanding a client with CBD is not hopeless. In fact, there are a number of useful tools and techniques that, when combined with financial planning best practices, can help get the client on track. If these disordered money behaviors are identified through client interactions, there are several ways in which a financial planner may choose to proceed; (1) refer to a mental health professional (for severe disorders), (2) communicate with the clients using motivational interviewing and other awareness techniques designed to decrease their denial and increase their readiness to change, or (3) use logic-based education and information (for actively engaged customers).

In terms of financial planning, the financial management best practice of preparing and tracking a monthly household budget and statement of cash flow (CFP Board, 2015) is a primary tool for the identification and assessment of overspending and compulsive buying behavior. The completion of a statement of personal net worth (CFP Board, 2015) can also provide a strong indication of money status and money worship script behaviors by the types of assets held, and the way in which they were financed. Finally, a ratio analysis (CFP Board, 2015) can also be an effective tool in identification of overspending and inadequate savings levels relative in income and overall assets.

FINANCIAL DENIAL OR AVOIDANCE

Case Study

A CFP® professional has started working with a new client, a young lawyer. The client provides all of her financial statements and for the most part seems very organized. Her main reason for working with a financial planner is that she would like to pay off her home faster as well as her remaining college loan debt. In reviewing her employment benefits, though, the financial planner notices that she is not contributing anything to her firm's 401(k) plan, and the employer matches up to 4%. As part of her financial review, the financial planner notes that she should begin contributing to the employer plan and to make her lack of contribution a point of discussion at your upcoming meeting. When they meet, she remarks that her father is a lawyer and is still working today. She does not need to start saving now, she still has plenty of time and truly believes she will want to work up until the day she dies—"Who needs retirement savings when you have no plans to retire?"

Financial and Psychological Symptoms

Money avoidance and money worship beliefs have been found to be associated with lower levels of net worth and income, and positively predict financial denial behaviors (Klontz & Britt, 2012; Klontz et al., 2011). People who use denial as a way of solving their money-related problems typically exhibit money-avoidance reasoning (Klontz et al., 2016). It has been hypothesized that clients who lack engagement in one of the most foundational retirement savings behaviors, participation in an employer 401(k) plan, suffer from money avoidance beliefs (Horwitz & Klontz, 2017). This lack of engagement was thought to result from the lack of conceptualizing a desired retirement vision, consistent with financial denial beliefs.

Money avoidance beliefs and money denial behaviors are problematic for clients and planners alike. Avoiding thoughts of money issues, denial of the need to plan for retirement, and using cognitive dissonant reasoning to support these beliefs, all illustrate a lack of engagement. While life events and motivated spouses may provide the impetus for an initial visit to the financial planner, avoidance beliefs and denial behaviors will be important for the planner to identify.

Possible Actions

Financial psychology assessment tools such as the KMSI–R and KMBI can be used during the data-gathering step of the financial planning process to identify financial beliefs and behaviors in at-risk clients. Identification of disordered money beliefs and behaviors can be used to formulate the proper tools and methods needed to address these concerns.

Helping the client better understand the consequences of the underlying financial beliefs using MI techniques can be useful in a discussion toward making lasting change. Building intrinsic motivation to achieve a desired goal is a critical factor in managing behavioral change (Horwitz & Klontz, 2013). Likewise, the vision of that desired goal has proven to be a strong motivator for achievement. The financial planner could benefit from being versed in client-visioning exercises and the use of scaling questions found in MI, to facilitate the clarification of retirement and other goal establishment (Horwitz & Klontz, 2013).

Not all behaviors associated with money avoidance are negative. For example, if you can assist clients with money avoidance behaviors to establish a systematic savings plan, they may be less likely to open and read their statements and thereby more likely to not be affected by market fluctuations. This behavior may allow clients to tolerate a higher level of risk needed to reach their long-term financial goals, and reduce panic selling in times of higher market volatility.

FINANCIAL ENABLING AND DEPENDENCY

Case Study

A CFP® professional is getting ready for a meeting with long-time clients. They are in their mid-to-late 50s and are getting really excited for their retirement, but there is a problem. Lately the clients have been calling and asking to take money out of their accounts in order to help their two adult children. Their son and daughter have just both graduated and are having trouble finding consistent work. The clients are regularly supporting their children and the financial planner believes it is starting to get out of hand. Further, the clients' daughter is planning a large wedding and the expenses are becoming more and more extravagant. The son hasn't worked in 2 years and the last time the financial planner met with him, it did not appear he was even looking for work. How does the financial planner talk with his clients about the fact that they won't be able to retire if they keep up supporting their children? How might the CFP® professional talk to the children about becoming more financially responsible?

Financial and Psychological Symptoms

Parents who enable financially dependent children are common financial family dynamics seen by financial planners (Klontz & Canale, 2016).

Another source of financial dependency may come from nonwork income associated with an illness, accident, or disability. These disorders create problems for your clients in that needed cash flow for savings and attainment of financial goals are being consumed by the needs of the person they are trying to help. Furthermore, when enabling becomes overspending beyond the established budgets or income, interest and debt payments create on ongoing drag against savings ability.

Financial enabling is defined as the inability to refuse when a friend or family member asks for money (Klontz et al., 2016). Enablers can experience significant financial challenges and potential bankruptcy as a result of having to cover their expenses and the person they are trying to help (Klontz et al., 2012). Financial enabling behaviors can threaten the financial health of individuals and families and cause significant negative impacts on the attainment of financial goals (Klontz & Canale, 2016). Financial enablers are the counterparts to financial dependents, and both suffer the negative impacts of this unhealthy codependent financial relationship (Klontz et al., 2012).

Possible Actions

The financial management best practice of preparing and tracking a monthly household budget and statement of cash flow (CFP Board, 2015) can be helpful in the assessment of financial dependency, financial enabling, and overspending behavior. The preparation of financial forecasts of retirement accounts can help illustrate the impacts the gifted money is having on the clients' financial goals. Establishing a monthly, quarterly and/or annual limit of gifts to children can also be very useful. Specific group communication, delivered with an explanation from the parents, can illustrate the financial impact of the gifts on the parents' financial well-being. This communication can also highlight the need to establish limits to future gifts in the future. Proper communication and expectation setting is critically importance to bring about positive change for both parties.

Also, a referral to a mental health professional may be in order for a severe dependency situation. The financial planners can help to identify the dependency dynamic, educate their clients on the negative impacts of these maladaptive behaviors, and help facilitate the needed behavioral change (Klontz & Canale, 2016).

Financial planners frequently see clients whose behaviors are not in line with good financial health or even their stated financial goals. In some cases, these behaviors cause them significant impairments in their emotional, relational, and financial lives. When planners see chronic self-destructive financial behaviors that are resistant to change, this could be indicative of a money disorder. An increasing array of assessments and tools are available to planners to help them identify disordered money behaviors and work with clients to encourage them to gain insight and increase their motivation to change. Planners will benefit from knowledge of behavioral patterns indicative of money disorders and know when they may need to bring in the assistance of, or make a referral to, a financial behavior and/ or mental health professional. The financial planning profession would benefit from further research exploring money disorders and their intersection with financial planning. For example, prevalence data on the manifestation of various money disorders in financial planning practice would help researchers and practitioners alike by raising awareness and targeting future research efforts. For money disorders that are seen more frequently by financial planners, research could explore the impact these conditions have on the financial planning process. This data could help the field further develop, implement, and measure the effectiveness of financial planner-specific interventions on money disordered behaviors such as the effectiveness of a financial planner's approach and efforts in making a successful referral to a mental health professional and the effectiveness of financial planning efforts to shape financial behaviors.

REFERENCES

Aboujaoude, E., Gamel, N., & Koran, L. M. (2003). A 1-year naturalistic follow-up of patients with compulsive shopping disorder. *Journal of Clinical Psychiatry, 64*, 946–950.

American Psychiatric Association. (2013). *Diagnostic and statistical manual of mental disorders* (5th ed.). Washington, DC: Author.

Andreassen, C. S., Griffiths, M. D., Hetland, J., & Pallesen, S. (2012). Development of a work addiction scale. *Scandinavian Journal of Psychology, 53*(3), 265–272.

Archuleta, K., Dale, A., & Spann, S. (2013). College students and financial distress: Exploring debt, financial satisfaction, and financial anxiety. *Journal of Financial Counseling and Planning 24*(2), 50–62.

Baker, H. K., & Ricciardi, V. (Eds.). (2014). *Investor behavior: The psychology of financial planning and investing*. Hoboken, NJ: John Wiley & Sons.

Black, D. W., Shaw, M., & Allen, J. (2016). Five-year follow-up of people diagnosed with compulsive shopping disorder. *Comprehensive Psychiatry, 68*, 97–102.

Blanco, C., Hanania, J., Petry, N. M., Wall, M. N., Wang, S., Jin, C. J., & Kendler, K. (2015). *Addiction 110*(8), 1340–1353.

Britt, S. L. (2016). The intergenerational transference of money attitudes and behaviors. *Journal of Consumer Affairs 50*(3), 539–556.

Britt, S. L., Klontz, B. T., Tibbetts, R., & Leitz, L. (2015). The financial health of mental health professionals. *Journal of Financial Therapy, 6*(1), 17–32.

Canale, A., Archuleta, K. L., & Klontz, B. T. (2015). Money disorders. In B. T. Klontz, S. L. Britt, & K. L. Archuleta (Eds.), *Financial therapy: Theory, research, and practice* (pp. 35–68). New York: Springer International Publishing.

Canale, A., & Klontz, B.T. (2013). Hoarding disorder: It's more than just an obsession—Implications for financial therapists and planners. *Journal of Financial Therapy, 4*(2), 43–63.

CFP Board. (2015). *CFP Board Financial Planning Competency Handbook.* Hoboken, NJ: John Wiley & Sons.

Consumer Financial Protection Bureau. (2017). *CFPB financial well-being scale: Scale development technical report.* Retrieved from https://www.consumerfinance.gov/data-research/research-reports/financial-well-being-technical-report/.

Furnham, A., von Stumm, S. & Milner, R. (2014). Moneygrams: Recalled childhood memories about money and adult money pathology. *Journal of Financial Therapy, 5*(1): 40–54. doi: 10.4148/1944–9771.1059.

Horwitz, E. J., & Klontz, B. T. (2013). Understanding and dealing with client resistance to change. *Journal of Financial Planning, 26*(11), 27–31.

Horwitz, E. J., & Klontz, B. T. (2017). *A financial psychology intervention for increasing employee engagement in a retirement plan meeting: Results of three trials.* Manuscript under review.

Kemnitz, R., Klontz, B., & Archuleta, K. L. (2016). Financial enmeshment: Untangling the web. *Journal of Financial Therapy 6* (2), 32–48.

Klontz, B. T., Bivens, A., Klontz, P. T., Wada, J., & Kahler, R. (2008). The treatment of disordered money behaviors: Results of an open clinical trial. *Psychological Services, 5*(3), 295–308.

Klontz, B., Britt, S. L., Archuleta, K. L., & Klontz, T. (2012). Disordered money behaviors: Development of the Klontz Money Behavior Inventory. *Journal of Financial Therapy, 3*(1), 2. doi:10.4148/jft.v3i1.1485.

Klontz, B. Britt, S. L., Mentzer, J., & Klontz, T. (2011). Money beliefs and financial behaviors: Development of the Klontz Money Script Inventory. *Journal of Financial Therapy, 2*(1), 1–22. doi:10.4148/jft.v2i1.451.

Klontz, B., & Canale, A. (2016). When helping hurts: 5 recommendations for planners with financial-enabling clients. *Journal of Financial Planning 29*(3), 24–28.

Klontz, B. T., Horwitz, E. J., & Klontz, P. T. (2015). Stages of change and motivational interviewing in financial therapy. In B. T. Klontz, S. L. Britt, & K. L. Archuleta (Eds.), *Financial therapy: Theory, research, and practice* (35–68). New York: Springer

Klontz, B. T., & Klontz, T. (2009). *Mind over money: Overcoming the money disorders that threaten our financial health.* New York: Crown Business.

Klontz, B. T., Kahler, R., & Klontz, T. (2016). *Facilitating financial health: Tools for financial planners, coaches, and therapists.* Erlanger, KY: National Underwriters Company.

Lawson, D. R., & Klontz, B. T. (2017). Integrating behavioral finance, financial psychology, and financial therapy theory and techniques into the financial planning process. *Journal of Financial Planning, 30*(7), 48–45.

Iervolino, A. C., Perroud, N., Fullana, M. A., Giupponi, M., Cherkas, L., & Collier, D. A. (2009). Prevalence and heritability of compulsive hoarding: A twin study. *American Journal of Psychiatry, 166,* 1156–1161.

Mueller, A., Mueller, U., Silbermann, A., Reinechker, H., Bleich, S., & Mitchell, J. E. (2008). A randomized, controlled trial of group cognitive behavioral therapy for compulsive buying disorder: Posttreatment and 6-month follow-up results. *Journal of Clinical Psychiatry 69*, 1131–1138.

Newcomb, M.D., & Rabow, J. (1999). Gender, socialization, and money. *Journal of Applied Social Psychology, 29*(4), 852–869.

Oates, W. E. (1971). *Confessions of a workaholic: The facts about work addiction.* Cleveland: World Publishing.

Odean, T., & Barber, B. (1999). Do investors trade too much? *American Economic Review, 89,* 1279–1298.

Prochaska, J. O., & Velicer, W. F. (1997). The transtheoretical model of health behavior change. *American Journal of Health Promotion, 12*(1), 38–48.

Tolin, D. F. (2011). Understanding and treating hoarding: A biopsychosocial perspective. *Journal of Clinical Psychology, 67*(5), 517–529.

Tolin, D. F., Frost, R. O., & Steketee, G. (2007). *Buried in treasures: Help for compulsive acquiring, saving, and hoarding.* New York: Oxford University Press.

Townsend, B. B., & Silver, N. C. (2015). Compulsive hoarding as a function of money attitudes. *Journal of Psychology and Clinical Psychiatry 4*(4), 00228.

Taylor, C. D., Klontz, B., & Britt, S. L. (2016). Reliability and convergent validity of the Klontz Money Script Inventory–Revised (KMSI–R). *Journal of Financial Therapy, 6*(2), 1–13.

CHAPTER 18

Situation Awareness in Financial Planning

Research and Application

Charles R. Chaffin, EdD
CFP Board Center for Financial Planning

John Grable, PhD, CFP®
University of Georgia

Although the focus of this book is clearly on client psychology, it would be remiss to address this important financial planning topic without reviewing tools financial planning practitioners can use when working with clients. It is worth noting that while researchers working in the area of client psychology have done an excellent job of documenting client biases, behaviors, and perceptions, it is also important to use some of this same theory and apply it to financial planner behaviors, all in an effort to better serve clients. The purpose of this chapter is to introduce the concept of situation awareness to financial planning, which can assist practitioner decision-making when faced with complex environmental, social, professional, and client-specific decision-making inputs.

Financial planning in and of itself is a complex task environment and perhaps becoming more so. The variables associated with comprehensive financial planning are broad, taking into account a variety of client data points and measures, from a client's basic financial position to complex retirement and estate planning issues. Added to the multiple variables that exist within the financial life of a client are the written and verbal communication needs required to interact with that client. Success as a financial planner depends, in large part, on communicating both the current status of all relevant decision-making inputs and client-specific variables, as well as developing a plan of action that is forward thinking. Given the increasing partnerships that are emerging between practitioners and technology, there is more information available to a financial planner to consider when serving a client. Added to these data points are items related to interpersonal communication and the evolving dynamics of the life of a client, all of which require significant attentional resources and overall cognitive capacity.

The need to respond to multidimensional and fast-moving situational cues is not unique to the practice of financial planning. This is a standard situation among a diverse set of professionals, including pilots, physicians, and military leaders. Helping those who face complex decision frameworks, in which actions can have profound negative (as well as positive) outcomes, has been the focus of decision scientists over the past several decades. Consider the situation of a commercial airline pilot. The pilot must possess the requisite skills to make sense of the multiple data points presented in the cluster of dials and measurement indicators in the cockpit. The pilot must also have a keen perception of the physical environment in which the plane operates. Additionally, the pilot needs to comprehend how different factors influence not only the flight path of the plane but also how conditions affect the passengers. Finally, and maybe most importantly, the pilot must synthesize numerous data inputs that occur at constant, yet variable, rates and make predictions about future events. The pilot's short-term and long-term success depend on the ability to make reliable forecasts, execute tasks based on situational perceptions, and adapt to the changing environment (Carol, 1992).

A financial planner is in a similar position when working with a client. The planner must possess the basic skills and professional characteristics to differentiate between and among variables that are most relevant to developing client-specific financial recommendations. The financial planner must be able to perceive what environmental factors, regulatory events, client characteristics, and other elements will remain constant or change over time. The financial planner needs to exhibit a high level of comprehension of how multiple variables can influence a client's financial situation. Similar to a pilot, a financial planner must also develop recommendations based on predictions of future events. This aspect of financial planning incorporates the notion of continuous feedback in which the implementation of a recommendation changes the environment, which then alters the financial planner's predictions. In this sense, financial planning is a continuous process that involves the repeated application of perception, comprehension, and prediction.

The process of perception, comprehension, and prediction has been codified into a systems model: situation awareness. Situation awareness was first developed in the mid-1980s to explain and predict human performance within dynamic situations (Dalrymple & Schiflett, 1997; Endsley, 1995). Situation awareness has been defined many ways, but generally, situation awareness is thought to be a mental model or abstraction of an individual's environment (Billings, 1995). Endsley (1988a, 1988b) defined situation awareness as "the perception of the elements in the environment within a volume of time and space, the comprehension of their meaning, and the projection of their status in the near future." As just introduced, there are three levels of situation awareness: perception, comprehension, and prediction.

Situation awareness precedes any type of decision-making and is separate from the actual performance of any action. As Flach (1995) noted, situation awareness is not an objective cause of anything specific other than the ability to make appropriate forecasts and then implement suitable tasks based on those forecasts. Stated another way, situation awareness is merely a mental model of an individual's environment prior to a type of decision-making or performance of a task. It is possible for two practitioners with the same level of situation awareness to respond to their comprehension of the environment differently based upon their overall skill level or past experiences within a similar environment, explaining why some planes crash even when flown by very experienced pilots. Similarly, two experienced financial planners can synthesize the same economic information and arrive at widely different planning forecasts. With that said, situation awareness is linked to performance, as the more information and meaning that an individual is able to comprehend from the environment, the more likely the person is able to act appropriately, particularly when executing tasks during changing circumstances (McMillan, 1994).

One way to see how this works in practice is to observe battlefield operations. On the battlefield, situation awareness is critical to an understanding of all of the key components of an artillery operation. Here is what the *Army Field Manual* says about battlefield situation awareness (Department of the Army 1–02, 2004):

> *Knowledge and understanding of the current situation which promotes timely, relevant and accurate assessment of friendly, enemy, and other operations within the battlespace in order to facilitate decision making. An informational perspective and skill that fosters an ability to determine quickly the context and relevance of events that are unfolding.*

Situation awareness has been used by numerous other types of professionals, including airplane pilots, health practitioners, and military leaders. All of these disciplines, or task environments, require individual decision-makers to devote cognitive resources to a complex task environment before acting and responding. For example, in medicine, situation awareness is critical to patient safety. The physician must evaluate a patient's situation, often very quickly and without significant diagnostic tests. The physician must amalgamate multiple points of data and make a task recommendation. This decision-making process must include a subjective estimate of the possibility that the chosen course of action may not be correct. That is, the physician must be forward-thinking in order to anticipate additional courses of action in case the initial task decision is insufficient to alter the patient's situation. The same is true in the context of comprehensive financial planning. Financial planning is a future-oriented task, sometimes conflicting with the way in which clients view their financial situations. As noted throughout this book, clients often act in biased ways. A financial planner who operates with high situation awareness is able to account for client biases when making forecasts and recommendations. Further, a high-performance financial planner incorporates dynamic client characteristics into predictions and executes tasks based on well-developed perceptions (McMillan, 1994).

According to Taylor (1990), situation awareness is a prerequisite state of knowledge associated with making adaptive decisions in which outcomes are both uncertain and potentially negative. In the context of performing a military mission, flying a plane, or performing an operation, situation awareness incorporates perceptions and knowledge, comprehension and cognition, and the anticipation and prediction of events and variables that influence the safe and effective performance of the action. Within the context of comprehensive financial planning, the same elements are at play, with the effective implementation of strategies used to meet client goals as the mission. When viewed this way, situation awareness can be divided into three main stages.

PERCEPTION

Perception is the first stage, and the most basic element, of situation awareness, where a decision-maker monitors and recognizes the environment around him or her. At this stage, the individual has recognition of the placement and condition of objects and is able to place a quantitative value on a number of variables.

At this level of situation awareness, a soccer player, for example, knows the location of each of the players on both her team as well as the opposing team, as well as the speed and capabilities of each of the players. When driving a car, a perceptive driver knows where each of the other cars are on the road, their speed, as well as the speed of his or her automobile. It is important to note that it is possible to have excellent perception and still not be a good soccer player or driver. This can occur because of problematic coordination, attitudinal issues, or other factors (Tenney, Adams, Pew, Huggins, & Rogers, 1992). What is important to remember, however, is that it is not possible to exhibit situation awareness without having highly attuned and practiced perception.

Within the context of comprehensive financial planning, a financial planner who exhibits perception at level one of situation awareness has an understanding of the client's financial status, as well as a comprehensive knowledge of the many variables that are part of this book, including interpersonal relationships, behavioral tendencies, and client biases. It is understood that a highly perceptive financial planner intuitively understands the scope of his or her practice, and possesses the technical skills to perform financial planning tasks.

COMPREHENSION

As noted by Vidulich (1994), situation awareness requires more than the ability to perceive the environment and client situation. Situation awareness involves higher cognitive processing. Comprehension is the synthesis of the information perceived in the first stage of the process, but with an awareness of how these items interact to influence the status of the initiative or objective. The decision-maker at the comprehension stage of the process has a firm understanding of the status of the environment around her and the implications of that status on the larger environment.

An individual in level two situation awareness can pull together relevant pieces of information obtained through perceptions and understand the significance of these factors relative to broader objectives. As described by Endlsey, Farley, Jones, Midkiff, and Hansman (1998), high-level comprehension allows a financial planner to form patterns among elements of a client's situation and develop a holistic picture that includes an understanding of what information and events are most important. The decision-maker at level two situation awareness has a much more holistic view of the environment and can accurately detect deviations within the expected environment. A soccer player, for instance, who exhibits a proficient level of comprehension, can begin to anticipate weaknesses in an opponent's defenses by quickly evaluating movements of players on the field. A driver who has a comprehension of the driving environment can often anticipate when it is appropriate to accelerate or brake in order to avoid an accident.

Similarly, a financial planner who is operating with a high degree of perception and comprehension (stage two of the process) is better able to understand what data points are important in helping a client reach their financial goals. This often involves ranking and ordering environmental elements, client attitudes, behaviors, and biases in order to form meaningful patterns or pictures of the client's situation. Whereas gathering data in the financial planning process is akin to perception in the situation awareness process, analyzing client data within the macroeconomic and client-specific environment and developing plans and recommendations, as steps in the financial planning process, is similar to comprehension in the framework of situation awareness.

PREDICTION

Again, it is possible to be perceptive and to comprehend how multiple elements work together to shape plans and tasks, and yet still fail to exhibit situation awareness. It is prediction—the last stage of the situation awareness process—that is of critical importance. Prediction is the ability to project the future status of an operation based upon all of the relevant factors described in stages one and two. Essentially, the decision-maker has, at this stage of the process, an understanding of the implications of the environment on both the current status of the initiative as well as the future outcome of the project.

The decision-maker at level three of situation awareness has not only a comprehensive understanding of the environment, but can also predict the outcome of this environment given the current status. Stated another way, prediction allows the decision-maker to project the impact of implemented tasks within the environment. The ability to make forecasts is based on a thorough knowledge of the task at hand, the dynamics involved between and among the elements associated with the task, and the decision-maker's comprehensive understanding of the situation in which a decision is being made. Consider a driver who is operating at this level of situation awareness during a rainstorm on a busy highway. The driver is engaged in a series of subjective evaluations based on data inputs from the automobile, visual information, feelings, and knowledge of the situation. Perceptions of speed, conditions, and the abilities of other drivers is quickly transmitted and comprehended. It is this level of data synthesis that allows a driver operating at this stage of the situation awareness process to predict traffic flow and potential accidents. Additionally, the driver will use feedback obtained from the prediction to alter future perceptions, cognitions (that improve comprehension), and predictions. At this stage of the process, a decision-maker is constantly engaged in monitoring the current situation to predict what will happen in the future. This feedback mechanism is an important element of adaption exhibited by someone operating at this level.

Financial planners who possess and exhibit high levels of situation awareness have the ability to search for trends that can have a significant impact on the future status of their clients. They can detect patterns quickly and adapt to positive, negative, expected, and unexpected events. Consider the situation of a financial planner who recommends that a client pay off high-expense credit card debt with lower yielding monetary assets. This type of recommendation should only be made if the financial planner perceives that (1) her client is willing and able to implement the task; (2) the client is not exhibiting behavioral biases, such as mental accounting, which might prompt the client to re-engage in a spending pattern; and (3) the environment is conducive to the action (e.g., the interest rate gap between the debt and assets is sufficient to warrant liquidating assets). Answers to these and other related questions occur with comprehension. A situation-aware financial planner will use the data inputs to predict, in this case, that paying down the credit card debt will be in the long-run best interest of the client. Concurrently, the financial planner will be looking for outcome feedback to adjust, if necessary, future perceptions and comprehension of the client's situation.

Inherent within any model of situation awareness is competency. For example, an individual who has little competency as an airplane pilot will be unable to achieve any level of situation awareness. Similarly, an individual who knows very little about financial planning will be unable to synthesize elements of a financial plan or consider adequate measures in communicating with her client. Similarly, ethics within financial planning is a lens through which the individual examines all aspects and actions associated with the financial planning process, as well as communication.

Financial Planning Practice

Figure 18.1 illustrates the situation awareness process as it applies to financial planning. The process of situation awareness within any complex task environment repeats itself continuously as new information is presented to the

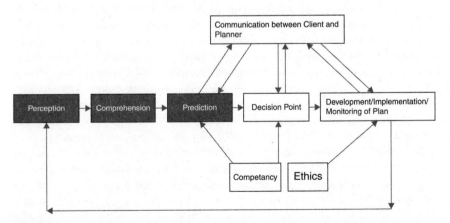

FIGURE 18.1   Situation Awareness Model in Financial Planning Based upon 1995 Model

individual. In financial planning, the client's ever-changing quantitative information and behaviors necessitate a repeat to the situation awareness process. Oral communication with the client also requires repetition of this cycle.

As illustrated, the process of situation awareness is a linear progression from perception to prediction. Predictions influence and are influenced by communications between the financial planner and client, whereas the financial planner's competency influences predictions. Decisions are jointly impacted by a financial planner's predictions, the planner's competency, and through dialog with the client and feedback of decision outcomes from the client. Decisions lead to the development, implementation, and monitoring of a client's financial plan. This too is associated with communication between the client and financial planner. The ethical perspective of the financial planner also has a direct association with these elements of the financial planning process.

Situation awareness can be useful in educating the next generation of financial planners, providing specific achievement benchmarks to individuals as they learn to perceive the components of an individual's financial status as well as many of the dynamics associated with their families, decision-making, and other variables that are part of this book. Financial planning educators can use case studies to not only provide valuable experiences and feedback to future financial planners, but also quantify their understanding of a given scenario outside of the actual performance of developing and presenting a comprehensive financial plan.

An Applied Example

While there are numerous ways in which situation awareness can be applied to the practice of comprehensive financial planning, one approach stands out as being aligned well with the theory. Yeske and Buie (2006) introduced the notion of policy-based financial planning as a framework to help financial planners and their clients formulate strategic plans. Their work was roughly based on the writings of Hallman and Rosenbloom (1987). A policy-based recommendation is one that combines a client's goals, values, biases, circumstances, and current and future financial situation into a concise set of decision rules. In order to arrive at a set of rules that are broad enough to account for unexpected events and specific enough to provide concrete guidance when a client needs to make a decision, a financial planner must exhibit perception, comprehension, and prediction proficiencies. A well-written policy "acts as a bridge between a client's core values and aspirations and the specific, concrete steps that should be taken at any given time to sustain progress toward achieving those aspirations" (Yeske & Buie, p. 51).

Consider the following example from Yeske and Buie (2014). Assume a married couple has retired and approached a financial planner to develop a retirement asset withdrawal strategy that will produce lifetime annual income. Further, assume that the financial planner has read the relevant literature on withdrawal strategies and decides to use a stochastic modeling approach that shows a 5.5% initial withdrawal is appropriate to meet the client's income needs while maintaining real portfolio values. If the financial planner bases recommendations only on perceptions and/or comprehension, the recommendation will likely be presented in a straightforward manner. Specifically, the client will be shown the results from the stochastic model, provided a withdrawal guideline, and encouraged to review spending on a regular basis to ensure that the portfolio is able to maintain the withdrawal rate in the future. This approach, while appropriate, fails to account for potential client biases that can lead to overspending or environmental changes that could negatively affect portfolio values in the future.

A financial planner who is working from a position of situation awareness would likely provide the client with greater actionable tasks and rules that incorporate predictions of future environmental changes and possible shifts in a client's attitudes and behaviors. The following is an example of a policy-based retirement withdrawal recommendation that fits well with the third stage of situation awareness (see Yeske & Buie, 2014, p. 203):

- Inflation rule: Target spending will be increased by the change in the Consumer Price Index for the preceding 12 months, except when the portfolio has had a negative return over that same 12 months and the current withdrawal rate is greater than the initial withdrawal rate.
- Capital preservation rule: If current spending as a percentage of the portfolio is more than 20% larger than the initial withdrawal rate, target spending is reduced by 10%.
- Prosperity rule: If current spending as a percentage of the portfolio is more than 20% smaller than the initial withdrawal rate, target spending is increased by 10%.

As noted by Yeske and Buie (2014), this policy is both broad and adaptable to changing circumstances. What makes this approach useful from a practice management perspective is that the policy is based on a financial planner's synthesis of data points in the formation of a forecast that results in implementable tasks and rules. The resulting policy is forward-looking but flexible enough to account for possibilities that may or may not happen once the recommendation is implemented. This financial planning approach is additionally helpful to clients because it reduces anxiety associated with determining when follow-up reviews and reanalysis are needed.

To summarize, situation awareness, as this example suggests, is a process, not a product or service. The process is adaptive. When viewed this way, financial planning recommendations account for predictions of future client behavior and changing environmental circumstances. The process also allows for feedback. Information obtained during monitoring activities within the financial planning process inform future recommendations.

FUTURE DIRECTIONS

Future research in financial planning can explore and define perception, comprehension, and prediction relative to the stages of a continuum in a career track of new financial planners, or within a variety of learning environments for future financial planners. These experiences would provide the new or preprofessional financial planners the opportunity to cognitively engage the many facets of the client financial profile and environment before then making a decision on an appropriate action.

Implicit in this model is the allocation of attentional resources that the practitioner utilizes in this complex task environment, shifting attention from the quantitative aspects of the financial plan to all aspects associated with communication with the client. By quantifying attention, new models of expertise specific to financial planning can be developed that would impact mentorship programs and potentially new methods of categorizing experience.

By defining these different stages of awareness of the practitioner, each of the elements associated with client–planner interaction can assist in helping the entire process to be more client-centered. Financial planning educator programs, most notably the CFP Board Registered Programs, along with new advisor training and induction programs, can be more effective in defining where each student or new advisor exists within the continuum of levels of situation awareness, providing opportunities to enhance the entire complex system of synthesizing all aspects of both a comprehensive financial plan as well as the cognitive requirements associated with client communication. Through these efforts, education programs and firms can be more precise in introducing new learning experiences, contextual or not, that enhance situation awareness and ultimately the level of service to each current and future client.

REFERENCES

Department of the Army. (2004). Operational terms and graphics, FM1-02 (FM 101-5-1) MCRP 5-12A. Washington, DC: Headquarters, Department of the Army.

Billings, C. E. (1995). *Situation awareness measurement and analysis: A commentary.* Proceedings of the International Conference on Experimental Analysis and Measurement of Situation Awareness. Embry-Riddle Aeronautical University Press.

Carol, L. A. (1991). Desperately seeking situation awareness. *TAC Attach* (TAC SP 127–1), *32*(3), 5–6.

Dalrymple, M. A., & Schiflett, S. G. (1997). *Measuring situational awareness of AWACS weapons directors.* Augmented proceedings of the Naval Air Warfare Center's First Annual Symposium. *CSERIAC SOAR Report #97–01*, WP-AFB: Ohio.

Endsley, M. R. (1988a). *Situation awareness global assessment technique (SAGAT).* Paper presented at the National Aerospace and Electronic Conference (NAECON), Dayton, OH.

Endsley, M. R. (1988b). *The functioning and evaluation of pilot situation awareness.* Northrop Technical Report: NOR DOC 88–30.

Endsley, M. R. (1995). Measurement of situation awareness in dynamic systems. *Human Factors, 37,* 65–84.

Endsley, M. R., Farley, T. C., Jones, W. M., Midkiff, A. H., & Hansman, R. J. (1998). *Situation awareness information requirements for commercial airline pilots* (ICAT-98–1). Cambridge, MA: MIT International Center for Air Transportation.

Flach, J. M. (1995). Situation awareness: Proceed with caution. *Human Factors, 37,* 149–157.

Hallman, V. G., & Rosenbloom, J. S. (1987). *Personal Financial Planning* (4th ed.). New York: McGraw-Hill.

McMillan, G. R. (1994). Report of the Armstrong Laboratory Situation Awareness Integration (SAINT) Team (briefing transcript). In *Situation Awareness: Papers and Annotated Bibliography.* Armstrong Laboratory, Wright-Patterson AFB: OH.

Taylor, R. M. (1990). Situation awareness rating technique (SART): The development of a tool for aircrew systems design. In *Situational Awareness in Aerospace Operations* (Chapter 3). Paris, France: Neuilly-sur-Seine, NATO-AGARD-CP-478.

Tenney, Y. J., Adams, M. J., Pew, R. W., Huggins, A. W., & Rogers, W. H. (1992). A principled approach to the measurement of situation awareness in commercial aviation. *NASA contractor Report 4451.* NASA: Langley Research Center.

Vidulich, M. (1994). Cognitive and performance components of situation awareness: SAINT Team Task One Report. In *Situation Awareness: Papers and Annotated Bibliography.* Armstrong Laboratory, Wright-Patterson AFB: OH.

Yeske, D. B., & Buie, E. (2006). Policy-based financial planning provides touchstone in a turbulent world. *Journal of Financial Planning, 60*(7), 50–58.

Yeske, D. B., & Buie, E. (2014). Policy-based financial planning: Decision rules for a changing world. In H. K. Baker & V. Ricciardi (Eds.), *Investor behavior: The psychology of financial planning and investing* (pp. 181–208). Hoboken, NJ: John Wiley & Sons.

CHAPTER 19

Final Remarks

Charles R. Chaffin, EdD
CFP Board Center for Financial Planning

Financial planning is a practitioner-based profession that, at its core, is a human endeavor. The human element brings with it all of the biases, behaviors, and perceptions that impact all aspects of the financial planning process and certainly the short- and long-term financial well-being of the individual. Each of those human activities is distinctive and representative of various motivations and interactions with others and the environment as a whole. As reinforced throughout this book, the action or decision of the client cannot be treated in isolation, but must be questioned and quantified based upon a number of factors, many of which are not present when the client sits down, or interacts electronically, with the financial planner.

Throughout this past year, I have thought many times that some practitioners may suggest that all of the research and ideas found within this book can be substituted for one word: experience. It could be argued that after 10 to 20 years, a practitioner can begin to intuitively know where to direct her thoughts when talking with a married couple or how to better understand a new client's motivations for saving and investing. However, client psychology brings new avenues for understanding the human element of financial planning and perhaps most important, can provide new hires with a level of understanding that can shorten the lengthy time it takes intuition to bear through experience. This new body of knowledge provides a rationale for the decisions of clients and the decisions of those who never become clients, both of which are important to the future of financial planning. Quite frankly, if we as a profession are going to be client-centered, then client psychology must not be secondary, but rather, receive equal billing alongside the traditional subject areas of financial planning.

Within other practitioner-based professions, individuals entering the workforce must know the individuals they are serving. For example, if one aspires to become a math teacher, she must obviously know the concepts of mathematics. If she is aspiring to become an elementary math teacher, then certainly addition, subtraction, and multiplication are key topics. However, she must also have years of study in educational psychology, focusing on how people learn; cognitive development; instructional techniques; and aspects of measuring student progress. It is therefore not enough to merely know the subject matter in order to effectively teach. We all have experienced teachers or professors who had deep knowledge of the content, but were not effective educators. What good is that content knowledge to the students if learning does not exist within the classroom?

Could that be the future direction of financial planning? Is it not enough for aspiring practitioners to know the basic tenets of investments, tax, insurance, and the other traditional content areas of financial planning? Should they also know the other humans in the room, understanding their biases, behaviors, and perceptions in order to mitigate their challenges and control for issues and dynamics that could impact their financial decision-making and overall financial well-being?

The present and future client is likely going to answer that question in the coming years. As the old saying goes, "People vote with their wallets." The integration of technology into financial planning has created both a challenge and an opportunity for the CFP® professional to exercise higher-order cognitive thinking, go beyond the transactional side of financial planning and focus on communication, counseling, and the innate and interpersonal psychological constructs associated with client decision-making and financial well-being. In talking with practitioners, firms, and scholars, it is clear that client psychology has immense opportunity for this growing profession. Learning about the biases, behaviors, and perceptions of our clients is not only the right thing to do, but as CFP Board CEO Kevin Keller says, it is a play for relevance for this profession. Having a deeper understanding of the people we serve can help us achieve relevance in the future.

Many practitioners, and even some scholars, suggest that financial planning is both an art and a science. The notion of the science of financial planning is pretty straightforward. As stated earlier, within our sphere exists the content areas of estate planning, taxation, investments, retirement planning, and communication, all part of the lexicon of practice and significant components of requirements for CFP® certification. These content areas are integral parts of the competency of a CFP® professional and will likely always be integral to any individual entering the profession.

The term *art* is a bit more nebulous. *Merriam–Webster* provides several definitions, two of which are relevant to this argument within financial planning. It defines art as "-a skill at doing a specified thing, typically one acquired through practice" (Merriam–Webster, 2017) and "subjects of study primarily concerned with the processes and products of human creativity and social life, such as languages, literature, and history (as contrasted with scientific or technical subjects)." Art suggests a planner-centered action that is indescribable with words and not subject to scientific inquiry. As Michael Finke (2013) writes:

> *Art implies subjectivity. If financial advice is an art, then it is different from a science-based profession like medicine. Doctors vary in their ability to communicate effectively with patients, but the advice they give tends to be consistent because it is based on sound theory supported by evidence. What would happen if doctors stopped reading medical journals, didn't receive training in science-based techniques and relied instead on their instinct? Plenty of holistic medical professionals practice healing techniques that have no proven effectiveness (and they also have many loyal customers). (Finke, 2013, p. 1)*

Given that the stakes in managing the financial future of clients are so high, it seems questionable to rely fully on instinct in this profession.

Our hope is that future research will explore many of the questions that have emanated from this book. We hope that some practitioners will become doctoral students and dedicate the next 30 years of their research to this new interdisciplinary line of inquiry. Researchers from cognitive psychology will partner with financial planning scholars and those from sociology to answer some of these new questions about the human client. We as an evolving academic discipline are uniquely positioned to build a theoretical base for this new area of work, essentially marrying multiple disciplines under one umbrella. Financial planning's roots in academia started in Human Ecology—previously known as home economics, where students first learned basic budgeting in order to manage the household. Human Ecology has evolved considerably since those early days of the last century in taking a lead in policy research relative to a variety of different academic disciplines and professions, including financial planning. The overwhelming majority of graduates with a PhD (whether degree, concentration, or cognate) in financial planning have come from Human Ecology.

At the same time, the growth of financial planning within the business schools is occurring at a very rapid pace. Within the past 7 years, the majority of new degree programs are coming from schools of business. Our past, present, and future with one foot in the human sciences and another in business make us perfectly positioned to build a new body of knowledge specifically for client psychology. Researchers from both of these colleges need to have the opportunity to work together to develop and refine this new theory and perhaps most importantly, outline the implications of such theory in practice. Papers in both areas need to be cited across campus, rather than within the traditional silos that tend to occur with all academic disciplines across campuses.

It is not lost on us at the CFP Board Center for Financial Planning that this research must be supported through platforms that are recognized for tenure and promotion, both for research presentation and publication. Hence, we are excited to launch *Financial Planning Review*, our double-blind, peer-reviewed academic journal that is committed to research in this area, as well as the broader spectrum of interdisciplinary inquiry that directly or indirectly relates to financial planning practice.

For practitioners, we hope that you will be inspired to think about these broader disciplines and the questions posed. We hope that CFP® professionals will continue to work to not only be regular consumers of research in this new area, but also participate in discussions and clinical and experimental research that answers many of the questions about the human client.

The human being, and therefore our clients, is complex. Human beings and ideas should be viewed, as Seltzer (2015) suggests, kaleidoscopically, where "there is no single turn, or focal point, that enables some defining pattern to emerge. Rather, each pattern is equally 'true,' equally descriptive— and whether one is better, or more valid, than another depends solely on the perceiver" (p. 1). We hope that we have begun to at least define some of the patterns and colors of this kaleidoscope here.

REFERENCES

Finke, M. (2013). Financial planning: Art or science. *Think Advisor*. Retrieved from http://www.thinkadvisor.com/2013/05/28/financial-planning-art-or-science.

Merriam-Webster (2017). Art [def. 1]. In *Merriam-Webster Online Dictionary*. Retrieved from https://www.merriam-webster.com/dictionary/art.

Seltzer, L. F. (2015, December 10). Why—with humans—it's all so complicated. *Psychology Today*. Retrieved from https://www.psychologytoday.com/blog/evolution-the-self/201512/why-humans-it-s-all-so-complicated.

Index